Publications
Of
The Colonial Society of Massachusetts

VOLUME LXXXVII

The Papers of Francis Bernard

Governor of Colonial Massachusetts, 1760-69

VOLUME 5: 1768-1769

Sir Francis Bernard, 1772. By John Singleton Copley.
By permission of the Governing Body, Christ Church, Oxford.

EDITED BY COLIN NICOLSON

The Papers of Francis Bernard
Governor of Colonial Massachusetts, 1760-69

VOLUME 5: 1768-1769

Research Assistants:
Stuart Salmon
Christopher Minty
Robyn Leith Stewart

BOSTON The Colonial Society of Massachusetts 2015
Distributed by the University of Virginia Press

DEDICATION

To John W. Tyler

© Colonial Society of Massachusetts 2015
ISBN 978-0-9852543-5-3
Published from the Income of the Sarah Louise Edes Fund
Library of Congress Cataloging-in-Publication Data is available
from the Library of Congress.

CONTENTS

APPENDICES

ILLUSTRATIONS

ACKNOWLEDGMENTS

I am delighted once again to thank everyone who has assisted in the publication of this volume of *The Bernard Papers*. Firstly, my sincere thanks to the Colonial Society of Massachusetts for financing the project, and to John W. Tyler, editor of publications, for his guidance and encouragement. This volume is dedicated to him in acknowledgement of his contribution to this project and to the history of Colonial America. Owen Dudley Edwards and Neil Longley York diligently read the manuscript, and the book is all the better for their generosity. My thanks also to Stuart Salmon, Christopher Minty, and Robyn Leith Stewart for their excellent research assistance: they helped transcribe documents, check facts, and proof-read drafts with little fuss and much care. John Catanzariti, former editor of the Jefferson Papers, shaped editorial policy, while colleagues contributed in various ways, notably Emma Macleod and Ben Marsh. My sincere thanks also to Jeanne Abboud for her splendid work in designing this volume, and to Kyriaki Tsaganis at Scribe for the digital edition. Key support was provided by the UK Arts and Humanities Research Council; a generous Research Fellowship provided relief from teaching commitments during 2011, enabling me to conduct research for this volume. I am especially pleased to acknowledge the many librarians and archivists who answered my enquiries at the Houghton Library, Harvard University, the Massachusetts Historical Society, the UK National Archives, the National Library of Scotland, the University of Stirling, and the William L. Clements Library of the University of Michigan.

Permission to publish material from the following collections is herewith acknowledged: the private collections of Robert Spencer Bernard; the Massachusetts Archives Collection, courtesy of the Massachusetts Archives; the Thomas Gage Papers, by permission of the William L. Clements Library.

My last debts are the greatest: to my dear wife Catherine and my wonderful daughters, Catriona and Kristen.

LIST OF ABBREVIATIONS

Acts and Resolves	*The Acts and Resolves, Public and Private of the Province of Massachusetts Bay, 1692-1776.* 21 Vols. Boston, 1896-1922.
Adams, *American Independence*	Thomas R. Adams, *American Independence, The Growth of an Idea: A Bibliographical Study of the American Political Pamphlets Printed Between 1764 and 1776 Dealing with the Dispute Between Great Britain and Her Colonies.* Providence, R.I., 1965.
ADM 2/1057	Admiralty: Out-Letters: Legal Correspondence, 1762-1776. ADM 2/1057. TNA
APC	W. L. Grant and James Munro, eds., *Acts of the Privy Council of England: Colonial Series, 1613-1783.* 6 Vols. Vols. 4-6. London, 1909-1912.
Appeal to the World	Samuel Adams, *An Appeal to the World; or A Vindication of the Town of Boston, From Many False and Malicious Aspersions Contain'd in Certain Letters and Memorials, Written by Governor Bernard, General Gage, Commodore Hood, the Commissioners of the American Board of Customs, and Others, and by Them Respectively Transmitted to the British Ministry. Published by Order of the Town.* Boston: Edes and Gill, 1769.

Barrington-Bernard	Edward Channing and Archibald Cary Coolidge, eds., *The Barrington-Bernard Correspondence and Illustrative Matter, 1760-1770.* Harvard Historical Studies Series. Vol. 17. Cambridge, Mass., 1912.
Bernard Papers	Colin Nicolson, ed., *The Papers of Francis Bernard, Governor of Colonial Massachusetts, 1760-69.* 6 Vols. The Colonial Society of Massachusetts; distributed by the Univ. of Virginia Press. Boston, 2007-.
BL	The British Library.
BL: Add	The British Library; Additional Manuscripts.
Boston Gazette	*Boston Gazette and Country Journal.*
BP	Bernard Papers, 13 Vols. Sparks Papers, MS 4. Houghton Library, Harvard University.
Bowdoin and Temple Papers, Loose MSS.	Bowdoin and Temple (Winthrop Papers). Loose Manuscripts, 1580-1900. MHS.
Bowdoin and Temple Papers	*The Bowdoin and Temple Papers. Collections of the Massachusetts Historical Society,* 6th ser. Vol. 9. Boston, 1897.
CO 5	Colonial Office Records, Colonial Office Series. TNA.
CO 5/757	Massachusetts, Original Correspondence of Secretary of State, 1767-1768. CO 5/757. TNA.
CO 5/766	Letters to Secretary of State, 1766-1768. CO 5/766. TNA.
CO 5/823	Massachusetts, Council Executive Records, 1760-1766. CO 5/823. TNA.[1]

CO 5/827	Massachusetts, Council Executive Records, 1766-1769. CO 5/827. TNA.
CO 5/828	Council in Assembly, Massachusetts, 1767-1768. CO 5/828. TNA.[2]
CO 5/829	Massachusetts, Council Executive Records, 1769-1774. CO 5/829. TNA.
CO 5/893	New England, Original Correspondence of Board of Trade, 1767-1770. CO 5/893. TNA.
CO 700	Colonial Office and predecessors: Maps and Plans: Series I. CO 700. TNA.
Coll. Mass. Papers	Collection of Papers relating to Massachusetts History, 1749-1777. Ms. N-2193. Massachusetts Historical Society.
Copies of Letters from Governor Bernard to Hillsborough	*Copies of Letters from Governor Bernard, &c. to the Earl of Hillsborough.* [Boston: Edes and Gill], 1769.[3]
Customs GB II	Great Britain Commissioners of Customs letters [typescripts], 1764-1774. Formerly cataloged as "G.B. Customs II." Includes typescripts of the Bowdoin and Temple Papers. Massachusetts Historical Society.
DCB	*Dictionary of Canadian Biography Online.* Toronto, 2003, http://www.biographi.ca.
Dorr Collection	The Annotated Newspapers of Harbottle Dorr Jr. 4 Vols. Online edition. Massachusetts Historical Society, http://www.masshist.org/dorr/.
Early American Imprints, Series 1	*Early American Imprints, Series 1: Evans, 1639-1800.* Online edition. Readex, Archive of Americana. Newsbank Inc., http://infoweb.newsbank.com.

ECCO	Eighteenth Century Collections Online. Available at Historical Texts published by JISC Collections https://historicaltexts.jisc.ac.uk/#!/home.
FB	Francis Bernard (1712-79).
Gage	Thomas Gage Papers. American Series. 139 Vols. Vols. 73-88 (1768-1769). William L. Clements Library, University of Michigan.[4]
HCJ	*Journals of the House of Commons, 1688-1834.* 89 Vols. Vols. 30-34. London, 1803-1835. House of Commons Parliamentary Papers. ProQuest and University of Southampton, http://parlipapers.chadwyck.co.uk.
HLJ	*Journals of the House of Lords, 1688-1834.* 66 Vols. Vols. 30-32. London [1771-1808].[5] House of Commons Parliamentary Papers. ProQuest and University of Southampton, http://parlipapers.chadwyck.co.uk.
HLL	House of Lords Library
HLL: American Colonies Box 1	The House of Lords Library: American Colonies Box 1, 28-30 Nov. 1768. HL/PO/JO/10/7/286.
HLL: American Colonies Box 2	The House of Lords Library: American Colonies Box 2, 28-30 Nov. 1768. HL/PO/JO/10/7/287.
HLL: American Colonies Box 3	The House of Lords Library: American Colonies Box 3, 28-30 Nov. 1768. HL/PO/JO/10/7/288.
Hutchinson Transcripts	Malcolm Freiberg, ed. and comp., Transcripts of the Letterbooks of Massachusetts Governor Thomas Hutchinson. Edited transcripts of originals in the Massachusetts Archives Collection. Vols. 25-27. Microfilm P-144. 3 Reels. Massachusetts Historical Society.

JBT	*Journal of the Commissioners for Trade and Plantations.* 14 Vols. London, 1920-1938.
JHRM	*The Journals of the House of Representatives of Massachusetts, 1715-1779.* 55 Vols. Boston, 1919-1990.
KJV	Authorized or King James Version of The Bible.
Letters to Hillsborough (1st ed.)	*Letters to the Right Honourable the Earl of Hillsborough, from Governor Bernard, General Gage, and the honourable His Majesty's Council for the Province of Massachusetts-Bay. With an appendix, containing divers proceedings referred to in the said letters.* Boston: Edes and Gill, 1769.[6]
Letters to Hillsborough (repr.)	*Letters to the Right Honourable the Earl of Hillsborough, from Governor Bernard, General Gage, and the honourable His Majesty's Council for the Province of Massachusetts-Bay. With an appendix, containing divers proceedings referred to in the said letters.* Boston: Edes and Gill, 1769; repr. London: J. Almon, [1769?].[7]
Letters to the Ministry (1st ed.)	*Letters to the Ministry from Governor Bernard, General Gage, and Commodore Hood. And also Memorials to the Lords of the Treasury, from the Commissioners of the Customs. With sundry letters and papers annexed to the said memorials.* Boston: Edes and Gill, 1769.[8]
Letters to the Ministry (repr.)	*Letters to the Ministry from Governor Bernard, General Gage, and Commodore Hood. And also Memorials to the Lords of the Treasury, from the Commissioners of the Customs. With sundry letters and papers annexed to the said memorials.* Boston: Edes and Gill, 1769; repr. London, J. Wilkie, 1769.[9]
M-Ar	Massachusetts Archives. Boston.

Mass. Archs.	Massachusetts Archives Collection, Records, 1629-1799. 328 Vols. SC1-45x. Massachusetts Archives.
MH-H	Houghton Library, Harvard University.
MHS	Massachusetts Historical Society.
MiU-C	William L. Clements Library, University of Michigan.
MP	Member of Parliament.
ODNB-e	*Oxford Dictionary of National Biography Online.* London, 2004-2006, http://www.oxforddnb.com.
OED	*Oxford English Dictionary Online.* London 2004-2006, http://dictionary.oed.com.
NEP	Papers Relating to New England, 1643-1768. 4 Vols. Sparks Papers, MS 10. Houghton Library, Harvard University.
Papers of John Adams	Robert J. Taylor, Mary-Jo Kline, Gregg L. Lint, et al., eds., *Papers of John Adams.* 17 Vols. to date. Cambridge, Mass., 1977-.
PDBP	Peter D. G. Thomas and R. C. Simmons, eds., *Proceedings and Debates of the British Parliament respecting North America, 1754-1783.* 6 Vols. Millwood, N.Y., 1982.
Prov. Sec. Letterbooks	Province Secretary's Letterbooks, 1755-74, Secretary's Letterbooks, 1701-1872. 4 Vols. SC1-117x. [Vols. 1, 2, 2A, & 3]. Massachusetts Archives.
Reports of the Record Commissioners of Boston	*Reports of the Record Commissioners of the City of Boston.* 38 Vols. Boston, 1876-1909.

Select Letters	[Francis Bernard], *Select Letters on the Trade and Government of America; and the Principles of Law and Polity, Applied to the American Colonies. Written by Governor Bernard in the Years 1763, 4, 5, 6, 7, and 8. London, 1774. First edition. W. Bowyer and J. Nichols. London, 1774.*[10]
Spencer Bernard Papers	Spencer Bernard Papers D/SB. Centre for Buckinghamshire Studies, Aylesbury, Buckinghamshire, England.
T 1	Treasury: Treasury Board Papers and In-Letters, 1557-1922. T 1. TNA.
Temple Papers, 1762-1768: JT Letterbook	Bowdoin and Temple (Winthrop Papers). Bound MSS. Temple Papers, 1762-1768: Letter book of John Temple and other manuscripts. MHS.
TH	Thomas Hutchinson (1741-80).
TNA	The National Archives of the UK: Public Record Office, London.
WMQ	*The William and Mary Quarterly: A Magazine of Early American History and Culture*, 3d ser.

---

1. The Council's record books are Council Executive Records, 1760-1769, CO 5/823 and CO 5/827. There is also a set of nineteenth-century transcripts in Council Executive Records, 1692-1774, 13 vols. [vols. 2-14], GC3-327, M-Ar. The corresponding volumes for 1760-69 are vols. 15 and 16.

2. There are two contemporaneous sets of the Council's legislative records. One was kept in Boston and is in Council Legislative Records, 1692-1774, 24 vols., GC3-1701x, vols. 23-28, M-Ar. The other was sent to London: Council in Assembly, Massachusetts, 1760-1769, CO 5/820-CO 5/828. This project utilizes the London copies, for it was this set that was prepared for and consulted by ministers and officials.

3. This was the first publication in the Bernard Letters pamphlet series, printing six of Bernard's letters to the earl of Hillsborough **Nos. 706, 708, 709, 711, 717**, and **718**, *Bernard Papers*, 5: 96-101, 103-109, 111-114, 128-133; and Thomas Gage to Hillsborough, Boston, 31 Oct. 1768. The compositors'

copy texts were transcripts of copies of original correspondence presented to Parliament on 20 Jan. 1769;* the transcripts were prepared and authenticated by the clerk of the papers of the House of Commons on 27 Jan. William Bollan, acting as London agent to the Massachusetts Council, sent them to Samuel Danforth, the "president" of the Council, on 30 Jan.; the parcel arrived on 8 Apr. and Danforth subsequently passed them to fellow councilor James Bowdoin, in whose keeping they remained. Thus, the printed versions of the first batch of Bernard Letters were three steps removed from the original letters received by the secretary of state: the differences between them generally are not substantive (viz. missing or additional words, grammatical alterations) and consistent with accidental copying errors (misspellings) or incidental practice (orthography, punctuation). There are three imprints, listed as items 68a-68c in Adams, *American Independence,* 51-52. Copies of all the imprints are available in *Early American Imprints, Series 1*, nos. 41911, 11178, and 11179. The first was an unnumbered four-page folio pamphlet, the second a sixteen-page quarto, and the third a twenty-eight-page quarto. The first imprint was published between 10 and 17 Apr.; all three would have been distributed to newspapers for reprinting.

    * These are no longer extant. The Parliamentary archives in the House of Lords Library holds the American correspondence laid before Parliament on 28 Nov. but not the letters presented on 20 Jan. 1769. HLL: American Colonies Boxes 1-3.

4.   The Gage Papers were being reorganized when this volume was in preparation. I have retained the abbreviation "Gage" for consistency across the *Bernard Papers* series but have added additional information to this section summarizing the collection.

5.   The editors of this online resource advise that "the Journals of the House of Lords follow the same model as for those of the House of Commons. . . The volumes are from the Hartley Library [*Univ. of Southampton*], but give no information as to date, order or printer." http://parlipapers.chadwyck. co.uk/infoCentre/about_long18.jsp. The first thirty-one volumes (covering the period up to 1767) were published between 1771 and 1777; vol. 36, published in 1808, took the series up to 1779. See H. H. Bellot, "Parliamentary Printing, 1660-1837," *Bulletin of the Institute of Historical Research* 9 (1933-34).

6.   The Boston first edition included all the correspondence printed in *Copies of Letters from Governor Bernard to Hillsborough*, and added several documents framing and constituting the Massachusetts's Council's response to their governor's reports: James Bowdoin's letter to Hillsborough (**Appendix 3**); the Council's letters to Hillsborough (**Appendices 4** and **5**); and an appendix of the Council's proceedings, Jun-Dec. 1768. For copy text the printers again used the transcripts made by the House of Commons' clerk plus author copies of the Council's documents, both sets probably supplied by James Bowdoin. Publication was advertised in the *Boston Weekly News-Letter*, 27 Jul. 1769. The first edition is listed as 68d in Adams, *American Independence,* 53. Several US libraries have copies of this rare pamphlet, including the Library of Congress and the Boston Public Library. The project utilized the digitized version available in *Early American Imprints, Series 1*, no. 49926 (digital supplement).

7.   The London reprint is listed as 68e in Adams, *American Independence,* 53. The British Library microfilm copy (166p in reel no. 1870) is available in ECCO. The page sequence is different from the first edition, but the content is the same. It was first advertised for sale at 3s. in the *Public Advertiser*, 31 Oct. 1769.

8.   Pamphlet 69a in Adams, *American Independence,* 53. The project used the digitized version of the pamphlet held by the Bodleian Library (Oxford) available in ECCO. This was a new edition of correspondence based on a second batch of transcripts supplied by the Commons' clerk of papers and again transmitted to Boston by William Bollan, on 21 Jun. It included thirty of Bernard's letters to the secretaries of state (the earls of Shelburne and Hillsborough)* and two in-letters from Hillsborough (**Nos. 722** and **727**); Gage to Hillsborough, Boston, 3 and 5 Nov. 1768; letters received by Philip Stephens, the secretary of the Admiralty, from Royal Navy officers stationed in Boston (including Commodore Samuel Hood, 22 Nov. to 7 Dec. 1768); memorials of the American Board of Customs to the Treasury (including **Appendix 6**, *Bernard Papers*, 4: 373-374) and their enclosures, and correspondence with Gov. Bernard (**Nos. 624** and **626** ibid., 190-192, 194-195). It was first advertised for sale in the *Massachusetts Gazette and Boston Weekly News-Letter*, 7 Sept. 1769 and the *Boston Evening-Post*, 11 Sept. 1769.

* To Shelburne: **Nos. 585, 589, 593, 596, 600, 601,** plus FB's letter of 2 Feb. 1768, CO 5/757, f 24 (omitted because it merely acknowledged receipt of correspondence). *Bernard Papers*, 4: 86-88, 98-99, 112-118, 121-124, 129-139. To Hillsborough: **Nos. 623, 630, 632, 633, 638, 646, 648, 654, 656, 660, 663, 664, 668, 672, 681, 686, 690,** and **691**. *Bernard Papers*, 4: 185-190, 201-205, 207-214, 220-230, 242-246, 248-249, 255-257, 259-261, 266-270, 277-282, 288-290, 295-300, 318-324, 331-337, 347-353. In this volume, to Hillsborough: **Nos. 694, 698, 700,** and **703**.

9. Pamphlet 69c in Adams, *American Independence,* 53. The project used the digitized version of the copy in the Houghton Library (Harvard), (146p in microfilm reel no. 1471), in ECCO. The London reprint included three additional letters from Commodore Hood to Philip Stephens. Advertised for sale at 2s. 6d. in the *Public Advertiser,* 15 Nov. 1769.

10. A second edition was published in 1774 with a variant title and additional papers. *Select Letters on the Trade and Government of America; and the Principles of Law and Polity, Applied to the American Colonies. Written by Governor Bernard, at Boston, In the Years 1763, 4, 5, 6, 7, and 8. Now first published: To which are added The Petition of the Assembly of Massachuset's Bay against the Governor, his Answer thereto, and the Order of the King in Council thereon* (London: T. Payne, 1774). It was reprinted in Boston by Cox and Berry and advertised for sale on 27 Oct. 1774.

INTRODUCTION

A sense of crisis prevailed in the political world of London during the autumn of 1768. Because armed conflict with the colonies did not commence until 1775, it is easy to overlook the circumstance that as far as people in Britain knew it had already begun seven years earlier. . . . The prospect of war with the colonies was viewed with horror, but seen as a regrettable necessity, and in London there was every confidence that the army and navy would succeed in restoring Britain's authority in America.

(PETER D. G. THOMAS, *The Townshend Duties Crisis: The Second Phase of the American Revolution, 1767-1773* [OXFORD, 1987], 91-92.)

When British Regulars marched into Boston at midday on Saturday 1 Oct. 1768 they did so without incident. For three weeks, there had been rumors that the landing would be resisted and loose talk in the town meeting of arming the inhabitants. Governor Bernard took of all this seriously, as did the soldiers' commanders. By four in the afternoon the two regiments were parading on the Common, the landing accomplished "not only without Opposition but with tolerable good Humour" (**No. 694**). The troops were a deterrent to those who would break the king's peace; the Governor and Council could call upon their assistance in the event of civil disorder. Beyond that Bernard was unsure what the soldiers would actually do other than guard key positions and conduct parades. There was no revolt to crush, though Bernard trusted a garrison of Regulars would dispel once and for all the seditious tendencies of the town's radicals he had often cited in his reports to ministers. Two more regiments soon followed, bringing the total number of troops to around 2,200; in a town of 16,000 inhabitants this was roughly one soldier to four adult residents. Colonists, understandably, came to view the British regiments as an army of occupation, but got on with their lives and endured the tribulations and perils of having regular soldiers billeted among them.

The British government had given Governor Bernard what he wished. With the troops at his back—but not at his beck and call—the Chatham administration (then from 14 Oct., the Grafton administration) expected Bernard to turn things around: to protect Crown officers, to restore popular respect for the institutions of royal government, to remind radicals of their loyalties, and to enforce "due Obedience to the Law" in the streets and in the debating chambers. It was a tall order. On top of that Bernard was to undertake an investigation of the *Liberty* riot of 10 Jun. and bring the ringleaders and participants to justice. (**Nos. 661** and **699**.)[1] The new administration of the duke of Grafton also began discussing other ways and means of reestablishing equilibrium in British-American relations, and the debate would endure long after Bernard left the province of Massachusetts. No one in London or Boston expected war in 1768 or 1769; but it was no longer unthinkable to Boston citizens living cheek by jowl with soldiers or British politicians unable to understand why the colonists remained so resentful of parliamentary authority.

Both sides knew their differences hinged on what Francis Bernard had been telling the British government in the course of 1768. Colonial grievances and British impatience are manifest in the extensive documentary record for that signal year of Bernard's administration, much of which is published in the fourth volume of the *Bernard Papers* series. The colonists believed their governor had misrepresented their case to the secretary of state for the Colonies, portraying them as disorderly radicals and would-be rebels—all to the single purpose of getting London to send in the troops. They were not far wrong. But they lacked evidence. In the summer of 1768 Bernard's enemies began a slow-burning campaign to expose their governor's machinations. Bernard, for his part, responded with a bitter counteroffensive that caught the full attention of the British government and Parliament. He, too, lacked evidence and proceeded to gather what he could of the radicals' seditious activities and treasonable proclivities. This fifth volume of the *Bernard Papers* examines the political debates as they unfolded in Boston and London, and reviews the evidence gathered by the governor and his enemies in their efforts to besmirch each other. It would be foolish to dismiss the mud-slinging as irrelevant to the enlargement of the Imperial Crisis, for Bernard's letters were considered and debated by the Parliament in late 1768 and early 1769. The stakes could not have been higher: whose version of events in Boston would Parliament accept—the governor's or his enemies'?

Boston, October to December 1768

Bernard did not stick around after the soldiers paraded on the Common, and that evening retreated to his farm at Jamaica Plain, some four miles out of town. Open "talk of rising" had ceased (**No. 695**). But having requisitioned the town's Manufactory House as barracks for one of the regiments, Bernard did not anticipate the occupants staging a sit-in. When the squatters could not be evicted by the law officers, he allowed the commanding officer of the 14th Regiment of Foot, Lt. Col. William Dalrymple, to set up temporary barracks in Boston's most commodious public buildings, the Town House and Faneuil Hall, the very places where the House of Representatives and town meeting normally convened. But the circumstances were anything but normal. And in the days and weeks ahead the governor seemed to stumble from one potential flashpoint to another. Lt. Col. Maurice Carr's 29th Regiment and the artillery train set up camp on the Common, their drills and billets a stark reminder to the townsfolk of the harshness of military life (**No. 694**). Several weeks later these soldiers moved into outhouses, barns, and sugar houses hired by the army, thus rendering daily contact with the citizenry unavoidable. The 64th and 65th Regiments started arriving in the second week of November (**No. 715**) and were billeted in both the hired premises and Castle William barracks.

Bernard's month-long tussle with the Council to secure town barracks for the soldiers, before winter set in, revealed how little sway the governor now had with the province's elite politicians. While Dalrymple was privately unimpressed by the governor's evasiveness during the troop landing (**No. 751**), his superior General Thomas Gage[2] was more direct in recommending how Bernard should deal with the councilors.

> Considering what has passed, how short a time it is, that a Resolution was taken to rise in Arms in open Rebellion. I don't see any Cause to be Scrupulous in doing what is judged absolutely necessary for the Service, and for the security of the King's Government, which has been so highly invaded, and so insolently threatened. (**No. 697**.)

Gage's engineers, meanwhile, proceeded to repair Castle William's defences. Dalrymple was ordered to take possession of the Castle (since it was a Crown installation), though the provincial garrison was allowed to continue at Bernard's request. Gage wanted to put his soldiers straight into public buildings and to fortify the town, but the Council managed to frustrate that scheme.

The negotiations can be followed in Bernard's correspondence (**Nos. 700, 701, 706, 708**, etc.) and the Council's official proceedings,[3] but a fair amount of bargaining went on behind the scenes. Of particular note is the emergence of wealthy merchant James Bowdoin, who, in the governor's estimation was the prime mover in the Council's opposition (**Nos. 703** and **717**). The Quartering Act directed that soldiers be put in "barracks, or in hired uninhabited houses, outhouses, barns, or other buildings." The councilors and selectmen argued that the barracks at Castle William should be filled first, since Castle Island was within

Boston's original municipal boundary. While everyone knew the Castle barracks could not accommodate both regiments already in the town (let alone the two others on their way from Ireland) the municipal officials and councilors used the act to frustrate the governor and regimental commanders. The most they could have expected was to have one of the regiments placed in town, another at the Castle, and the others withdrawn for lack of accommodation; they did not achieve any of that although managed to evade paying for the billets and provisions, as the law required.

Whereas Bernard strove to follow the procedures set out in the American Quartering Act, Gage and Dalrymple were quite prepared to evade legal objections raised by the Council and selectmen. Ostensibly, that was because the councilors' objections limited the army's and the governor's discretionary authority to distribute the soldiers between town and Castle. The first set of orders issued by the secretary of state for the Colonies, the earl of Hillsborough,[4] specified only that at least one regiment should be stationed in the town, while the second set allowed Gage to decide how the regiments from Ireland should be deployed.[5] Since Boston did not have military barracks in the town itself and the governor could not clear squatters from the Manufactory House, a public building, Bernard's default position was to hire premises at the Crown's expense (**No. 706**). Neither Bernard nor Gage seemed particularly worried that billeting in public houses would likely increase the risk of violent clashes between drunken soldiers and citizens. At no point, it should be stressed, did Gage and Bernard plan to put British soldiers into private houses (despite what American folk history has since claimed), but there is no doubting that, as the Declaration of American Independence later maintained, the British had connived at "Quartering large bodies of armed troops among us." The Council, as well as the House of Representatives, suspected Bernard of plotting with the Customs commissioners to bring the troops to Boston, as the address to Gage, signed by a majority of members, intimated (**Appendix 1**).

From November 1768 until August 1769, Bernard obtained little active assistance from the Council on imperial affairs. Council business on issues connected with the Imperial Crisis was dominated by a group of between eight and eleven members who met regularly and separately from the Governor. They styled themselves the "major part" of the Council, although they did not actually constitute a majority of members. Most lived in or near Boston: radicals James Bowdoin, Samuel Dexter, James Pitts, and Royal Tyler; moderates William Brattle (whose recent radicalism had cooled somewhat), Samuel Danforth, John Erving, Harrison Gray, and Isaac Royall; and former friends of government Thomas Hubbard and James Russell. They claimed to act "individually, and not as a body," and convened under the presidency of the longest-serving member, Samuel Danforth. Bernard refused to countenance their irregular, unconstitutional proceedings from which he and the other members were excluded. (Under the Province Charter, executive meetings of the Council were to be chaired by the governor and legislative sessions were to be held only when he was present.)

For all that he was pleased to have the regiments, Bernard wanted out of Boston before isolated contretemps between soldiers and civilians turned nasty. He no longer expected the British government to fulfil former Chancellor of the Exchequer Charles Townshend's promise to institute Crown salaries for royal governors, and certainly did not look forward to the moment when he would have to go cap in hand to the assembly for his annual salary (**No. 766**). Perhaps before then, he hoped, he might be brought home on leave; such would depend on being able to persuade the British government that Boston was now reduced to a state of compliance, if not the "Obedience" that Hillsborough's instructions demanded. In rejecting Lord Barrington's[6] proposal that the governorship of South Carolina was a possible alternative, Bernard protested that what came first were

> two of the greatest Comforts of my Life, my Health
> & my Wife. The former indeed would depend upon a
> Trial: but the latter would have none; for I could not
> ask her to go with me. And as after 27 Years Cohabi-
> tation, We are still as desirous to continue together as
> we were the first Day. (**No. 705**.)

Nonetheless, when his recall came eight months later, he was quite prepared to return home at once with Thomas, his third son and secretary, and leave his wife Amelia and the other children to make their own way back.

Boston, December 1768-January 1769

While Bernard's family relationships remained strong throughout his last, difficult year in the province, the internal affairs of his administration were prone to tension. The return of the American Board of Customs to Boston in the first week of November further unsettled Jonathan Sewall,[7] the province's chief law officer, whose relationship with the Board had deteriorated since the spring. Sewall was right in thinking that the commissioners had questioned his commitment to the imperial cause when a legal opinion he proffered to the Board initially hampered its legal pursuit of John Hancock (**No. 678**).[8] John Hancock looms large in Bernard's story as much as he did in Boston's prerevolutionary politics. One of Boston's wealthiest merchants, the commissioners believed Hancock an arrogant and prolific smuggler who, with Bernard's assistance, they would bring to book after seizing his vessel the *Liberty*. Hancock was a wily opponent, and probably knew the essentials of admiralty law as well as any trained lawyer, including Sewall. It was

Sewall who, as advocate general, oversaw the prosecution of Hancock and five of his men in one of the most controversial trials to come before a colonial court: the defendants each faced inordinately high penalties of £9,000, from which Bernard (as governor) and Sewall (as prosecutor) each stood to benefit from their entitlement to one-third of the total fines. The proceedings lasted on and off until 25 Mar. 1769, when Sewall abandoned the action for lack of evidence, something which had troubled Sewall and Bernard throughout.

Nonetheless, Bernard was disappointed in Sewall. He had molded Sewall's career in hopes of encouraging other lawyers—even the Whig John Adams[9]—to serve the Crown. Since the autumn of 1768 Bernard harbored doubts about Sewall's reliability (**No. 719**). Promoting Sewall to judge of the Vice Admiralty Court at Halifax was preferment of a rather odd kind; for it obliged his chief law officer to sojourn in Nova Scotia for weeks at a time (**No. 752**). Nevertheless, Bernard and Hutchinson helped broker a settlement of sorts between Sewall and the Customs commissioners, albeit that two middle-ranking customs officials lost their jobs as a result (**No. 728**).

Hillsborough never instructed the provincial government to go after Hancock, but he did require Bernard to pursue the *Liberty* rioters. That too, came to naught under Sewall's stewardship. Bernard did what he could to fulfil Hillsborough's other directive about reforming the province magistracy (**Nos. 711** and **724**). The bottom line, as both Bernard and Sewall well knew, was that the British government had no idea how colonial government operated in practice (irrespective that Hillsborough subscribed to Bernard's notion that the government had been long subject to undue popular pressures). From here on, Bernard advocated revising the Province Charter to permit the Crown to appoint the Massachusetts Council directly, an idea that had considerable appeal to Hillsborough, Secretary at War Lord Barrington, and Secretary to the Board of Trade John Pownall, though its introduction would have required parliamentary legislation (**No. 715**). A private and confidential letter to Pownall,[10] reveals that Bernard held exploratory talks— "divers Conferences"—on such matters with "some of the cheif Members of the Government & the principal Gentlemen of the Town." The subject of these discussions can only be guessed at, but they resulted in a secret memorandum offering "Hints" on Massachusetts's "future Connexion" to Great Britain. Constitutional matters aside, the memorandum may also have touched upon the trial of John Hancock, though it is impossible to say if Bernard was hoping to unearth new evidence against Hancock or other Whigs (**No. 721**).

Governor Bernard had learned to live with the fact that, while residing in Boston, he was disconnected from the nuances of British high politics. Colonial newspapers did what they could to keep readers informed of current affairs, printing long extracts from the *London Gazette*, summaries of parliamentary debates taken from private letters, and travelers' gossip. Such news was invariably three months out of date. Journalism for journalism's sake focused largely on what the provincial government was doing rather than guessing what the British might be up to. Bernard did not plan a counter-offensive in print, however. "Philanthrop," Jonathan Sewall's *alter ego*, who had rushed to the governor's defense in the aftermath of the Stamp Act Crisis, was noticeably silent. Sewall had been the most effective of a small cadre of government writers in deflecting attention away from the governor and exposing some of the contradictions in the Whig polemics.[11] But with Sewall holding down three government jobs (and a fourth on the way) and conducting the prosecution in the Hancock trial, he had little if any time to spare for political writing. Even so, the shroud of anonymity under which polemical writing normally proceeded invites speculation as to Sewall's loyalty toward Bernard (**No. 762**). In the end, Bernard relied on his own judgment and his own private writings to keep the British on his side.

In January 1769, the news from London could not have been more encouraging. King George III's speech to Parliament of 8 Nov. raised Bernard's hopes that the British would tackle the "Disobedience" the king believed was manifest in Boston (**No. 729**).[12] The king, according to Hillsborough, approved Bernard's seeking the Council's advice as to whether or not to request soldiers from General Gage, thus excusing the governor from any accusation of tardiness. Bernard was also spared the trial of having to meet the assembly until the following May at the earliest (**No. 702**). Hillsborough further provided Bernard with a credible excuse as to why the king could not accept the House's petition for repealing the Townshend duties—thus apparently negating the effectiveness of the House's London agent Dennys DeBerdt (**No. 730**).[13] Hillsborough could not have made it any clearer that Bernard had the king's backing.

> In the very unpleasant & critical situation in which you stand at present, it will, I apprehend, be a great support and consolation to you to know that the King places much confidence in your prudence and caution on the one hand, & entertains no diffidence of your spirit and Resolution on the other, and that His Majesty will not suffer these sentiments to receive any alteration from private misrepresentations, if ^any^ such should come, that may flow from Enmity to you, or self interested Views in those who transmit them; and, for my own part, Sir, I take the Liberty to add that I will not fail to do Justice to your Conduct in every representation that I have occasion to make of it to His Majesty. (**No. 712**.)[14]

The endorsement would certainly have pleased; so too would the realization that the British government seemed responsive to what he had been writing since the late summer and autumn. Bernard did not realize that the reception accorded his reports was more complicated and the outcomes more complex, as events in London unfolded.

Meanwhile, in Boston, Bernard brought a renewed vigor to his official duties. Hillsborough had instructed him to extend his enquiries into any "illegal and unconstitutional Acts" committed since the *Liberty* riot. After consulting his cabinet council (of Thomas Hutchinson, Andrew Oliver, and Robert Auchmuty),[15] Bernard dispatched depositions provided by his informers: one could have been used to indict Samuel Adams for sedition (**No. 732**) while another revealed how far Adams and other radicals had scared moderates like Thomas Cushing with talk of resisting the troops (**No. 733**).[16] His next letter to Hillsborough railed at the "trumpeters of Sedition" in the *Boston Gazette* and its printers, Benjamin Edes and John Gill, who somehow had been able to print copies of six of Bernard's recent letters to the secretary of state in the issue of 23 Jan. How Edes and Gill managed this is uncertain, though they must have been assisted by someone with access to the governor's papers, and someone with the clout to manage the espionage, perhaps even James Bowdoin (**No. 734**).[17]

The six letters, dated 1 Nov. to 5 Dec. 1768, largely concerned Bernard's disputes with the Council (**Nos. 706, 708, 709, 711, 717, and 718**). Their publication predated the first of the Bernard Letters pamphlets by two months (an important fact that historians have hitherto missed), and was probably an immediate response to knowledge that the governor had been engaged in "divers Conferences" with his cabinet council and selected local dignitaries. Four of the six letters detailed how the Council hampered the governor's efforts to secure barracks for the British soldiers (**Nos. 706, 708, 709, and 711**); the two most recent letters complained of the irregular manner in which the councilors had drawn up petitions to Parliament for presentation via William Bollan, whom they hoped would become the Council's agent (**Nos. 717 and 718**). The governor's critics made much of a brief comment in **No. 709** where Bernard recommended a royally-appointed Council, observing to Hillsborough "how necessary it is become that the King should have the Council Chamber in his own hands. How this can be done may be a question; the Exigency of it is none." What the Whigs never got to know—but which they correctly deduced—was that their governor had made specific recommendations for appointing the Governor's Council by royal writ of mandamus, providing Hillsborough with the names of likely councilors—judges, officers, and friends of government he wished restored (**Nos. 737 and 738**).

Publication of Bernard's six letters thus marked a turning point in the Whigs' campaign against their governor. Risking prosecution, the printers were able to present to the public for the first time evidence of the governor's alleged wrong-doings (**Nos. 741** and **747**). The accusations mounted in the months following, as Whig polemicists tried to counteract news and rumor that Bernard's correspondence had been discussed in Parliament (**No. 742**). Bernard had to bide his time and endure the insults (in which he presumed his old adversary John Temple had a hand),[18] confident that he could take a leave of absence in the spring (**Nos. 746** and **762**). Both sides suspected, but did not know for certain until early April, that British politicians had also been wrangling over what Governor Bernard had written about the province of Massachusetts Bay over the past year.

London, November 1768-January, 1769

The king's speech at the opening of Parliament on 8 Nov. was a major turning point in the Imperial Crisis, for it brought the recent troubles in Boston to the center stage of British politics. Delivered in the House of Lords to the assembled Lords and newly elected members of the Commons, George III declaimed that Boston "appears, by late Advices to be in a State of Disobedience to all Law and Government." Having just read Bernard's report on the town meeting of 12 Sept. (**No. 681**),[19] the king and his ministers were convinced that Bostonians would stage a "Rebellion."[20] Not until 4 Nov. did they learn that the troop landings on 1 Oct. had been peaceful (**No. 694**); this outcome they presumed owed much to Bernard. Evidence of wrongdoing in the colonies, as Hillsborough quickly established, was mired in interpretation.[21]

Over the next six months the cabinet considered American affairs in more depth than any time since the Stamp Act Crisis, while Parliament subjected the government's colonial policy to a stern examination.[22] Bernard's conduct as governor figured prominently in these discussions and debates. Bernard had his advocates inside and outside the cabinet. While he received the backing of the secretary of state for the Colonies, other ministers were more ambivalent. There is no official record of cabinet discussions but private accounts of Parliament's debates reveal that opposition MPs highlighted inconsistencies in the governor's reports while government men defended the governor as a faithful servant of the Crown. Both sides found evidence in Bernard's copious correspondences to justify their respective positions, particularly on the question of whether or not to make concessions to the American colonists.

The king's speech gave no indication that the new prime minister, the duke of Grafton, and his cabinet would substantially change the direction of American policy. The decision to send the troops into Boston was taken by the previous administration, under the earl of Chatham's nominal leadership.[23] Grafton's cabinet[24] continued to support the troop deployment for the same reasons that they were sent there: Boston, they believed, was prone to civil disorder. Bostonians did not cast their opposition in that same light, and it took a while for Grafton and his colleagues to appreciate how far ministers' perceptions had been influenced by the hostile reports provided by Governor Bernard and the American Board of Customs.

Wills Hill, the earl of Hillsborough, the architect of Britain's hard-line approach, remained as colonial secretary under Grafton and looked set to continue to lead in formulating policy. Lord Hillsborough was by no means a bucolic aristocrat, untutored in political wiles; but for this Irish landlord the display of force remained an essential political tool to cow popular dissent, whether at home or in America.[25] He listened to Crown servants far more than his predecessor Shelburne,[26] though never uncritically, as his reception of Bernard's reports indicates; and it was in his domain, he told Bernard, to decide if their correspondence should ever be presented to Parliament (**Nos. 681**,[27] **712**, and **713**). Hillsborough pushed the cabinet to consider some of the root and branch reforms of colonial government advocated by Bernard; in this he was supported by the governor's friends John Pownall and Lord Barrington (**Nos. 723** and **740**). But Grafton's cabinet shied away from further intervention. In part that was because Grafton and the king instinctively favored conciliation with the colonists (and both certainly doubted the wisdom of punitive measures advanced by Hillsborough and others during 1769). But it was also because the administration had to tread carefully.

> Under one administration the stamp act is made; under the second it is repealed; under the third, in spite of all experience, a new mode of taxing the colonies is invented, and a question revived, which ought to have been buried in oblivion.

This first letter by the mysterious "Junius," who would go on to become a prolific critic of the Grafton and North administrations, encapsulated the frustration of many Britons with Hillsborough's handling of American affairs. "Junius," in common with the parliamentary opposition, blamed Hillsborough for having "driven" the colonists "into excesses little short of rebellion." Hillsborough's dismissal would not of itself "remove the settled resentment of a people . . . outraged by an unwarrantable stretch of prerogative."[28] For the moment, the administration could afford to ignore what "Junius" and other critics in the newspapers were saying about American affairs, though they felt their barbs more keenly in domestic matters, above all the controversy surrounding John Wilkes's libel trial and expulsion from the House of Commons.[29]

The general election did not provide Grafton with an unassailable majority in the House of Commons. While government won votes on American affairs, the opposition seemed to grow stronger and bolder with each division. Old Whigs in the House of Lords, including the Rockinghamite and Chathamite factions, pressed for a parliamentary inquiry into American affairs, only to find government men ready to support a declaration chastising the Americans. This demonstrative turn brought independents, Grenvillites, and Bedfordites alongside the King's Friends in defense of the principle of parliamentary supremacy. There was, overall, a strong sense that the Americans should be punished for their transgressions. Of course, that was not the view of the small band of American-born MPs, notably Barlow Trecothick, and their friends and sympathizers: generally they advocated compromise where possible, urging pragmatism and expediency when questions of principle promised only impasse.

The problem for Grafton, therefore, was not to appease the factions or fashion a united front but sustain a working majority from disparate groups.[30] Beginning with King George's public condemnation of Boston, the Grafton administration practiced an imperial rhetoric that imagined colonial opposition would wither in the shade of disapproval. In replying to the king's speech of 8 Nov., the House of Lords regretted the "Circumstances" in the American Colonies "which manifest a Disposition to throw off their Dependence" on the Crown.[31] When the Commons prompted a debate on the speech, the government went on the defensive to win Commons' approval for its American policy. Repeal of the 1767 Townshend Acts (listed in *Bernard Papers*, 4: 50n) was not on the cabinet's agenda in the winter of 1768-69. Despite attracting widespread criticism in America, ministers were obdurate on the question of colonial taxation.

The government assembled an extensive portfolio of evidence to justify why the troops should remain in Boston and why Massachusetts was unworthy of His Majesty's favor. On 28 Nov., Lord North, the chancellor of the Exchequer and leader of the Commons, and Hillsborough in the Lords, laid before Parliament over sixty items of American correspondence. The list included twenty-nine letters (plus their enclosures) Bernard had written to the secretaries of state Shelburne and Hillsborough between 21 Jan. and 5 Oct.[32] One additional letter of Bernard's (**No. 703**) and a file of papers received by the Admiralty were presented on 7 Dec.[33]

All of this was a prelude to the Lords' consideration and adoption of eight resolutions presented by Hillsborough on 15 Dec. The first resolution proposed that the proceedings of the Massachusetts House of Representatives had denied Parliament's legislative supremacy. The second denounced the Massachusetts Circular Letter as "unwarrantable and dangerous" for encouraging an "illegal Combination" to defeat the Townshend Acts. The third resolution proclaimed Boston "for some Time past" to have "been in a State of great Disorder and Confusion" on account of riots and obstructions offered the officers of Customs. The fourth accused the Council and the justices of the peace of a dereliction of duty in "suppressing" such disturbances. The fifth justified the use of "Military Force" to "Aid" the civil government and Customhouse; the sixth declared the proceedings of the Boston town meeting of 14 Jun. and 12 Sept. "illegal and unconstitutional, and calculated to excite Sedition and Insurrection." The seventh castigated the Convention of Towns for exhibiting a "Design" to establish a "new and unconstitutional Authority, independent of the Crown." The eighth accused the towns who elected delegates to attend the Convention and the Convention itself of "audacious Usurpations of the Powers of Government."

Finally, an accompanying address to the king urged that the Massachusetts governor be directed to conduct an investigation into treasonable activities in the province:

> to proceed in the most speedy and effectual Manner for bringing to condign Punishment the chief Authors and Instigators of the late Disorders . . . to take the most effectual Methods for procuring the fullest Information that can be obtained, touching all Treasons or Misprisions of Treason, committed within his Government since the Thirteenth of *December* last [*1767*], and to transmit the same, together with the Names of the Persons who were most active in the Commission of such Offences, to One of His Majesty's Principal Secretaries of State, in order that His Majesty may issue a Special Commission for enquiring of, hearing, and determining, the said Offences, within this Realm, pursuant to the Provisions of the Statute of the Thirty-fifth Year of the Reign of King *Henry* the Eighth.[34]

The following day, the resolutions and address were sent down to the House of Commons for concurrence; there they lay, out of public view, over the Christmas holidays, awaiting consideration by the whole House.[35]

While it is difficult to establish if the governor's letters were of material significance to the Lords' debate, Bernard's correspondence briefly captured parliamentarians' attention.[36] Several critics of the proposed treason commission, who were familiar with Bernard's reports, expressed concern that he would likely be put in charge of any investigation.[37] (Bernard's reservations were rather different for he had no power to compel people to testify before any such commission, **No. 753**.) Meanwhile, more of Bernard's letters arrived. On 20 Jan., Hillsborough and North presented Parliament with another batch of American correspondence, including six of Bernard's letters to Hillsborough (**Nos. 706, 708, 709, 711, 717, and 718**), plus ten other letters from senior military and naval officers stationed in Boston.[38] These constituted the most up-to-date information on the situation in

Boston available through official channels. Some fears would have been laid to rest, not least that Bostonians would resist the soldiers or seize the governor and other officials; the armed revolt that Bernard hinted at in **No. 681**[39] had not transpired. But ministers' concerns would not have been dispelled by what the letters also told them: that the Council had obstructed attempts to find quarters for the troops and that the justices of the peace neglected their duty to apprehend rioters. While a revolt did not seem (and was not) imminent, the perception remained that Boston was a disorderly and hostile place for the king's men.

Interruptions in the Commons' discussion of the American correspondence had nothing to do with ministers' management of the order of business. Members were advertised of an opportunity to review all the American correspondence on 25 Jan. The following day it was debated by a committee of the whole House, prior to consideration of the Lords' resolutions and address to the king, just as the Commons had insisted. The long delay in the Commons attending to the Lords' papers was largely due to the lengthy proceedings concerning John Wilkes. His expulsion from the Commons (which Bernard approved of)[40] preceded final consideration of the resolutions and address, both occurring within the first eight days of February (**No. 740**).

During this period, Hillsborough continued to express support for Bernard. With each letter to the governor, he promised Parliament would give American affairs its full attention, perhaps anticipating that the debate would vindicate not only his handling of the Imperial Crisis but Bernard's too. Yet he chose not to reveal how many of the governor's letters were presented to Parliament (**Nos. 722** and **727**). Hillsborough told Bernard only what he thought he needed to know. His early letters to Bernard were characterized by their tactical effusiveness (as much as any official communication could be), but letters from 2 Sept. onwards were studiously evasive with regard to what the administration was planning; perhaps that was how it ought to have been for a minister concerned with the security of transatlantic mail (**No. 670**).[41] John Pownall, however, provided a glimpse of the extent to which Hillsborough was pushing Bernard's reform ideas in cabinet (**No. 743**). But on 13 Feb. the cabinet pulled back from antagonizing the colonists further. Hillsborough too kept his options open. Bernard was expendable, and could be removed if the cabinet deemed it expedient to placate the opposition. Bernard's enemies had already provided Hillsborough the required ammunition, having blamed Bernard for misleading ministers in order to get troops sent to Boston. For all that Bernard presumed an affinity with Hillsborough, fed by Barrington's professions of friendship with the secretary (**Nos. 597** and **605**),[42] he was as dispensable as any other colonial governor.

Bernard was cautiously critical of Parliament's resolutions on Massachusetts, thinking them a dead letter unless the British government was prepared to follow them up with concrete measures (**No. 723**). He still preferred a centralizing reforming program based on strengthening royal government and introducing American representation in Parliament, though he knew the latter idea no longer counted for anything with his British friends. He was not blind to the efficacy of repealing the Townshend Acts, however. But he favored punitive legal action against the radical ringleaders, provided that trials could be conducted in England (**Nos. 753** and **758**). Bernard's comments on these issues during the winter of 1768-1769 are hazy and opaque because he never obtained a clear account of Parliament's proceedings until mid-April. He kept to himself any misgivings about Hillsborough keeping him in the dark.

London, January-February 1769

The Massachusetts Whigs might never have learned the full story of their governor's epistolary campaign against them had it not been for William Bollan. While historians have long acknowledged Bollan's part in the acquisition of Bernard's letters, they have had little to say about the intrigue surrounding their disclosure; nor has anyone provided a close reading of how the Bernard Letters fit with transatlantic political developments.[43] Unaware of Parliament's deliberations, the colonists were anxious to put the case for the repeal of all the American revenue acts following the Christmas recess. Uninformed of how hostile Bernard's reports were, the Massachusetts Whigs nonetheless long suspected their governor of complicity in bringing the troops to Boston and of turning ministers against them. Unwilling to wait on news of Parliament's proceedings, however, they set out to obvert ministers' preoccupation with their governor's advices. To that end, they enlisted the assistance of William Bollan.

Bollan had strong personal connections with Massachusetts, having represented its interests in London as province agent for over twenty years. He also nursed a grievance. He held Bernard personally responsible for his dismissal from the agency in 1762. Bollan, according to one biographer, grew "resentful during . . . years of vexatious leisure."[44] But his interest in colonial affairs never abated, and he penned several pamphlets during the Imperial Crisis. While Bollan's publications focused more on economics and imperial administration than constitutional issues he nevertheless came to share the radicalism of Massachusetts's leading Whigs in challenging Parliament's legislative authority in the colonies. When penury bit as retirement approached, Bollan gratefully accepted the Massachusetts Council's invitation to act as its first agent, in early 1769.[45] He may not have appreciated that he might not be paid for his services, for hitherto the governor had refused to recognize or authorize salary grants for any agent whom he had not approved or who was not jointly appointed by both houses of the legislature.[46] The professed "diligence" with which Bollan went about Council business, however, was testimony to his desire to play a part in resolving British-colonial disputes—and also his zeal to exact revenge on Bernard. Bollan's first epistolary report was calculated to ruin the governor's reputation.

Bollan was already deeply troubled by the direction of the Grafton administration's American policy. In a letter to senior Massachusetts councilor Samuel Danforth, dated 30 Jan. 1769 (**Appendix 2**), he expressed "great surprise & concern" at the hardening of British attitudes towards the Americans, prompting him to declare his determination to aid the "comon cause" of American liberty.[47] Bollan was especially worried by the recommendation in the Lords' address to the king for bringing felons to trial in England under a treason statute of Henry VIII, 35 Hen. 8, c. 2 (1543). Bollan called in the "favour of a principal member" and firm friend of the Americans (probably William Beckford) who undertook to provide him with "proper office copies" of the resolutions and address. These he received during or shortly after the Christmas recess. Upon reflection, he decided to submit his own petition, as a former resident of Boston, arguing against concurrence by the House of Commons. Hitherto Bollan's personal quest and the colonists' cause were parallel endeavors. But they became linked on 16 Jan., when Bollan received a letter of invitation to present to the Commons the Council's petition calling for the repeal of all the American revenue acts. The Council also alerted him to the necessity of by-passing the governor, who, they believed, would have misrepresented this petition (as he had others, they claimed) had he been entrusted with its transmission.[48] Four days later, Bollan was reminded why the Council were so wary of their governor, when Lords Hillsborough and North laid before Parliament another six of the governor's letters, in which Bernard fulminated on the Council's obduracy in the matter of finding quarters for the British soldiers.[49]

With American affairs scheduled for discussion on Monday 23 Jan., Bollan had to move quickly if the colonists' voice was to be heard. He also knew there was a strong possibility the Commons would refuse to accept the Council's petition. Not only was the protocol of transmission highly unusual, the petition's diplomatic form was irregular: the engrossed copy was signed by Samuel Danforth as "president"—an apparently spurious title—and a professed majority of councilors. There was another issue too: the petition's language was suitably deferential but the prayer reflected a shift in the colonists' argument against parliamentary taxation. The Council pressed for the repeal of all the American revenue acts, not just the Townshend Acts; the prayer thus called into question the continuance of the Navigation Acts and every operative trade law. Because he shared the Council's views Bollan did not think these matters were insurmountable obstacles to presenting the petition (and he reserved his strongest criticism for the Council's predilection for publishing its proceedings). So, Bollan arranged for William Beckford,[50] the city of London's Lord Mayor and MP, to present the Council's petition on the 23rd.

But "by a singular event" Beckford was "prevented" doing so. The Commons' votes and proceedings on John Wilkes's libels continued through the night until 3 AM, pushing American affairs back until the Wednesday.[51]

The first order of business on 25 Jan. was the reading of the American correspondence. It took the entire day. Proceedings concluded with a resolution that the committee of the whole House should consider the papers at noon the following day, as a prelude to a subsequent (and overdue) debate on the Lords' resolutions and the king's address. Beckford was finally able to present the Council's petition at 7.30 PM on the 25th, the House accepting it as a prayer from Samuel Danforth in the "Name" of individual councilors. Many of the objections against receiving it, Bollan later noted, "rested in a good measure on the representations of Gov[r] Bernard" (**Appendix 2**), whose official correspondence from 1768 had been read in the chamber, earlier that day. (Two of the six letters presented on 20 Jan. complained of the petition's irregular presentation [**Nos. 717** and **718**].) After Barlow Trecothick, another prominent friend to the Americans, read the Council's petition Beckford moved to refer it to the debate on the American correspondence scheduled for the Thursday.[52] While the motion failed, it did not extinguish Bollan's hopes of aiding the colonists.

The Commons' proceedings of 26 Jan. were taken up with a host of petitions on domestic affairs, before attention turned to Bollan's own petition late in the day. Bollan requested the House postpone consideration of the Lords' resolutions and address. To do so, he challenged the legal basis by which 35 Hen. 8, c. 2 (1543) could be applied to the colonies. That also failed. Bollan probably never expected the House to act upon either his or the Council's petitions. But he thought they might energize opposition to the administration's American policy—and in that he succeeded. Later that day, when the Commons debated the American correspondence, several speakers rose to question the dubious rationale by which the Grafton administration justified the proposed treason commission and the resolutions on Massachusetts.[53]

Sir Henry Cavendish's detailed private accounts[54] reveal that the opposition contended the American correspondence was problematic evidence, specifically questioning the probity of Bernard's letters. Judging by their reported comments, speakers had listened carefully when the letters had been read on the 25th, particularly attentive to what the governor had written about the *Liberty* riot, the Sons of Liberty, the Boston town meeting, and the Convention of Towns. However, the debate was not preeminently about the governor's rectitude but the credibility of the British government's American policy. No one appeared to doubt that the Chatham and the Grafton administrations had acted in response to what the governor had reported; and if Bernard had erred, the opposition argued, then ministers should accept responsibility.

The first speaker, William Dowdeswell,[55] the leader of the Rockingham Whigs, began by attacking Hillsborough's "rash and inconsiderate" handling of the Massachusetts rescinding controversy and the "cruel" proposal to apply the Henrician treason statute to North America.

> I never was more in earnest in all my life, than I am when I declare, that I was always for maintaining the authority of this country over the colonies, by every reasonable means: but the mode now proposed to us cannot be justified at the bar of justice or of reason.— After referring to the letters of Governor Bernard [*Cavendish noted*], and pointing out the tone of irony and contempt towards the Americans in which they were dictated, . . . [*he*] concluded with a recapitulation of his arguments.

Responding, Attorney General William de Grey[56] doubted the Bostonians were "guilty of an overt act of treason," but had "come within an hair's breadth of it," citing Bernard's letters. But "If the letters of Governor Bernard contain what is false, punish him, impeach him; proceed in a regular way against him." De Grey's purportedly judicious evaluation of Bernard's interpretations also offered the administration a way out, should the debate turn against the government. Bernard was potentially a convenient scapegoat, as much as he was actually a target of the opposition.

As the chorus grew, speaker after speaker followed Dowdeswell (in criticizing the resolutions and the address) and de Grey (in defending them), many on both sides commenting on the veracity of Bernard's reports. Preferably, Bostonians should be treated leniently, but if treasonable investigations were to proceed be sure to take them out of Bernard's "angry hands" and give them to Parliament, declared Charles Cornwall in support of Dowdeswell.[57] Having supported the repeal of the Stamp Act and having expected the Declaratory Act to end disputation about Parliament's authority, Richard Hussey[58] (for the administration) demanded the colonists be "taught . . . a lesson." But avoid commitments "to measures which you cannot see the consequences of," the sagacious Edmund Burke[59] warned the House, beware of "falsehoods" perpetrated by Bernard or any other governor.

> Whatever acts of injustice you commit in America will react upon yourselves. . . . Governors will not grow wise, so long as you fortify their folly with your approbation. . . . By your resolution you suppose and presume treason, at the same time that you acknowledge you have no proof.

The former prime minister George Grenville[60] condemned the Lords' failure to tackle the inadequacies of the Boston magistracy and professed to "lament" the general orders to enforce the law sent to Bernard; yet even he noted that

> Governor Bernard cannot be in the right. He and the council quarrel. Cannot you see the cause in the letters? I think the Americans, thus encouraged, could do no otherwise than they have done.

Solicitor General John Dunning[61] intervened to defend the proposed Crown commission on treason: "not all cases" of treason would be "sent for," only those where the king saw "sufficient ground for such a proceeding."

The clarification prompted William Beckford to urge that any treason trial must take place in America. Doubting that the government would risk provoking the Americans, he continued to question the legality of any treason commission when the Bostonians had not actually resisted the landing of the troops, despite what Bernard had said about seditious views being aired in the town meeting of 12 Sept. "Do not let there be fresh grounds of dispute," he warned, "and especially let us not give way to force." Instead, Beckford urged a parliamentary inquiry into the troubles reported by Bernard, a "measure" whose merit "does not leave the Americans in the hands of an angry man." Thereupon, former Massachusetts governor Thomas Pownall undertook a detailed examination of each of the resolutions, arguing that the Boston selectmen who drafted the precepts summoning the Convention of Towns—the single piece of felonious evidence submitted by Bernard—did not actually realize that the forms were in themselves seditious. (Bernard had made the same point when pleading for the Convention to break up, **No. 685**.)[62]

The crescendo of the opposition's tirade against the "angry man" in Boston was a speech by war veteran and warm friend of the Americans, Isaac Barré.[63] After years disputing Parliament's authority to tax them, and with Boston now enduring military occupation brought on by Bernard, the American Colonies were "ripe for revolt."

> As to governor Bernard, let him have what merit he will, he appears, from these papers, to be peevish and litigious; glad to find things wrong, on purpose to represent them to the government at home. If we are to believe him, there must be a revolution somewhere. 'I expect,' he says, 'to be stormed by the sons of liberty.' You might as well expect an account of his being murdered, together with the last words of governor Bernard. He mentions every little dirty story, and writes of an intention to seize Castle William. Sir, all this is in-

excusable, unless, in the following post, he could give us the names of the conspirators. . . . After these ridiculous resolutions, and this strange address, can any gentleman imagine that the colonies will not have a contemptible notion of us, all put together? A passionate governor may wish to see America chained down like a conquered province; but, can any man believe that that would heal the wound, that that would restore order? If we do not change our conduct towards her, America will be torn from our sides.

The penultimate exchange descended into farce before the concluding scene. Dowdeswell demanded to see the Boston selectmen's precept. When the ministry were unable to furnish it, the leading independent Sir George Savile[64] quipped that "If governor Bernard by letter could induce the secretary of state to believe false facts, we should be careful not to be led into the same error." With reference to the missing precept, Lord Barrington[65] and Thomas Pownall were able to explain "how the mistake had arisen," thus allowing the chamber to proceed (whether with or without the precept, we do not know). When the votes were cast, 155 favored proceeding to consider the Lords' resolutions and address, 59 were against. Sitting until 3 AM, the Commons finally resolved, without a division, to consider the Lords' papers in a week's time.[66] The censure of John Wilkes delayed American business, however, until 8 Feb.

That day, the debate on the Lords' resolutions and address commenced with a motion by an American sympathizer, Rose Fuller,[67] to recommit the report (that is, to postpone the decision taken by the committee of the whole House to consider the papers). In trying to delay consideration, opposition MPs once again condemned the harshness of the king's address, with Beckford urging Bernard's immediate recall. Imagine how the Americans would react to their countrymen being transported to England under the Henrician statute, Capt. C. J. Phipps[68] asked the House. "Will they not think these men are brought over here to be murdered?" Barlow Trecothick astutely observed that Bernard's comment (in **No. 632**)[69] on the Customs Board's removal to Castle William after the *Liberty* riot—that "the retreat of the commissioners will tend to serve our purposes"— raised questions of his "fidelity, or duty to government"; for as the colonists continued to pay the Townshend duties, the commissioners and the governor plotted against them, Trecothick implied. The remainder of the debate ranged over the colonists' disputation of parliamentary taxation and the validity and propriety of the Henrician statute, until Thomas Pownall delivered a long speech defending the colonists.

Pownall, as was his wont, commenced with a legal fact. A statute of 8 Will. 3, permitted treasonable cases to be heard in the colonies. But, he stressed, "rebellion was not in their hearts; independence is not in their heads," although with a military force already deployed in Boston, conflict was not unlikely. "In such a state of inflammability . . . the smallest spark would give it fire — it will break out into a flame, which no reason, no prudence, no force can restrain." His principal message was that the government, at this juncture, should avoid "innovation" and propose conciliation on "the ground that this business actually now stands": that meant accepting the convenient distinction between internal and external taxes, and forever giving up introducing the former. He echoed Burke's warning that the Declaratory Act should never be enforced, thus studiously avoiding in the near future contests over the principle of Parliament's legislative supremacy. "Do nothing which may bring into discussion questions of right, which must become mere articles of faith." While Pownall and other opposition speakers thus tried to undermine the credibility of Grafton's American policy (as Bollan hoped), they did not (as Bollan and the Massachusetts Council wished) urge the repeal of all revenue acts currently in force. In the end, the Commons approved both the resolutions on Massachusetts and the address to the king with minor amendments.[70]

Ultimately, the government majority was too solid for the opposition to defeat on any division. But there is little doubt the opposition succeeded in warning the government about the dangers of escalating tensions in British-American relations. The relationship was by no means critical, but certainly in need of repair. Many in government and out must have doubted the wisdom of letting Hillsborough lead American policymaking. The colonists knew nothing of this and little of Parliament's debates, which were never reported in detail in any newspaper. (The adoption and text of Parliament's resolutions and address were not reprinted in Boston until 17 Apr.) Their most important source of information was William Bollan's letters to Danforth and the Council. But Bollan's other sterling service to his New England friends, however, was to provide them with the means by which to expose Bernard as the king's villainous adviser.

It was Bollan who first discovered that Bernard's correspondence with Hillsborough had been of material significance to ministers. He did not know exactly what the governor had been telling the British government; for, like all visitors, he was excluded from the Strangers' Gallery during Commons' debates. But he was able to rely on his parliamentarian friends to brief him. Knowing that MPs were entitled to request from the clerk of papers copies of any item tabled,[71] Bollan enlisted help to get copies of the governor's six letters that had been presented to the Commons on 20 Jan. The clerk, George White, countersigned the transcripts on 27 Jan., and three days later Bollan sent them, unopened, to Danforth in Boston. It is odd that Bollan did not read the letters. Likely, his friends in Parliament told him that these particular letters concerned Council business and would be of value in challenging Bernard's interpretation of events. He may also have decided not to break the clerk's seal before transmitting the parcel. Bollan was not yet able to supply documentation revealing Bernard's allegations about Bostonians' sedition, which several MPs had referred to, and the next batch of the governor's letters he made sure to read before transmission.

What Bollan did not know, however, was that the Boston Whigs already knew what the six letters contained. It is a puzzling coincidence that Bollan purloined copies of the same six letters the Whigs published in the *Boston Gazette* on 23 Jan., a fact hitherto ignored by historians. The most logical explanation is that publication in the *Gazette* was arranged by the leading opposition councilor, James Bowdoin. Bowdoin may have learned of the governor's "divers Conferences" with senior officers and local gentlemen, in which they discussed reforming the Council and disqualifying the governor's opponents (**No. 721**). Nursing a personal grievance and determined to prove the governor had misrepresented the Council, Bowdoin or an accomplice may have accessed Bernard's private letterbooks and surreptitiously made copies of the relevant letters. If so, the espionage apparently remained undetected until the letters appeared in the *Gazette*. It is most unlikely the newspaper's copy text (which is not extant) was based on transcripts sent over from England. The Whigs did not have a spy in the secretary of state's office (as far as is known) who could supply the printers of the *Gazette* with copies of the governor's letters as soon as the originals or their duplicates arrived in London. In any case he or she would have had to have overcome the limitations of transatlantic communication to ensure that copies of letters received in January were transmitted to Boston in time for publication on the 23rd. An alternative, speculative explanation is that Bowdoin used Bollan to acquire authenticated copies of the letters from the clerk of the papers of the House of Commons in order to cover his own crime: that were he prosecuted for libel he might defend himself by protesting the clerk's transcripts postdated publication in the *Gazette*. (On the points above see the source note to **No. 734**.) Equally valid is the possibility that one of the Boston selectmen was involved in the procurement. For in responding to the six letters' publication the selectmen eagerly challenged the governor to produce evidence denying he had misrepresented the province in the rest of his correspondence (**Nos. 741** and **747**).

Bollan was not the Bostonians' dupe and acted of his own volition in supplying the Council with the first of two batches of Bernard's letters. Eighteen months later, Bollan clarified how he procured copies of the governor's letters.

> I obtained them in the same manner wherein from time to time I obtain'd copies of papers in my former agencies. The first parcel [*was*] sent by direction of a knight of the shire for the county of Wilts, and the second by direction of the present Lord Mayor. The clerk wou'd have had me receive the latter copies without his authentication, which with difficulty I obtain'd.[72]

These "two worthy members" used their privileges on "various attendances" to conduct "examination of the papers in the drawer of the House of Com^s, and, insisting with resolution, [*on*] authentic copies of Govr Bernard's letters." Bribes were essential, for the documents prepared by the clerk "cou'd not be had at a small expense." [73]

The "first parcel" of Bernard Letters—the six letters Bollan dispatched to Boston on 30 Jan.[74]—was obtained through the intercession of one of Bollan's long-standing contacts (and whose contribution hitherto has escaped historians' notice). Bollan chose not to name him, but gave Danforth clues sufficient to deduce his identity, describing him a "knight of the shire" of Wiltshire. Knights of the shire were MPs for English counties, and most counties, including Wiltshire, had two. Edward Popham (?1711-72) of Littlecote, Wilts., was the more likely of Wiltshire's MPs to have been Bollan's accomplice in respect of both the Bernard Letters and Bollan's "former agencies." [75] While Popham's family had strong historical connections with America, Edward Popham's motivation in aiding Bollan was largely political (at least we must presume it was in the absence of any other documentary evidence left by Popham or Bollan). Independent for most of his parliamentary career, Popham subsequently gravitated toward the Chathamite Whigs, first supporting Chatham's administration then the opposition, and generally voting against the government. [76]

It is possible Edward Popham was the "principal member" who also procured copies of the Lords' papers for Bollan, but William Beckford seems a more likely candidate. By "principal member" Bollan may not have been alluding to an *éminence grise* so much as a member whose eminence derived from longevity of service. Even so, by also describing this MP to Danforth as "one of your best friends" (meaning he was a firm supporter of the Americans' cause) Bollan gave the impression that the "principal member" was indeed an *éminence grise*. These particular epithets are more readily applicable to Beckford than to Popham. Elected lord mayor of London later that year, Beckford made no secret of his support for the Americans. As a wealthy West Indies merchant, plantation owner, and slaveholder, Beckford was regarded as a parvenu and social outsider by the English aristocracy, and though he went to considerable lengths to cultivate friendships his Jamaican accent and reputedly vulgar manners drew hostile comment. Beckford, as Bollan made clear, subsequently acquired for him a second batch of Bernard Letters. Beckford's conduct fitted easily with his strident criticism of the government's American policy. He may have shared the colonists' hope that the dismantling of mercantilism would usher in a new age of commercial prosperity for British North America. His domestic politics were also tinged with radicalism. By the spring of 1770, he was the foremost advocate for restoring fellow alderman John Wilkes to the House of Commons, Wilkes having been expelled after winning the Middlesex elections. [77]

William Beckford. Mezzotint by John Dixon, published 1769. © National Portrait Gallery, London.

Boston, April-May 1769

Historians have tended to conflate the colonists' reactions to both parcels of the Bernard Letters and have ignored entirely the significance of the prior publication in the *Boston Gazette*. Generally, they have assumed that the letters' publication in a series of pamphlets from April onwards constituted the governor's disgrace, forever sullying his reputation as chief executive and justifying the colonists' opposition to British colonial policies; and, that the evidence of the governor's perfidy was (and is) plain to see in the published correspondence.[78] That is only part of the story, for historians have not fully accounted for the Whigs' management of their campaign against Bernard, nor connected it to the chronology of events in Britain, nor considered what the published letters did not reveal. Popular reaction to the Bernard Letters was actually less demonstrative than historians have allowed, not because there was any significant support for the governor but because public condemnation was channeled effectively through local institutions. The campaign against Bernard was carefully managed—as it had to be if the Whigs were ever to get rid of him. It is easy for us to forget that the stakes were high: for this was a Crown servant who had brought troops to Boston streets, who had dissolved the legislature, and whose correspondence had left British ministers thinking of treason trials.

Speculation about the content of Bernard's letters abounded in early April. This followed publication on 3 Apr. of both the full list of American correspondence presented to Parliament on 28 Nov. and the resolutions on Massachusetts passed by the House of Lords.[79] (Confirmation of the resolutions' adoption by the Commons followed on 17 Apr.). The "first parcel" of letters arrived in Boston on Saturday 8 Apr.[80] Danforth and Bowdoin met with their fellow councilors the next day to strategize a counter-offensive. Moderates like Thomas Flucker were excluded from these discussions, and in the coming days and weeks the Whigs utilized the press to undermine the few friends of government left in the House of Representatives (**No. 765**). The strength of partisan condemnation was only to be expected (though Bernard also had his critics among the friends of government). The most striking aspect of the Whigs' initial reaction, as reported by Bernard, was how the Council stage-managed their governor's denouement. That Sunday, the authentic copies prepared by the Commons' clerk of papers were given to Edes and Gill with instructions to print three copies for each councilor (which would amount to a total of sixty-six copies if they were distributed regardless of political allegiance). The authentic copies, however, Edes and Gill put on public view at their Queen Street office, where "many Hundreds of People" flocked "to read them" over the next two or three days, "with some justifying others condemning the Letters according to the Part they take" (**No. 765**). Bowdoin was then allocated the task of drafting the Council's response (**Appendix 4**), for which he took possession of the authentic copies; the publication of transcripts of Bernard's letters was purposely delayed until Bowdoin had finished.

Edes and Gill had always been the printers of choice for the Whig faction. The public display of evidence purporting to show the governor's treachery helped the Whigs in the upcoming elections, but also served an additional purpose: it vindicated the printers' long opposition to the governor. Edes and Gill may or may not have been aware of Bernard's more recent attacks on them, in which he urged the case for restricting press freedoms (**No. 734**), following publication of the governor's six letters on 23 Jan. But for the moment, at least, the disclosure of the authentic copies of these letters gave them the upper hand in the contest. For those colonists, if any, who doubted that the letters published on 23 Jan. were accurate transcripts of genuine letters, here was proof provided by the clerk of the papers of the House of Commons. Such proof would not in itself have saved the printers from a libel trial had the British government gone after them, but it certainly turned the heads of the governor's remaining friends, as Bernard conceded (**No. 765**). Bollan's letter enclosing the authentic copies broke the news that these particular letters had been laid before Parliament on 20 Jan. (following those presented on 28 Nov.)[81] We can assume that most readers of the governor's letters would have given little or no thought as to how the printers of the *Gazette* acquired copies of the same letters before then.

The Council too used the "first parcel" of Bernard Letters to deflect criticism from within Whig ranks. The first newspaper commentary on the letters allowed that Bernard's predilection for instituting a royal Council ought to spur the Council into action to defend their reputations; the Council's Whig credentials had been blunted by the cautious language—but not the sentiments—of their recent petitions for repealing the revenue acts.[82] The Council's response to the Bernard Letters, contained in a letter to the earl of Hillsborough, went some way to restoring the reputation of Bowdoin and other Whig councilors (**Appendix 4**). It provided an enlightening counter-narrative to Bernard's hostile rendition of his difficulties in procuring quarters for the troops. (In this volume the Council's commentary has been cross-referenced to the governor's six letters). James Bowdoin also prepared a lengthy vindication (**Appendix 3**) against personal criticism made by Bernard in **No. 717**. Researchers ought to read both missives in conjunction with the governor's letters—as they should all the Whig responses—not only as a corrective to the bias in the governor's reports but to appreciate what the colonists had to do to repair their deteriorating relationship with Britain.

In the first instance, the Council had to sacrifice Bollan's anonymity in order to prove the copies' authenticity. It seemed not to concern the agent if the British or the colonists learned of his part in acquiring the letters. The second imperative, having seen the full list of American correspondence, was to acquire more material from Bollan as quickly as possible.[83] These letters concerned provincial matters far beyond the business of the Council. Bowdoin, Danforth, and the others took it upon themselves to expose the scale of Bernard's machinations against "this Country." Since the troops arrived, they had been living "as if in an Enemy's Country,[84]

> We do not yet certainly know all the means by which this has happened: nor do we yet certainly know all our accusers. But we apprehend the representations and memorials, that have been made by Governor Bernard, the Commissioners of the Customs, and some other Persons, concerning the disorders and riotous proceedings, which happened in the Town of Boston in March and June 1768, have brought upon them that misfortune.

The Council never managed to undertake the detailed, careful examination of the governor's other correspondence that Bollan wanted. For sure the Council had already addressed issues pertinent to their own governmental role (**Appendix 4**), and took the discussion forward in a follow-up letter to Hillsborough of 12 Jun. (**Appendix 5**). But when the second parcel sent from London arrived in August, the Council stood back; Danforth and Bowdoin gave way to radical Whigs in the town meeting and House of Representatives, notably Samuel Adams, who hereafter fashioned the public responses to the governor's letters.

While the Council waited expectantly for more material, the "first parcel" of Bernard Letters was published as *Copies of Letters from Governor Bernard to Hillsborough.* Printed by Edes and Gill it was issued within a week or so of the letters' arrival in Boston.[85] The copy text was prepared from the authentic copies provided by the Council; subsequent reprints in colonial newspapers followed the imprints issued by Edes and Gill.[86] Included with Bernard's six letters was a copy of General Gage's letter to Hillsborough of 31 Oct.[87] But there was no extended commentary on the governor's correspondence, as Bernard had anticipated: that appeared in the next pamphlet in the series. *Letters to Hillsborough*, on sale by 27 Jul., included Bowdoin's and the Council's letters to Hillsborough (**Appendices 3** and **4**) and an appendix of the Council's proceedings from July to December 1768. The printers hinted more would follow, claiming the governor's "other letters are said to contain high charges against, and gross misrepresentations" of the "people of this province."[88]

Public defenders were nowhere to be seen. "Officers of the Crown & the Friends of Government are very loud" in their condemnation, Bernard noted (**No. 765**). Sewall, while he did not openly criticize the governor, was unwilling to risk further opprobrium defending him. Bernard's observation, however, likely had more to do with Thomas Hutchinson's reaction to the letters' publication. Bernard's assertion to Hillsborough that Hutchinson "well understands my System" glossed over palpable differences between them (**No. 767**). By his own account Hutchinson had never seen

> a Line of any of the Letters until I saw them in Print nor did I know such Letters had been wrote unless perhaps some mention might have been made in Company by the Governor of his having wrote to such purpose which he is sometimes apt to do though I had no particular Remembrance of it.

The disclaimer of foreknowledge may have been willful dissembling. But entrusted to a confidant, Israel Williams (who, though a friend of government, had been a lukewarm advocate for Bernard), it also projects sincerity and in doing so puts considerable distance between the lieutenant governor and the governor. Bernard, Hutchinson continued, did not understand the colonists' reverence for the Province Charter when he called for a royal Council.

On that issue, Bernard and Hutchinson remained far apart, the governor evincing an imperialist outlook, his lieutenant an American-centered and identity-laden provincialism. "I am not desirous of a change in the Constitution," Hutchinson insisted, concluding with the assurance that it is "natural to suppose I have attachments to old modes and customs, civil and religious which are not to be expected in him."[89] While publication of the Bernard Letters did not jeopardize their relationship, their friendship nevertheless cooled during Bernard's last months in the province. Bernard's dull, matter-of-fact account of the affair in his private letters confessed his disappointment with Crown officers, without naming Hutchinson or Sewall, and reinforced his determination to be rid of the troublesome province (**Nos. 763 to 765**). Hutchinson, meanwhile, was left pondering how Britain would manage to establish the "dependence" of its colonies without further alienating the Americans.[90] In repudiating the necessity of special measures, he led himself, inexorably, to defending imperialism in the abstract: that British rule emanated from an indivisible and indissoluble British sovereignty.

It is curious how few commentaries on the Bernard Letters were published in the provincial press in the first four months of 1769.[91] We should not accept this as a yardstick of popular opinion, but an indication as to how far criticism of the governor was being managed. Back in February, when the Boston selectmen taunted the governor to make his correspondence public, they initiated a campaign to oust him from office that gathered speed over the spring and summer and continued after his departure. On 4 Apr., before the six letters arrived, the town meeting voted to petition the king for Bernard's removal.[92] Much of the credit for organizing the opposition against the governor has been attributed to Samuel Adams, who had unrivaled influence in the assembly and among the Boston populace.[93] Adams drafted and wrote many important papers as clerk of the House of Representatives, though historians have tended to lose sight of the fact that these documents were the productions of committees. Adams was certainly a leading figure in the deliberations of the assembly respecting Bernard, when it opened on 31 May, nearly a year after its dissolution. Adams's brand of radicalism had not gone down well with the Americans' friends in London, but publication of the Bernard Letters probably softened their attitudes. Bernard's last letter to Richard Jackson, one of the more conservative British defenders of the Americans, closed with a plea to accept that colonial-British relations could never be the same again.

> A good Friend of yours observed t'other day upon your still being an Advocate for the Constitution of this Government, that if you had seen the Effects of it upon the Spot, for these last 3 Years you would be of the same Opinion with us. (**No. 772**.)

On 29 Apr., Bernard received news he had long desired (**No. 757**). Six weeks earlier, the ministry decided to recall him to England and allow him to make a personal report. More than that, the king created him a baronet—paying the expenses to boot. Bernard took satisfaction in Hillsborough's assurances that the king had "not been influenced by the Malevolence & Misrepresentation" emanating from the Boston Whigs (**No. 768**). He soon learned the British government was still interested in prosecuting leading American Whigs. On 20 May, Bernard received Hillsborough's instructions (**No. 745**) to investigate treasonable activities committed since 30 Dec. 1767 (in line with Parliament's resolutions). Hillsborough did not spell out the procedural arrangements that Bernard was to follow. Initially the governor set to collecting evidence since he was not directed to head up a royal commission (which Parliament had suggested). While Bernard assumed that any treason trial would take place in England, Barrington offered a corrective. "Five or Six Examples are sufficient," Barrington confided, and "it is right they should be made in Boston, the Only place where there has been actual Crime" (**No. 740**). Bernard replied forcefully to Hillsborough (**No. 778**), highlighting the unlikelihood of persuading any Whigs to bear witness against another. Nor would he be able to collect sufficient evidence for a trial, "tho their Practices were treasonable yet I cannot fix upon any Act that seems to me to be actual Treason." Bernard knew he would be in England by the time any royal commission could be established, thus automatically casting Thomas Hutchinson as a chairman in waiting. (Thankfully, a Massachusetts treason commission was never established. But a royal commission of inquiry met in Rhode Island in 1772 to consider the burning of HMS *Gaspee*, though it did not proceed with prosecutions largely to avoid the political consequences of any treason trials.)[94]

London, March-May 1769

Meanwhile, in London, Bollan advanced the colonists' cause. Much of the information about British politics Bollan sent to Boston was gleaned from regular conversations with the coterie of pro-American MPs who had distinguished themselves in the debates on the American correspondence. All of them were familiar with what the Massachusetts governor had written. It would not have taken Bollan long to ascertain the contents of the full range of Bernard's correspondence with Hillsborough that had been read to the House of Commons. The friends of America were not a lobby group, but a congeries of opposition MPs with varying degrees of interest in how the disputes over American affairs were affecting the American colonists.[95] Bollan also worked in parallel with the agent of the Massachusetts House, Dennys DeBerdt, though their relationship was often strained. On one thing they were agreed: "The greatest resentment" the colonists "have reason to fear will arise from Gov'. Bernards representations in his Letters."[96]

The most enigmatic of Bollan's contacts was the former Massachusetts governor Thomas Pownall. If Edmund Burke was the most erudite of parliamentary commentators on American affairs, Pownall was the most knowledgeable. His reputation rested upon his wide-ranging if verbose *Administration of the Colonies* (1764; 4th ed., 1768). Pownall had come to share Bollan's dislike of Bernard (see **No. 607**),[97] irrespective that his brother John remained Bernard's confidant. Indeed, Pownall was better placed than Bollan to procure Bernard's correspondence for the colonists had he been so motivated. (Pownall had once before undermined a governor, his predecessor William Shirley, and might have done so again if he had been approached to take on the agency. He was listed among the supposed authors of the "Junius" letters and later assisted Benjamin Franklin in acquiring the *Hutchinson-Oliver Letters*.)[98] Although Pownall had his supporters in Massachusetts—and he maintained contact with James Bowdoin—he also had his enemies from his days as governor (Thomas Hutchinson among them). Pownall's appointment as Council agent would have divided the Massachusetts Whigs, whereas Bollan's previous experience outweighed objections about his court party connections. Having been Shirley's man, Bollan never really trusted Thomas Pownall. Pownall made only a brief but important contribution in the Commons' debate of 25 Jan., and took no part in Bollan's plan to promote the Council's petition and discredit Bernard. Bollan, therefore, was taken aback when, on 19 Apr., Pownall moved the repeal of the Townshend Revenue Act in the House of Commons.[99]

Bollan was disappointed Pownall did not make the most of the opportunity to get at the root causes of the colonists' discontent. Pownall did not propose the repeal of all the revenue acts, which the Council's petition had requested, nor did he address the principle being contested—Parliament's authority to tax the colonists. Bollan and a "sincere friend," probably Beckford, suspected Pownall of acting at the behest of the administration—that he was secretly prompted by Hillsborough to test parliamentary opinion on conciliating the Americans.[100] It was a plausible deduction.

At a meeting on 1 May Grafton's cabinet decided to move for the partial repeal of the Townshend duties. By embracing conciliation the cabinet repudiated Hillsborough's hard-line proposals for a permanent solution to the Imperial Crisis. Reform of the colonial governments would certainly have provoked Massachusettensians, Virginians, and New Yorkers. Instead, government aimed to "assuage" the Americans (as King George III put it), calm apprehensions, and restore trust. All of this was to be achieved without making concessions on principles or engaging in sustained dialogue with the Americans. Hillsborough and North, with seven others, won a majority vote to retain the tea duty, defeating Grafton and three others. While the tea duty was to be retained largely on principle—to demonstrate Parliament's legislative supremacy in the American Colonies—there was also a more practical aspect to the retention.[101] Chancellor Lord North was returning to former Chancellor Townshend's original idea (written into the 1767 American Revenue Act) of using revenue from the duty to pay the Crown salaries of colonial governors and other officials. Thus, the retention of the tea duty was in fact a defeat for the prime minister and those of his colleagues who favored its removal.[102]

The conciliatory message, however, was given prominence in a circular to the colonial governors dated 13 May (**No. 773**) formally announcing the administration's intention to repeal the Townshend duties in the next session of Parliament. The cabinet hoped that the news would dampen the opposition in the colonial assemblies and weaken the colonial nonimportation agreements. They also expected to satisfy criticism from British merchants angered by the disruption to trade caused by the American boycotts. Ministers let it be known privately that henceforth Parliament would effectively leave the colonies alone. The professed rationale did not concede ground on constitutional principles but on commercial expedience, accepting the colonists' oft-stated grievance that since the colonies were a growing and important market for British manufactures the Atlantic trade ought not to be comprehensively taxed.

While Bollan was not privy to cabinet deliberations, his parliamentarian friends would have kept him informed of the change of policy. He also managed to find a way of linking the campaign for repealing the Townshend duties to the Whigs' campaign against Governor Bernard.

In mid-May, Bollan received fresh advices from the Massachusetts Council. He was requested to present the Council's commentary on the six Bernard letters to Hillsborough (**Appendix 4**) and to procure more of Bernard's letters.[103] Bollan personally delivered the Council's letter to Hillsborough at his London residence in the last week of May, but was refused an audience. A second visit, in mid-June, gained him admission. Hillsborough knew of Bollan's part in obtaining the six letters. But rather than question Bollan's integrity or contest his agent's credentials (as the governor's honor demanded) Hillsborough engaged Bollan in a long conversation.[104] Bollan, by his own account, seized the moment to press the repeal of the "whole Grenvillean system," as the Council had urged. While Hillsborough seemed sympathetic to the idea of freeing American trade from all mercantilist restrictions, he was noncommittal on the "total repeal" of the American revenue acts. He also refused Bollan's request for copies of state papers the Council wanted—"sundry" letters of Hillsborough's to Bernard and two memorials of the American Board of Customs.[105]

This was more than a probe for information. Bollan could hardly have expected the secretary of state to be forthcoming. Hillsborough knew any material gifted to Bollan would be transmitted to Boston and used against Bernard. If all that mattered to Bollan was obtaining copies of the letters, he could have enlisted the help of a friendly member of Parliament. The whole point of approaching Hillsborough was likely to intimate that Bernard was a convenient scapegoat for the past follies of the Chatham and Grafton administrations. Bollan knew that Hillsborough had recalled Bernard. He was also convinced that with Bernard out of the way and his reputation discredited reconciliation with Massachusetts stood a better chance. Hillsborough, however, was tactfully evasive and "express'd a very high regard for the conduct of Govr Bernard." Even if Hillsborough were tempted to scapegoat Bernard in order to boost his own flagging reputation, he could not confide in Bollan. After discussing the encounter with friends, Bollan sanguinely concluded that Hillsborough's influence was waning. Bollan was only partially correct, and was not aware that Hillsborough had won the contest to retain the tea duty. Still, he highlighted two indicators pointing to British willingness to accommodate the Americans' grievances. The first was that the Grafton administration was not opposed to repealing the Townshend Revenue Act. The second was that the British government was not inclined to levy further taxes, provided the colonists ceased challenging parliamentary authority.[106] A third but unspoken indicator in Bollan's rationale was whether or not Hillsborough and the administration would stand by the beleaguered governor. That test would not be resolved for another six months.

By the time Bollan's assessment reached Boston in mid-August, these promising indicators were already obsolete. Colonial demands had progressed beyond the terms proffered in the circular to the governors. Boston Whigs were insisting on the withdrawal of the troops, the repeal of the tea duty, the dismantling of the Navigation Acts, and an acknowledgement of colonial rights of legislative autonomy. And they were also plotting Bernard's disgrace, regardless of what Hillsborough might do.

Boston, June–August 1769

Governor Bernard made only two speeches at the General Court during its final session: one to open it and one to close it. To some, the lame duck governor cut a dejected figure, bereft of meaningful support and wedded to his uncompromising tactic of vetoing the election of radicals to the Council (**No. 776**). When the House refused to proceed to business in protest at the presence of the British soldiers, he moved the assembly to Harvard College and was obliged to continue the assembly until the House passed the annual supply bill on 15 Jul. (but not the salary bill for acting governor Thomas Hutchinson). Such a frustrating session prompted Bernard to deliver a fusillade of accusations in letters to Hillsborough. His enemies were humiliating him and embarrassing their own supporters by bringing government to a fiscal cliff. They pulled back only when they had sated their pride with a series of impertinent resolves further challenging parliament's authority to tax Americans and accusing Bernard of conspiring with ministers to bring troops to Boston (**Nos. 779, 797**, and **792**). Otis and Adams were "now in full Possession" of the provincial government, Bernard declaimed to John Pownall (**No. 780**), "driving over every one who has loyalty & Resolution" to defend the King and Parliament (**No. 784**).

Unknown to Bernard, in March Hillsborough had broached the possibility of withdrawing the regiments from Boston. He left it to General Gage to decide how many regiments should be withdrawn and when. Gage did not consult Bernard on the question of withdrawal but engaged him in discussion as to how many troops should remain (**No. 782**). Bernard predictably objected, claiming that "*all*" the principal provincial and Crown officers feared "very dangerous Consequences" (**No. 787**), and managed to win the argument that two regiments should be kept in the town and Castle (**Nos. 785, 786, 790**, and **792**). In mid-July the 64th and 65th Regiments of Foot were removed to Halifax (with the agreement of both Bernard and Hutchinson) but the 14th and 29th remained, testament to their governor's nervousness (**Nos. 793** and **796**). The House of Representatives continued protesting at the presence of the Regulars for the next three years until all the soldiers were withdrawn.[107]

News of Bernard's impending departure triggered the Whigs' decision to call for their governor's permanent removal. Samuel Adams had already drafted a document when the motion for drawing a petition was unanimously approved on 27 Jun. (The engrossed copy is printed as **Appendix 6**, and was considered by the Privy Council in London on 28 Feb. 1770.)[108] Bernard's last words to his enemies in the Massachusetts House breathed defiance.

> By your own acts you will be judged:[109] you need not
> be apprehensive of any Misrepresentations; as it is not

in the power of your Enemies, if you have any, to add
to your Publications: they are plain and explicit and
need no comment.[110]

While both Bernard and his enemies indulged in political theater the seriousness of the moment was not lost on the governor. Powerless to prevent the posturing, Bernard nevertheless railed at the House for insulting his office and status as the king's representative. In the wider context of the Imperial Crisis, the petition to remove Bernard might be counted as a delayed emotional reaction to the king's speech of 8 Nov., Parliament's resolutions on Massachusetts, and British deliberations on pursuing colonists for treason. The petition was a symbolic attack on royal authority, the start of an ideological journey that was to culminate in an attack on the person of the king in the American Declaration of Independence of 1776.

Governor Bernard had started planning his departure in the first week of June (**No. 783**). Son Thomas, he decided, would accompany him (though it would mean Thomas would graduate from Harvard M.A. *in absentia*); the rest of the family would follow once Bernard had found a suitable residence in England. He had about six weeks or so to put his affairs in order, appointing agents to manage his several land grants and property in Mount Desert. He probably did not expect to return to Massachusetts, though had not ruled out the possibility of a posting elsewhere. Public affairs he largely dispensed with after proroguing the General Court on 15 Jul.

Uppermost in Bernard's mind, however, was the need to preserve what he termed "a Union of Sentiments & Coalition of Interests" with the man whom he assumed would eventually succeed him, Thomas Hutchinson (**No. 788**). But Hutchinson was without any guarantee that the assembly would vote him a salary. Bernard had weakly recommended that Hutchinson should insist the House enact a permanent governor's salary, in keeping with the provisions of the Townshend Revenue Act. Of that there was no chance, as both men knew, but it was Bernard's crude way of excusing his failure to persuade the House to make provision for the acting governor or the British government in London to pay Hutchinson a salary from the tea duty. The auguries that Hutchinson was to be allowed a fresh start were not good. Not only was Hutchinson without a salary; he was going to find himself bereft of significant political support when facing an unmanageable assembly, a popular nonimportation movement, and a province eager to condemn him for having faithfully served his governor and king. In his final letter to Hillsborough Bernard hoped his successor would find "fair Play in the Opening of his Administration": in truth, the tribulations of his predecessor ensured that Hutchinson would never enjoy the peaceful start that Bernard had enjoyed when he assumed the governorship (**No. 797**).

After a final public appearance at the Harvard College commencement, Bernard took his leave of the province. He boarded HMS *Rippon* on 1 Aug. nine years to the day that he entered the province in a procession of promise. The *Rippon* did not sail for another day, and Bernard would have witnessed from distance the pageantry heralding his departure: the cacophony of town batteries, the church bells ringing out, and the Union flag atop the Castle. These arrangements conformed to British tradition, but the symbolism sent a mixed message, of British rule and American defiance. Unfurling the St. George's flag on Liberty Tree and Hancock's Wharf, Bernard's enemies sent a clear signal that the province was relieved to be rid of a governor who had apparently trampled on the rights and liberties of their English heritage.[111]

London, June–August 1769

Had Hillsborough been more accommodating in providing Bollan with the advices he wanted perhaps Bollan might not have attended to the Council's request that he obtain more of Bernard's letters. But he did not hold back, having sensed an opportunity to aid the colonists by disparaging the governor and criticizing the secretary of state. Shortly after meeting with Hillsborough, Bollan requested William Beckford's assistance to obtain authentic copies of "all" the governor's letters that had been presented to the House of Commons since the previous November.[112] Upon encountering some "unexpected difficulties" (perhaps occasioned by the promotion of the clerk of papers, George White, rather than any ministerial hand), Beckford was obliged to place his request in writing. The transcripts were then prepared by White's successor, John Rosier.[113]

This time Bollan familiarized himself with what Bernard had written. Troubled by poor eyesight and pushed for time, the sixty-four year old Bollan arranged for an acquaintance or secretary to read the letters to him.[114] Bernard's candid reporting and dramatized style of writing left a lasting impression on Bollan.

> I have scarcely had time to hear the letters now sent once read, & therefore can say nothing in consideration; their contents & bare reading[115] astonish'd me extremely.

After discussing the letters and the Council's rebuttal (**Appendix 4**) with a "member of the first character"—Beckford again, probably—Bollan assured Danforth and his colleagues that they would be gifted the evidence to assail the integrity of Bernard's correspondence. The entire second batch, he wrote, "will probably explain the proceedings relative to your distress."[116] Even the House of Commons' clerks were "stagger'd" by what the governor had written, Bollan noted, a comment which may also reflect Beckford's own feelings.[117] Bollan's reaction to the Bernard Letters was similar to those of the opposition MPs who had listened intently when the Commons Speaker read them aloud on 25 Jan. Government men were less affected by the publication of Bernard's letters, and Barrington for one was unperturbed. He supposed Bernard was just as "obnoxious" to the colonists as he was before. Since Bernard was preparing to leave Massachusetts, Barrington could "not see how the knowlege of your Correspondence can do you any harm" (**No. 781**). Barrington's reaction might have been different had his letters been purloined and published. It was not that Barrington or Hillborough failed to anticipate that the colonists, with Bollan's aid, would capitalize on the governor's letters; rather, they no longer cared what the Bostonians did with the material.

The second "parcel" of Bernard's letters that Bollan dispatched to Boston on 21 Jun. has not survived intact. But it would have contained transcripts of thirty letters Bernard had written to Shelburne and Hillsborough during 1768.[118] Bollan sent duplicates by another vessel, along with copies of Hillsborough's out-letters, the memorials of the American Board of Customs, and other items concerning Massachusetts that were on Parliament's list of American correspondence.[119] Both ships arrived in Boston on or shortly before 19 Aug., by which time Bernard was already on his way back to England.[120] Bollan received a further request came from councilor John Erving, seeking copies of Bernard's letters concerning the court cases generated by the Benjamin Barons controversy and disputations over the writs of assistance between Jun. 1761 and Feb. 1762. This time Bollan was unable to oblige.[121]

Sensing "victory," as he wrote much later, Bollan had striven to influence the course of events in both Boston and London.[122] Bollan exposed Bernard's machinations against the Council and the province of Massachusetts in order to give the British government and the colonists a chance to settle their differences by scapegoating Bernard. For the moment Bollan advised the Council against publishing their letter to Hillsborough lest it be considered critical of the secretary (which in sum it was) and damage the case for repealing the Townshend Revenue Act. Far better, he advised, was for the Council to use all the information they had been supplied to build a solid case against Bernard and publish that instead, if possible in time for the next session of Parliament.

> A removal of all unjust impressions, prejudicial to its
> Council, magistrates, & inhabitants, wou'd be very
> beneficial, if obtainable, and I beg leave to submit to
> the consideration of those who are able to make it,
> the utility of a plain, clear, distinct & candid narrative

> of all the material facts placed in their natural order,
> attended with decent and pertinent observations, & a
> constant regard for future as well as past proceedings.

The idea of publishing a "useful narrative," he admitted, had come to him whilst writing, certain as he was that he would not able to obtain any further copies of official letters. If this was his personal day of reckoning with Governor Bernard it was also, Bollan knew, time for the colonists to heap righteous indignation upon Secretary of State Hillsborough for turning the British government and Parliament against them.[123] His preferred outcome was a parliamentary inquiry into the governor's administration which, even if Bernard were not impeached, would nevertheless highlight how far ministers were viewing events in Boston through the lens of an "angry man" (as William Beckford called Bernard).

Bollan's faith in Parliament was not misplaced. Hillsborough might not have survived a second debate on the American correspondence, given the strength of feeling evident in January. But even as Bollan advised the Council to trust in the opposition MPs, events in Boston undermined the case he was building. The Council had already published their commentary (**Appendix 4**) on the "first parcel" of Bernard Letters as *Letters to Hillsborough*. It did not meet Bollan's requirements for a critique simply because the councilors were unable to address the full range of the governor's correspondence. In gifting the rest of the materials to the Council, Bollan urged councilors to "exercise . . . wisdom, diligence & caution":[124] that did not mean they should keep the transcripts out of public view, but that they should use them judiciously to undermine Bernard and Hillsborough—and to manage that they needed Parliament's support. But the Council had already ceded its lead role to the Boston town meeting and the House of Representatives. It was Samuel Adams, not James Bowdoin, who led the campaign to vindicate the province. Bollan's advice was not ignored, but in the autumn of 1769 it was no longer relevant to developments in Massachusetts.

Boston, September-October 1769

With Bernard out of sight but not out of mind, the Massachusetts Whig exploited their acquisition of the governor's correspondence. Publication of the first batch further undermined the credibility of friends of government, who were reduced a rump faction in the House.[125] The second batch Bollan sent Danforth was received on 19 Aug. and quickly turned into a pamphlet by Edes and Gill. *Letters to the Ministry*[126] was advertised for sale on 7 Sept. at the price of "One Pisterene and Half."[127] It contained thirty of Bernard's letters to Shelburne and Hillsborough,[128] the correspondence of the American Board of Customs relating to the *Liberty* riot,[129] several letters from Commodore Samuel Hood to the Admiralty, and Bollan's letter to Danforth of 30 Jan. (**Appendix 2**). It was reprinted in London on 15 Nov.[130] Boston shopkeeper Harbottle Dorr characteristically annotated his copy of the Boston edition with colorful declamations: the former governor was a "Vile Traytor."[131] On 18 Oct., the Boston town meeting directed Samuel Adams to produce a vindication of the town from the "many base insinuations and virulent charges" contained in the Bernard Letters.[132] Adams's detailed report was appended to the town records[133] and subsequently published in Boston and London as an *Appeal to the World*.[134]

Adams's appraisal of the governor's letters shaped both contemporaries' and historians' perceptions of Governor Bernard. The *Appeal to the World* delivered the most articulate and lucid of all contemporary critiques of the Bernard Letters. While William Bollan may not have approved its strident language, *Appeal to the World* probably matched his expectations as to what a detailed commentary should be. Adams undertook a close reading of the governor's interpretation of events as presented in his letters. While Adams skirted around some of the more problematic issues, notably the bravado display of arms at the Boston town meeting of 12 Sept. 1768, he nonetheless undertook a compelling deconstruction. (Adams's commentaries have been collated with the editorial notes to several of the letters published in volumes four and five of the *Bernard Papers*.)[135] True or not, Adams's perceptive observations contradicted Bernard's version of recent history and, Adams declared, exposed a guilty conscience. More than any other polemic from prerevolutionary Boston, Adams's *Appeal to the World* exemplifies the conspiracy theory at the heart of Bernard Bailyn's enduring interpretation of American revolutionary ideology.[136]

> It is remarkable that Governor Bernard, not long before these letters were made public, expressed to a certain gentleman, his earnest wish, that the people of this Province could have a sight of all his letters to the Ministry, being assured that they would thereby be fully convinced that he was a friend to the Province— Indeed he made a declaration to the same purpose, in one of his public speeches to the House of Representatives. Upon the Arrival of the letters however, he discovered, as some say, a certain Paleness, and complained of as an hardship that his letters, wrote in confidence, should be exposed to the view of the Public.— A striking proof of the Baseness, as well as the Perfidy of his heart![137]

It is puzzling why the administration took so long to stop the leaks of American correspondence. In the spring of 1770, Hillsborough "censured" Bollan for his part in the procurement of the Bernard Letters.[138] No action was taken against the printers in Boston or London who published the Bernard Letters. But by then Bernard was no longer important to the British government. Rather than antagonise the Bostonians with an investigation, the easiest course of action was to defend Bernard against the accusations made in the House of Representatives' petition calling for his removal and impeachment (**Appendix 6**).[139] The Privy Council found the accusations groundless. On 5 Mar., Parliament fulfilled Grafton's promise to repeal the Townshend duties, save that on tea. That same day in Boston, the troops Governor Bernard had brought to Boston fired on a crowd of protestors, killing three instantly and mortally wounding two others. The Boston Massacre was Francis Bernard's legacy.

Historians familiar with Samuel Adams's critique of the Bernard Letters have underplayed William Bollan's role. Bollan was much more than a messenger, and in the winter of 1768-69 probably the colonists' most important friend in London. There was no grand plan to seize the Bernard Letters, but in capitalizing on Bollan's initiative, Adams and his associates fashioned a careful and measured transatlantic campaign to undermine both Governor Bernard and Secretary of State Hillsborough. The imperative, in short, was to negate Bernard's depiction of them as would-be rebels. Bernard's removal and the sidelining of Hillsborough constituted a fresh beginning of sorts for colonists anxious to effect reconciliation and press the repeal of all the revenue acts. The incoming North administration met them halfway by repealing the Townshend duties except that on tea, while leaving the rest of the mercantilist system untouched. But North's overtures fell far short of colonial aspirations for legislative self-government. Hillsborough remained in office, trusted by North but without exerting much influence on American policy; he resigned in Aug. 1772 after a dispute over American land grants.[140]

The Bernard Letters series could not provide all the answers the colonists sought about what their governor had said and why. Despite what historians have said, they did not contain information that was already publicly known.[141] The "first parcel" of six letters dealt mainly with Council business. Bernard's proposals for reforming colonial government and his disparaging comments about Whig leaders were not as prevalent in the "first parcel" as has been assumed.[142] But none of that really mattered at the time, however. For the Whigs long suspected their governor of malfeasance. In the much larger second "parcel" they found plenty of evidence seeming to justify accusations of misrepresentation, misinformation, and disinformation. Closer examination, however, suggests that on balance the evidence was "misrepresentation more than misinformation . . . and not the conspiracy of disinformation as Samuel Adams later claimed."[143] But the amount of evidence gathered was undoubtedly impressive, despite some significant gaps. The pamphlet series published forty-eight of Bernard's letters to Shelburne and Hillsborough, about 72 per cent of all of Bernard's out-letters to the secretaries of state during 1768.[144] The omission of **No. 657**[145] from the series was surely deliberate, for its contents addressed a potentially embarrassing issue: the rejection of the first motion in the Massachusetts House of Representatives proposing the Circular Letter. (While the defeat was overturned readers of the letter might have been prompted to ask an awkward question as to why it was necessary to have the motion expunged from the House journals.)[146]

The pamphlet series contained only two of Hillsborough's letters to Bernard (**Nos. 722** and **727**). Neither was a major policy document, and both were printed probably because they were the only full copies of Hillsborough's out-letters that the Council had acquired.[147] Hillsborough wrote nine other letters to Bernard during 1768 and all were presented to Parliament.[148] Given the controversial subject matter of some of them—information about troop orders to Boston and Hillsborough's instructions for rescinding the Circular Letter[149]—it can be assumed that Bernard's enemies would have been delighted to publish material confirming their governor's influence on British policy.[150] It is probable, then, that Bollan was not able to obtain copies of these letters from the Commons' clerk of papers. Or, Bollan may have baulked at traducing Hillsborough in this way, at least until he read what the other letters contained.[151]

The full range of American correspondence printed in the fourth and fifth volumes of the *Bernard Papers*, would certainly have enabled the American Whigs to piece together the transatlantic dialogue that brought British Regulars to Boston and persuaded the British government that Boston was on the verge of revolt. Had they been able to do so, it is doubtful if the Chatham or Grafton administrations would have survived the hot coals of an indignant opposition. Perhaps with Bernard and Hillsborough both out of the way and with full evidence to hand, the Massachusetts Whigs would have been able to dispel the myth of their proclivity for sedition. Perhaps, then, history would have turned out rather differently.

EDITORIAL APPARATUS

Editorial policy has aimed to preserve the integrity of manuscripts by printing them in full (except where noted) and depicting their content as accurately as possible with limited editorial intervention.

Whenever possible, autograph out-letters and in-letters have been used as authoritative texts—the actual manuscripts upon which the transcripts are based. When the receiver's copy (**RC**) or its duplicate were not extant, contemporary copies were substituted from the preserved record in the receiver's or author's letterbook (**RLbC** and **LbC**). In the absence of a letterbook, the transcript was based on a copy of an original made by a third party; printed versions (**PC**) were used in the last resort—contemporary imprints taking precedence over modern imprints and transcriptions.

Bernard's letters to the secretaries of state were his primary means of communication with the British government. He wrote regularly to the secretary of state for the Southern Department, whose portfolio included the American Colonies, and also, from 1768, to the newly-created secretary of state for the Colonies, whose first occupant was the earl of Hillsborough. Bernard usually wrote out his own letters to the secretaries of state in a fine, easy to read script. Numbered sequentially, his first official letter to Hillsborough is dated 12 May 1768; he restarted the sequence at the beginning of 1769. In-letters from the secretary of state were numbered in sequence regardless of the year or the minister, reaching No. 11 before Shelburne left office and No. 27 by the time Bernard returned to England. This volume has printed most but not all of the extant correspondence from this period between Governor Bernard and Hillsborough, omitting letters of acknowledgment (concerning appointments or receipt of correspondence) and several circulars; these items, however, are mentioned in the editorial commentaries and listed in **Appendix 7**.

The secretaries of state probably read every one of Bernard's holographs before passing the letters to their clerks so copies could be made and the originals filed. Letters to the earl of Halifax, Henry Seymour Conway, and the earl of Shelburne are in CO 5/755-CO 5/757; letters to the earl of Hillsborough, the first colonial secretary, are in CO 5/758. The secretaries' clerks were not required to keep a minute-book (as was the case with clerks attached the Board of Trade and the Board of Admiralty); nor did they did maintain correspondence entrybooks (either a ledger or letterbook); however, correspondence that the secretary of state referred to other departments (that is, the Treasury, the Privy Council, the Admiralty, the War Office, and the Board of Trade) can usually be traced in the administrative record of these departments.

The filing system for original incoming letters was thorough, by the standards of the day. The secretary of state's clerks routinely endorsed in-letters on the back leaf of the letter when folded (usually its last verso page) thus providing a convenient docket for filing. A date of receipt was written at the top, sometimes with one or two lines summarizing the letter's subject matter; a filing reference was added at the bottom. For example, Bernard's letter to the earl of Hillsborough of 26 Dec. 1768 (**ALS, RC**) is endorsed "Governor Bernard (N°. 37) R 24th: Feb[y] 1769. B.9." The first figure, "N°. 37", indicates that this letter was the thirty-seventh that Bernard had sent to Hillsborough in 1768. "R" prefaces the date of receipt and "B.9." is the bundle of correspondence in which the letter was filed. The numbering of letters was established by the earl of Shelburne in 1766, but the docketing procedure was operational before then. Bernard's letters were later re-bound but the original ordering of materials in the collections was preserved, more or less. The letter to Hillsborough is now contained in a bound volume of papers, CO 5/758, with a modern folio reference, ff 38-39.

In the aftermath of the Stamp Act Crisis, colonial governors were required to communicate directly with the secretary of state in all matters. Bernard continued to send copies to the Board of Trade, but with one important difference: the addressee was the secretary of state, not the Board. For example, the Board's file copy of Bernard's letter to Hillsborough of 26 Dec. 1768 is in CO 5/893, ff 92-94; it is a letter handwritten by a clerk and signed by the governor (**dupLS, RC**). I have catalogued it not as a distinct item of correspondence but as a variant of the original letter in CO 5/758. This particular manuscript was laid before a meeting of the Board of Trade on 6 Dec. 1769 (*JBT*, 13: 35) and subsequently endorsed by a clerk in the Plantation Office: "Boston Dec[r]. 26. 1768 Gov[r] Bernard (N° 37) Dup Reced Read Dec[r]: 6. 1769. N.n. 28."

Several people were involved in the composition of the original letters and papers authored by Bernard. Bernard himself wrote out the majority of his out-letters; not only the originals going to the secretary of state and to the Board of Trade, but also the duplicates and the triplicates of these letters that were conveyed separately. He also made letterbook copies of much of this material. Before 1768, Bernard was also heavily reliant on clerks to make letterbook copies of routine correspondence and prepare copies of out-letters for dispatch. But concerns over security and "not daring to trust Strangers" (**No. 744**) meant that he became dependent upon his third son Thomas Bernard (27 Apr. 1750-1 Jul. 1818). In the period covered by this volume of *The Bernard Papers* Thomas was responsible for over 88 per cent of letterbook entries and over 38 percent of out-letters, including duplicates (with Bernard penning over 46 percent of out-letters).

In transcribing manuscripts for *The Bernard Papers*, the authoritative texts were systematically compared with the extant variants composed by the clerks. Substantive differences in content were rare. Contemporary emendations to letterbook copies (**LbC**) were usually incorporated in the fair versions dispatched to and received by correspondents (**RC**). Major differences among the variant texts are discussed in the endnotes and source notes, and an editorial comment clarifies scribal involvement. Near-contemporaneous transcripts[152] and modern versions, including *Barrington-Bernard* are listed only when cited or discussed.

Transcripts are presented in chronological order, according to the first given date. Non-epistolary enclosures follow the covering letter, while letters that were themselves enclosures have been placed in sequence by date. With letters bearing the same date, out-letters take precedence over in-letters (unless the out-letter is a reply to the in-letter); thereafter, out-letters are sorted by the likely order of composition (for which Bernard's letterbooks provide a rough guide); date of receipt has been used to sort in-letters; the remainder have been sorted alphabetically by correspondent. Transcripts have been allocated numbers in a sequence than runs across the series of published volumes, in this volume beginning with **No. 694**.

Editorial practice is to show the whole text plus any substantive emendations made by the author—the person(s) on whose authority a document was prepared or under whose signature it was sent—and by any clerk who drafted or copied the document. (Noncontemporaneous annotations on manuscripts have been excluded.) Obvious slips of the pen have been ignored. When the source note reports "minor emendations not shown," the editor is referring to corrections of oversights and grammatical errors made by the scribe or author of the manuscript that have no bearing on the meaning of the text or the author's perceived intention. Generally, original emendations, including scribal corrections, are reconstituted when this might help to illuminate authorial intention or when the additions suggest ambiguity or invite alternative interpretations: the representations follow the editorial apparatus set out in Table 1.

Grammar and spelling were transcribed with limited modernization. Orthographical idiosyncrasies have been retained, save for the kind of transparent mistakes mentioned above. Abbreviations, contractions, and terminal punctuation (and its absence) follow the manuscript, as does capitalization (when the writer's intention can be determined) and the underlining of dates. Emphasis is rendered in italics. Superscripts have been preserved but with all accompanying punctuation lowered to the line. Accidentally conjoined words have been separated. Eighteenth-century spelling, such as "highth" for "height" is readily understood; however, instances confusing to the reader are clarified by an interpolation or an endnote. Original forms have been reproduced, such as the ampersand (&) and the thorn ("y" for "th"), but not the long "s." Confusing punctuation in numbers has been silently corrected, with period separators being replaced by commas (thus "20.000" becomes "20,000"). Where symbols are used in the original to indicate pounds sterling, they are lowered to the line, and silently corrected to "£ s. d." Clarification on currency and monetary values is provided in endnotes.

The layout of the transcripts has preserved some common features of manuscripts and standardized others. The location and punctuation of salutations and datelines have been preserved, but placed in one line; the addressee's name is at the end of the closure (where it usually is) and above the postscript regardless of its location in the manuscript. Original lineation has not been retained but paragraphing sequencing has. Epigraphs, foreign language phrases, and postscripts have been formatted. Closures have been centered, except those running on from the last sentence of a letter. Tabulated information is presented in a form as close to the original as possible. Quotation marks placed at the beginning of every line of quoted material have been silently relocated to the beginning and end; block quotations have been indented. Flourishes have been omitted, as have brackets in dockets and closures. All transcripts have been given a caption; original titles have been transcribed and placed with the main body of text except entrybook titles, which are given in the notes.

The source note at the end of each transcript provides information about the provenance and location of the authoritative text. Table 2 is a list of descriptive acronyms used to indicate the typology of authoritative texts. The acronyms representing manuscript collections and archives are explained in the List of Abbreviations, above. (Pagination and folio descriptors have been omitted except when required by a repository's citation style). Where possible, the source note provides some clarification as to the processes of composition and preservation, noting among other things differences in handwriting styles, the extent of authorial emendation, and the location of variant texts. Endorsements added by the recipient confirming receipt and dockets added by the sender have been transcribed in accordance with editorial method. These are not enclosed in quotation marks but are easily recognizable since they are prefixed with "endorsed" or "docket" and offset from the editor's comments. When Bernard marked a letter with "r" he meant "received" and with "a" "answered." Extant enclosures are briefly described, and should be assumed to be manuscript copies (usually third-party copies) unless otherwise indicated. Relevant historical and administrative information is provided at the end of the source note. Guidance is given as to where to find any replies and rejoinders. The order of discussion varies, according to the requirements of each transcript.

Endnotes to source notes follow in sequence those for the transcript. Endnotes aim to clarify obscurities in the transcript and direct the reader to additional material. Cross-references to transcripts published in this volume are indicated by bold numerals, thus, **No. 694**. Citations of manuscripts not printed in this volume direct the reader to the authoritative version; in many cases there is only one extant manuscript; source text typology is included where it may help the reader. "Not found" is used to signal the absence of a manuscript.

Appendix 7 is a list of Bernard's extant correspondence for the period covered by this volume. This list is an interim calendar. The information has been checked as fully and thoroughly as all the other material printed in this volume; it is possible, however, that some typological classifications may change, if further handwriting analysis can identify the clerks who scribed the copies. Any such revisions will be reported in the Calendar volume.

Acts of the English, Irish, Scottish, and British parliaments are cited according to regnal year, with dates where appropriate, and with modernized titles; the index provides both the dates and a short-title. Provincial legislation is not normally calendared by regnal year but by date, although Bernard's contemporaries used regnal codes when referring to historic acts.

Biographical information is provided at the first mention of a person in the correspondence; rare sources are cited but standard reference works are not.[153] Online directories and newspaper collections proved to be particularly useful.[154] Francis Bernard is referred to throughout as "FB" and Thomas Hutchinson as "TH".

I have tried to record information and transcribe manuscripts as accurately as possible, but it is inevitable that there will be errors in a project of this scale. I am grateful to everyone who has helped me to correct them, and I take full responsibility for those that remain.

TABLE 1
EDITORIAL SYMBOLS

Additions (insertions, interlineations, and substitutions) are marked with carets "^"at the intended location. When it is necessary to distinguish different hands or differentiate between insertions and substitutions the following will be used: ↑roman↓.

Bold type or heavily-inked letters are set in **bold**.

Canceled text is shown in ~~strikethrough font~~.

Confusing passages are described "thus in manuscript" in an endnote.

Conjectured readings for illegible material that can be inferred from the source text are in [roman text within square brackets]; there is a question mark before the closing bracket if there is considerable doubt as to the accuracy of the reading, [roman?].

Editorial interpolations have been italicized and placed in square brackets, [*editor's comment*].

Ellipses signify material that is either illegible or missing. The number of suspension points corresponds to the number of missing letters or numbers, e.g. [. . .] for three letters missing. Missing words are rendered thus, [_ _ _].

Emphasis is conveyed by *italics* and double underlining by SMALL CAPITALS.

Lacunae are represented by [*blank*].

Passages marked for deletion are indicated by <angled brackets>.

Underlining in authorial tables, numbers, dates, and punctuation has been retained.

TABLE 2
SOURCE TEXT TYPOLOGY

The first set of acronyms in table 2 describes the nature of the authoritative text on which the transcript is based. The second set categorizes documents by their administrative history and preservation.

ADft	Author's Draft Manuscript.
AL	Autograph Letter (text in the hand of the author, but unsigned).
ALS	Autograph Letter Signed (text and signature in the hand of the author).
AMs	Autograph Manuscript (text in the hand of the author but unsigned).
AMsS	Autograph Manuscript Signed (text and signature in the hand of author).
Dft	Draft
dup/trip	duplicate/triplicate
extract	An extract of a source text.
L	Letter (text not in the hand of the author and unsigned).
LS	Letter Signed (text not in the hand of the author but signed by the author).
Ms	Manuscript.
MsS	Manuscript Signed.
précis	A summary.
noted	A documentary record of the existence of a nonextant source text.
Prt	Contemporary Printed version of manuscript.
AC	Author's Copy (loose file or bound copies usually found in a personal collection).
Copy	Third Party Copy.
LbC	Author's Letterbook or Entrybook
PC	Published Copy.
RbC	Recordbook Copy.
RC	Receiver's Copy.
RLbC	Receiver's Letterbook Copy.

ENDNOTES

➤➤➤ ⸨⸨⸨

1. **No. 661** in *Bernard Papers*, 4: 271-276.

2. Thomas Gage (1721-87), British military commander in chief in North America, 1764-75.

3. CO 5/827, ff 59-66.

4. Wills Hill (1718-93), first earl of Hillsborough, was the first secretary of state for the Colonies, 21 Jan. 1768-15 Aug. 1772.

5. Hillsborough's orders to Gage were dated 8 Jun. and 30 Jul. 1768. **Appendices 4** and **12**, respectively *Bernard Papers*, 4: 373-374, 397-399.

6. William Wildman Barrington (1717-93), second Viscount Barrington, MP for Plymouth, and secretary at war, 1755-61 and 1765-78.

7. Jonathan Sewall (1729-96) was the province attorney general, 1767-75, and the advocate general of Vice Admiralty, 1767-68.

8. *Bernard Papers*, 4: 307-313.

9. John Adams (1735-1826) was one of the province's most successful lawyers, but did not pursue Crown or provincial offices. He served one term in the House of Representatives as a member for Boston, 1770-71.

10. John Pownall (1724/5-95), undersecretary of state for the Colonies, 24 Jun. 1768 to 5 Apr. 1776.

11. See *Bernard Papers*, 3: 310-312.

12. *HJL*, 32: 165-166, and *HCJ*, 32: 21-22.

13. Dennys DeBerdt (d.1770), a Dissenter and London merchant, was appointed agent of the House of Representatives on 12 Mar. 1767, and held the position until his death.

14. John Pownall further reassured Bernard that his remaining in Boston to await the troops' arrival was "highly approved & commended," and that the British government believed his handling of the situation helped to ensure that the landing was not resisted. Those who contemplated resistance, Pownall continued, might well be pursued for "high Crimes & misdemeanors which have been committed." Pownall to FB, Whitehall, 19 Nov. 1768, BP, 12: 21-24, received 16 Jan. 1769.

15. Thomas Hutchinson (1711-80), lieutenant governor of Massachusetts, 1760-69, and chief justice since 1760. He is referred to as "TH" in the editorial commentaries to this volume. Andrew Oliver (1706-74) was province secretary, 1756-70. Robert Auchmuty (1724-88) was appointed judge of the Vice Admiralty Court in New England in 1768.

16. Samuel Adams (1722-1803), elected to the House of Representatives in 1765, was one of the leaders of the Boston Faction. He was also clerk of the House and author of numerous papers issued by it. Thomas Cushing (1725-88) was a representative for Boston between 1761 and 1774, and Speaker of the House, 1766-70 and 1772-74.

17. James Bowdoin (1726-90), a prosperous merchant, served in the Council 1757-68 and 1770-73.

18. John Temple (1731-98) had been appointed to the American Board of Customs in 1767, but his professional relationship with FB had long since soured. His marriage to Elizabeth Bowdoin (1750-1809), daughter of Whig councilor James Bowdoin, earned him the distrust of his fellow commissioners of Customs who came to suspect him of leaking damaging information to the Whigs. Temple was replaced by the Treasury in 1771.

19. *Bernard Papers*, 4: 318-324.

20. See **No. 707**.

21. See especially **Nos. 713** and **722**.

22. Peter D. G. Thomas, *The Townshend Duties Crisis: The Second Phase of the American Revolution, 1767-1773* (Oxford, 1987), 104-105.

23. William Pitt (1708-78) had been secretary of state and leader of a Whig administration formed with the duke of Newcastle (as first lord of the Treasury), between 1757 and 1761. He was raised to the peerage as first earl of Chatham upon forming a second administration in 1766, taking office as Lord Privy Seal. But the Chatham administration was dogged by factionalism and infighting, and during the prime minister's long incapacity was led by the duke of Grafton. Chatham resigned on 14 Oct. 1768.

24. The key personnel in Grafton's cabinet who were involved in formulating American policy were:

    Augustus Henry FitzRoy (1735-1811), third duke of Grafton (and descendant of King Charles II), first lord of the treasury from 14 Oct. 1768 to his resignation on 30 Jan. 1770. He delayed resigning until the succeeding prime minister, Lord North, formally accepted the king's request to form an administration. After leaving office, Grafton supported North's administration.

    Wills Hill (1718-93), the first earl of Hillsborough in the Irish peerage, baron Harwich in the British peerage, and later first marquess of Downshire in the Irish. He was the first secretary of state for the American Colonies, 21 Jan. 1768-15 Aug. 1772.

    Frederick North (1732-92), second earl of Guilford, chancellor of the Exchequer from 6 Oct. 1767 to 1782, and prime minister from 28 Jan.1770 to 27 Mar. 1782.

    William de Grey (1719–81), MP for Newport, 1761-70, and Cambridge University, 1770-71. He was attorney general from 1766 to 1771, and though not formally in the cabinet was an important adviser to Hillsborough. He left the House of Commons to become lord chief justice of the Common Pleas and was knighted in 1771. He was created first Baron Walsingham in 1780.

25. Hillsborough's responses to the situation in Massachusetts from Sept. 1768 until FB's departure in Aug. 1769 are cursorily discussed in Sian E. Rees, "The Political Career of Wills Hill, Earl of Hillsborough (1718-1793) With Particular Reference to His American Policy," unpublished PhD diss., Aberystwyth Univ., 1976, 164-171.

26. William Petty (1737-1805), second earl of Shelburne, was secretary of state at the Southern Department, 30 Jul. 1766-21 Oct. 1768. He relinquished responsibility for colonial affairs on 21 Jan. 1768, when they were taken over by the new American Department under the earl of Hillsborough.

27. This letter is in *Bernard Papers*, 4: 318-324.

28. Letter I appeared on 21 Jan. 1769. John Cannon, ed., *The Letters of Junius* (Oxford, 1978), 30.

29. The reputation of John Wilkes (1725–97) reached across the Atlantic, where Americans viewed him as the embodiment of their struggle for Liberty. Having been found guilty of obscene and seditious libel *in absentia,* Wilkes returned to England to face arrest, but also to stand for Parliament; his subsequent imprisonment and election for Middlesex in Mar. 1768 prompted popular demonstrations of support from Londoners defending the rights of constituents. His expulsion from the House of Commons in Feb. 1769 precipitated a round of disputed elections; but after his release from prison, he managed a successful campaign to permit his return to Parliament.

30. Thomas, *Townshend Duties Crisis*, 93, 104-106, 121-129; Charles R. Ritcheson, *British Politics and the American Revolution* (Norman, Okla., 1954), 120-130.

31. *HJL*, 32: 165.

32. *HCJ*, 32: 74-76; *HLJ*, 32: 182-185. **Nos. 581, 585, 589, 593, 596, 600, 601, 623, 630, 632, 633, 638, 646, 654, 656, 657, 660, 663, 664, 668, 672, 681, 690, 691, 686, 694, 698,** and **700**. *Bernard Papers*, 4: 71-76, 86-88, 98-99, 112-118, 121-124, 129-139, 185-190, 201-203, 206-214, 220-230, 242-246, 255-257, 259-263, 266-270, 277-282, 288-290, 295-300, 318-324, 331-337, 347-353; 5: 63-68, 75-77, 79-82. To this list should be added FB's letter to Shelburne of

2 Feb. 1768, which was omitted from *Bernard Papers*, 4, since it merely acknowledged receipt of correspondence.

33.   *HCJ*, 32: 91-92; *HLJ*, 32: 192-193.

34.   35 Hen. 8, c. 2 (1543).

35.   *HLJ*, 32: 209-210.

36.   For a brief summary see Colin Nicolson, *The 'Infamas Govener': Francis Bernard and the Origins of the American Revolution* (Boston, 2001), 186-187.

37.   The duke of Richmond, briefly secretary of state under Rockingham in 1766, "seemed to think Governor Bernard might misconstrue that to be treason which was not so." Lord Weymouth, secretary of state for the Southern Department (1768-70) replied that "the governor was only to transmit informations and whether the riot[s] were treasonable or not would be judged here." In criticizing the address to the king, former secretary of state Shelburne supposed the administration "negligent" if they had not already given FB "directions" to investigate treasonable activities. "He and Lord Hillsborough had some sparring about the conduct of Governor Bernard." This likely concerned the accuracy of FB's observations on crowd action. Quoted in the Hardwicke Papers (BL), cited in J. Wright, ed. *Sir Henry Cavendish's Debates of the House of Commons, during the thirteenth Parliament of Great Britain, commonly called the unreported Parliament; to which are appended illustrations of the parliamentary history of the reign of George the Third; consisting of unpublished letters, private journals, memoirs, &c*, 2 vols. (London, 1841), 1: 193-194.

38.   *HCJ*, 32: 123-124; *HLJ*, 32: 229.

39.   *Bernard Papers*, 4: 318-324.

40.   "The Censure of Wilkes is considered here as a good Assurance of the firmness of Government." **No. 761**.

41.   *Bernard Papers*, 4: 292-293.

42.   Ibid., 292-293.

43.   William Bollan (1705-82). Born in England and a lawyer by profession, Bollan settled in Boston in 1740 and married the daughter of the governor, William Shirley. He was province agent from 1743 to 1762. Bollan's signal achievements were in helping negotiate two reimbursements from the British government for the province's wartime expenses: first after the successful Louisbourg campaign of 1745 and then at the conclusion of the French and Indian War. Bollan never returned to his adopted province, however. His dismissal from the province agency can be followed in *Bernard Papers*, 1: 200–203, 237, 239–240. His career is detailed in Malcolm Freiberg, "William Bollan, Agent of Massachusetts," *More Books: The Bulletin of the Boston Public Library* 23 (1948): 43- 53, 90-100, 135-146, 212-220. Bollan's writings are carefully examined in Joel D. Myerson, "The Private Revolution of William Bollan," *New England Quarterly* 41 (1968): 536-550. Bollan's part in the acquisition of the Bernard Letters is mentioned but not examined in Francis G. Walett, "Governor Bernard's Undoing: an earlier Hutchinson Letters Affair," *New England Quarterly* 38 (1965): 217-226. The best account of British politics and America is Thomas, *Townshend Duties Crisis*.

44.   Myerson, "The Private Revolution of William Bollan," 544.

45.   The Council's invitation was made in Samuel Danforth to Bollan, Boston, 5 Dec. 1768, *Bowdoin and Temple Papers*, 113-115. The letter explained why, on c.30 Nov., the Council drafted a new petition to Parliament. From Hillsborough's letter to FB of 14 Sep. 1768 (**No. 679**), the Council learned that the king had "graciously" received the Council's petition to the king, dated 7 Jul., (**Appendix 11**, *Bernard Papers*, 4: 392-396), and that it would be considered. But from one of the governor's letters (**No. 654**) councilors concluded that FB was likely to have misrepresented the petition's prayer for relief from taxation. (See *Bernard Papers*, 4: 255-257; the source note to **No. 717**.) The petition to Parliament, though moderate in language, unequivocally called for the repeal of all the American revenue acts. Bollan's appointment as agent was later communicated in a letter from John Erving dated 26 Jul. 1769. Ibid., 149-150.

46. The acquisition of the first parcel of the Bernard Letters demonstrated Bollan's capabilities and roundly won the councilors' approval. A majority in the House of Representatives, however, favored continuing with their own agent, Dennis DeBerdt, partly persuaded by letters of commendation supplied by Thomas Pownall. Ibid., 151. Bollan's relationships with both Pownall and DeBerdt (who, on his decease in 1770, was replaced by Benjamin Franklin) were strained at times, though all three were advocates of the American cause. The suspicion remains that Bollan, already in financial difficulties, used the Bernard Letters primarily to get his appointment confirmed in the hope of getting a stipend or grant. But to suggest he was motivated by lucre misses the point: he would have expected that FB (and his successor) would, at the very least, object to his appointment and more likely delay or refuse any provincial payment—regardless of his personal involvement in the exposure of the governor's letters. Bollan had to lobby strenuously for the Council to reimburse his expenses, let alone pay him a salary, and in both was unsuccessful; a House resolve in Apr. 1771 for a salary grant of £300 for the year commencing 12 Jul. 1769 also came to naught. *JHRM*, 47: 127, 242. On Bollan's earlier problems in obtaining his salary as province agent and disagreements over expenses, see Freiberg, "William Bollan, Agent of Massachusetts," 143; *Bernard Papers*, 2: 235, 404.

47. Bollan to Danforth, Henrietta Street, 30 Jan. 1769, *Bowdoin and Temple Papers*, 121-125.

48. *Bowdoin and Temple Papers*, 121-122.

49. *HCJ*, 32: 123-124. The letters were **Nos. 706, 708, 709, 711, 717**, and **718**, dated 1, 5, 12, 14, and 30 Nov., and 5 Dec. 1768, respectively.

50. William Beckford (bap.1709-1770), a former West India sugar planter and a wealthy merchant, was the City of London's MP, 1754-70, and its mayor, 1769-70.

51. *HCJ*, 32: 130; Wright, *Cavendish's Debates*, 1: 185.

52. *HCJ*, 32: 136-137. Barlow Trecothick (?1718-75), an alderman of London and MP 1768-74, was a leader of the Rockingham faction in the House of Commons, and had been instrumental in coordinating the merchants' support for the repeal of the Stamp Act. Peter D. G. Thomas, *British Politics and the Stamp Act Crisis: The First Phase of the American Revolution, 1763-1767* (Oxford, 1975), 144-150.

53. Government speakers may have been aided by a briefing note probably prepared by the undersecretary of state for the Colonial Department, John Pownall, summarizing "The Intelligence of the State of the Colonies received from His Majesty's Governors." One of the four surviving copies is annotated: "This Paper is given to you in great confidence of your Secrecy, with a request that You will not communicate it to any person whatever." *Narrative of Facts Relative to American Affairs* ([London?], 1768), 15p, Bodleian Library: Ms. D. D. Dashwood, c.3, B/5/1/4. It is not listed in Adams, *American Independence*.

54. Sir Henry Cavendish (1732-1804) was a member of the Irish House of Commons, 1766-68, and an MP in the British Parliament for the Cornish rotten borough of Lostwithiel, 1768-74. His voluminous short-hand notes of Parliamentary debates, deciphered and published, are a fecund historical resource. Wright, *Cavendish's Debates*, 2 vols.

55. William Dowdeswell (1721-75), MP for Worcestershire, 1761-75. See Neil Longley York, "William Dowdeswell and the American crisis, 1763-1775," *History* 90 (2005): 507-531.

56. William de Grey (1719-81) was MP for Merton, Norfolk, and attorney general, 1766-71; in 1771 he was appointed Lord Chief Justice of the Common Pleas and subsequently raised to the peerage as baron Walsingham.

57. Charles Cornwall (1735-89), MP for Grampound, Cornwall, 1768-74, a constituency with fifty freehold voters, he was subsequently elected for the Winchelsea and Rye constituencies and sat until 1789 (serving as Speaker 1780-89).

58. Richard Hussey (?1715-70), MP for East Looe, Cornwall, 1768-70.

59. Edmund Burke (1729-97), MP for Wendover, Bucks., 1765-74, formerly private secretary to the first lord of the Treasury (the marquess of Rockingham), 1765-66. Burke has been celebrated for

his towering intellect and outstanding skills as a parliamentary debater; also, in 1770 he was elected agent for the province of New York and acquired considerable knowledge of American affairs.

60. George Grenville (1712-70), MP for Buckinghamshire, 1741-70; first lord of the Treasury and chancellor of the Exchequer, 1763-65.

61. John Dunning (1731-83), MP for Calne, Wilts., 1768-82, and solicitor general, Jan. 1768-Jan. 1770. Famous for carrying the Commons' resolution amid the American war "that the influence of the Crown has increased, is increasing, and ought to be diminished" (1780); created Baron Ashburton in 1782.

62. *Bernard Papers*, 4: 330-331. Thomas Pownall (1722-1805), was MP for Tregony, Cornwall, 1767-74, having been governor of Massachusetts, 1757-59. Pownall's speech was later printed and read by FB. See **No. 771**.

63. Isaac Barré (1726-1802) was an Irish-born veteran of the French and Indian War, promoted to lieutenant-colonel of the 106th Regiment of Foot. He was MP for Chipping Wycombe, Bucks., 1761-74, and a loyal ally of Pitt (having initially criticized him) and Shelburne (his most important patron). Celebrated for describing the Americans as "Sons of Liberty," the town of Wilkes-Barre in Pennsylvania was named in his and John Wilkes's honor in 1769. He was represented in Benjamin's West famous painting *The Death of General Wolfe* (1770).

64. Sir George Savile (1726-84), MP for Yorkshire, 1759-83, and an American sympathizer in 1775.

65. There is a biographical note in n6 above.

66. Wright, *Cavendish's Debates*, 1: 191-207.

67. Rose Fuller (?1708-77), MP for Maidstone, Kent, 1761-68, and Rye, 1768-71, was a Jamaican planter who supported the administration on most issues except American policy.

68. Constantine John Phipps (1744-92), a Royal Navy officer and MP for Lincoln. 1768-74.

69. *Bernard Papers*, 4: 207-212.

70. Wright, *Cavendish's Debates*, 1: 207-225; *HCJ*, 32: 151.

71. Members of the public were excluded while the House was sitting. *HCJ*, 32: 20. The American correspondence was not printed in advance for the members, although that had been the case in Jan. 1766 when the House debated the Stamp Act Crisis. *Bernard Papers*, 3: 128. While Hillsborough had promised to prevent copies of FB's correspondence being distributed from his office (**No. 653**, *Bernard Papers*, 4: 254-255), he could not prevent MPs requesting copies from the Commons' clerk of papers and letting others view them.

72. Bollan to Danforth, Fludyer Street, 1 May 1770, *Bowdoin and Temple Papers*, 179.

73. Bollan to Danforth, Nassau Street, Soho, 28 Jan. 1771, *Bowdoin and Temple Papers*, 257. Freiberg mistakenly conflated the information Bollan provided in his letters to Danforth of 30 Jan. and 1 May 1770 and 28 Jan. 1771 to suggest that Beckford, "representing the county of Wiltshire," was Bollan's sole contact. "William Bollan, Agent of Massachusetts," 179-180. The transcripts Bollan dispatched were made by four different scribes. White attested that each was a true copy, signing and dating them 27 Jan. 1769. Bowdoin and Temple Papers, Loose MSS. On White see Orlando Cyprian Williams, *The Clerical Organization of the House of Commons, 1661-1850* (Oxford, 1954), 143, 182-183.

74. They were probably sent with Capt. Lyde on 4 Feb. See **No. 765**n1.

75. Popham was MP for Wiltshire between 1741 and 1772, and theoretically available to assist Bollan during his terms as Massachusetts's province agent (1743-62) and the Council's unofficial agent (1769-74). Thomas Goddard, the county's other sitting MP in 1769, was first elected in 1767, too early to fit the profile constructed by Bollan.

76. George Popham, an ancestor of the MP, had led the first English settlement to New England (the future Maine) in 1607-08, where he died in Feb. 1608 after which the English left. In 1762, Edward Popham joined the followers of the ousted Whig prime minister the duke of Newcastle in voting

against the peace policy of Lord Bute, the Tory prime minister. Thereafter, Popham voted with the opposition on the question of general warrants (during the Wilkes controversy) and was counted among the Chathamite Whigs who formed a government in the summer of 1766. When Chatham's frequent incapacity left the duke of Grafton de facto leader of the administration in 1767, Popham voted against the government, alongside other disgruntled backbench Chathamites. Mary M. Drummond, "Member Biographies: Edward Popham (?1711-72)," *History of Parliament Online* (http://www.historyofparliamentonline.org/volume/1754-1790/member/popham-edward-1711-72, accessed 30 Dec. 2013); Donald E. Ginter, *Voting Records of the British House of Commons, 1761-1820*, 6 vols., (London, 1995), 4: 1204.

77. Richard B. Sheridan, "Beckford, William (bap.1709, d.1770)," *ODNB-e* (http://www.oxforddnb.com.ezproxy.stir.ac.uk/view/article/1903, accessed 8 Feb, 2014).

78. James K. Hosmer, *Samuel Adams* (Boston and New York, 1885), 126-127; Leslie Thomas, "Partisan Politics in Massachusetts During Governor Bernard's Administration, 1760-1770," 2 vols., unpublished PhD diss., Univ. of Wisconsin, 1960, 2: 689-694; Walett, "Governor Bernard's Undoing," 217-226; Bernard Bailyn, *The Ordeal of Thomas Hutchinson* (Cambridge, Mass., 1974), 130-131, 137, 222n; Ira Stoll, *Samuel Adams: a Life* (New York, 2008), 74-78; John K. Alexander, *Samuel Adams: the Life of an American Revolutionary* (Lanham, Md., 2011), 89-93, 98.

79. *Boston Chronicle*, 3-10 Apr.; *Boston Gazette* and *Boston Post-Boy and Advertiser*, 3 Apr.; *Essex Gazette*, 4 Apr. 1769.

80. See **No. 765**n1.

81. Confirmation of their presentation on 20 Jan. was provided in the *Boston Chronicle*, 10-13 Apr.

82. "Protographos," *Boston Gazette*, 17 Apr. 1769.

83. The cover letter of 15 Apr. is not extant. Bollan noted receipt of the package in his letter to Danforth, et al., Henrietta Street, 21 Jun. 1769, *Bowdoin and Temple Papers*, 145.

84. This lament provided an apposite title for a thorough account of the British military occupation of Boston by Richard Archer, *As If an Enemy's Country: the British Occupation of Boston and the Origins of Revolution* (Oxford, 2010).

85. On 12 Apr., Bernard noted that Edes and Gill had delayed issuing a pamphlet of the letters until they were able to include detailed "Observations" on his correspondence (**No. 763**). *Copies of Letters from Governor Bernard to Hillsborough* was printed and circulated within a few days either side of 12 Apr. An annotated copy is filed with the *Boston Evening-Post* of 10 Apr. in the Dorr Collection, 2: 463-466.

86. For example,

  No. 706: *Boston Chronicle*, 13-17 Apr. 1769; *New-York Gazette, and Weekly Mercury*, 22 May 1769; *Boston Gazette*, 31 Jul. 1769.

  No. 708: *Boston Chronicle*, 13-17 Apr. 1769; *Providence Gazette*, 22 Apr. 1769; *New-York Chronicle*, 22-29 May 1769; *Boston Gazette*, 31 Jul. 1769.

  No. 709: *Boston Chronicle*, 17-20 Apr. 1769; *Providence Gazette*, 22 Apr. 1769; *New-York Chronicle*, 29 May-5 Jun. 1769; *Boston Gazette*, 31 Jul. 1769.

  No. 711: *Providence Gazette*, 22 Apr. 1769; *New-York Chronicle*, 15-22 May 1769; *Boston Gazette*, 31 Jul. 1769.

  No. 717: *Providence Gazette*, 22 Apr. 1769; *Boston Chronicle*, 27 Apr.-1 May 1769; *New-York Gazette, and Weekly Mercury*, 29 May 1769; *Boston Gazette*, 31 Jul. 1769.

  No. 718: *Boston Evening-Post*, 10 Apr. 1769; *Boston Chronicle*, 27 Apr.-1 May 1769; *Boston Gazette*, 31 Jul. 1769.

87. They are listed as items 68a-68c in Adams, *American Independence*, 51-52. Copies of all the imprints are available in *Early American Imprints, Series 1*, nos. 41911, 11178, and 11179. For further details see the **List of Abbreviations**, above, xxivn3.

88. *Letters to the Right Honourable the Earl of Hillsborough, from Governor Bernard, General Gage, and the honourable His Majesty's Council for the Province of Massachusetts-Bay. With an appendix, containing divers proceedings referred to in the said letters* (Boston: Edes and Gill, 1769), quotation at 22. The London reprint by J. Almon ([1769?]) did not include any additional material. The pamphlet was reissued in *A Collection of Tracts, on the Subjects of Taxing the British Colonies in America, and Regulating Their Trade*, 4 vols. (London: Printed for J. Almon, 1773), vol. 4, no. 2.

89. Thomas Hutchinson to Israel Williams, Boston, 6 May, 1769, Israel Williams Papers, MHS.

90. TH to Thomas Whately, Boston, 20 Jan. 1769, Hutchinson Transcripts, 2: 709.

91. See the newspapers listed in note 87, above, plus "Bostonian," *Boston Gazette*, 24 Apr. 1769. On 24 Apr., news arrived that FB had been created a baronet. *Boston Post-Boy and Advertiser,* 1 May 1769. The fact that the costs were paid from the "Privy Purse" seemed "additional Proof" of the king's regard for FB, reported the *Boston Evening-Post*, 8 May 1769. FB's preference for a "new-modeled" constitution drew lengthy comment in a letter addressed "To the Sons of Liberty" in the *Boston Evening-Post*, 15 May 1769. Anonymous attacks on FB were more prevalent after his departure from the province on 2 Aug. and the arrival of the second parcel of letters on the 18 Aug.

92. *Reports of the Record Commissioners of Boston*, 16: 274.

93. See Alexander, *Samuel Adams*, 83-118.

94. See Neil Longley York, "The Uses of Law and the *Gaspee* Affair," *Rhode Island History* 50 (1992): 3-21.

95. On the friends of America see Julie M. Flavell and Gordon Hay, "Using Capture-Recapture Methods to Reconstruct the American Population in London," *Journal of Interdisciplinary History* 32 (2001): 37-53; John Derry, *English Politics and the American Revolution* (London, 1976), 129-173; Julie M. Flavell, "American Patriots in London and the Quest for Talks, 1773-1775," *Journal of Imperial and Commonwealth History* 20 (1992): 335-369; idem, "Lord North's Conciliatory Proposals and the Patriots in London," *English Historical Review* 107 (1992): 302-322; Frank O'Gorman, "The Parliamentary Opposition to the Government's American Policy, 1760-1776," *Britain and the American Revolution*, edited by H. T. Dickinson (London and New York, 1998), 97-123.

96. DeBerdt to Thomas Cushing, London, 25 Feb. 1769, in Albert Matthews, "Letters of Dennys DeBerdt, 1757-1770," *Publications of the Colonial Society of Massachusetts* 13 (1911): 290-461.

97. *Bernard Papers*, 4: 147-149.

98. See Eliga H. Gould, "Pownall, Thomas (1722–1805)" *ODNB-e* (http://www.oxforddnb.com.ezproxy.stir.ac.uk/view/article/22676, accessed 28 Dec. 2013). "Junius" was probably Sir Philip Francis (1740-1818), a Dublin-born writer and clerk in the War Office under Lord Barrington, whom he bitterly attacked in print. On the disputed identities of "Junius" see Cannon, *The Letters of Junius*, 539-572.

99. Bollan wrote Danforth on 22 Apr. describing Pownall's preparations to introduce the motion.

> I understood from a principal member, & one of your chief friends, that Mr Pownal mention'd a proceeding of this kind to him, who answer'd, this tended to rivet the chains upon the Colonists, that he wou'd oppose it if made, but would second a motion for general relief, and that Mr Pownal afterwards enlarged his idea, & declared he wou'd make a motion in the House on Wednesday last . . .

Bowdoin and Temple Papers, 134.

100. Bollan to Danforth, Henrietta Street, 6 May 1769, *Bowdoin and Temple Papers*, 137-138. Bollan's presumption was not without foundation. On 18 Mar. 1769, Pownall informed Danforth that

> The ministers, I understand, are desirous of concluding the dispute with the Colonists, for the present at least, in their own way, and at different times it has been said they wou'd promote a repeal in case the Colonies wou'd petition for it on the foot of inexpediency, relinquishing or waving their claim of exemption from taxation; whether by waving they mean a temporary or perpetual relinquishment, or none at all, I leave to your judgment, & likewise whether they intend such a palliative as may prevent the stagnation of trade which they fear, & possibly regard more than your welfare, and whereby they may gain time to carry on other designs.

Bowdoin and Temple Papers, 132. Historians, however, have not considered the possibility that Pownall was acting with ministers' tacit approval or active encouragement. Peter D. G. Thomas concluded that "Pownall's motion fell on stony ground. It was not supported by any of the opposition factions nor accepted by the ministry." Thomas, *Townshend Duties Crisis*, 134.

101. Ritcheson, *British Politics and the American Revolution*, 124-132; Thomas, *Townshend Duties Crisis*, 129-147. George III quoted by Thomas, ibid., 129. Hillsborough's reform proposals are discussed in the source note to **No. 743**.

102. Thomas, *Townshend Duties Crisis*, 138.

103. The Council's request for more of FB's correspondence was made in a letter of 15 Apr. (not found), to which Bollan replied on 21 Jun. 1769. *Bowdoin and Temple Papers*, 144-146.

104. On 29 Mar., Hillsborough received FB's account of the publication of his letters in the *Boston Gazette*. 23 Jan. 1769 (**No. 734**). Bollan's report of the meeting with Hillsborough indicates that the secretary of state was aware that the Council's letter to him of 15 Apr. had been published, in *Letters to Hillsborough*. Bollan to Danforth et al., Henrietta Street, 21 Jun. 1769, *Bowdoin and Temple Papers*, 144-146.

105. Bollan was trying to obtain copies of the Customs commissioners' memorials to the Treasury concerning the *Liberty* riot, dated 16 Jun. and 11 Jul. 1768, which he later acquired: the originals are in T 1/465, ff 120-122, 179-180.

106. Bollan to Danforth et al., Henrietta Street, 21 Jun. 1769, *Bowdoin and Temple Papers*, 144-146.

107. The 64th and 65th Regiments were withdrawn from Boston to Halifax in July 1769. After the "massacre" of civilians by soldiers of the 29th, that regiment was deployed to New Jersey and the 14th Regiment put into the barracks at Castle William until 1772 when it was sent to the West Indies. British marines were stationed on board the several Royal Navy ships that visited Boston harbor, but after the withdrawal of the 14th Regiment there was no garrison of Regulars in Boston until April 1774, when the 64th returned to Castle William. When General Thomas Gage arrived in June that year as Massachusetts's new military governor, he initially brought four regiments. By November 1774, there were ten British regiments (plus two companies of the 65th) stationed in Boston, making upwards of three thousand soldiers. I am grateful to Neil Longley York for his advice on this matter. The troop movements can be followed in Walter S. Dunn, *Choosing Sides on the Frontier in the American Revolution* (Westport, Conn, 2007), 101-102.

108. The resolves of 27 Jun. are in *JHRM*, 45: 168-172, and the petition at ibid., 197-199.

109. "Judge not, that ye be not judged." Matthew 7.1, KJV.

110. On 15 Jul. 1769. *JHRM*, 45, 196-197.

111. Bernard's arrival and departure are described in Nicolson, *The 'Infamas Govenor,'* 4-5, 49-50, 203.

112. Bollan to Danforth et al., Henrietta Street, 21 Jun. 1769, *Bowdoin and Temple Papers*, 144-146.

113. The authenticated transcripts are not extant. Rosier's attestation was reproduced in the printed versions published in *Letters to the Ministry*. A court calendar for 1770 indicates that George White was one of four "Clerks without Doors, attending Committees." *A New Edition of the Royal Kalendar; Or Complete And Correct Annual Register for . . . 1770* (London, 1770), 68. Rosier's position came with a £100 salary, which was raised to £200 in 1770 in respect of his due diligence, and he rose through the ranks of the Commons' officers. Williams, *Clerical Organization of the House of Commons,* 169-170.

114. After preparing the copies for dispatch, Bollan noted that "being so straiten'd in time that I shall not be able to read any of the fresh copies now sent." By "fresh copies" Bollan was probably referring to the transcripts prepared by the House of Commons clerk; alternatively he could have meant Hillsborough's out-letters and the commissioners of Customs' memorials which he had recently obtained. Bollan to Danforth et al., Poland Street, 23 Jun. 1769, *Bowdoin and Temple Papers,* 148.

115. The term "bare reading" is ambiguous. Bollan may simply be referring to the act of reading. But it may also record how he felt the first time he heard the contents read aloud: that the letters were bereft of morality. "Bare in thy guilt how foul must thou appear?" John Milton, *Paradise Regain'd, a poem in IV books: to which is added Samson Agonistes* (1671): *Samson Agonistes,* 1:902, cf. *OED*.

116. Bollan to Danforth et al., Henrietta Street, 21 Jun. 1769, *Bowdoin and Temple Papers,* 144-146.

117. Bollan to Danforth, Poland Street, 23 Jun. 1769, *Bowdoin and Temple Papers,* 147.

118. The package was sent under cover of Bollan's letter to Danforth et al., Henrietta Street, 21 Jun. 1769. It was carried by Capt. Smith, who arrived in Boston on Tuesday 15 Aug. Bollan insisted the transcripts be shown to the Boston selectmen because of the "charges" made against them. *Bowdoin and Temple Papers,* 144-146. It is possible, therefore, that the selectmen were the final recipients of the parcel (although this is not recorded in *Reports of the Record Commissioners of Boston,* vol. 23).

119. The duplicates were carried by Capt. Scott, master of the *Boston Packet,* which arrived on Thursday 10 Aug. after a six-week crossing. *Boston Chronicle,* 7-10 Aug. 1769. The cover letter was Bollan to Danforth et al., Poland Street, 23 Jun. 1769, *Bowdoin and Temple Papers,* 146-148. Some of the additional papers may have included items later issued as a pamphlet. *A Third Extraordinary Budget of Epistles and Memorials between Sir Francis Bernard of Nettleham, Baronet, some Natives of Boston, New-England, and the present Ministry; against N America, the True Interest of the British Empire, and the Rights of Mankind* ([Boston]: [Edes & Gill], [1770]). Despite what its title stated the pamphlet did not include any of FB's letters but copies of Benjamin Hallowell's examination before the Treasury on 21 Jul. 1768, depositions of customs officers, Hillsborough to Gage of 8 Jun. 1768 (**Appendix 4**), the lords of the Admiralty to Hillsborough of 14 Dec., and correspondence between Thomas Bradshaw and John Pownall.

120. John Erving acknowledged receipt with a letter of that date. *Bowdoin and Temple Papers,* 153-154.

121. Erving to Bollan, Boston, 26 Jul. 1769. *Bowdoin and Temple Papers,* 149-150. Erving's personal request was only partly driven by curiosity, having been a defendant in one of the cases reported by FB. The relevant letters were **Nos. 52, 54, 60,** and **64.** *Bernard Papers,* 1: 119-123, 132-135, 140-142.

122. Bollan to Danforth, Nassau Street, Soho, 28 Jan. 1771, *Bowdoin and Temple Papers,* 257.

123. Ibid., 148.

124. Bollan to Danforth et al., Henrietta Street, 21 Jun. 1769, *Bowdoin and Temple Papers,* 146.

125. See Nicolson, *The 'Infamas Govener,'* 198-200.

126. *Letters to the Ministry from Governor Bernard, General Gage, and Commodore Hood. And also Memorials to the Lords of the Treasury, from the Commissioners of the Customs. With sundry letters and papers annexed to the said memorials* (Boston: Edes and Gill, 1769).

127. *Massachusetts Gazette and Boston Weekly News-Letter,* 7 Sept. 1769; *Boston Evening-Post,* 11 Sept. 1769.

128. To Shelburne: **Nos. 585, 589, 593, 596, 600, 601**; To Hillsborough: **Nos. 623, 630, 632, 633, 638, 646, 648, 654, 656, 660, 663, 664, 668, 672, 681, 686, 690, 691, 694, 698, 700**, and **703**. *Bernard Papers*, 4: 86-88, 98-99, 112-118, 121-124, 129-139, 185-190, 201-214, 220-230, 242-246, 255-257, 259-263, 266-270, 277-282, 288-290, 295-300, 318-324, 331-337, 347-353; 5: 63-68, 75-77, 79-82. Also printed in the pamphlets was FB's letter to Shelburne of 2 Feb. 1768, which was omitted from *Bernard Papers* volume 4 since it merely acknowledged receipt of correspondence.

129. Including **Nos. 624 to 628**, *Bernard Papers*, 4: 190-198; and **Appendix 6**.

130. *Letters to the Ministry from Governor Bernard, General Gage, and Commodore Hood. And also Memorials to the Lords of the Treasury, from the Commissioners of the Customs. With sundry letters and papers annexed to the said memorials* (London, J. Wilkie, 1769).

131. Dorr's copy is in the MHS catalogue, reference E187, f 894.

132. On 18 Oct. the town adopted four resolves. First, that Bernard's letters and the Customs commissioners' memorials to the ministry had "misinform[ed]" the king about "Affections and loyalty" of American colonists and revealed the authors had "discovered an implacable Enmity to this Town." Second, the town "rejoice[d]" in the House of Representatives' petition of 27 Jun. calling for the governor's removal. Third, Gen. Thomas Gage and Commodore Samuel Hood entertained "unreasonable prejudice against the Town." Fourth, much of the correspondence contained "false scandalous and infamous Libels" upon the inhabitants of Boston, about which the selectmen were instructed to begin legal proceedings. *Reports of the Record Commissioners of Boston*, 16: 299-300.

133. Adams's report was read and unanimously accepted at the town meeting of 18 Oct. The town ordered its publication and that copies be transmitted to Isaac Barré, William Bollan, Dennys DeBerdt, Benjamin Franklin, Thomas Pownall, and Barlow Trecothick—but not William Beckford, whose role in the procurement of the Bernard Letters Bollan did not fully reveal until May 1770; Edward Popham, Bollan never mentioned by name. *Reports of the Record Commissioners of Boston*, 16: 299-302. The report was appended to ibid., 303-324, and printed in the province newspapers, including the *Boston Weekly News-Letter*, 26 Oct. 1769. *Reports of the Record Commissioners of Boston*, 16: 302.

134. *An Appeal to the World; or A Vindication of the Town of Boston, From Many False and Malicious Aspersions Contain'd in Certain Letters and Memorials, Written by Governor Bernard, General Gage, Commodore Hood, the Commissioners of the American Board of Customs, and Others, and by Them Respectively Transmitted to the British Ministry. Published by Order of the Town* (Edes and Gill; Boston, 1769); appendix to the *American Gazette* containing An Appeal to the World: or, a vindication of the town of Boston, from many false and malicious aspersions, contained in certain letters and memorials, written by Governor Bernard, . . . and others (London, 1769).

135. **Nos. 600, 623, 625, 630, 632, 646**, and **681**. *Bernard Papers*, 4: 129-134, 185-190, 192-193, 201-205, 207-212, 242-246, 318-324.

136. Bailyn, nonetheless, did not discuss the *Appeal to the World* in his seminal monograph, *The Ideological Origins of the American Revolution* (Cambridge, Mass., 1967).

137. *Appeal to the World*, 23n.

138. "Pray do not let this matter be divulged," Bollan warned in a letter to Danforth, Fludyer Street, 1 May 1770, *Bowdoin and Temple Papers*, 179.

139. Lord North, who had succeeded Grafton as prime minister on 28 Jan. 1770, was unwilling to prosecute the Boston Whigs for libel or sedition. Any prosecution would certainly have undermined the reconciliation that North expected from a partial repeal of the Townshend duties. But his hesitancy to pursue the Boston printers may indicate sensitivity to criticism by "Junius" concerning censorship of the British press and prohibitions on the reporting of Parliamentary debates. On the wider issues of press freedoms see Robert Right Rea, *The English Press in Politics* (Lincoln, Neb. 1963); Jeremy Black, *The English Press in the Eighteenth Century* (London, 1987).

140. Publicly and in cabinet, Hillsborough opposed the establishment of a new colony on the Ohio River. Privately, however, he encouraged the scheme's backers to seek unfeasibly large grants in the expectation that they would be refused. His duplicity was exposed and exploited by his enemies. See Peter Marshall, "Hill, Wills, first marquess of Downshire (1718–1793)," *ODNB-e* (http://www.oxforddnb.com.ezproxy.stir.ac.uk/view/article/13317, accessed 6 Feb. 2014).

141. See the works cited above in n75.

142. Only in one of the six letters did FB provide names, and that was in the context of discussing divisions with the Council during the preparation of the petitions to Parliament in Nov. 1768 (**No. 718**). He briefly recommended a royally-appointed Council in **No. 709** and the reform of justices of the peace in **No. 711**; but the six letters did not provide a comprehensive discussion of the reform of colonial government.

143. *Bernard Papers*, 4: 22.

144. The sixteen unpublished letters had not been presented to Parliament because they did not directly comment on provincial affairs, or were private, or in two cases (**Nos. 719** and **724**) were received on 10 Feb. after the debate on the American correspondence was over.

145. *Bernard Papers*, 4: 261-263.

146. In **No. 657**, FB defended himself against the House's accusation that he had incorrectly reported the rejection of the first motion to prepare the Circular Letter. Ibid., 261-263. A copy of the letter was presented to Parliament on 28 Nov. *HLJ*, 32: 184.

147. **No. 722** was an end of year notification that the king approved FB's conduct as governor and that FB's recent correspondence was being considered by Parliament. It also condemned the "unwarrantable & unjustifiable behaviour of the Council upon many occasions," notably with regard to the quartering of the British regiments. **No. 727** was essentially an update about Parliament delaying deliberations on American affairs, again acknowledging that two of the governor's letters (**Nos. 709** and **711**) confirmed the Council's "determined resolution" to defeat British policy. The letters were printed in *Letters to the Ministry* (1st ed.), 76-77.

148. **Nos. 603, 608, 622, 651, 653, 661, 679**, *Bernard Papers*, 4: 142-143, 149-152, 181-184, 252, 254-255, 271-276, 313-315; and **Nos. 702**, and **712**, in this volume.

149. **No. 603** disapproved of the House of Representatives petitioning the king without going through the governor; **No. 608** was Hillsborough's controversial instruction to FB to have the House rescind the vote approving the Circular Letter; **Nos. 622** and **661** informed that orders had been issued to locate British regiments to Boston; **No. 651** was a circular to the colonial governors; **No. 653** covered administrative matters; **No. 679** indicated that the Council's petition to the king had been laid before His Majesty; **No. 702** instructed FB not to summon the assembly until May 1769; **No. 712** discussed the king's speech to Parliament of 8 Nov. 1768.

150. The Whigs did not flinch at printing the two out-letters they acquired, and there is no evidence to suggest that they were keeping ammunition in reserve. Indeed, the House of Representatives continued to press their governor to release Hillsborough's letter on the rescinding controversy. **No. 608**, *Bernard Papers*, 4: 149-156; *JHRM*, 45: 68.

151. This may have been what he meant by "unexpected difficulties." Bollan to Danforth et al., Henrietta Street, 21 Jun. 1769, *Bowdoin and Temple Papers*, 145.

152. George Chalmers, "Papers relating to New England, 1643-1786," Sparks MS 10, MH-H; John Almon, *A Collection of Interesting, Authentic Papers, relative to the Dispute between Great Britain and America; shewing the causes and progress of that misunderstanding, from 1764 to 1775* (London, 1777).

153. Standard biographical directories include: Mark Mayo Boatner, ed., *Encyclopedia of the American Revolution* (New York, 1966); Joseph Foster, ed., *Alumni Oxonienses: the Members of the University of Oxford, 1715-1886*, 4 vols. (Oxford and London, 1888); Edward A. Jones, *The Loyalists of Massachusetts: Their Memorials, Petitions and Claims* (London, 1930); David E. Maas, ed. and comp., *Divided*

Hearts: Massachusetts Loyalists, 1765-1790: A Biographical Directory (Boston, 1980); Sir Lewis Namier and John Brooke, eds., *The House of Commons, 1754-1790*, 3 vols. (London, 1964); John A. Schutz, ed., *Legislators of the Massachusetts General Court* (Boston, 1997); Search & ReSearch Publishing Corp, *Early Vital Records of the Commonwealth of Massachusetts to About 1850* (Wheat Ridge, Conn., 2002); John L. Sibley, Clifford K. Shipton, Conrad Edick Wright, Edward W. Hanson, eds. *Biographical Sketches of Graduates of Harvard University* [title varies], 18 vols. to date (Cambridge, Mass., 1873-); James H. Stark, *The Loyalists of Massachusetts and the Other Side of the American Revolution* (Boston, 1910); Nancy S. Voye, *Massachusetts Officers in the French and Indian Wars, 1748-1763* (microfiche, Boston, 1975).

154. *American National Biography Online* (New York, 2005-, at http://www.anb.org); *Dictionary of Canadian Biography Online* (Toronto, 2003-, http://www.biographi.ca); Newsbank Inc., *America's Historical Newspapers. Archive of Americana. Early American Newspapers Series 1, 1690-1876* (2008-, available via subscription at GenealogyBank.com, http://www.genealogybank.com/gbnk/newspapers/); *Oxford Dictionary of National Biography Online* (London, 2004-2006, http://www.oxforddnb.com) (hereafter *ODNB-e*). The British Army Lists, published annually since 1740, are not online, but Worthington C. Ford, *British Officers Serving in America, 1754-1774* (Boston, 1894) is available at the Internet Archive.com. Also useful for establishing dates of British government appointments is the authoritative J. C. Sainty, et al., eds., *Officeholders in Modern Britain, 1660-1870*, 11 vols. (London, 1972-2006), available at British History Online (via http://www.british-history.ac.uk/catalogue). Contemporary almanacs and court-registers are accessible through ECCO. For example, *The Court and City Kalendar: or, Gentleman's Register, for the year 1766* . . . (London, 1765).

The Papers of
Governor Francis Bernard

1 OCTOBER 1768-29 JULY 1769

694 | To the Earl of Hillsborough

Boston Oct 1 1768

My Lord

The Day my last Packet[1] went out of the Harbour, brought in the Fleet from Halifax with two Regiments on board under the Command of Lieut Colonell Dalrymple. As soon as I was informed of it I went to the Castle and got there before the Ships got to Anchor. Soon after I saw Colonell Dalrymple and informed him of all the Proceedings of the Council concerning his Quarters and the Difficulties he was to encounter. And it was agreed that I should call a Council at the Castle the next Morning and invite the Colonell and the commanding Officer of the Fleet to attend the Council.[2]

The Council accordingly met at the Castle the next Morning being Thursday Sep 29: The commanding Officers likewise attended. After the Business was opened, the Colonell acquainted them in a very genteel Manner that he was ordered to quarter one of the Regiments at Boston; that he hoped he was going among Friends and that his Men would on their Parts behave as such; that he should be glad if he could have Quarters in the Way of Barracks where he could keep his Men under the Eyes of their Officers and then he would engage that his Men should be kept in good Order. He added several kind Expressions signifying his Desire to conduct the Business in a Manner that should be most easy and agreeable to the Town. He was answered that they hoped he would observe the Act of Parliament; and if he did, he would put both his Regiments in the Barracks at the Castle which were in the Town of Boston and capable of holding two Regiments. That when the Barracks were full the Council had Nothing to do with the quartering Troops untill the public Houses were full. The Colonell said that he would not dispute whether the Castle Island was in the Town or not; they certainly were distinct Places in his Orders: that he was not used to dispute about his Orders but obey them and therefore should most assuredly march his Regiment into the Town, and if they assigned him Quarters in the public Houses he should take them: but then he could not be answerable for the good Order of his Men, which it would be impossible to preserve if they were intermixed with the Townspeople and separated from their Officers. I then interrupted and asked whether as the Colonell had now told them that he must and would march his Regiment into the Town it would not be best to reconsider my Proposal for fitting up the Manufactory House for a Barrack. It was observed that it was not regular to put a Question untill the Board was cleared: The Gentlemen thereupon withdrew.[3]

I then desired that in reconsidering my Proposal for fitting up the Manufactory House they would let me know what Objections they had to it: The only Objection worth Notice was that they had no Power to draw the Money. I told them that there was an appropriation in the Treasury for contingent Services which had much more Money upon it than would be wanted for this Business, which was a contingent Service: They still declined it. I then told them that I would make but one more Proposal to them, which was that it [*if*] they would authorise me to fit up this Building, I would be answerable it should be done at the Charge of the Crown. This also they refused in a Writing referring to their former Answer. I then gave them to understand that those Subterfuges should not disappoint the Execution of the King's Commands; and that I by myself would assign the House in Question for a Barrack.[4]

The next Morning when I got to the Castle as usual to hold a further Consultation, Captain Montresor an Engineer[5] arrived here and brought Letters ^from Genl Gage^ for me and the Colonell;[6] wherein the General says that by a Number of private Letters from Boston to New York and from the Narrative of the Proceedings of the Town Meeting at Boston it was reported and beleived at New York that the People in and about Boston had revolted; he therefore sent Captain Montresor to assist the Forces as Engineer and to enable them to recover and maintain the Castle and such other Posts as they could secure. As Things were not so bad as this came to, the Colonell thought proper upon the Authority of these new Orders, to alter his Plan and land both Regiments at Boston without Loss of Time. I gave him a positive Order to take Possession of the Manufactory House for one; and the other Regiment was to be encamped. This being resolved, the Fleet was immediately put into Motion and by the next Morning commanded the whole Town. And this Day at Noon the Troops began landing and were all paraded on the Common by four in the Afternoon. This was done not only without Opposition but with tolerable good Humour. Thus this Business has been effected for the present; which would have had none of these Difficulties, nor have occasioned such a Parade, if it had not been for the undutiful Behaviour of the Council.

I am, with great Respect, My Lord, your
Lordship's most obedient & most humble Servant

Fra Bernard

The Right honourable The Earl of Hillsborough

dupLS, RC   CO 5/757, ff 434-436.

In handwriting of Thomas Bernard. Endorsed: Boston October 1ˢᵗ. 1768. Govʳ. Bernard (Nᵒ. 26). R 4ᵗʰ: Novᵇᵉʳ: Dupˡ. _ origˡ not reced _ A.53.   Enclosed a copy of the minutes of the Massachusetts Council of 29 Sept. 1768, CO 5/757, ff 437-438. Variants of letter: CO 5/767, ff 119-124 (L, RLbC); BP, 7: 67-70 (L, LbC); *Letters to the Ministry* (1st ed.), 66-68; *Letters to the Ministry* (repr.), 89-92. Hillsborough acknowledged receipt with **No. 712**. Copies of the letter and enclosure were laid before both houses of Parliament on 28 Nov. 1768. HLL: American Colonies Box 3.

On Wednesday 28 Sept., there arrived in Boston harbor His Majesty's ships the forty-gun *Launceston*, *Mermaid* (28 guns), *Glasgow* (20), *Beaver* (14), *Senegal*, and *Bonetta* (10), with two armed schooners and "several Transports" bringing some one thousand troops: the 14th Regiment of Foot commanded by Lt. Col. William Dalrymple, the 29th Regiment under Lt. Col. Maurice Carr,[7] plus the Grenadiers, a company of the 59th Regiment, and a detachment of the Royal Regiment of Artillery. It was reported that on the Thursday, the boats from the fleet "came up and sounded the Bay all round the Town, and on Friday the Ships of War came up and ranged themselves on the North East Side of the Metropolis, as if intended for a formal Siege." When HMS *Romney* and HMS *Martin* moved up from the Castle eight warships lay anchored in the inner harbor. Lt. Col. Dalrymple came ashore an hour before his troops landed, presumably with a small advance guard.[8] At noon on Saturday 1 Oct., the 14th Regiment "landed at the Long Wharf, and having formed, marched with Drums beating, fifes playing, and Colors flying, up King Street to the Town-House." There they awaited the 29th Regiment; both thence proceeded to Boston Common, and were joined by the rest of the troops and the artillery train with two field guns.[9]

Dalrymple fully expected to put most of his men into the Manufactory House, situated on the east side of Tremont Street. One of his officers inspected the building at 2 PM, and shortly thereafter Dalrymple gave John Brown, the factory overseer, and other tenants and their families, two hours' notice to vacate the premises. But Dalrymple responded sympathetically to Brown's complaint, for, according to historian Richard Archer, he was anxious to "avoid a confrontation" with the townsfolk by forcing an eviction. He promptly negotiated with the selectmen to place some of the 14th Regiment in Faneuil Hall, promising to be out by the following Monday; his soldiers "stood 2 or 3 Hours before admission could be obtained" (TH noted) and did not enter the Hall until 9 PM (according to one newspaper). With space limited, on the evening of 2 Oct. Dalrymple (with FB's permission) moved some of the regiment into the Town House. The soldiers remained at Faneuil Hall for four weeks and at the Town House for seven until barracks were found in "converted warehouses" and other private buildings. The 29th Regiment and the artillery train, meanwhile, (which, unlike the 14th Regiment, had brought tents) set up an encampment on the Common for several weeks, before being moved into "sugarhouses and commercial buildings."[10] The transports from Ireland bringing the 64th and 65th Regiments started arriving in the second week of November.[11]

This letter provides an account of the soldiers' arrival up to 4 PM on 1 Oct. During this time, FB remained in Boston, probably at the Province House, but evidently left the town for Jamaica Farm, shortly thereafter.[12] FB was unaware that Dalrymple "had been put to Difficulties in providing a temporary Shelter" for his men, assuming that they would be placed in the Manufactory House under the direction of Sheriff Stephen Greenleaf (**No. 696**). FB wrote to Gen. Gage that evening (**No. 695**) without mentioning Dalrymple's

British Troops Landing in Boston. "A View of Part of the Town of Boston in New England and Brittish Ships of War: Landing Their Troops! 1768." Engraving by Paul Revere. Courtesy of the American Antiquarian Society.

"Difficulties." FB came into Boston on the morning of 2 Oct., whereupon he authorized the Town House for the soldiers' use,[13] before again returning to his country estate in the evening.

1. **Nos. 690**, **691**, and **693**. *Bernard Papers,* 4: 347-353, 355-356.

2. Lt. Col. William Dalrymple commanded the land force and Capt. Henry Smith the naval ships. FB and Dalrymple urged Smith to keep his vessels in the harbor until all the troops had arrived in Boston, including the two regiments from Ireland expected the following month. FB to Henry Smith, Boston, 8 Oct. 1768, BP, 7: 212.

3. FB's account summarizes the proceedings of the meeting at Castle William on 29 Sept., for which see CO 5/827, ff 62-63.

4. Ibid.

5. John Montresor (1736-99) was a captain in the 48th Regiment of Foot and one of Gage's senior engineers.

6. **No. 689**, *Bernard Papers*, 4: 345-346; Gage to Dalrymple, New York, 25 Sept. 1768, MiU-C: Gage, vol. 81.

7. Maurice Carr (1730-1813), lieutenant colonel of the 29th Regiment of Foot.

8. No. 751.

9. *Boston Evening-Post*, 3 Oct. 1768.

10. For these proceedings see Archer, *As If an Enemy's Country*, 110-115, including a social profile of the regiment at 106; *Boston Evening-Post*, 3 Oct. 1768; TH to Richard Jackson, 5 Oct. 1768, Mass. Archs., 25: 282, in Hutchinson Transcripts, 1: 283.

11. **No. 715**n1.

12. **Nos**. **695** and **696**.

13. FB to William Dalrymple, Province House, 2 Oct. 1768, BP, 7: 209.

695 | To Thomas Gage

Roxbury near Boston. Oct 1 1768

S[r].

I received your Letter of Sep 25[1] by Capt Montresor & that of Sep 26,[2] by an express. I wrote to you a letter dated Sep 24[3] considering an Account of what had passed between me & the Council concerning providing quarters for the troops to that day. This Letter I sent by Maj[r] Bayard who was to meet his Brother at Hertford who was to return to New York about the same time as the post.[4] The pretences upon which the Council refused quarters to the troops at Boston you will find published ^by themselves^ in all the Newspapers.[5]

On Wednesday last[6] the Fleet from Halifax came in. I immediately met Col Dalrymple at the Castle, when I stated to him the difficulties We were under in regard to quarters. We agreed that I should call a Council at the Castle the next day, & admit to it the Colonel & Capt Smith comm^r of the Navy.[7] We accordingly met the next day: the Council[8] endeavoured to put the Col off with barracks at the Castle for both regiments. He told them he should certainly obey his Orders by carrying one of his regiments to Boston & pressed them to find them barracks instead of open quarters. I urged them again to assist me in fitting up the Manufactory; they pleaded that they had no money. I at last told them that it should be done at the Kings Expence: they still refused to concur in it. At last I told them that the Kings Commands should not be disappointed; and I would myself assign the ~~barracks~~ ^manufactory^ for the use of the troops.

We were met the third day[9] to consult what to do; when Capt Montresor brought your letters;[10] when it was immediately resolved to land both regiments at Boston next day: and I gave the Col a power to take possession of the Manufactory. Accordingly both regiments were landed this ^day^ at Boston without opposition, or any great appearance of ill humour. As the Col will give you an exact Account of this, I have been Very short in it.

We have still quarters to provide for the two regiments from Ireland which will occasion much difficulty, unless the breaking the charm in the present instance shall facilitate it. There will be wanting a few Companies for Salem & Newbury; but they cant be spared as yet. There is no talk of rising; tho' 3 weeks ago the time was appointed & the Men enrolled to storm the Castle, but they are greatly lowered since that, the Country having failed them.

I am with great regard S^r your most obed^t humble Servant

Fra. Bernard

His Excellency Genl Gage.

ALS, RC   Gage, vol. 81.

Endorsed: Govr Bernard, Roxbury near Boston 1st: Oct 1768 Received 7th: Octr __ 1768.   The second paragraph and the last three sentences of the final paragraph are extracted in CO 5/86, ff 205-206. Another variant in BP, 7: 203-204 (L, LbC).

1. **No. 689**, *Bernard Papers*, 4: 345-346.

2. There is an AC in MiU-C: Gage, vol. 81.

3. **No. 687**, *Bernard Papers*, 4: 338-342.

4. Robert Bayard (1739-1819), a major in the 59th or Royal American Regiment of Foot, was a neighbor of FB's at Jamaica Plain.

5. *Boston Post-Boy and Advertiser*, 26 Sept.; *Boston Weekly News-Letter*, 29 Sept.; *Boston Chronicle*, 19-26 Sept. 1768.

6. 28 Sept.

7. Lt. Col. William Dalrymple and Capt. Henry Smith.

8. The proceedings of the meeting at Castle William on 29 Sept. are in CO 5/827, ff 62-63.

9. 30 Sept. FB is referring to a meeting with Dalrymple and Smith.

10. **No. 689**, *Bernard Papers*, 4: 345-346; Gage to Dalrymple, New York, 25 Sept. 1768, MiU-C: Gage, vol. 81.

696 | To William Dalrymple

Roxbury Oct 2 1768

S^r

Upon my Return from Boston in the Afternoon of this day I received your letter dated at Boston the same day[1] wherein you acquaint me with the Want of quarters & other accommodations for all the troops under your Command and say you fear the public Service will be retarded by my absence.

When I assigned the manufactory house for Barracks for the Troops as far as it would go[,][2] It was all that I could possibly do for providing barracks, & as it will be generally said, probably more than I had a right to do. When that was done the billeting the troops did not in the first Instance belong to me; and you must know that I exerted the utmost influence I had over the Council to prevent there being any occasion for resorting to billeting.

I also sent an Order to the Sheriff and afterwards gave him verbal instructions to attend the Destination of the Troops and provide Carriages &c, which I understand, he has done to the full Satisfaction.

When I went to town this morning to attend the Service at the King's Cha^p^pel I learned that you had been put to Difficulties in providing a temporary Shelter for your men and I, of my own accord, inclosed in a Letter to you[3] an order to the doorkeeper of the Courthouse[4] to open that building and all the spare rooms in it for the accommodation of the Men untill they could be encamped and quartered.

In regard to the accommodations required by law, I ordered a Council to be summoned to meet on Monday next,[5] which was the earliest time I could appoint. And I shall at such Meeting lay your Requisition before th[em?][6] and do the best I can get it fully complied with.

After having ever since your Arrival given my whole time and attention to the particular Business of accommodating your Troops, and having in no^one^

Instance that I know of, neglected any one thing that belonged to me, I shall be sorry to be really chargeable with the publick Service being retarded by my Neglect.

I am &c

Lt Col Dalrymple

L, LbC   BP, 7: 209-211.

In handwriting of clerk no. 9. Minor emendations not shown.
    FB was not fully aware of the problems Dalrymple had encountered in trying to place his soldiers in quarters on 1 and 2 Oct (see the source note to **No. 694**). But soon after writing this letter, FB permitted some of the soldiers to billet in the Town House, temporarily.

1. Not found.

2. Editorially supplied.

3. FB to Dalrymple, Province House, 2 Oct. 1768, enclosing FB's order to William Baker of the same date. BP, 7, 209.

4. The Town House, known today as the Old State House.

5. 3 Oct., for which proceedings see CO 5/827, ff 63-64.

6. Obscured by tight binding.

697 | *From Thomas Gage*

New York Oct^r $\underline{2}^d$ 1768.

Sir,

    I was yesterday favored with your's of the $\underline{24}^{th}$: ul^{mo}:,[1] and am sorry you meet with so many Obstacles in providing Quarters for the Troops. The Declaration of the Council that Castle William is in the Town of Boston is indeed pretty remarkable.

    I am to observe on these matters, that most of the Troops are ordered to the Town of Boston, and to be quartered therein; that they will agreeable to their orders disembark, and march into what is litterally meant to be the Town of Boston, and not to an Island seven miles distant from it, and if any Disturbances shall happen thro' the want of Quarters for the Troops, the Gentlemen of the Council and the magistrates must be answerable for it. The Officers will do every thing in their Power to prevent Disturbances, and I shall readily concurr with you in every measure that can be thought of to prevent mischief.

After using every Endeavor to provide Quarters for the Troops in the Town of Boston, and that you shall fail therein, we must be reduced to the Necessity of quartering them at the Expence of the Crown.

You seem assured that you will receive no assistance from the Council or magistrates, and therefore resolved to appropriate the manufacturing house for the purpose of quartering. And I wish in that case you could also do the same by the work-house and poor House,[2] as it would save both time and Expence: But you are apprehensive of Clamour, which it would, no doubt, be best to avoid, tho' I don't see how it is possible to act in any shape, that will prevent Clamour for whatever is done, will be construed into evil Designs. And Considering what has passed, how short a time it is, that a Resolution was taken to rise in Arms in open Rebellion. I don't see any Cause to be Scrupulous in doing what is judged absolutely necessary for the Service, and for the security of the King's Government, which has been so highly invaded, and so insolently threatened.

Whatever you shall at length find absolutely necessary to be done in this Affair of quartering on the Town's Account, when all other Expedients fail, you will be so good to acquaint Lieu^t Col^o. Dalrymple therewith that he may execute your Resolves whatever they shall be. And Captain Montresor will be ready likewise to assist you. I must leave the Determination of these matters to you who are upon the spot, and therefore best able to determine. But I would mention, if the Proposal of running up slight Barracks in a hurry cannot be avoided, whether they could not be erected on some advantageous spot for Defence or Offence vizt on Fort Hill, or Beacon Hill, such a Circumstance if the Distemper of the Times increases, may prove usefull.

His Majesty's Secretary of State in His Letter to me on the subject of ordering Troops to Boston,[3] recommends the taking Possession of Castle William, and repairing it, as it belongs to the Crown. Upon your Appearing unwilling to let the King's Forces go into the Fort, to avoid giving umbrage Colonel Dalrymple was only ordered to take Possession of it, in Case of Emergency; but upon the late Resolution[4] to take Arms, I sent the Engineer to repair it, and ordered the Colonel to take Possession, which order he will shew you. And I hope you will approve of it.

I am with great Regard, Sir, your most obedient, and most humble Servant

Thos: Gage

His Excellency Governor Bernard.

ALS, RC   BP, 11: 315-318.

Endorsed: [General Gage][5] Oct[r] 2nd 1768.   There is an extract in CO 5/86, ff 198-200.

The 14th and 29th Regiments had disembarked and moved into temporary accommodation by the time FB received Gage's letter. But the logistical problem still remained as to how they could be accommodated in barracks within the town. Gage's preference was to concentrate the soldiers in public buildings and to fortify the town lest his men encounter armed resistance. And with winter approaching, Gage was determined to avoid further wrangling over the legalities of establishing permanent quarters for his soldiers in the town. "I don't see any Cause to be Scrupulous in doing what is judged absolutely necessary for the Service, and for the security of the King's Government, which has been so highly invaded, and so insolently threatened." (**No. 697.**)

---

1. **No. 687**, *Bernard Papers*, 4: 338-342.

2. The workhouse and almshouse were situated on the eastern edge of the Common near the Old Granary Burial Ground, no more than one hundred yards from the Manufactory House.

3. **Appendix 4**, *Bernard Papers*, 4: 373-374.

4. Gage is not referring to a specific resolve of the town, but to the determination voiced at the town meeting of 12 Sept., as reported by FB in **No. 680**, *Bernard Papers*, 4: 316-318.

5. Obscured in the fold of the binding.

British Troops on Boston Common. Engraving by Sidney L. Smith, 1902, after "A Prospective View of Part of the [Boston] Commons." Watercolor, c.1768. By Christian Remick. I. N. Phelps Stokes Collection, Miriam and Ira D. Wallach Division of Art, Prints and Photographs, The New York Public Library, Astor, Lenox, and Tilden Foundations. Dedicated "To John Hancock, Esq. This prospective view of part of the Commons, and the encampment of the 29th Regiment and Field Pieces etc., as taken from the grove on ye first of October, 1768, is most humbly dedicated, by his most Faithful Servant Christian Remick." Hancock's mansion on Beacon Hill is at the top right of the painting.

698 | *To the Earl of Hillsborough*

N.º 27

Boston Oct 3 1768

My Lord

In my letter No 25[1] I gave your Lordship an account of the proceedings of the Convention; in this I propose to finish it. They set[2] exactly a week; and their last Act I hereby send your Lordship a printed Copy of; this & what I before sent being all that has been printed. They have besides, as I am told, prepared a Petition to the King in the same or nearly the same terms as the former & have sent it ^to Mr Deberdt^ with a long letter of instructions, among which is, as is said, a direction to give it into the Kings own hands. But I am not certain of this, as all this business was done with a kind of Secrecy, into which it is scarce Worth while to pry.[3]

The cheif Observation upon these writings is of their moderation so Very different from the temper of those who called this meeting. This is accounted for many ways: Many of the deputies came down with instructions & disposition to prevent the Bostoners involving the province in the Consequences of their own mad devices; Many of them were, from the beginning, sensible of ^the^ impropriety & danger of this proceeding & were desirous by a moderate conduct, to correct the one & ward off the other; My Message, which was said to be Very high (tho I hope not too high for the occasion) although it did not disperse them, had the good effect to keep them in awe. Hence it was that Otis, when he joined them, was perfectly tame; and his Collegue Adams when he attempted to launch out in the language used in the house of representatives, was presently silenced: And now these people assume to themselves merit of the moderation of those, whom they called together for very different purposes.[4]

However therefore this temperate Conduct of these Deputies may in some measure apologise for the Towns who deputed them & for themselves who assembled, It makes no excuse for those who took upon themselves to call them together. For whoever reads the minutes of the Town Meeting in which the Summoning this Convention was ordered, will easily perceive that It was intended to have Very different effects from those which it was issued in.[5]

I am, with great respect, My Lord, Your Lordships most obedient & most humble Servant.

Fra. Bernard

the right honble the Earl of Hillsborough.

I inclose in this an original Circular Letter, the only one I have been able to get as people Don't care to appear to ask for them.[6]

ALS, RC   CO5/757, ff 439-440.

Endorsed: Boston October 3[d]: 1768. Gov[r]. Bernard (N[o] 27) R 4th: Nov[ber] A.54.   Enclosures: resolves of the Massachusetts Convention of Towns, Boston, 29 Sept. 1768, CO 5/757, f 441, extracted from the *Boston News-Letter,* 3 Oct. 1768; also enclosed the circular of the Boston selectmen to the Massachusetts towns, 14 Sept. 1768[7] (**Appendix 13**, *Bernard Papers,* 4: 400-401; also sent under cover of **No. 681**).[8] Variants of letter in: CO 5/767, ff 124-126 (L, RLbC); BP, 7: 70-72 (L, LbC); *Letters to the Ministry* (1st ed.), 69; *Letters to the Ministry* (repr.), 92-93. Hillsborough acknowledged receipt with **No. 712**. Copies of the letter together with the enclosures were laid before both houses of Parliament on 28 Nov. 1768. HLL: American Colonies Box 3.

House agent Dennys DeBerdt endeavored to transmit to Secretary of State Hillsborough the Convention's petition to the king, but Hillsborough delayed responding until he was able to consult with the cabinet. On 6 Dec., Hillsborough finally refused to accept the petition on the grounds that the Convention was an "unlawfull assembly."[9]

---

1. **No. 691**, *Bernard Papers,* 4: 352-353.

2. Thus in manuscript.

3. The Convention's petition to the king was never printed in the province or British newspapers, and a copy has not been found. The original was forwarded to Dennys DeBerdt for transmission to the king. Thomas Cushing (as chairman for the Convention of Towns) to Dennys DeBerdt, Boston, 27 Sept. 1768, printed in the *Boston Chronicle*, 10-17 Oct. 1768.

4. The Convention's resolves of 29 Sept., which FB included as an enclosure, cited the governor's order that the Convention should disperse as grounds for petitioning the king. The Convention reiterated the case against the Townshend duties "very clearly set forth" in the House of Representatives' petition to the king of 20 Jan. and public letters of Feb. 1768. The resolves further disputed any need for a "standing army" to suppress riots and stressed the loyalty of the colonists in making dutiful "Supplications" to the king. What probably impressed FB most was the concluding section, the humble language of which contrasted with the bullish attitude of the Boston town meeting.

    > While the People wisely observe the Medium between an abject Submission, and a slavish Stupidity, under grievous Oppression on the one Hand, and irrational Attempts to obtain Redress on the other, and steadily persevere in orderly and constitutional Applications, for the Recovering the Exercise of their just Rights and Liberties, they may promise themselves Success.

    Boston Weekly News-Letter, 3 Oct. 1768.

5. The Whigs expected the governor to make political capital from the Convention having met in defiance of his orders. The Convention's letter to DeBerdt (probably drafted by its clerk, Samuel Adams, and signed by Thomas Cushing) provided the House agent with further clarification on the disorders of 18 Mar. and 10 Jun., from which, the Whigs (rightly) believed FB had constructed a case for having troops sent to Boston. The Convention left DeBerdt in no doubt that the Convention expected FB to misconstrue their work in much the same way that he exaggerated the threats to law and order posed by the riots.

We cannot indeed wonder, that when such false representations are made by persons, as we have reason to believe, of rank and figure here, our mother country should for a while give credit to them, and under an apprehension of a general insurrection, should send a military force to subdue a people . . .

Boston Chronicle, 10-17 Oct. 1768; *Boston Gazette*, 10 Oct. 1768; Harry Alonzo Cushing, *The Writings of Samuel Adams*, 4 vols. (New York, 1904), 1: 241-247.

6. Not found. This refers to the printed precept dated 14 Sept. distributed by the Boston selectmen and inviting towns to send a delegation to the Convention. See **Appendix 13**, *Bernard Papers*, 4: 400-401.

7. Not included in the list of American correspondence presented to Parliament on 28 Nov. 1786. *HCJ*, 32: 76.

8. *Bernard Papers*, 4: 318-324.

9. Dennys DeBerdt to Thomas Cushing, London, 18 Nov. and 7 Dec. 1768, Matthews, "Letters of Dennys DeBerdt," 345-348.

699 | *From Lord Barrington*

Beckett October the 3ᵈ. 1768

Dear Sir,

Since my last I am to acknowlege your Letters of the 20[1] & 30[th2] of July. I agree entirely with your reasonings about sending Troops to Boston: The late Violences made it proper to send them, orders went accordingly to General Gage,[3] but he had not received those orders when you wrote the above mention'd Letters to me. He was right in not sending any Troops without either orders or requisition.[4] I find near three Regiments are assembled at Halifax, & two saild from Ireland the 10th of last month. I hope this will furnish us sufficient Strength for you; but when they come, how will you quarter them, or where will you find a Civil Magistrate to use them? If the Act for quartering Troops in N. America had been alter'd as I proposed, the first difficulty would not have existed.[5] I hope you will be able to remove the Second difficulty.

I long to hear that things are quiet, I mean *permanently* quiet in your part of the world, & I wish it may be without any bloodshed. Beleive me ever

Dear Sir Your Excellency's most faithful & most obedient Servant

Barrington

Cannot a Governor make what Justices he pleases, & is he not himself a civil Magistrate? The Commissioners of the Customs at Boston may also be justices of the Peace and act as such, both for quartering & directing the Troops: At least I conceive they may.

ALS, RC   BP, 11: 319-322.

Endorsed by FB: Lord Barrington d. Oct 3 1768 r Jan 4 1769.
    Barrington's enthusiasm for putting troops into Boston may have owed something to his determination to justify his own conduct in deploying troops to disperse the Wilkesite protestors gathered in St. George's Fields on 10 May. "Five or six" were killed that day and dozens injured, including bystanders, and the "massacre" provoked weeks of sporadic crowd action. (See also the source note to **No. 740**.) Barrington's letter of congratulation of 11 May to the commanding officer of the Scots Guards deployed against the protesters was subsequently printed by Wilkes's supporters.[6] Barrington took a lead role in Wilkes's expulsion from the House of Commons, proposing the government's motion to that effect on 3 Feb. 1769. Before then, however (during the Commons debate on the king's speech of 8 Nov.), Barrington reportedly

> gave a very long account of the disturbances in America. He said, he wished the Stamp act had never been passed. He called the Americans traitors, worse than traitors, against the Crown—traitors against the legislature of this country. He said, the use of troops was to bring rioters to justice. I wish, continued his lordship, that Parliament would enter into an examination of all these matters.[7]

---

1. **No. 658**, *Bernard Papers*, 4: 263-265.

2. **No. 659**, *Bernard Papers*, 4: 265-266.

3. **Appendices 4** and **12** in *Bernard Papers*, 4: 373-376, 397-399.

4. FB had reported to Barrington his exchange of letters with Gen. Gage, in which Gage insisted that any requests for military assistance to suppress riots must come from the Governor and Council. FB had stressed, however, that his requirements went beyond

    > sending to New York or Halifax for Troops to quell a Riot at Boston. . . . In Short, my Lord, Troops are not wanted here to quell a Riot or a Tumult, but to rescue the Government out of the hands of a trained mob, & to restore the Activity of the Civil Power, which is now entirely obstructed.

    No. 658, *Bernard Papers*, 4: 263-265. However, with two further regiments on the way to Boston from Ireland, Barrington believed that the British government had now met FB's desire to have the military quartered in the town, as a bastion of imperial power.

5. The Quartering Act, 5 Geo., c. 33 (1765). For details of amendments that Barrington proposed in 1769 see **No. 754**n1.

6. Barrington wrote

> I have great pleasure in informing you, that his majesty highly approves of the conduct of both officers and men [. . .] Employing the troops on so disagreeable a service always gives me pain, but the circumstances of the times make it necessary [. . .] I beg you will be pleased to assure them, that every possible regard shall be shewn to them; their zeal and good behaviour on this occasion deserve it.

Quoted in David J. Cox, *Crime in England*, 1688-1815 (Oxford and New York, 2014), 25. Printed in John Wilkes, *The North Briton, from No. I. to No. XLVI. Inclusive with several useful and explanatory notes, not printed in any former edition: to which is added, a copious index to every name and article* (1769), lxxvii.

7. Wright, *Cavendish's Debates*, 1: 41.

700 | *To the Earl of Hillsborough*

N° 28

Boston Oct 5. 1768

My Lord

The landing the two regiments at Boston on Saturday last with such dispatch & parade, which I informed your Lordship of by N° 26,[1] is like to have good effects; & will at last, tho' it has not done it at present, produce quarters for the troops. On the Monday following, I called the Council together & laid before them a requisition of Col Dalrymple's for the usual allowances under the Act of parliament.[2] Against this it was argued that they were ready on their parts to comply with the Act of parliament, if the Colonel would on his. If therefore the Colonel would remove both the regiments to the Castle, they would provide the allowances, otherwise not. This produced a good deal of Debate, af[ter][3] which I told them that the Col had desired that if they were disposed to refuse, he might be heard before the refusal was made absolute; and I accordingly sent for the Colonel.

He came with Captn Smith: and I informed him of what was passing. He enforced his requisition in Very strong Words, not without some hints of the ^Kings^ resentment which would follow their refusal. He said that he had encamped one of the regiments & was providing barracks for the other; that they might be both considered to be in barracks. If therefore they refused the allowances because they were not in the barracks at the Castle, they took upon themselves to determine upon the propriety of the Kings stationing his troops at this or that place, & to presume to dispense with an Act of parliament unless the Troops were stationed at such places as they thought fit; altho' such proposed stationing directly contradicted the intention of the Kings ordering the Troops to be stationed here at all. This was the substance of the Colonel's & my own reasoning upon the occasion which had much weight; so to induce the Council to desire me to give them time to consider further of it; which I did upon their assuring me that they would draw up no more papers for publication. Accordingly the Council was adjourned to this day.

Upon this day the Council met by themselves in the Council chamber;[4] & two of the Council came to me to know if I could engage the Colonel to send one of the regiments to the Castle if they would provide for the other. I said I could make no such Terms with the Colonel; but as he happened then to come in, they might hear from himself. He said that his orders were to station the two regiments in the Town: but if things were quiet & the Troops well received & accommodated, he made no doubt but the General would allow one regiment to go [*to*] the Castle; for which purpose he had allready wrote. The Gentlemen returned to the Council they continuing to Sit by themselves at the Council chamber; when after many debates, it was determined to supply the troops by 8 against 5 in the Council then assembled.

After noon they came to me in a body & gave me an answer in writing, wherein they resolved that I should appoint a person to provide the allowances, "he undertaking to *run the risk* of the Assembly paying the charge of it".[5] I told them that this clause was disabling as well as enabling; for by inserting such a terrifying ~~clause~~ proviso I should not be able to get any one to undertake it. If they meant nothing but to indemnify themselves, from being personally answerable for this charge, I would recommend this clause, "that such provision should be made *on the credit of the Assembly* & not of the particulars of the persons composing the Gov[r] & Council." Some Gentlemen approved of this: but it was greatly opposed, & it was urged, that as there really was a great risk that the Assembly would not pay this Money, ~~& that~~ it was fitting that the undertaker should know it. I asked them, if the Troops were barracked at the Castle, whether they would have inserted this clause: they freely answered no; for then, there would have been no doubt of the legality of making such allowances; now there was. I then told them that it plainly appeared that this discouraging Clause was put in as a prejudgement of what the Assembly had to do in providing for this expence & a dictation to them not to discharge it: and so it would be understood by all knowing of this proceeding. However I insisted upon the question of the amendment I proposed being put, & it passed in the negative. Upon which upon the unamended Answer, I proposed a person for Commissary for this purpose; & he was approved.[6] So here is a subject for dispute laid in store against the next meeting of the Assembly.[7]

Oct 6

This morning I had with me Col Dalrymple & Mr Goldthwait[8] the person I appointed to make provision for the troops. And being informed of the terms upon which the Council had made this appointment, Mr Goldthwait with the advice & approbation of the Colonel declined undertaking this business: And the Colonel told me that he thought it was to no purpose for me to apply any more to the Council, upon this or any other provision for the troops; for He saw that they were determined to do Nothing. And I must add myself that I am certain that the proviso was put in to defeat the whole purpose. I am assured that at first they resolved to make a positive refusal, & had drawn up near 2 sheets of paper of arguments to justify this refusal. But this paper being much excepted to & generally disapproved; and a Vote being obtained to make a provision, the Opponents hit upon this expedient to annul the Vote & render it ineffectual, & the Affirmers of the Vote with their Eyes open came into this expedient.

I am with great respect My Lord, Your Lordships most obedient
& most humble Servant

Fra Bernard

The right honble The Earl of Hillsborough

ALS, RC   CO 5/757, ff 442-444.

Minor emendations not shown. Endorsed: Boston October 5th: 1768. Govr Bernard (N°. 28) R 4 Nov^ber: A.55.   Enclosures: minutes of the Massachusetts Council of 3 and 5 Oct. 1768, CO 5/757, ff 445-446; the selectmen of Hatfield to the selectmen of Boston, 22 Sept. 1768, printed in the *Massachusetts Gazette and Boston News-Letter*, 6 Oct. 1768, ibid., CO 5/757, f 447. Variants of letter in: CO 5/767, ff 126-132 (L, RLbC); BP, 7: 72-76 (L, LbC); *Letters to the Ministry* (1st ed.), 70-72; *Letters to the Ministry* (repr.), 94-97. Hillsborough acknowledged receipt with **No. 712**. Copies of the letter together with the enclosures were laid before both houses of Parliament on 28 Nov. 1768. HLL: American Colonies Box 3.

Whilst FB remained in negotiation with the Council over quartering the troops, Col. Dalrymple urged that the Royal Navy ships should remain in the harbor.[9] FB, meanwhile, delayed advising the commissioners of Customs that they could return to the town in safety.[10]

1. **No. 694**.

2. FB laid before the Council a letter from Dalrymple dated 30 Sept. (not found) in which he stated that his express orders from Gen. Gage were to land both regiments in the town and to procure quarters and supplies from the province. For the proceedings of 3 Oct. 1768 see CO 5/827, f 63. The Quartering Act, 5 Geo., c. 33 sect. 7 (1765) specified:

   > That all such officers and soldiers, so put and placed in such barracks, or in hired uninhabited houses, outhouses, barns, or other buildings, shall, from time to time, be furnished and supplied there by the persons to be authorized or appointed for that purpose by the governor and council of each respective province, or upon neglect or refusal of such governor and council in any province, then by two or more justices of the peace residing in or near such place, with fire, candles, vinegar, and salt, bedding, utensils for dressing their victuals, and small beer or cyder, not exceeding five pints, or half a pint of rum mixed with a quart of water, to each man, without paying any thing for the same.

3. Smudged.

4. The proceedings of 5 Oct. 1768 are in CO 5/827, ff 63-64.

5. RbC: "Provided the Person or Persons so to be appointed will take the risk of the Province's paying to him or them all such sum or sums of money so by them laid out or expended for the purpose aforesaid." 5 Oct. 1768, CO 5/827, f 63.

6. Joseph Goldthwait (1730-79).

7. The Council objected to Dalrymple's comment in his letter of 30 Sept. that a "bad spirit prevailed" in Boston. They requested of Dalrymple that he relay to Gen. Gage that the town was "in a state perfectly peaceful and quiet" and to ask of Gage that "at least" one of the regiments currently in the town be ordered Castle William and the two expected from Ireland be sent to Nova Scotia. (The Council were probably aware that the regiments from Ireland were originally intended as relief for the Halifax garrison.) CO 5/827, f 63.

8. Joseph Goldthwait.

9. FB to Henry Smith, Boston 8 Oct. 1768, BP, 7: 212. His Majesty's Ships *Mermaid* and *Bonetta* remained in Boston harbor and were unrigged over the winter. The *Launceston* and *Romney* sailed for Halifax before 17 Oct. and the *Glasgow* before 4 Dec. The *Romney* returned on 17 Nov. and she too was unrigged for the winter. Only the *Senegal* and the *Beaver* remained on patrol. *Boston Chronicle*, 17-24 Oct.; *Boston Weekly News-Letter*, 17 Nov.; *Boston Evening-Post*, 5 Dec.; *Essex Gazette*, 6–13 Dec. 1768. I am grateful to Stuart Salmon for compiling this information.

10. FB to the American Board of Customs, Boston, 8 Oct. 1768, ibid., 211.

701 | To Thomas Gage

Boston Oct 9 1768.

S^r.

You are allready informed of the resolution taken upon the arrival of Capt Montresor of landing both regiments at Boston.[1] This, altho' subject to temporary inconveniences, will produce quarters in time.

As the Council has desired that I would send you a Copy of the Minutes of their proceedings since the landing the troops, I shall have the less to say upon this subject. But I must tell you, what will appear plainly enough of itself, that the proviso that the proveditor[2] should act *at his own risk* was inserted on purpose to defeat the business of carrying the order into execution. And that the intent might not be mistaken, the Gentlemen[3] who had opposed making the provision & afterwards proposed & introduced that proviso, have declared both in Council & out of it that the Assembly would not discharge the expence. By flinging such a discredit upon the undertaking It was impossible for any one, who had nothing but credit to carry it out with, to undertake it. And the only chance I have now of getting it done, will be by engaging a person who has such a command of money as to enable him to wait for payment, & who also can persuade himself that this money will be paid by the Crown, if refused by the Assembly.[4]

When I gave an order for the Manufactory house, it was the only building in Boston that I could pretend an Authority over & even in that I stretched my power in appropriating a provincial building without the concurrence of the Council. The Colonel however is going on pretty well, in hiring buildings for barracks, of which he will give you an Account. We all seem to agree that building should be avoided as much as possible: because if the Crown should be obliged to build barracks it would be better that it should be done in a manner durable and defencible. In regard to taking the Fort on the Castle Island out of the hands of the provincial Garrison, It is agreed on all hands that it will answer no good purpose whatever; whereas it will certainly have effects inconvenient & disagreable. Two or three Companies in the barracks there with the Kings ships which will remain here will make that place perfectly secure.

As for the desire which the Council express that I should interpose with you to order the two regiments from Ireland to Nova Scotia &c, I must beg to be excused: I certainly shall not make myself answerable for the consequences which may follow a reduction of the forces which his Majesty has been pleased to order for the Support of his Authority in this Town; especially as the Season is approaching which will cut off all communication for relief or reinforcement. I am sensible however that it will be extremely difficult to find barrack-quarters for 3 regiments in this Town, under its present want of buildings for that purpose. And if my Opinion should be asked, I should recommend that only 2 regiments should be quartered in the Town; which with one regiment at the Castle, would ^in my opinion,^ make this Capital perfectly secure. And the other Regiment might be cantoned in the Towns which have lately shown that Spirit of contempt of Government & Law which has heretofore singularly distinguished this. But this for the present I wholly submit to you. I this day delivered your letter to Col Dalrymple[5] & had a talk with him upon the subject: I beleive our Ideas of this Service are quite the same.

I am with great regard, S[r] Your most obedient and most humble Servant.

Fra. Bernard

His Excellency Gen[l] Gage

ALS, RC   Gage, vol. 81.

Variant in BP, 7: 204-207 (L, LbC). Enclosures (not found): copies of the minutes of the Massachusetts Council of 3 and 5 Oct. 1768 (for which see CO 5/827, ff 63-64).

---

1. By **No. 695**.

2. A purveyor or official in charge of municipal supplies. *OED*.

3. FB did not identify the councilors by name in his report to Hillsborough in **No. 700**.

4. The Crown was eventually obliged to shoulder the cost of quartering the troops. In Jun. 1769, FB presented a British Army account to the assembly for payment, which was refused. See **No. 787**.

5. Gage to Dalrymple, New York, 2 Oct. 1768, MiU-C: Gage, vol. 81.

702 | *From the Earl of Hillsborough*

(N^o: 20.)

Whitehall Octo^r: 12th. 1768.

Sir,

Since my last Letter to you, N^o: 19,[1] I have received and laid before the King your Dispatches from N^o: 14 to N^o: 18.[2]

The King approves your having asked the advice of the Council, whether you should, in consequence of General Gage's Letter, require Troops from Halifax to support the execution of the civil power, and preserve the peace of the Town of Boston; and His Majesty laments that their advice should upon this occasion so little correspond with what His Majesty conceives to be the duty of their Station, and what they owed to the safety of a Colony, in which the exercise of all civil power and authority was suspended, by the most daring acts of force and violence. What remedy it may be proper to apply to an evil of such a magnitude must remain for the consideration of Parliament.

Your request to have instruction whether you should or should not issue Writs for a new Assembly to meet in January has been fully considered, together with the observations upon this matter contained in your letter N^o: 15;[3] and I am to signify to You His Majesty's commands that no new Assembly should be called before the Month of May, the time prescribed by the Charter for the election of a new Assembly, unless you should receive His Majesty's directions for calling such Assembly before that time comes.[4]

I am with great truth & regard Sir Your Most Obedient Humble Servant

Hillsborough

Governor Bernard

LS, RC   BP, 12: 1-4.

Endorsed by FB: Earl of Hillsborough N° 20 –12 Octr. 1768 r Jan 4 1769. Docket by Thomas Bernard: dated Octr. 12. 1768 Direct^g not to call the Assembly till May —   Variants: CO 5/757, ff 386-387 (LS, AC); CO 5/765, ff 43-44 (L, LbC). Copies were laid before both houses of Parliament on 28 Nov. 1768. HLL: American Colonies Box 3.

As Hillsborough indicated, the situation in Boston and FB's handling of it were of prime interest to the king and cabinet. But they would soon garner Parliament's full attention when FB's reports of the Boston town meeting of 12 Sept. and the Convention of Towns reached London at the end of October.

1. **No. 679**, *Bernard Papers*, 4: 313-315.

2. State papers Nos. 14 and 15, 17 and 18 are **Nos. 660**, **663**, **664**, and **668**, respectively. *Bernard Papers*, 4: 266-270, 277-282, 288-290. In **No. 660**, FB discusses presenting Gage's letter of 2 Jul. 1768 (**No. 637**) to the Council. State paper No. 16 was dated Boston, 8 Aug. 1768 and is a letter of recommendation on behalf of Edmund Quincy et al. regarding their memorial to establish a silver mine in Massachusetts.

3. **No. 663**, *Bernard Papers*, 4: 277-280.

4. The paragraph is marked by a line in the left margin, which might have been added by FB.

703 | *To the Earl of Hillsborough*

N⁰ 29

Boston Oct 14. 1768

My Lord

I find myself obliged to continue my informations of the Councils separation from and opposition to the Governor in the execution of his Majesty's commands. I should have been glad to have been excused carrying the account any farther than where I have allready laid it: but my Duty & the Importance of the Subject will not admit of my not proceeding.

In my letter N⁰ 24[1] I informed your Lordship that I had prevented the publication of the proceedings of the Council on July 27 & 29 last, by ordering the Secretary to deliver no Copies thereof; which I then thought was an effectual means of prevention. Also in my Letter N⁰ 28[2] I informed that I consented to the Councils taking time to consider of my proposal for their providing the Allowances for the troops, upon their assuring me that ^they^ would draw up no more papers for publication. And I might have added that I expressly stipulated that they should deliver into the Secretary's hands *all papers* which they should use upon this occasion, without keeping *Any Copies* thereof. And this Stipulation was, as I understood, unanimously assented to before we parted.

Nevertheless there appeared on Monday last Oct 10 in 3 of the News papers of that day a publication of all the proceedings on July 27 & 29 & also the entire Minutes of the Council on Oct 3 & 5,[3] which were the Subject of the stipulation before mentioned. Upon my enquiring of the Secretary how these papers came to be published, He said he understood that it was done by *order of the Council* but how they came by the Copies he did not know. He was sure that no Copies came out of his office; for he had kept the Originals in his own Custody & never suffered them to be out of his sight when they were in use.[4]

The next Council day Oct 12[5] I took an Opportunity to observe upon this publication & reminded them of the Assurances they had given that no Papers or copies of papers should be kept out of the custody of the Secretary; & I desired to know from whom the Copies used for these publications were procured as they did not come from the Secretary; and who committed them to the press. No Answer was given for the present: but when the Business of the Council was over & we had rose from the table, Mr Bowdoin, who upon this Separation of the Council has been the perpetual President, Chairman, Secretary & Speaker of this new Council, addressing himself to me, said that he was desired by the Council to inform me, that they had caused this publication judging it necessary to quiet the minds of the people. Upon my observing that they had promised to keep no Copies of the papers they had used upon the last occasion, He answered that the publication was not from copies but the Originals.[6] I answered that they had promised to deliver to the Secretary *all papers* used in that business; but that I was obliged to him for being so explicit: For their declaring that the Original papers of these Minutes of Council were with them; and that those remaining with the Secretary were only copies was such an avowal of their being a board separate from and independant of the Governor as I did not expect. But they were in the right to speak out. I added that It might be doubted whether the Council by any separate Act of their own could create a Forfeiture ^of the Charter^: but If they could, I should have no doubt, but that their separating themselves from the Governor & acting as a compleat body by themselves would amount to such a forfeiture. And, I either added, or had it strongly in my mind (I cannot say which) that these their proceedings would probably be joined with other extraordinary proceedings on the part of the people, to infer a general departure from the constitution of the Government & an invasion of the royal rights contrary to the Tenor of the Charter.

Mr Bowdoin in justification of himself and his associates say that the people in their present temper would not bear with the keeping the proceedings in Council secret; for this reason, to quiet the people, they found themselves obliged to make their doings public & could not submit to an injunction of Secrecy. I answered that if they would show me any civilised Government upon earth that did or could support itself under a continual & immediate publication of the resolute[ions][7] of its most intimate Councils, so that before any of its orders could be carried into execution they should be canvassed by Tavern Politicians & censured by News-paper libellers, I would submit to their prescriptions. But as I knew that Government could not be carried on upon these terms, I should be obliged to desire his Majesty's instructions how to conduct myself under these difficulties.

I should have before observed that in opening this Council I ordered the Secretary to read the Oath of a Councillor, part of which is that *they shall not reveal what shall be committed to them in Secrecy*, and I added that what I was now going to commit to them was in Secrecy. I added that I was sorry to observe that some matters which I had heretofore committed to them in Secrecy, had not only transpired, but been published with particulars which could not have been known abroad if a due regard had been paid to the Oath. Upon this Mr Bowdoin said that the Council were of opinion that the Oath of Secrecy related only to such Matters as *they* should think & advise ought to be kept Secret; and that the Governor had no power to enjoin them [*to*] Secrecy without their own consent. I told them that this their Resolution, which I now heard the first of, was Very extraordinary: for 1. It argued That Matters committed *to* the Council in ^secrecy^ should be committed *by* themselves, which was a contradiction in terms; 2. That if Secrecy was not to be injoined till after the Matters had been considered of & debated upon they could not be *committed* in Secrecy; 3. That according to this the Governor could not commit any Matter in Secrecy to the Council, tho' enjoined by the King himself.[8]

Besides the merits of the subject matter, your Lordship will observe the extraordinary Circumstance of a Councellor denouncing to the Governor the resolution of the Council upon a Question, or a distinction of a Question, which tho' relative to the conduct & Duty of the Council was never moved or argued in Council before the Governor, & concerning which he has neither had an opportunity to hear the Reasons which induced the Council to be of that Opinion or to offer his own reasons against it; & in consequence can make no report of the principles & arguments upon which such Opinion was founded.

Before I finish this subject I must mention a fact of their Treatment of Mr Oliver the *King's* Secretary. This New Council met in the Council chamber by themselves[9] & by their own appointment & sent for the Secretary. When he came, they examined him concerning an entry in the Minutes of the Council, which to my knowledge was read & approved before they parted, but which upon recollection did not suit their purpose, & therefore they disavowed. During this examination they kept him standing at the end of the table, & at last asking him to set[10] down at the bottom of the table, He said he knew of no Council where the Governor was not present & withdrew. Mr Oliver by his rank in the list of Councellors & the usage of the Country had a right to take place of much the greatest part of the Councellors present in all indifferent places. But being full of their own self assumed dignity they treated this Gentleman with a rudeness, which I should have been ashamed to have seen practised upon ^a Man of ^much less rank & merit, if I had been in the Chair.

The difficulties I meet with in carrying his Majestys orders for quartering the Troops into execution will, I foresee, occasion my being behind hand in letters due to your Lordship. If therefore you should observe in me a want of punctuality, You must not impute it to Idleness: for I was never harder worked than I am at present.

THE PAPERS OF GOVERNOR FRANCIS BERNARD

I am, with great respect, My Lord, your Lordships most obedient
and most humble Servant

Fra Bernard

The right Honourable the Earl of Hillsborough

ALS, RC   CO 5/757, ff 492-495.

Endorsed: Boston. October 14th. 1768. Governor Bernard. (N[o] 29) R 6th Decem[r]:
A.63.   Enclosed a copy of the *Boston News-Letter*, 13 Oct. 1768, CO 5/757, ff 496-497.
Variants: CO 5/893, ff 86-90 (dupLS, RC); CO 5/767, ff 139-147 (L, RLbC); BP, 7: 76-83
(L, LbC); BL: Add 35912, f 151 (L extract, Copy); *Letters to the Ministry* (1st ed.), 72-75;
Letters to the Ministry (repr.), 97-101. Hillsborough acknowledged receipt with **No. 722**.
Copies of the letter together with the enclosure were laid before both houses of Parliament
on 28 Nov. 1768. HLL: American Colonies Box 3.
    James Bowdoin (1726-90), a wealthy Boston merchant, had been the most active of
FB's opponents within the Council since 1766. Family considerations carried as much
weight as politics in turning Bowdoin against FB, at least according to TH. Bowdoin was
married to Elizabeth Erving (1731-1809), the daughter of fellow councilor John Erving
Sr.; their daughter, Elizabeth Bowdoin (1750-1809) married FB's implacable enemy John
Temple in 1767. The "high resentment" of this "particular family" toward the governor, TH
supposed could help explain much of the Council's animus toward the governor in which
James Bowdoin took a lead role.[11] Bowdoin drafted a number of important Council papers,
including the petition to the king of 7 Jul. 1768[12] and a letter to Hillsborough of 15 Apr.
1769 commenting upon FB's misrepresentations (**Appendix 4**). Historians, following TH,
have probably exaggerated James Bowdoin's influence within the Council, for he, like FB,
was obliged to compete for the political allegiances of the moderates and friends of government.[13] Nevertheless, Bowdoin's emergence as a leader of an opposition group meeting
separately from the governor is clearly enunciated in this letter.

1. **No. 690**, *Bernard Papers*, 4: 347-351.

2. **No. 700**.

3. The *Boston Evening-Post, Supplement*, the *Boston Post-Boy and Advertiser*, and the *Boston Gazette*, 10
    Oct. 1768.

4. The versions of the minutes authorized by the Council were printed in the *Massachusetts Gazette*, 10
    Oct. 1768, while one of their members (Bowdoin probably) distributed copies to the printers of the
    other newspapers noted above. Thereafter, the material was reprinted in other newspapers, including
    the *Boston Weekly News-Letter, Postscript*, 13 Oct. 1768.

5. The proceedings described here by FB were not recorded in the official minute. But the minute did
    note an incident of popular hostility toward the troops when, on 9 Oct., timber to be used in the con-
    struction of a guard house was "destroyed"; a reward of £20 was advertised for information concerning
    the perpetrators. CO 5/827, ff 64-65.

6. FB seems to suggest that by "Originals" James Bowdoin meant that since July he had been working from his own file of Council proceedings, which he spuriously termed an original minute. Bowdoin and fellow councilor John Erving (Bowdoin's father-in-law) kept their own set of minutes, at least for the period 19 Sept. to 5 Oct., some of them in Bowdoin's handwriting and signed by Erving "In the Name of the Committee." Bowdoin and Temple Papers, Loose MSS. The version published by the Council was not an exact transcript of the executive record, yet differed only in incidentals and lay out rather than in substance; this suggests that Bowdoin probably was not working from his own minutes but from the official set kept under lock and key by Province Secretary Andrew Oliver (and now filed at CO 5/827) or a third-party copy. The question remains unanswered as to how Bowdoin obtained access to Oliver's papers.

   TH also blamed Bowdoin for his "artful management" in leading otherwise "honest men . . . into wrong measures," a hint, perhaps, that he doubted Bowdoin's integrity. TH to unknown, n.d. Nov. 1768, Mass. Archs., 25: 324-325, in Hutchinson Transcripts, 1: 672.

7. Manuscript torn.

8. Councilors were obliged to swear the oath of allegiance and abjuration under 1 Geo. 1, c. 13 (1714).

9. This meeting probably took place the day after the Council meeting in response to FB's proposal to summon a full Council for 26 Oct. to consider "matters of importance" that he would lay before them (and which concerned the quartering of the troops). CO 5/827, f 65.

10. Thus in manuscript.

11. TH to unknown, 16 Feb. 1769, Hutchinson Transcripts, 2: 726. TH was wont to "believe" that "the majority" of councilors were "honest men" whose opposition could be attributed to "the artful management of one of the Council [*Bowdoin*] whose general conduct" had not been "unfriendly to Government" until he "engaged" with the Boston faction. To unknown, Boston, Nov. 1768, Hutchinson Transcripts, 2: 672.

12. **Appendix 11**, *Bernard Papers*, 4: 392-396.

13. Colin Nicolson, "The Friends of Government: Loyalism, Ideology and Politics in Revolutionary Massachusetts," 2 vols., unpublished Ph. D. diss., Univ. of Edinburgh, 1988, 1: 152-156, 163, 170-182; Francis G. Walett, "James Bowdoin: Patriot Propagandist," *New England Quarterly* 23 (1950): 320-328.

704 | To the American Board of Customs Commissioners

Roxbury Oct[r] 22 1768

Gentlemen,

I have just now received your Letter dated yesterday[1] desiring that I would advise with the Council concerning the Propriety of your leaving the Castle & resuming the Exercise of your Commission at Boston. I will accordingly take such Advice with all proper Expedition. I have appointed a General Council to meet next Wednesday, to whom I shall communicate such of his Majesty's Commands as I have hitherto thought fit to defer making public. And that will be a most suitable Time for asking the Advice which you desire concerning the Removal of you & your Office to Boston. And I shall then be at Liberty to make further Communications to you of the Commands I have received from his Majesty.

I am &c_

The hon'ble The Comm'rs of the Customs__

L, LbC   BP, 7: 213-214.

In handwriting of Thomas Bernard.

At the 26 Oct. meeting, following a two-hour debate, the Council answered in the affirmative FB's question as to whether "they would Advise him" to inform the commissioners that "in their opinion" they could resume their duties in the town without "resistance or danger" to themselves or their officers. The divisions are discussed in **No. 708**.[2]

---

1. Not found.
2. CO 5/827, ff 65-66.

705 | To Lord Barrington

Boston Oct[r] 20 [22][1] 1768

My Lord

I deferred writing to your Lordship on the Subject of Lord Botetourt's Promotion untill I could receive from your Lordship as I expected I should, an Explanation of it. This did not come to my Hand untill 4 Days ago when I received your Letter of Aug 13[2] by that tedious Conveyance the Packet. I should not deal sincerely with your Lordship if I was to say that it has not proved a Disappointment to me. But I am quite sincere, when I assure your Lordship that it will have no Influence upon my Conduct, & that it will never appear from my Actions that I have received any Disappointment at all. And indeed it will soon wear off by my reflecting that it has arose from my Lord Hillsboroughs favorable Intention towards me, which has itself received no Abatement, tho' it has been prevented being carried into Execution in the Manner proposed by unforeseen Circumstances.[3] And therefore I should be inexcusable, if I did not dispose myself to wait chearfully for a more suitable Opportunity of it's exerting itself towards me.

The Expectation of this becoming an agreeable Government, tho at best it would be very unpromising, seems to be entirely cut off by the Disposition which appears in the present Administration not to carry into Execution M[r] Townshend's Act[4] for settling adequate civil Lists for each Government. For if I should reconcile myself to the People which considering the fresh Tasks I have now sat me, is not as yet to be expected, I don't see how I am to be relieved in Regard to the Deficiency of my Income, concerning which I sent a Petition to the King about 2 Years ago, which by the Act that passed the Session after, I flattered myself had been favorably received.[5] For my own Part I cannot now live upon the Income of my Government, which by Means arising from the Troubles of the Times & the ill Temper of the People is now reduced to under 1000 Guineas a year, as I proved by authentic Vouchers annexed to my Petition. And I suppose it is not intended that the Income of any Government shall fall short of a full Subsistance to the Governor.

My Idea of M[r] Townshend's Plan for settling fixt civil Lists in the Governments is very different from that which now prevails: and it seems that a Departure from it will be very contrary to the Rules of true Policy. But as I have had more than any Governor whatsoever, an Intrest in its being carried into Execution, I have for that Reason only, avoided expressing my Sentiments upon it. But my Lord I am persuaded that the Time is coming, if not allready come, when the very Opposition to that Establishment, will evince the Necessity of carrying it into Execution. It was some Years before the passing of the Stamp Act that I was convinced that establishing certain civil Lists in America was indespensably necessary to the Reformation

& Regulation of the Governments. This is become much more so now than it has been heretofore: and if the Perverseness of the Americans in their Treatment of the supreme Legislature should oblige the Ministry in Order to vindicate the Authority of Parliament to carry this Act into its full Execution it would be an happy Effect of a bad Cause. For if it is not executed the Want of it will often be felt. In this Province particularly, the Want of Pay for proper Officers will be found among the cheif Causes of the Imbecillity of Government. If Punishments & Rewards are the two Hinges of Government, as Politicians say, this Government is off of its Hinges; for it can neither punish nor reward. In short my Lord if this Act should be laid aside either by Repeal or Non-Execution, we shall have Reason to be sorry that it ever passed. For the Disappointment of it will cast such a Damp upon the few People which remain faithful to the King, that he will soon be without Servants. The Laws of Trade will be executed, because there the Officers are paid. But in all other Departments of civil Policy the Service of the Crown will be defeated: for it cannot be expected that Officers should act in Opposition to the Humours of the People on the Behalf of the Crown, when they are left by the Crown to the People for scanty & precarious Salaries.

We have got two Reg^{ts} from Halifax landed at Boston: those from Ireland are not yet come in. So that the Persons of the Crown Officers are safe as I beleive; tho' that is still doubted. But Security alone will not restore the Authority of Government; especially as the Council has now gone over to the People, thinking, as I suppose, the Cause of the Crown to be desperate. And indeed the long Delay of parliamentary Resentment & of military Protection together with the non-execution of the Salary Act has caused a General Despondency. And this will be compleat if it is confirmed, as I have just now heard that the Charter of this Government is still considered as sacred. For most assuredly if the Charter is not so far altered as to put the Appointment of the Council in the King, this Government will never recover itself. When Order is restored it will be at best but a Republic, of which the Governor will be no more than President. I have sent My Lord H Matter enough to support this Assertion;[6] I have still more of the same Kind to follow. I shall herewith enclose some printed Papers to this Purpose.

As for my Voyage to England, I had fixed upon the Ship & the Day of sailing; when about a fortnight before the Day I received a long Letter from Lord Hillsborough which contained Orders of such a Kind that I could not but consider it as a Suspension of my Leave.[7] This Letter also brought the first Advice of Lord Botetourt's Promotion. I thereupon sat down (with an heavy Heart I must own) to spend another Winter here & how much more I know not, under the gloomy Prospect of encreasing Trouble & decreasing Health & Fortune. In this Temper I wrote to my Lord Hillsborough with as chearful a Countenance as I could.[8] So that by this Time he must be satisfied of my not returning to England.

I have often reflected with Concern upon what your Lordship informed me that there were not 10 Persons in either House that were favorable to an American Representation.[9] I conceive it to be unfortunate for Great Britain that this Expedient meets with no better a Reception. For it seems to me that this Measure is not only the most proper to remove the Causes of the present Dissentions; but that an incorporating Union is the *only* Provision which can prevent a Separation of the Colonies from Great Britain. If it is not done soon, it will be too late; & a Separation will take Place at no great Distance of Time. I shall enclose an Extract of a Letter to me from a Member of Parliament well acquainted with America, observing that his Opinion & mine was not taken one from another; but we were each confirmed in it before we knew the other's Opinion.[10]

I am &c

The Right honble The Lord Visc[t] Barrington

P S Oct 29

I am just now informed ~~by~~ ^from^ Letters now arrived that the Government of S Carolina is at this Time proposed for me.[11] I have in former Letters particularly excepted to that Government, not upon Account of the Value but the Climate. But as your Lordship may not have this in Memory, I think it proper to repeat my Reasons why I must desire to decline it. I have made myself so well acquainted with the Nature of that Country, that I am persuaded it would deprive me of two of the greatest Comforts of my Life, my Health & my Wife. The former indeed would depend upon a Trial: but the latter would have none; for I could not ask her to go with me. And as after 27 Years Cohabitation, We are still as desirous to continue together as we were the first Day. I cannot consider an Appointment which will separate us as a Reward or an Advancement, tho my own Health was out of the Question.

By my Letter of June 29th last[12] I informed your Lordship how great a Stress I laid upon an healthy Climate in my Idea of a good Government. And I added that I had rather return to my old Government of New Jersey with a Salary of £1500 a year (no more than that of Nova Scotia) than go to any other Government, Barbadoes excepted. Now, my Lord, if the Vacancy of S Carolina could be made the Means of removing Gov[r] Franklin,[13] & Means could be found to encrease the Salary of New Jersey to the Sum before mentioned or nearly towards the same, I should be better pleased with it than with a much larger Income in a worse Country. The present Salary allowed to the Gov[r] of New Jersey is £720 or £750, I am not certain which. The Assembly might be induced to raise it to 900: & if 600 or 500 could be added from the American Treasury it would quite compleat my Wishes. I still love the Place & am still beloved by the People. M[rs] B begs Leave to join in Compl[ts] to your Lordship. She has greatly recovered her Health by the Use of a mineral Spring in Connecticut & continual riding on Horseback

L, LbC   BP, 6: 156-163.

In handwriting of Thomas Bernard. Minor emendations not shown. Enclosures not found. A duplicate was also received by Barrington.[14]

---

1. The clerk first wrote "22", then corrected it by writing "0" on top of the second "2". The editors of *Barrington-Bernard* dated this letter as 20 Oct. Barrington, however, acknowledged receipt of an original letter and duplicate dated "22ᵈ. Oct" in **No. 726**; thus, I have taken 22 Oct. as the date of composition.

2. **No. 665**, *Bernard Papers*, 4: 284-285.

3. See **No. 661** and FB's reply **No. 683**, *Bernard Papers*, 4: 326-327.

4. The Revenue Act, 7 Geo. 3, c. 4 (1767).

5. There is no official record that FB's petition to the king and his memorial to Hillsborough of 4 Jan. 1767 requesting a Crown salary were considered by the Privy Council. For the memorial see **No. 524**, *Bernard Papers*, 3: 295-298; there is an undated draft of the petition in BP, 12: 297-299. However, Chancellor of the Exchequer Townshend was probably aware of FB's proposal. *Bernard Papers*, 3, 26-27.

6. **No. 703**.

7. **No. 661**, *Bernard Papers*, 4: 271-276.

8. **No. 683**, *Bernard Papers*, 4: 326-327.

9. In **No. 597**, *Bernard Papers*, 4: 124-125.

10. Not found, possibly from Richard Jackson (d.1787), formerly secretary to George Grenville and MP for the Cinque Port of New Romney, 1768-74.

11. It was reported that the governor of South Carolina, "George Grenville," had requested leave to resign. *Boston Post-Boy and Advertiser*, 17 Oct. 1768. Lord Charles Greville Montagu (1741-84) had been on leave of absence with Lt. Gov. William Bull deputizing; but Montagu returned and continued as governor until 31 Jul. 1769. FB wrote John Pownall on 29 Oct. urging him to act in concert with Barrington to prevent him being transferred to South Carolina. BP, 6: 155-156.

12. **No. 640**, *Bernard Papers*, 4: 233-235.

13. William Franklin (1730/31-1813), governor of New Jersey, 1763-76.

14. Noted in **No. 726**.

706 | To the Earl of Hillsborough

N.º 30

Boston Nov. 1 1768

My Lord

I now proceed to conclude my narrative of my endeavours to get quarters for the Kings Troops untill I found myself at the end of my String & could do nothing more.

On Saturday Oct 15 Gen.l Gage arrived here with his Officers to look to the quartering the troops himself. On Monday I called a Council in the Morning & introduced the General.¹ He told them that He was resolved to quarter the two regiments now here in the Town & demanded quarters; and that he should reserve the barracks at the Castle for the Irish Regiments or such part of them as they would contain; which has ^since^ been determined to be only one Regiment.² After the General left the board I sat at it untill 8 o'clock at night, 2 hours at dinner time excepted. The whole was a Scene of perversion, to avoid their doing any thing towards quartering the troops, unworthy of such a body. In the Course of the questions I put to them, they denied that they knew of any building belonging to the province in the Town of Boston that was proper to be fitted up for Barracks; and they denied that the Manufactory-House was such a building. This was so notoriously contrary to truth, that some Gentlemen expressed their concern that it should remain upon the minutes. And to induce me to consent to its being expunged, a Motion was made in writing³ that the Governor be desired to order the Manufactory-house to be cleared of its present inhabitants that it might be fitted up for the reception of such part of the two Irish Regiments as could not be accommodated in the Castle Barracks. This was Violently Opposed but was carried in the affirmative by 6 to 5: upon ^this^ I allowed⁴ the former Answers to be expunged. ~~otherwise they would have made a ridiculous figure upon the Council ^books^.~~ This Resolution amounting to an Assignment of the Castle Barracks for the Irish Regiments effectually put an End to the Objection before made that no Quarters were due in Town untill the Castle Barracks were filled.

The next thing to be done was to clear the Manufactory-House, the preventing of which was a great Object of the Sons of liberty. For this purpose about 6 or 7 weeks before, when the Report of Troops coming here was first Confirmed, All kinds of people were thrust into this building; and the Workhouse itself was opened & the people confined there were permitted to go into the Manufactory-House. This was admitted to be true in Council by one of the board who is an Overseer of the poor and a principal therein.⁵ And after the Order of the Council was known Sevral of the cheifs of the Faction went into the Manufactory-house, advised the people there to keep possession against the Governors order & promised them support. And when some of them signified their intention to quit the House, they were told that if they did so they must leave[6] the Town; for they would be killed if they staid in it.

I had the Advice of the best Lawyers[7] that according to the Law & Usage of this Country the Owners of an House occupied by Tenants at sufferance or wrongfull possessors might enter by any Means they could & turn them out of possession without bringing an Action. It was also certain that the Governor & Council when the Assembly was not sitting were perfect Owners of the Estates belonging to the Government[8] except for alienation. Upon these two principles I appointed the Sheriff & two of his Deputies, Bailiffs of the Governor & Council for the purpose of removing the People out of the Manufactory house. The Sheriff was refused Admittance; upon which the Cheif Justice went with him & advised them to give up the House; he was answered that they had the Opinion of the best Lawyer in the province to keep possession.[9] Upon a third attempt The Sheriff finding a Window open entered: upon which the people gather'd about him & shut him up; he then made a signal to an Officer without, who brought a party of soldiers who took possession of the yard of the building & releived the Sheriff from his Confinement. This occasioned a great Mob to assemble with some of the Cheifs of the Faction. They were Very abusive against the Soldiers, but no Mischeif was done. They kept the House blockaded all that day & best part of the next day. When some of the Council declaring that it was not intended to use ^Force^, altho' they knew that it could not ^be done^ without, & the building not being immediately wanted, The Soldiers were withdrawn on the Evning of the Second day. Thus this building belonging to the Government & assigned by the Governor & Council for his Majesty's Use, is kept filled with the Outcast[10] of the Workhouse & the Scum of Town to prevent it's being used for the Accommodation of the Kings Troops[.][11]

After this was over, there was nothing more to be done with the Council untill the Soldiers were billeted in the publick houses as far as they would go. This we knew would Never be done; but it must be attempted; & the Council left this business to me alone without offering me their Assistance; which in other cases has been usual. Indeed I did not ask them, as I did not think the business would be forwarded by my associating them. I therefore summoned all the acting justices to meet me in the Council chamber: Twelve of them appeared; I acquainted them that the General demanded quarters for two regiments, according to the Act of parliament;[12] they desired to take it into Consideration Among themselves; I consented, & We parted. Two justices, 2 days after this, attended me with an Answer in writing, whereby the whole body refused to billet the Souldiers.[13] But these Gentlemen informing me that the Justices had been much influenced by the Argument that the barracks at the Castle ought to be first filled &c, I showed them the Minutes of the Council whereby the barracks at the Castle were assigned for the Irish Regiments;

and they must be considered as full. This was quite new to them, the Council themselves having overlook't this effect of their Vote.[14] I gave them a Copy of this Vote & returned the Answer desiring them to reconsider it. Three days after the same Gentlemen informed me that they ^had^ resolved against billeting the Souldiers but could not agree upon the reasons to be assigned for the refusing it: but the next day they gave me an Answer in writing ^(a Copy of^ which is here inclosed) signed by 8 of the Justices; [15] 2 others were against billeting & gave other reasons for their refusal; 2 others argued for billeting, but declined acting by themselves after so large a Majority of the whole body had declared for the contrary Opinion.

To show the futility of these pretences I must observe that the Act directs the billeting to be by Constables tything men Magistrates & other Civil Officers & in their default or absence by any one Justice of peace. The usual Construction of this Act has been that Magistrates ^should^ grant the billets & Constables deliver them; and the latter being ministerial[16] cannot grant billets without a Magistrate or Justice ^ordering them^; By Magistrates have been allways understood the Magistrates of Corporations, & where A Town is not a corporation The justices are the only Magistrates who are applied to in England & they deliver the billets to the Constables who serve them upon the public houses. Now in this Town of Boston there are no persons who come under these denominations but Justices and Constables. As to the Select men to whom the Justices are Supposed to refer, they have been declared by themselves, by the Council & by the Governor to be neither Magistrates nor Civil Officers; and they Certainly are not, for they can ^neither^ grant nor execute a Warrant. This I explained fully to the Justices before they gave their final Answer; but to no purpose, they being determined to refute at all events. Thus we have an Act of parliament which is become a great favourite; for with the Comments it has received here it is become in fact "An Act to *prevent* his Majesty's troops being quartered in the Town of Boston."

Immediately after, I held a Council[17] & informed the Board of the refusal of the Justices to billet the Soldiers I said that I was now at the End of my tether: for as they had declared before, that they would adhere to the Act of parliament, and had refused to act in that liberal Way which I thought was their duty when the King's Necessary Service was obstructed, I could propose nothing farther to them. For I foresaw that if I proposed to hire & fit up houses &c for the troops, they would answer that did not become their business till the public houses were full. But if any Gentleman thought it was to Any purpose to put such a question I was ready to do it: this was declined by Silence. I then informed them that by reason of this general refusal of quarters the General found himself obliged to hire & fit up houses at the expence of the Crown for the reception of the troops, who now ^(Oct 26)^ especially they who were encamped, began to feel the Want of Warm quarters; and as he thought the Expence would ultimately fall upon the province; He desired that I would appoint a Commissary to join with & assist his officers in providing such houses, especially with regard to the Œconomy of the Expences. I therefore desired their Advice & Assistance in making such appointment. This after a long debate was refused, they saying that if they should join in such appointment, it would be admitting that the province ought to be charged with the Expence; and I could appoint Auditors to examine the Accounts without them. I thereupon put an End to this Business, having been employed in it from Sep 19 to Oct 26 in all 38 days, without any prospect of doing Any thing to purpose, but under an Obligation of trying evry Effort, before I gave it up.

During this time the General, who foresaw how this Negotiation would end, had employed his Officers to hire & fit up houses for the Troops: so that by the time I had received the definitive refusal, Compleat Quarters were provided for all the troops. But now another Difficulty arose: If the Soldiers should he put into barracks, tho' provided by the Crown, without the intervention[18] of a Magistrate, The Military Officer who placed them there would be chargeable with taking upon them to quarter Soldiers otherwise than by this Act, & being Convicted of it by 2 justices of peace would be cashiered *ipso facto*. This Clause was much depended upon to oblige the Soldiers to quit the Town after they had found it impracticable to get quarters according to the Act of parliament; & was part of the Original plan which I mentioned to your Lordship Very early. And It could not be expected that the Justices who had refused to billet the Soldiers would place them in other quarters: for that would be to contradict themselves.[19] I therefore took upon myself to remove that difficulty, and by a Commission, wherein I recited his ^Majesty's^ Commands to me to take evry Necessary step for the Accommodation of the said troops,[20] & the sevral Means by which the Execution of the Act for providing quarters for the troops was defeated, & the obligation I was thereby put under to provide quarters for the troops in the best Manner I could, I authorized a person therein named, to place the said two regiments in such buildings & houses as could be procured at the expence of the Crown with the Consent of the Owners. Thus has ended the Business of quartering the two regiments. As for provision for them at Boston; according to the Act of parliament, I have already shown how the order of Council for that purpose was annulled & avoided in the origination of it. Provision has been made at Castle William by an order of Council being made that the provincial Commissary should take care of it. But they have refused to make such an order for the troops at Boston; & therefore it is not done, nor like to be done.

I am, with great respect, my Lord, your Lordship's most obedient,
and most humble Servant

Fra. Bernard.

the right honble the Earl of Hillsborough

ALS, RC   CO 5/757, ff 497-502.

FB numbered the pages from 1 to 9. Endorsed: Boston Nov[r]. 1st: 1768. Gov[r]. Bernard (N[o]. 30) R 23[d] December. A.64. Encl[d].   Enclosures: minutes of the Massachusetts Council of 12 Oct.1768, CO 5/757, ff 503-508; orders to Joseph Goldthwait, 27 Oct. 1768, ibid., ff 509-510; the justices of the Peace of Boston to FB, 24 Oct. 1768, CO5/757 ff 511-512. Variants of letter in: CO 5/767, ff 152-162 (L, RLbC); BP, 7: 83-93 (L, LbC); Bowdoin and Temple Papers, Loose MSS (L, Copy); BL: Add 35912, ff 132-137 (L, Copy); *Boston Gazette,* 23 Jan. 1769;[21] *Copies of Letters from Governor Bernard to Hillsborough; Letters to Hillsborough* (1st ed.), 3-7; *Letters to Hillsborough* (repr.), 3-11. The RC was finished and sealed ready for dispatch c.7 Nov.[22] Copies of the letter together with the enclosures were presented to Parliament on 20 Jan. 1769.[23]

FB was less preoccupied with the legality of the disputes surrounding the placement of British soldiers that in finding winter quarters for them. The position that he and Gage took was that Castle William was not situated in the town and thus they were not required (as the Council had earlier insisted) to fill the barracks before quartering the soldiers in public houses and rented warehouses.[24] The failed clearance of the Manufactory House (reluctantly supported by the Council) was frustrating for the governor,[25] but ultimately unimportant, for by then other barracks had been secured for the two regiments already in town and the two expected from Ireland.

---

1. The proceedings of 17 Oct. are in CO 5/827, f 64.

2. FB stressed the point at the meeting. Ibid.

3. The written answer was composed and delivered in the afternoon. Ibid.

4. Copies and PC: "ordered".

5. The Council, however, denied that Tyler, elected a town overseer of the poor the previous March, had admitted any such thing, in **Appendix 4**.

6. Copies, LbC, and PC: "quit".

7. Not identified, but Chief Justice Hutchinson attended the Manufactory House on 19 Oct. to explain in person the government's legal entitlement to clear and occupy the building. TH was not a trained lawyer and FB probably sought advice from Attorney General Jonathan Sewall and other pro-government lawyers.

8. Copies and PC: "province" or "Province".

9. James Otis Jr.

10. Punctuation supplied.

11. The confrontation at the Manufactory House on 19 Oct. between John Brown, the tenant occupier, and Sheriff Greenleaf, began with a "scuffle" as Greenleaf tried to enter by a window. It is described in the *Boston Evening-Post,* 24 Oct. 1768. During the day, troops had been called to assist Greenleaf take possession of the yard, and FB withdrew them at 7 PM, leaving only a "small guard" in the cellar and at the windows. Samuel Adams later reported that others "give a very different account": that the sheriff forced entry to the premises, that he was resisted by the people already inside (wherefrom Brown commenced the trespass suit), whereupon the sheriff signalled to the troops for assistance, which was provided (as FB in fact mentions). *Appeal to the World,* 31n. See the recent account in Archer, *As If an Enemy's Country,* 114.

12. The American Quartering Act (1765).

13. Thus in manuscript.

14. The minute of the Council meeting of 17 Oct. does not vindicate FB's opinion. The Council expressly advised that the Manufactory House be cleared "so that it may be ready to receive those of the said Regiments [*from Ireland*] as cannot be conveniently accommodated in the Barracks at Castle William." CO 5/827, f 64.

15. Justices of the Peace of Boston to FB, 24 Oct. 1768, CO5 /757, ff 511-512. The signatories were William Stoddard, John Hill (1703-72), John Avery, John Tudor (1709-95), Richard Dana (1700-72), John Ruddock (1713-72), Nathaniel Balston (b.1730), and Edmund Quincy (1703-88).

16. That is to say, without independent authority and acting as an agent under direction.

17. This paragraph provides a summary of what evidently comprised an introductory speech, and which is unrecorded in the minutes of 26 Oct. CO 5/827, f 370.

18. Editorially altered. This word is located at the line break and may have been hyphenated.

19. FB also put it to the Council that they should seek the opinion of the Superior Court justices, which the Council declined.

20. FB read the Council an extract of **No. 661**, probably the following passage concerning the regiments from Ireland.

> I am to signify to You His Majesty's Commands, that you do, in Concert with the Commander in Chief, take every necessary Step for the Reception and Accommodation of these Troops.

Bernard Papers, 4: 271-276.

21. Also published in *Boston Chronicle*, 13-17 Apr. 1769; *New-York Gazette, and Weekly Mercury*, 22 May 1769; *Boston Gazette*, 31 Jul. 1769.

22. CO 5/757, f 520.

23. *HCJ*, 32: 123-124; *HLJ*, 32: 229.

24. Archer suggested that FB and Gage accepted they were acting illegally in contravening the terms of the Quartering Act, 7 Geo. 3, c. 33. That is not my reading of the situation, as I explain in the source note above, which establishes the legality of the governor's and general's positions. However, I also appreciate that the Council later claimed that it was they, and not the governor or the military officers, who were acting in accordance with a *strict* interpretation of this statute. Archer, *As If an Enemy's Country*, 115.

25. John Brown unsuccessfully sued Sheriff Stephen Greenleaf for damages. Greenleaf's request for financial assistance toward the cost of his defense was refused by the Council, on 28 Dec. 1768. CO 5/827, f 70.

707 | *From Lord Barrington*

Cavendish Square Novr. the 1^t 1768.

Dear Sir,

I am to acknowlege your letter of the 27th. of August, the last received, and the only one unanswered.[1]

I have before acquainted you of the necessity of sending a *Governor* to Virginia which has put an End to the Idea of your succeeding M^r. Fauquier. The unexpected and extraordinary behaviour of the Council and assembly of that Province, made it thought necessary to send a man of Quality thither in a more eminent station than has been usual for many years past.[2] The News Papers &c have assigned other reasons for Lord Botetourt's appointment; but without the least ground. He never had an Idea of going to America till it was proposed to him.[3] I hope some other good thing will soon open for you, and the *Title* is ready whenever you are on the whole inclined to accept it.

You mention in the Letter I am now answering, an intention of making use of the discretional leave sent you by Lord Hillsborough, tho' not then received: When this leave was granted, the Province under your Government was tolerably quiet; but the Riots which have since happen'd, particularly the Rebellion in September last,[4] and the expected arrival of the Troops who will stand in great need of your Excellency at their arrival and in their proceedings, will undoubtedly keep you at Boston till better times. I most sincerely feel for your difficulties and distresses there; But it is such a situation that shews Virtues & talents in their true light. I am with my best Comp^t. to all my Cousins

Dear Sir Your Excellency's most faithful & most obedient Servant

Barrington.

ALS, RC   BP, 12: 5-8.

Endorsed: Lord Barrington dat Nov 1 & Nov 9 1768 r Jan 25 1769.   Variant in BL: Add 73634, f 63 (ALS, LbC).

---

1. **No. 666**, *Bernard Papers*, 4: 285-287.

2. Francis Fauquier (1703-68), acting governor of Virginia from 1758 until his death on 3 Mar. 1768. The suggestion that an aristocrat was now required to sort out the Virginians probably rankled with FB. He had delayed responding to Hillsborough's query (made via Barrington in **No. 610**), although a prompt reply probably would not have changed ministers' preference for Lord Botetourt. See **Nos. 665** and **666**. *Bernard Papers*, 4: 283-287.

3. Lord Botetourt was not party to the displacement of the honorific governor and former commander in chief of North American forces, Gen. Sir Jeffrey Amherst, who took offence at Hillsborough's lack of consultation over the decision to appoint a resident Virginia governor. The cabinet had assumed that Amherst would be unwilling to return to America to take up such duties. But after being deprived of the governorship, Amherst resigned his regimental commands and pension in protest and demanded financial compensation; he eventually persuaded the ministry to restore his pension and commands, and raise him to the peerage. The controversy was widely reported in the British newspapers, for example the *Gazetteer and New Daily Advertiser*, 30 Aug. and 8 Sept., and the *Public Advertiser* 2 and 6 Aug. 1768. See Thomas *Townshend Duties Crisis*, 88-91.

4. As Barrington indicates, the proceedings of the Boston town meeting of 12 Sept. as reported by FB had so alarmed ministers as to suppose that armed resistance to the government had already taken place. See Thomas *Townshend Duties Crisis*, 91-92.

708 | To the Earl of Hillsborough

Nº 31

Boston Nov 5 1768.

My Lord,

When I received your Lordship's letter Nº 16[1] I immediately communicated it to the Lieut Governor; and we both agreed in Opinion that it would not be advisable to lay before the Council any part of it, except what related to the providing for the troops, untill the troops were got into quarters: as we foresaw that the Business of quartering the troops would occasion a good deal of trouble & possibly some commotion; and it would not be advisable to bring on too much business at once; at least untill the town was a little settled. This Business of quartering, your Lordship will observe, kept me employed till Oct 26, on which day I had summoned a general Council.[2] On this day I had 19 Councellors, ^that is^ all but 3: I therefore chose this time to communicate the other parts of your Lordship's letter; except what relates to the calling the Assembly, which I had reserved untill I receive further orders about it. I made this communication by an extract, which ^after it was read^ I left in the Secretary's hands, that the Gentlemen might peruse it at leisure.[3] I cautioned the Secretary against suffering a Copy to be taken, but did not restrain him from permitting it being read. I also gave another copy of the same extract to the first Commissioner of the Customs,[4] engaging him to keep it in his own hands & not let a Copy be taken.

Immediately after, I had an occasion to move a matter that would show their disposition to pay a proper regard to his Majesty's commands. The Commissioners had wrote to me[5] desiring that I would take the advice of the Council whether they might return to Town and reassume their functions with safety to themselves & Officers. I communicated this Letter to the Council & put the question to them.[6] This was very embarrasing: if they answered yea, they would be chargeable with advising the return of the Commissioners; if they said No, they would contradict all their assertions, that there was no occasion for troops to support the Civil Power. They therefore, for above 2 hours together used all kinds of evasions to avoid giving an Answer. I was told that they were not obliged to give opinions: I answered that they were obliged to give Advice; and the Question was[7] whether they w^d advise me to assure the Commissioners that they might return ^with safety^. At last I was obliged to tell them that if they would not give me an Answer, I would take their refusal for an Answer in the Negative; for if they could answer in the affirmative no reason could be supposed why they should not give an answer. And if they could not answer in the affirmative, they must reconcile it with their public declarations of the loyalty & peaceableness of the Town as well as they could. At length I got an Answer, 12 answering in the affirmative, 5 declining answering because they lived out of Town, and 2 giving written Answers[8] condemning the Commissioners for going out of the town & therefore refusing advise about their return, but concluding that all persons would be safe. In this Council I sat from 11 to 9, 2 intermediate hours excepted: and all the business might have been Very well done in an hour or two by practicable Men.

Before this Council met I had been informed that some of the board had been preparing an Address to the General to remove the troops from hence, that at this meeting they might get a great Number of hands to it.[9] When the Council broke up, I heard some of them making an appointment to meet there the next Morning. I told them that I understood that they were going on with business as a Council separately from me; but I cautioned them against proceeding. It was answered that they should not act as a Council but as private Gentlemen. I then desired that they would not give their meetings the appearance of a Council by holding them in the Council Chamber. They met the next day and settled the address, which was Very much softened from the first draught, which I am told was much more Virulent against the Commissioners. It was signed by 15 of the Council, among whom were the 5 who knew not enough of the Town to Vote for the safety of the Commissioners returning, but knew enough to join in an invective against them:[10] 4 refused to sign.[11] It was then presented to the General, who observed to them, that the resolves of the Town meeting were a sufficient cause for sending troops here, though there had been no riots: It was answered that they were the productions of a few imprudent wrong-headed men. The General replied that they were said to be *unanimously* resolved, in a *full* Town meeting.[12] The next Monday It appeared in all the public papers, from whence I send your Lordship the enclosed copy.[13]

I shall make but a few observations on this writing, the intent of it being plain enough, —1. It is well known to your Lordship that this kind of writing is designed for the people, and not for the persons to whom they are addressed. This is Notorious in the present Case: the Gentlemen who moved this business knew Very well that the General could not remove the troops from this Town, if ^he^ could have been disposed to do it; because they were sent hither by order of his Majesty, & not placed here by the discretion of the General. The General himself had told them ^so^,[14] and I had repeated it to them again & again, to induce them to assist the quartering. As therefore they could not expect the troops would be withdrawn we must look for another purpose of this address; and that appears to be, as it is indeed the principal subject of it, the Abuse of the Commissioners. — 2. This was surely very ill timed: the Very day after they had been made acquainted with his Majesty's command & expectation that the Commissioners should return to Boston & resume their function & would return without resistance & with safety, to publish a Manifesto against them, which as it had nothing new in it, could only serve to revive the popular prejudices against them & thereby encourage resistance & make their safety precarious, is unaccountable in Men of this rank & inconsistent with their public professions of their regard for the King's Service. — 3. This is also Very unseasonable in being done the day after the Commissioners had signified their apprehensions of danger in returning to Boston & desired the Advice of the Council concerning it and the Council had given their opinion that they might return in safety. For these Councellors who had one day encouraged their coming to Town, the Very next day to issue a writing under their hands holding ~~forth~~ them forth to the people as "Men whose Avarice having smothered in their breasts every sentiment of humanity towards this province, has impelled them to oppress it to the utmost of their power,"[15] is utterly irreconcilable with my Ideas of truth justice & humanity; & shocks me the more, as I know that the wives of two of the Commissioners, who have young children,[16] did not want to have their fears increased by this publication.

It would be unaccountable how so many persons of so respectable a station & many of them of a respectable character could join in signing such a paper if We did ^not^ consider that in public & popular proceedings the leaders are few & the followers many: and people called upon to sign papers frequently ^act^ without consideration & sometimes against their judgment. And the Virulence with which the Commissioners have been treated seems to be too Violent to be the effect of public Zeal only without the interference of private animosity, which at present I cannot take upon me to account for. I can only condemn & lament such proceedings in a body for which I have allways had & still retain a great regard.

> I am with great respect, my Lord, your Lordship's most obedient
> & most humble Servant
>
> Fra Bernard.

The right honble the Earl of Hillsborough.

ALS, RC CO 5/757, ff 513-516.

Endorsed: Boston Nov[r]. 3[[d]]. 1768. Gov[r]. Bernard. (N[o] 31) R 23[d] December A.65. Enclosures: minute of the Massachusetts Council of 31 Oct. 1768, CO5/757, ff 517-518; Massachusetts Council address to Thomas Gage, Boston, 27 Oct., printed in the *Boston Post-Boy and Advertiser,* 31 Oct. 1768, CO 5/757, f 519 (see **Appendix 1**); committee of the Boston town meeting to FB, 13 Sept. 1768 (not found, for which see *Reports of the Record Commissioners of Boston,* 16: 263). Variants of letter in: CO 5/767, ff 163-169 (L, RLbC); BP, 7: 93-99 (L, LbC); Bowdoin and Temple Papers, Loose MSS (L, Copy); *Boston Gazette,* 23 Jan. 1769;[17] *Copies of Letters from Governor Bernard to Hillsborough; Letters to Hillsborough* (1st ed.), 7-10; *Letters to Hillsborough* (repr.), 30-33. The RC was finished and sealed ready for dispatch c.7 Nov.[18] Copies of the letter together with the enclosures were presented to Parliament on 20 Jan. 1769.[19]

The Council's address to Gage was signed by sixteen councilors, indicating that the governor was now facing opposition from a clear majority. (See **Appendix 1**.)

---

1. **No. 661**. Hillsborough's letter of 30 Jul. 1768, not only announced that two regiments were being sent to Boston from Ireland; it also lamented Boston's disobedience and the "illegal & unwarrantable" opposition to the officers of the Customs and exhorted the governor to "Firmness" in punishing "Disaffection or Opposition." FB was instructed to investigate treasonable activities, with the suggestion that perpetrators be brought to trial in England. *Bernard Papers,* 4: 271-276.

2. The minutes of the meeting are in CO 5/827, ff. 65-66.

3. The extract probably concerned the recommendation that in light of the Boston riot the Governor and Council undertake a "Reform in the Commission of the Peace for that Town." Ibid.

4. Henry Hulton.

5. On 21 Oct. (not found, but noted in BP, 7: 213).

6. "Whether they would advise him to acquaint the Commissioners that in their opinion they may resume the execution of their Office in the Town without resistance or danger to themselves and Officers?" CO 5/827, ff 65-66. This was answered in the affirmative. The Council, however, later suggested that the vote was taken on a revised question put by FB, viz., "Whether they would advise him to assure the Commissioners that they might return with Safety?" This the Council answered affirmatively. **Appendix 4**.

7. LbC: "and the Question was put"; PC: "and the question was put".

8. The five abstainers would have been drawn from the following list of councilors resident outside Boston: Gamaliel Bradford (from Duxbury), John Bradbury (York), Samuel Danforth (Cambridge), Samuel Dexter (Dedham), John Hill (Berwick), Benjamin Lincoln Sr. (Hingham), Isaac Royall (Medford), James Russell (Charlestown), Nathaniel Sparhawk (Kittery and Boston), and Samuel White (Taunton). If so, then the group of twelve included James Bowdoin, John Erving, Thomas Flucker, Harrison Gray, Thomas Hubbard, Timothy Paine, James Pitts, Nathaniel Ropes, and Royal Tyler, plus three of the out-of-towners listed. The identities of the two who tendered written answers are unknown.

9. **Appendix 1**.

10. The Council later defended the position of the five, seeing "no Inconsistency in their Conduct." They knew little of the state of Boston but much more about the how the "haughty and insolent Behaviour" of the commissioners' had "expose[d] them to the Resentments of the People." But neither they nor anyone else could be certain that upon the commissioners' returning "the People will offer the least Insult or Violence to them." **Appendix 5**.

11. These were Benjamin Lincoln (who had left town before the address was prepared), Thomas Flucker, Timothy Paine, and Nathaniel Ropes. The Council later asserted that the four had not "refused": they did not sign because they were not present, in three cases "business" calling them home to the "country." (**Appendix 4**.) Their places of residence were, respectively, Hingham, Charlestown, Worcester, and Salem.

12. Gage replied to the Council on 28 Oct., but FB is probably recounting an exchange of opinions between the Council committee presenting the address and the general. CO 5/86, f 222 and *Boston Weekly News-Letter,* 3 Nov. 1768.

13. Address of the Council to Thomas Gage, Boston, 27 Oct., in *Boston Post-Boy and Advertiser,* 31 Oct. 1768. See **Appendix 1**.

14. At the Council meeting of 17 Oct.

15. **Appendix 1**. The accusation could equally have been intended for FB.

16. Elizabeth Hulton (1739-1805), wife to Henry Hulton, and Ann Burch (d.1806), wife to William Burch.

17. Also published in *Boston Chronicle,* 13-17 Apr. 1769; *Providence Gazette,* 22 Apr. 1769; *New-York Chronicle,* 22-29 May 1769; *Boston Gazette,* 31 Jul. 1769.

18. CO 5/757, f 520.

19. *HCJ,* 32: 123-124; *HLJ,* 32: 229.

709 | *To the Earl of Hillsborough*

N° 32

Boston Nov 12 1768

My Lord,

After I had communicated your Lordships letter to the Council,[1] I considered that some farther notification of it would be necessary in regard to what related to the preservation of the peace & the protection of the Officers of the Revenue: especially as the Commissioners had fixed upon this week for their return to Boston. A proclamation was not thought proper, as the business was in a manner confined to the Town of Boston. I thereupon thought of a Letter from myself to the Justices of Boston, & accordingly drew one up: wherein I recited such part of your Lordship's letter as related to them & their business & thereto added injunctions & Admonitions of my Own. I communicated this to the Council last Wednesday,[2] proposing, ~~that~~ if it had their approbation, to call the Justices together & deliver it to them by Word of Mouth & then give them Copies of it. But tho' no exceptions were taken to particulars, the whole was objected to strongly for this reason: that if they were to consent to this Letter, they should appear to approve of the Censures your Lordship had passed upon the Town, which they could not admit it had deserved. I told them I would not enter into an Argument which might tend to impeach the truth or justice of your Lordship's letter; but I observed that both of them were Very defencible being founded upon Notorious Facts which could not be denied or doubted.

I then proposed another Method of informing the justices; which was to call the Justices together & after reading such parts of your Lordship's letter as related to their business, to give them a general Admonition concerning their future conduct. This was objected to, for that an Admonition implied a Censure: this I answered by showing that they did really deserve Censure, & by declaring that I should use them tenderly in that respect. But I found that I should never prevail with the Council to *act* in this business; that they would not *advise* to any method of notifying injoining or enforcing the orders contained in your Lordship's letter; and that I could make nothing of them but *passive* Associates. I proposed therefore that they should meet in Council the next morning; and I would of my own accord & without their advice order the justices to attend, & would admonish them as I had before proposed. This was at length assented to: tho' not without one Gentleman's protesting against it. I accordingly the next day[3] assembled the Justices & in the presence of the Council ^having^ caused an Extract of your Lordships letter to be read, I entered into a full explanation of the Nature of their office & their Duty therein; & avoiding, as much as I could, censuring them for their former conduct, I showed what would be expected of them for the future; and I concluded, that If they had a mind to retrieve the credit of the Town, It was not to be done by denying what was passed, but by regulating what was to come. As soon as I had done, a Gentleman of the Council[4] who had opposed this business said aloud that he liked this Very well: and the Justices seemed satisfied with this proceeding; and sevral of them gave assurances that they would do their best to preserve the good order of the Town.

These two conferences with the Council passed with good humour: and in the course of them I had an opportunity to observe upon & lament the servility, in regard to the people, with which the Business of the Council was now done, in comparison to what it used to be. This was not denied: and one Gentleman said, that he did not now enter the Council chamber with that free mind he used to have; but he liked to be concerned in public business, & did not chuse to quit his place in the Council; and therefore must be content to hold it upon such terms as he could. So fair a Confession deserves not to be passed unnoticed. But I should not trouble your Lordship with such trifling Anecdotes, if they did not seem to me ^to be^ the best Method to convey a true Idea of the present state of this Government, & to point out the chief Causes of its disease. And I must myself resort to the cause I am now treating of, to show why I have not executed all the Kings commands in as full a manner as may be expected from me. But, My Lord, the Council themselves have for above 4 months past taken great pains to show from whence the imbecillity of this Government arises; & have brought more forcible Arguments, than any one else could have urged, to show how necessary it is become that the King should have the Council chamber in his own hands. How this can be done may be a question; the Exigency of it is none.

I am with great respect, My Lord, Your Lordship's
most obedient & most humble servant,

Fra Bernard

The right honble the Earl of Hillsborough.

ALS, RC   CO 5/757, ff 524-525.

Endorsed: Boston Nov[r] 12th. 1768. Gov[r]. Bernard (N[o]. 32) R 30 Decem[r]. A.67.   Variants: CO 5/767, ff 171-174 (L, RLbC); Bowdoin and Temple Papers, Loose MSS (L, Copy); BP, 7: 100-103 (L, LbC); *Boston Gazette,* 23 Jan. 1769;[5] *Copies of Letters from Governor Bernard to Hillsborough; Letters to Hillsborough* (1st ed.), 10-11; *Letters to Hillsborough* (repr.), 18-21. Copies were presented to Parliament on 20 Jan. 1769.[6]

1. **No. 661**, on 3 Nov. *Bernard Papers,* 4: 271-276.

2. On 9 Nov. 1768, CO 5/827, f 67. The draft letter to the justices has not been found.

3. 10 Nov. 1768, CO 5/827, f 67.

4. The gentlemen mentioned here and below have not been identified. The Council's criticism of FB's account in **Appendix 4** also preserved their anonymity.

5. Also published in *Boston Chronicle,* 17-20 Apr. 1769; *Providence Gazette,* 22 Apr. 1769; *New-York Chronicle,* 29 May-5 Jun. 1769; *Boston Gazette,* 31 Jul. 1769.

6. *HCJ,* 32: 123-124; *HLJ,* 32: 229.

710 | *To the American Board of Customs*

Jamaica plain. Nov. 12. 1768

Gentlemen

I have not neglected the business I have undertaken, & I desired M[r] Robinson to inform you of what had passed therein. I met M[r] Sewal with the Lieut. Governor on Wednesday ~~next~~ last[1] & had a Conference with him on your Subject: after which the L[t] Governor undertook to write to you or one of you concerning what had passed;[2] I therefore saw no occasion to write to you myself. I went to Town

Yesterday to see M[r] Sewal, but found he had left the Court very ill, & was gone home: I could not pursue him to his Bedchamber. If he recovers himself, I shall see him next Monday.[3] When you come to Town, I shall report to you what I have done in this business. But I cannot sit down to write a detail of matters which are more proper for a conversation. All the time I have for writing is insufficient for the Kings ^immediate^ business; & tho no Governor writes more than I do, I am still in great arrears to the Secretary of State. I therefore cannot undertake to be punctual in writing letters which may be spared without an injury to business.

I am with &c.

The Honble the Comm[rs]. of the Customs.

L, LbC   BP, 7: 214-215.

In handwriting of clerk no. 3.

As this letter indicates, FB and TH continued to mediate in the dispute between Jonathan Sewall and the commissioners of Customs, concerning Sewall's allegations that the commissioners had questioned his competency as Massachusetts's chief law officer (see the source note to **No. 678**).[4] When FB wrote this letter, the commissioners had started to blame their own secretary, Samuel Venner, for deliberately misleading Sewall in retaliation for alleged personal slights and for undermining his seniority among the Board's administrators. While not specifically identifying Venner as the original source of his information, Sewall nevertheless reported to the Board the sum of their conversation of 20 Jul. in which Venner and Lisle confirmed Sewall's questions about the content of the commissioners' memorials to the Treasury in which he was supposedly maligned. Venner contradicted Sewall's account of the meeting, but on 15 Nov. the Board approved charges against their secretary. Initially Venner refused to answer questions and defended himself in writing by challenging the veracity of Sewall's narrative. Neither FB nor TH appeared concerned by the possibility that Sewall had exploited Venner's vulnerability to conceal his own lack of evidence with which to substantiate his accusations against the Board (no matter that Sewall was correct in supposing he had been criticized in the commissioners' memorials).[5]

The commissioners, however, remained anxious about Sewall's management of the upcoming trial of John Hancock, the wealthy merchant and prominent Whig. Sewall's illness (mentioned in this letter) may have been exacerbated by the stress of handling such a controversial case. The commissioners had pressed Sewall, as advocate general of Vice Admiralty, to file *in personam* actions against Hancock and five of his men on 29 Oct.; they were bailed until the informations against them were read in the Vice Admiralty Court on 7 Nov. The trial was continued over until 28 Nov., with Sewall leading the prosecution and John Adams defending Hancock. With the defendants each facing a penalty of £9,000 and FB (as governor) and Sewall (as prosecutor) entitled to one-third of the total, the trial became a *cause célèbre*. The proceedings lasted on and off until 25 Mar., when Sewall abandoned the action for lacking evidence necessary to secure convictions. (See **No. 719**.)

1. 9 Nov.

2. No such letter dated mid-November has been found. However, when Sewall delayed informing the Board that Venner and Lisle had aided his enquiries, TH took it upon himself to confirm their part in the affair (presumably with Sewall's approbation, for Sewall did not subsequently object). TH to the American Board of Customs, Boston, 29 Oct. 1768, T 1/471, ff 43-44.

3. 14 Nov., and the following day the Board drew up misconduct charges against Samuel Venner. T 1/471, f 45.

4. *Bernard Papers*, 4: 307-313.

5. The minutes of the American Board of Customs, 3 Nov.-20 Dec. 1768, T 1/471, ff 10-13.

711 | To the Earl of Hillsborough

Nº 33

Boston, Nov 14 1768

My Lord,

I come now to consider that part of my orders which relates to the reforming the bench of Justices: this is to be done by two ways, 1, by adding new Justices to the present bench, either by engaging Gentlemen who are allready in the Commission to qualify themselves, or by granting new Commissions to fit persons who will undertake to act; 2, by removing such persons in the commission who are known to be infected with principles of disaffection to the constitutional Authority of parliament. The first of these is practicable in both its branches; the second is at present absolutely impracticable, and will remain so whilst the Council make the humouring the people their cheif object.[1]

In regard to the first, I have allready made some attempts to engage some Gentlemen now in the Commission to qualify themselves & shall pursue it; and notwithstanding the undertaking is Very discouraging, I expect I shall have some success. I have also made an Essay to appoint new Justices who would engage to act, by naming one Very fit person. It was received Very cooly by the Council; & upon my asking the reason, I was told he was not popular; I replied that if he had been I should not have named him.[2] As He was allowed to be in evry other respect a most unexceptionable Man, it passed unanimously: but it gave me to know what I must expect if I proposed a Man *who was not popular* against whom Any exception could be taken. But I shall soon try again.

As for removing persons for their opposition to the Authority of Parliament by means of a Council[3] a majority of which has (indirectly at least) avowed the same principles, & now appears to act in concert with that party from whence the Opposition to Parliament originated, it would be an Attempt contrary to all rules of policy & prudence. It would be required to be done by a public Enquiry, which would receive all the obstruction & embarrassment which the Chicanery of Law could invent; and if after all, full proof of a disaffection to the authority of parliament should be made, it would be declared not to be relevant to infer such a Censure. It will therefore ^be^ in Vain to attempt to punish Disaffection to the Authority of parliament, untill the Criminality is better established than it is at present. To support this conjecture in what manner the Council would act in such a proceeding, I need only refer your Lordship to their conduct & the papers they have published within these two months last past.

And yet, my Lord, I would not insinuate that We have no fit objects for such a Censure: the Sons of Liberty have not been without Magistrates. We have seen Justices attending at Liberty tree; one to administer an Oath to the Stamp Master, when he was obliged to swear that he would not execute his Office;[4] another to perform the function of Toast Master; a third, but lately, to consult about fortifying the Town; others to make up' the procession of 45 carriages & 92 persons on the 14th of August last. All these are included in two lists which your Lordship has, that of the 5 select men who signed the circular letter for the convention, of which all but the first are in the commission, & that of the 8 Justices who signed the refusal to billet the Soldiers.[5] Now if the Censure of these proceedings should produce an Order to me to supersede the Commissions of these Gentlemen, It would be a trial of the power of the Governor: It seems at present that the Council would not enable me to execute such an order.

It is a great defect in this government, that the King has no power over the commissions, which are granted in his name & under his Seal. He can by order in Council disallow a Law which has been passed by the Governor Council & House of Representatives: but yet He cannot supersede a Commission which has been granted by the Governor & Council. And yet the Council of this province is as much out of the Controll of the King as the House of Representatives is. Wherefore It seems as reasonable that the King should be allowed to correct the mistakes of the Governor & Council, as of the Governor Council & House. As it is, when the Governor has once set the King's Seal to a commission, it is for ever out of the hands of the Crown, and the person who has obtained it may thenceforth defy the King, oppose his Laws & insult his Government & be in no danger of losing his Commission. It is true, the Governor with the advice of Council can supersede him: but if he acts in a popular Cause, under which Opposition to Government finds it easy to shelter itself, the Council, who are themselves the Creatures of the people, will never join with the Governor in censuring *the Overflowings of liberty.* It may be said that the Governor should take care not to appoint any one whose

Character is not well known. But the Governor does not personally know half of those whom he appoints to Offices: it is not therefore in his power to guard agst imposition, let him be ever so cautious. Besides, a Man's political Character often does not appear till he is got into an Office & thereby held forth to the publick. Hence It is not unusual for a person, who has not distinguished himself in political matters, to get himself recommended to the Governor, as a Man well disposed to government; and as soon as he has received his commission, to declare for the party of the Sons of Liberty. The Governor may resent the imposition as he pleases: but he cant undo what he has done. Thus the Commissions of the King, like his Cannon upon another occasion, are turned against him.

It would serve to remedy this abuse & strengthen Government if the King was enabled by order in his privy Council to supersede Commissions granted in his name & under his seal, when they shall appear to be granted to improper persons or made use of for improper purposes. This must be done by Act of parliament and I don't see the impropriety of such an Act; it seems to me to be a proper power to be vested in the Crown; especially at a time when the Crown wants to be strengthend by all legal Means, in this Country. And it seems[6] that it would be better to be done by a general ^Act^ than a partial one: for such a power may be wanted in the royal Governments, notwithstanding the controll the King has over the Councils. For It is Very possible, considering the Spirit which now prevails, that even a royal Council may support a popular magistrate against the intrest of the Crown. And if the Colonies should prevail to have the Judges Commissions during good behaviour, which some of them are now Very earnest about, It might be proper that the King in Council should be empowered to judge & determine upon such misbehaviour as would avoid the Commission. But this will not be necessary if the general instruction of granting No Commissions but during pleasure be continued & observed; Nor will it be necessary that such an act should be general; It is more wanted in this Government than in all the others together: and even here the Defect would be cured by a Royal Council.

I am with great respect, My Lord your Lordship's
most obedient & most humble Servant

Fra Bernard.

the right honble the Earl of Hillsborough.

ALS, RC   CO 5/757, ff 526-529.

Endorsed: Boston Nov.[r] 14th 1768. Gov.[r]: Bernard. (N.[o] 33) R 30 Decem.[r] A.68. Enc.[d]   No enclosures have been found. Variants: CO 5/767, ff 175-181 (L, RLbC); BP, 7: 103-108 (L, LbC); Bowdoin and Temple Papers, Loose MSS (L, Copy); *Boston Gazette*, 23 Jan. 1769;[7] *Copies of Letters from Governor Bernard to Hillsborough*; *Letters to Hillsborough* (1st ed.), 12-14; *Letters to Hillsborough* (repr.), 21-26. Copies were presented to Parliament on 20 Jan. 1769.[8]

In **No. 661**,[9] Hillsborough had instructed FB to "Reform" the province magistracy without fully appreciating the obstacles in the governor's path. The justification for reform arose from the apparent unwillingness of Boston's justices of the peace to disperse or arrest rioters, and in this letter FB set out his *modus operandi* for reforming the province magistracy. James Murray was the first of several new appointments in FB's "reforming plan," but many other friends of government refused the commission, some citing fear of being intimidated. Of the twenty-one new justices of the peace appointed by FB over the next ten months, only six were friends of government. His favored long-term solution, explained here, was an act of Parliament vesting authority in the royal governor to annul justices' commissions, effectively enabling him to by-pass the Province Charter's requirement that such appointments could only be made with the advice and consent of the Council. Any such measure would have constituted a significant extension of royal power.[10]

1. Hillsborough had proposed both options in **No. 661**, *Bernard Papers*, 4: 271-276.

2. James Murray (1713-81) was appointed a justice of the peace on 7 Dec. 1768. CO 5/827, f 69. Murray was a Scots-born merchant and proprietor of a sugar refinery, having moved to Boston from North Carolina in 1765. Widely regarded as a Tory, he was an outspoken critic of the Whig protest movement and hired out his sugarhouse as an army barracks. Soon after his appointment, he was ridiculed in the newspapers and jostled in the streets as he went about his business. Nina M. Tiffany and Susan I. Lesley, *Letters of James Murray, Loyalist* (Boston, 1901), 151-161; Oliver M. Dickerson, *Boston Under Military rule, 1768-1769, as revealed in a Journal of the Times* (Boston, 1936), 106; *Boston Evening-Post*, 29 May, 1769.

3. Hillsborough's recommendations for the reform of provincial magistracy are in **No. 661**, *Bernard Papers*, 4: 271-276.

4. Richard Dana (1700-72), on 17 Dec. 1765. *Boston Post-Boy and Advertiser*, 23 Dec. 1765.

5. Their names are given in **No. 706**n15.

6. The LbC is incomplete, missing the remainder of the letter from here to the end.

7. Also published in *Providence Gazette*, 22 Apr. 1769; *New-York Chronicle*, 15-22 May 1769; *Boston Gazette*, 31 Jul. 1769.

8. *HCJ*, 32: 123-124; *HLJ*, 32: 229.

9. *Bernard Papers*, 4: 271-276.

10. Nicolson, *The 'Infamas Govener'*, 186.

712 | *From the Earl of Hillsborough*

(N°. 21.)

Whitehall November 15th. 1768.

Sir,

His Majesty having thought fit to direct that your several dispatches to me from N°. 19 to N°. 28.[1] relating to the unhappy situation to which the Colony under your Government appears to be reduced, should be referred to His ∞ ∞ ∞[2] Servants in the Law department;[3] and that the Facts, relative to publick transactions in that Colony, from the meeting of the Assembly in Decr. last, to the arrival of the Troops at Boston, should be laid before both Houses of Parliament,[4] I have not at present anything in command from His Majesty to signify to you upon those dispatches, or any observations to make thereupon, lest any Instructions you should now receive, or any observations I might make, should not correspond with the result of their deliberations. It is however His Majesty's pleasure that you should punctually observe His Royal Commands signified to you in my former letters, & particularly in that of the 30th of July last, and that you should extend the enquiries you are therein directed to make to such illegal and unconstitutional Acts as have been committed since the disturbances which gave occasion to that letter, in such manner as that the perpetrators of them, may if possible be brought to justice.

In the present factious State of the Province of Massachuset's Bay, the propagation of every falsehood that malice can suggest, to exasperate & inflame the minds of the people is to be expected and therefore I was not surprized to find, that I have been represented, however unjustly and falsely, as having refused to lay before the King the Address of the Assembly in January last. — The Fact is, that M^r. De Berdt, the Agent of the Assembly had declined, for reasons best known to himself, to deliver this Address to me; & that I having mentioned the report of there being such an Address in M^r. De Berdt's hands to one M^r. Sayre,[5] who came to visit me, and as I have since found, is in connection with M^r. De Berdt, he told me there was such an Address, and if I had a mind, that he could procure me a sight of it, I said I should be glad to see it as the Accounts of the Contents were various, and the next morning M^r. Sayre inclosed the original Address to me in a Letter, the purpose of which very much surprized me, and of which I herewith send you a Copy.[6]

The manner in which this petition therefore came into my hands, not delivered by any person having Authority for that purpose, & unaccompanied with any Documents to authenticate it as the real Act of the Assembly, made it impossible for me to lay it before His Majesty in the usual course of Office; but neither this consideration nor the indignity offered to the Crown by the Assembly, in avoiding to transmit their petition through the Channel of the Gov[r]., and in printing and publishing it by way of appendix to the Minutes of their proceedings, before it could reach the Throne, prevented me from immediately communicating it to the King, but His Majesty not considering ^it^ as coming properly before him, did not think fit to signify to me any Commands thereupon.

I have the pleasure to acquaint you that the Queen was happily brought to bed of a Princess on Tuesday last,[7] and that both Her Majesty and the young Princess are as well as can be desired. I most heartily congratulate you upon this Increase of the Royal Family; an event that affords the greatest Satisfaction to all His Majesty's Subjects.

The inclosed Speech made by the King to His Parliament at their meeting on the 8th instant, and the Addresses of both Houses in answer thereto,[8] one of which Addresses passed *nemine contradicente*,[9] and the other without a Division, will point out to you the attention that has been given to the distracted State of your Government; and I trust that the unanimity and resolution to preserve entire and inviolate the supreme Authority of the Legislature of Great Britain over every part of the British Empire, so strongly expressed in these Addresses, will have the happy effect to defeat and disappoint the wicked views of those who seek to create disunion and disaffection between Great Britain & Her Colonies, and that all His Majesty's Subjects in America, who wish well to the peace & prosperity of the British Dominions, will give full Credit to Parliament for that affection towards the Colonies which appears in their declaration that they will redress every real Grievance of His Majesty's American Subjects, and give due attention to every complaint they shall make in a regular manner and not founded upon claims and pretensions inconsistent with the constitution.

In the very unpleasant & critical situation in which you stand at present, it will, I apprehend, be a great support and consolation to you to know that the King places much confidence in your prudence and caution on the one hand, & entertains no diffidence of your spirit and Resolution on the other, and that His Majesty will not suffer these sentiments to receive any alteration from private misrepresentations, if ^any^ such should come, that may flow from Enmity to you, or self interested Views in those who transmit them; and, for my own part, Sir, I take the Liberty to add that I will not fail to do Justice to your Conduct in every representation that I have occasion to make of it to His Majesty.

I am with sincere Esteem & Regard Sir Your Most Obedient Humble Servant

Hillsborough

Governor Bernard.

LS, RC   BP, 12: 11-16.

The last two paragraphs are marked by red line in left margin, possibly added by the recipient. Endorsed by FB: Earl of Hillsborough d Nov 15 1768 r Jan 25 1769. Docket by Thomas Bernard: Approv^g of his Conduct.   Variants: CO 5/765, ff 48-52 (L, LbC); CO 5/757, ff 454-457 (Dft, AC). FB received the duplicate first, on c.18 Jan. 1769 (not found).[10] Enclosures (not found): the king's speech to both Houses of Parliament, 8 Nov. 1768,[11] and the addresses of the House of Lords of 15 Dec. and the House of Commons of 16 Dec. 1768.[12] Extracts of the letter together with the enclosure were laid before both houses of Parliament on 28 Nov. 1768. HLL: American Colonies Box 3.

   The king's speech to Parliament of 8 Nov. 1768 (which FB did not read until 10 Jan.)[13] focused on the troubles in Boston. Four days earlier the cabinet had read FB's reports on the Boston town meeting of 12 Sept. and feared that FB's government had been toppled, and that armed insurrection was a distinct possibility. Boston, the king observed,

> appears, by late Advices to be in a State of Disobedience to all Law and Government; and has proceeded to Measures subversive of the Constitution; and attended with Circumstances that might manifest a Disposition to throw off their Dependance on *Great-Britain*.[14]

For three days, after **No. 712** was completed, the earl of Hillsborough and John Pownall sifted through FB's reports (listed in note 1) trying to separate fact from opinion. They drew up a list of items to lay before Parliament (**No. 713**), and which Lord North presented on 28 Nov.

---

1. **Nos. 672** to **674**, **681**, **690**, **691**, and **693**. *Bernard Papers*, 4: 295-304, 318-324, 347-353, 355-356; **Nos. 694**, **698**, and **700** in this volume.

2. These curious symbols may have been intended as a placeholder in the draft, perhaps indicative of uncertainty as to the proper terminology. "His Majesty's Servants" may not have been considered an appropriate term for provincial law officers, such as the attorney general, who were not appointed by the Crown, though from 1772 the attorney general's salary was paid by the Crown.

3. Hillsborough to the attorney general and solicitor general of England, Whitehall, 6 Nov. 1768, CO 5/757, ff 452-453.

4. On 28 Nov. 1768. While Hillsborough awaited Parliament's deliberations, this letter to FB extended the scope of the inquiry into the causes of the *Liberty* riot and other riots he had instructed the provincial government to undertake (in **No. 661**, dated 30 Jul.); it was widened to encompass "illegal and unconstitutional Acts."

5. Stephen Sayre (1736-1818), a London merchant and sheriff of the city, with strong American sympathies; he was arrested for treason in 1775 for allegedly planning to kidnap the king, though he was released after two weeks' detention.

6. Sayre's letter to Hillsborough of 2 Jun. 1768 confirms that Sayre sent to Hillsborough the House's petition of 20 Jan., undoubtedly with DeBerdt's backing and permission. CO 5/757, ff 458-459. DeBerdt's version of events is not unsympathetic to Hillsborough. The explanation Hillsborough provided here enabled FB to give a plausible excuse for the secretary of state's studied delay in drawing the king's attention to the petition. See **No. 730**. Albert Matthews, "Letters of Dennys DeBerdt," at 332.

7. The Princess Augusta Sophia (8 Nov. 1768-1840). She was the second daughter and sixth child of fifteen born to Queen Charlotte (1744-1818) and King George III.

8. Left marginalia: three diagonal lines probably indicating receipt of three enclosures.

9. Meaning "with nobody contradicting or dissenting," usu. *nem con*.

10. Noted in BP, 7: 254.

11. See *HJL*, 32: 165-166 and *HCJ*, 32: 21-22. The speech was reprinted in the *Boston Chronicle*, 9-12 Jan. 1769.

12. See *HJL,* 32: 209-210 and *HCJ*, 32: 107-108.

13. **No. 729**.

14. Printed in the *Boston Gazette*, 16 Jan. 1769.

713 | *From the Earl of Hillsborough*

Hanover Square 19th. Nov[r]. 1768

(Private)

Sirr[1]

I trouble your Excellency with a private letter to assure you of the concern I am under with regard to your disappointment of the Deputy-Government of Virginia which I had fully intended for you — but the State of that Colony is such that the King's Servants thought it necessary to lose no time in sending out a Governor. If the King should approve of making you a Baronet, as it will be mere honour without profitt to you I will take care it shall not be attended with expence.

M[r]. Pownal & I have spent some days in considering with the utmost attention your correspondence, to the end that we might lay before Parliament a State of the Facts relative to your Government & of the Arguments which have given rise to the several measures directed from hence, by Extracts from your Letters, without exposing the whole of each Letter, but we find you have so interwoven Facts with your own observations & opinions that it is altogether impracticable to seperate them. Many of your Letters may I hope however be entirely kept back — & you may depend upon the the[2] strenuous support, & entire approbation of both Houses. My Lord Barrington is of opinion you will be indifferent about your Letters, for he says you have nothing to manage with the Faction, nor now the Troops are arrived no^any^thing to fear. I shall however cautiously keep back every thing that I find I can. — A fortnight will enable me to acquaint you of the measures Parliament will take, it must give your Excellency pleasure to see us so firmly united in the resolution to support the Constitution & enforce obedience to the Laws — & if I am listened to the measure you think the most necessary[3] will be adopted — I beg the favour of you to acquaint me of your Inclination with regard to yourself, &

give me leave to assure you that as far as depends upon me you will find me eager to evince the Esteem & Respect with which

I am Sir Your Excellency's Most Faithfull & Most Obedient Servant

Hillsborough

ALS, RC   BP, 12: 17-20.

Endorsed by FB: [Hanover Square] Earl of Hillsborough d Nov 19 1768 r Jan 25 1769. FB replied with **No. 735**.

While Hillsborough expressed some concerns about FB's style of reporting, this letter nonetheless was an endorsement of the governor, as the promise to pay the expenses of his baronetcy indicated. Hillsborough could have made FB a scapegoat for the administration's difficulties with the American Colonies, but for the moment was prepared to wait and see how Parliament reacted to the Imperial Crisis. Hillsborough was rather hasty in dismissing FB's concerns about the possible publication of his correspondence, as demonstrated by the publication of FB's six letters in the *Boston Gazette*, 23 Jan. 1769.

1.   Thus in manuscript.

2.   Thus in manuscript.

3.   This is probably an allusion to FB's preference for reform of colonial government, as Pownall confirmed in **No. 714**.

714 | *From John Pownall*

Whitehall. Nov. 19. 1768

Dear Sir

Whatever other opinions may have been of the Spirit or want of Spirit in your answer to the committee of the Town meeting in June[1] and in the missives you penned upon that occasion; my opinion was & is still that your conduct in that business and in every other, throughout the whole of the very difficult part you have had to act, has been uniformly wise prudent & firm: _____ I had nothing in view in my letter of the 30 July[2] but to guard your mind against that diffidence and despondence which under such circumstances as attended your situation, the finest men might have yielded to: I am not however sorry that so much has been said to you by others, since it has produced the Letter from you now before me, which,[3] allow me to say, is filled with observations that do honour to your conduct & Sentiments.

It has been read by the -------[4] and has produced every consequence that your best friends could have wished; and you may rest assured that every favorable intention of my noble freind[5] towards you, will be not only kept alive; but cherished with the greatest good will & I hope e'er long will have its full Effect. Your resolution to continue at Boston some time longer is highly approved & commended & the good effects of it have been seen in every event that has happened from the 5 of Sept[r]. to the 8 of October.

For my own part I never had a doubt that the troops would ~~not~~ be opposed____ Such opposition appeared to me neither practicable nor consistent with the Views of the Enemys to the authority of Parliament. ____ If there is any settled resolution to resist that authority the Scheme must lye deeper than in fruitless struggle with two Regiments at Boston, & go further than the seeking a quarrel with them by creating perplexity and embarrassment in quartering ____ for as to that proceeding and every other transaction at Boston they are within our reach, but I have great ground to fear more dangerous Combinations than the self important Convention, that thing of Straw, which at last was afraid of it's own shadow. ____ Inclosed I send you a strong anonymous Letter from Boston; if you can guess at the author or procure any intelligence about it, it may be usefull.

It is impossible, in considering the State of Boston, with a view to measures, not to see the necessity of a reform in respect to the Council __ and the bringing to Justice the Persons guilty of possibly the Treasons, but certainly the high Crimes & misdemeanors which have been committed; — but what will be done I cannot yet say, — by the next opportunity you will hear further from

Your most faithfull & affc[t] Friend & humble Serv[t].

J Pownall

ALS, RC   BP, 12: 21-24.

Endorsed by FB: [_][6] d Nov 19 1768 r Jan 16 1769. Docket: approv[g] of Gov[r] B.   The enclosure (not found) was an "Anonymous Letter" in manuscript, "feigned" by one of FB's enemies.[7]

---

1. **No. 631**, *Bernard Papers*, 4: 205-206.

2. **No. 662**, ibid., 276-277.

3. **No. 684,** ibid., 328-329.

4. Probably an allusion to the "cabinet," if the number of dashes corresponds to number of letters omitted.

5. Hillsborough probably, described by Pownall "as our noble friend" in **No. 723.**

6. Obscured in the fold of the binding.

7. Quotation from **No. 742**.

715 | To John Pownall

Private

Boston Nov 25 1768

Dear S[r]

As this Packet conveys nothing but Duplicates to your Office I shall add to it a private Letter to you. This will inform you that of the Reg[ts] from Ireland the whole of the 64th & half of the 65th are arrived:[1] there are two Transports still out, one of which was seen about a fortnight ago partly dismasted in Lat 39 bearing for the Southward. We have now 3 Reg[ts] quartered in the Town in Barracks hired & fitted up by Order of the General at the Expence of the Crown; No other Quarters being to be procured for them. The Town is become very quiet except that abusive Publications in the Public Papers are continued, some of which directed against some of the Commissioners are supposed to come from Persons in the Pay of the Crown.[2] People in general are very well satisfied with the Troops being here, their Conduct being very orderly & decent: the Country is so well reconciled to them, that those who supply the Boston Markets wish there was more of them. However the Government, tho it is now protected, has not as yet recovered much of its former Energy: that must be a Work of Time if it can ever be done under the present Constitution.

I hereby inclose a fresh Publication which just at this Time is the Subject of general Talk. It has the common Fate of good Advice unseasonably urged, to be condemned by both Parties. It is said on one Side, that they don't want a Repeal upon such Terms; a Repeal procured by the Acknowledgement of the Parliaments Right to tax them would be worse than the Acts continued unrepealed. The Precedent is what they most complain of; the Burthen is trifling; & indeed the last ^Act^ is an Act of Bounty rather than of Burthen. Besides the Repeals expected in America greatly exceed the utmost Favor intended in England. Every Act imposing Duties must be repealed; there must not be one left as a Precedent for Acts of the same Kind. It is now 95 Years since the first Duties were imposed on the Colonies by Act of Parliament.[3] All Impositions of Duties during this long Interval must be abrogated at once. This is evident in their public Writings, as it is in their private Conversations. It is therefore no Wonder, that a Compromise of this Kind meets with a cold Reception even tho there was ~~no other~~ ^more^ Authority, than appears here, to propose it.

On the other Side it is said that the Writer ought not to have made such Proposals, tho but by Intimation, to People, whom he must know to be disposed by no Means to accept of the Terms. That it must tend to encourage them to persist in their Demands upon Great Britain, & to form Expectations of Compliances of such a Nature as it is impossible for the Parliament to accede to. That the Demands of the Americans were so widely distant from the most favourable Concessions which Great Britain could make consistently with the Safety of the Empire, that there was Nothing left for the Parliament but to speak with Authority. A Compromise is certainly very desirable: but to be succesful it must originate in America by withdrawing some of the most exorbitant Pretensions, which the Colonies have, within these 3 Years only, set up against the Imperial State. This is the Sentiment of the Friends of Government. M⟨r⟩ Rogers has all the Credit he can desire for his Candour & Integrity; but it has been wished that he had advised with his Friends concerning the Prudentiality of this Publication. Nevertheless as I have no Doubt of its being made with a good Intent, so I am not sure that it may not have some good Effect.

I asked M⟨r⟩ Rogers, whether his Hopes of the Colonies, & especially this Province, being treated with Indulgence had not been much abated by his being made acquainted with the Proceedings of the Town Meeting and the Calling the Convention in Consequence thereof. He owned that they were very much abated; & that he dreaded the Resentment of the Parliament against the calling & meeting of that Convention. For my Part I fear nothing from that Resentment if it shall be directed for the Purposes of Reformation & not of Punishment. If it shall be the Means of removing the Difficulties, which have hitherto prevented the making that necessary Amendment of the Constitution of this Government, the putting the Appointment of the Council in the Kings Hands, it will be an Event most happy for this Province. And if the Convention & the Proceedings of the Council about the same Time shall give the Crown a legal Right or induce the Parliament to exercise a legislative Power over the Charter, it will be most indulgently exercised, if it is extended no further than to make one Alteration in the Form of the Government which has been allways found wanting, is now become quite necessary & will really by making it more constitutional render it more permanent. With this Alteration I do beleive that all the Disorders of this Government will be remedied & the Authority of it fully restored. Without it there will be a perpetual Occasion to resort to Expedients, the continual Inefficacy of which will speak in the Words of Scripture "you are ^careful &^ troubled about many Things; but one thing is needful."[4]

I am D⟨r⟩ S⟨r⟩ &c

John Pownall Esq⟨r⟩

L, LbC   BP, 6: 165-168.

In handwriting of Thomas Bernard. Minor emendations now shown. Enclosed a copy of the *Boston Evening-Post*, 21 Nov. 1768.

Nathaniel Rogers had been in London for nearly a year, [5] *inter alia* attending to the affairs of his uncle TH. With letters of introduction to FB's friends he was able to meet with the earl of Shelburne and brief him on Massachusetts politics.[6] Rogers evidently did not consult FB before publishing an open letter in the *Boston Evening-Post*. The letter commenced with a warning of the widening breach in British-colonial relations: "sever reflections were thrown out upon our conduct, and the last summer, a general alarm appeared in the kingdom, that we were taking the most imprudent steps, and that matters would be carried to the last extremity." The newspaper obligingly carried digests of the London newspapers up to 19 Sept. reporting that dispatches of "great importance" from FB had arrived on "*Sept*. 14"[7] and that four days later it was "rumoured, that the people of Boston had set the Military at defiance." (Readers would automatically have assumed the rumor had been prompted by FB's reports.) And yet, Rogers opined, men of all parties in London were willing to listen to "reasonings as were admissible upon their ideas of the constitution." There existed strong support for the repeal of Townshend's Revenue Act, Rogers stressed. This was a prescription for *real politik* instead of a campaign resting on principle and an attack on unbridled parliamentary authority. FB was so far distant from the Whigs and the assembly as to preclude endorsing Rogers' proposal (indeed endorsement would have damned it in the eyes of many). He recognized too that Rogers would not have won converts among radical Whigs when "the Repeals expected in America greatly exceed the utmost Favor intended in England." But Rogers's invocation might yet have appealed to moderate Whigs as well as friends of government:

> that were we to adopt moderate and prudent measures, all our past
> warmth and heat would be forgot, and the Act with all its consequences, which now give so much concern, would be repealed.[8]

There was evidence to hand; the Council's respectful petition to the king (**Appendix 1**) had been received "in a most Gracious Manner" and was due to be considered by Parliament (on 8 Nov., Rogers suggested, though in fact it was 26 Nov.)

Newspaper readers could be forgiven for thinking that old news from London had little bearing on their current predicament or their contest with parliamentary authority. Rogers's optimism dimmed when FB informed him of the Convention of Towns and the reception accorded the Regulars' arrival. Furthermore, what FB, Rogers, and the readers of the province newspapers did not know was that British ministers and politicians experienced a second alarm, in early November (after Rogers' departure from London) and in the ensuing debates in Parliament opinion swung strongly against the colonies. To FB's dismay, constitutional reform was not advanced, while, as Rogers predicted, the repeal of the Revenue Act became central to the government's plans to improve British-colonial relations.

---

1. The first ships transporting the 64th and 65th Regiments arrived in the second week of November, a "few days" prior to 14 Nov., according to TH, and continued through 17 Nov., according to one newspaper. Hutchinson Transcripts, 2: 678; *Boston Weekly News-Letter*, 17 Nov. 1768. Col. Pomeroy's 64th Regiment was billeted in warehouses at Wheelwright's Wharf, with Col. Mackay's 65th destined for the barracks on Castle Island. Currently anchored in Boston harbor were His Majesty's Ships, *Romney* (recently returned from Halifax), *Mermaid*, *Glasgow*, *Beaver*, *Viper*, *Senegal*, and *Bonetta*; plus the armed schooners *Magdalene*, *Hope*, *Little-Romney*, and *Sultana*, and troops transports from Ireland. *Essex Gazette* 15-22 Nov. 1768. Alexander Mackay (1717-89) was promoted to major general on 30 Apr. 1770, while John Pomeroy (1724-90) saw service at the battles of Lexington and Bunker Hill.

2. "Candidus" began his attack on the American Board of Customs with a character assassination of Charles Paxton. *Boston Evening-Post*, 21 Nov. 1768. Purportedly authored by someone professing to have "always steadily adhered to the prerogative side of the question," FB appears to have given some credence to the notion (or rumor) that the author was a government man. He naturally suspected John Temple, but Temple's estrangement from the Board did not occur until after the turn of the year. If "Candidus" was a vexed officeholder, a more likely candidate was Attorney General Jonathan Sewall, presently in the midst of a long-running spat with the commissioners and (unlike Temple) a proven political writer. See **No. 678**, *Bernard Papers*, 4: 307-313. Another and more likely possibility is that Samuel Adams was "Candidus," given that Adams is said to have written at least nineteen letters as "Candidus" from 1771 (printed in the second volume of Cushing, *Writings of Samuel Adams*).

3. He is probably referring to one of the earliest Navigation Acts, the Encouragement of Trade Act, 15 Car. 2, c. 7 (1663).

4. The scriptural reference confirmed that FB's deluded opponents had chosen a path from which they could not easily be diverted.

> And Jesus answered and said unto her, Martha, Martha, thou art careful and troubled about many things:
>
> But one thing is needful: and Mary hath chosen that good part, which shall not be taken away from her.
>
> (Luke 10:41-42. KJV.)

5. He returned as a passenger on board the *Thames,* Capt. Watt, arriving on 17 Nov. 1768.

6. *Bernard Papers*, 3: 421.

7. Probably **No. 660**, dated 30 Jul., *Bernard Papers*, 4: 266-270.

8. *Boston Evening-Post*, 21 Nov. 1768.

716 | To John Pownall

Jamaica Plain Nov 26 1768

Dear S[r]

I am favored with your Letter by M[r] Rogers[1] & am much obliged to you for it. I am glad that my Conduct meets with your Approbation, as you are so good a judge of the Difficulties I have had to struggle with: they have been so many & so great, that it is no small Merit to have made no great Mistake. Nothing could be more embarrasing to a Governor than a Necessity for Troops to march to the Capital, heretofore unused to them except in Time of War. And yet tho the Necessity was real, I persisted in doing Nothing without the Advice of Council. I ran a Risk in this; but there would have been much greater Danger in acting otherwise. In either Way my Conduct would have been judged of by Events: but in the Way I took I could have justified myself by Orders, which might have been turned against me if I had acted otherwise. It seems that the General as well as myself judged right in waiting till Orders for marching Troops came from Home; which, as the People here went on, must have been sooner or later. The only Danger was of some great Mischeif being done in the Interval; which has not happened.

I cant now foresee where & from whence my Reward is to come. I liked the Proposal of sending me to Virginia & was disappointed at its being defeated. Perhaps it is better as it is: I want peace & Ease; I should ~~have~~ not probably have found them in Virginia under its present political Professions: but I should have got Affluence & Independency, neither of which are to be expected in this Government in its present State. I agree with you that it would be ~~better~~ best to look out for something on this Side of the Water: but I know not which Way to look. You ^must^ know that I am very exceptious in the Business of Governments: I set such a Value upon Health, that I think that no Emoluments whatsoever can make Amends for an Unhealthy Climate. For this Reason, although S Carolina would satisfy me in its Income, I should dread it as a Place of Residence, & would decline it if it was worth more that [than] it is. My former Government with an enlarged Salary would be the most agreeable Grant the King could make to me.

I was very near embarking for England before I knew any Objection to it. I had fixed upon the Ship & the Day of embarking, Oct 1st. A fortnight before that Day I received important Dispatches from Lord Hillsborough by a very quick Conveyance,[2] which immediately showed the Necessity of my putting off my Voyage. I accordingly wrote to Lord H[3] that I considered the Orders I had then received as a Suspension of my Leave of Absence & should continue here. Sometime after I received an Intimation[4] (not from himself) that Lord H was under Concern least I should have left Boston: But if I had not before determined this upon my own

Judgement the Hint would have come too late. And yet I want very much to go to England upon domestic Accounts as well as others: I am now in the 11th Year of my Peregrination. But I am quite reconciled to its being postponed for several Reasons: as I think it not improbable that Parliament will take some severe Resolutions against this Province, I am glad not to be on the Spot, that there may not be that Pretence for charging me with promoting them. I should also be very sorry to be publickly examined concerning the State of this Country: I should be obliged to speak the Truth; & the Truth wont bear to be spoken. So it is best that I should not be with you at present.

I dont wonder at your thinking of coming to America;[5] either with the Sagacity of a Rat quitting a falling House, or with the Prudence of one ~~quitting~~ ^changing^ an empty Granary for a full one. But I wonder at your Choice of Situation; surely Massachusets is rather too northerly for a chosen Spot. I should rather think of the Banks of the Delaware, or between that & the Hudson, particularily[6] the Passaik a Favorite of mine: I would not go much North of New York. However I will look out as you desire: Ready Money will purchase Lands cheap; the Difficulty is to get good Tenants. But there is no such Thing as getting so large a Tract of Land as you require in the old settled Country: among new Settlements it is to be had. I am concerned in a Town in the direct Road from Boston to Albany about 35 Miles from the latter & nearer to other Parts of the River Hudson. It is in the same Latitude with Boston.[7] It is settling apace & will be fully and well settled by next Summer. Our Lots are intermixed one with another: but I beleive I could prevail upon our Partners to join with me in laying you out an intire Tract of 2 or 300 Acres. There is also an entire Tract of 1500 Acres in the Middle of the Town not belonging to us, which has been offered for Sale to me by Col Israel Williams.[8] Col Partridge is our Manager. Sev'ral such Things as these are to be picked up. There are now good Purchases to be made on the River Penobscot from Col Waldo:[9] The Owls Head particularily, at the Mouth of the River containing about 6000 Acres of very good Land, may be had at between 1 Dollar & 2 an Acre. That River will soon be settled: There is a fine growing Town about Fort Pownall, in which I had a considerable Intrest; & another next to it is just now begun upon. There are also two large Islands the one just above & the other just below the Fort now to be sold by Col Waldo. They won't fetch above 2 Dollars if so much. I myself gave 6s. sterlg for the Neck at Fort Pownall before there was a single Settler there except at the Fort. You may consider of these Things.[10]

Mr Rogers has informed me of your View: I wonder at it, considering how Persons in that Station have been generally Treated. I had determined never to meddle with that Business again: but I shall depart from my Purpose to serve you. But if I can do any Service, it must be either by not appearing at all, or in the Light of an Opponent. If there should be such an Appearance it ~~must~~ ^will^ be for the

Purpose now professed: I have no one to serve in it but you. Mr. R will know my Sentiments from Time to Time. Upon this Account, if there was no other, it may be proper that as little Notice as may be, should be taken of our Correspondence.[11]

I have been much disappointed in my endeavours to procure American hemp. I got some seed last year & sowed it this: but it did not come up. The Indians have been offered a good price for a quantity of it but their Indolence & their Jealousy have prevented it. However We have learned where it grows.[12]

I am &c

J Pownall Esq

L, LbC   BP, 6: 168-173.

In handwriting of Thomas Bernard.

----

1. This private letter has not been found.

2. **No. 661**, *Bernard Papers*, 4: 271-276.

3. **No. 683**, ibid., 326-327.

4. Possibly from Nathaniel Rogers upon his return from London. See **No. 715**.

5. Pownall had evidently expressed interest in retiring to an American estate or at the very least investing in a land grant scheme with FB as partner (having spent many years assisting other speculators make application to the Board of Trade).

6. Thus in manuscript.

7. Township No. 2, included in grants of nine townships in Berkshire County in 1762. The principal proprietors were Oliver Partridge (1712-92) and Elisha Jones (1710-75), and the township was incorporated as Partridgefield in 1771 and renamed Peru in 1806. Chester Dewey, David D. Field, and the Berkshire Association, *A History of the County of Berkshire, Massachusetts* (Pittsfield, Mass., 1829), 443.

8. Israel Williams (1709-88).

9. Samuel Waldo Jr. (1723-70), proprietor of the Waldo Patent in Maine.

10. Joseph Chadwick surveyed the area for FB in 1765. Plan of lands belonging to the heirs of Brigadier Samuel Waldo (1696-1759), Spencer Bernard Papers, EM2.

11. The opaque explanation in this paragraph nevertheless seems to convey FB's willingness to act as Pownall's agent in the matter of securing land grants in the American Colonies.

12. The last paragraph and closure are in FB's hand.

717 | To the Earl of Hillsborough

[*Boston, 30 Nov. 1768.*]

My Lord

I think it proper to inform your Lordship that I communicated to the Council that part of your Lordship's Letter No. 19,[1] in which your Lordship Signified his Majesty's gracious reception of the Petition of the Council which I transmitted in July last,[2] and added that the Petition with my reasoning in support of it would have full consideration. Upon which Mr Bowdoin, who has all along taken the lead of the Council in their late Extraordinary proceedings, charged me with having misrepresented the purpose of their Petition by taking advantage of an Expression of theirs, "drawing a Revenue from the Colonies," and therefrom insinuating that their objection lay not so much against the raising money as the Carrying it out of the Country, and not expending it here. And to Justify this, He quoted a transitory Conversation he had with me on the day of the Public Commencement at the College in July last. I told him that if that Conversation had made such an impression upon him, it was a pitty that he had not mentioned it before, whilst my memory could interpose on my behalf. That at this distance of time, 5 Months, I could not recollect every trifleing Conversation; for such I was assured this was, from his report of it. But I could be very Certain whether I had or had not misrepresented their Petition by inspecting my own Books. And before I looked at them I could declare that I had not.

My Letter Books were at my Country House, where I generally write all my Letters. As soon as I got at them, I had the Letter in question N°. 11, July 16th, Copied: and as soon as I returned to Town I read that part of it, which related to this business, to 3 or 4 of the Council; and I let 2 of them and the Secretary read the whole Letter: The[y] were greatly surprised to find it so very clear of M^r: Bowdoin's charge. At the next Council I produced the Letter and read the whole passage referred to; from whence it appeared that in mentioning the prayer of their petition, I used their own words without adding a single word of my own; and also that the argument I used in behalf of the prayer went against Taxation in general, more than the disposal of the money; This appeared satisfactory to the whole Council except M^r. Bowdoin. But he still persisting in justifying himself mentioned something more of the Conversation referred to, which explained the whole, and shewed that what I had said upon that occasion was entirely in joke. ^This was confirmed by a Councillor, who recollected that on that Day, being a day of festivity, I did joke ^3 with some of them upon their Petition, to the same purpose as M^r. Bowdoin quoted, but in Terms that one could not have Imagined could have been taken seriously, and really were quite inoffensive to every one else.

This is a very trifleing matter to trouble your Lordship with: but it has already been the subject of debates in Council, and Libells in the News Papers.[4] It would have also produced a formal remonstrance to your Lordship, which I am told was actually prepared by the Gentleman who made the charge, if it had not been prevented by my making Communications, which, but for saving trouble to your Lordship, I would not have submitted to. But it will vent itself in another and more public way; of which I shall be able to give your Lordship an Account in a few days. Your Lordship may depend upon it, that my informations have been and shall be dictated by the Spirit of Truth and Candor: but I cannot make facts other than they are, nor can I excuse myself Communicating such observations and reflections as occur to me and appear to be material to the subject.

I am with great respect &c

Fran^s. Bernard.

L, RLbC   CO 5/767, ff 185-188.

Entrybook title: Governor Bernard Boston November 30th 1768 (N° 34) R 16 January 1769. The RC has not been found. Variants in: BP, 7: 109-111 (L, LbC); Bowdoin and Temple Papers, Loose MSS (L, Copy); *Boston Gazette*, 23 Jan. 1769;[5] *Copies of Letters from Governor Bernard to Hillsborough*; *Letters to Hillsborough* (1st ed.), 14-16; *Letters to Hillsborough* (repr.), 27-29. Copies were presented to Parliament on 20 Jan. 1769.[6]

The matter which FB considered "trifleing"—his summation of the prayer of the Council's petition to the king—James Bowdoin argued was a willful attempt to undermine the petition. The incident served to justify Bowdoin and his Whig colleagues taking action on a far more serious matter: that of circumventing the governor's control of information being transmitted to ministers and Parliament. To that end, on c.30 Nov., the group drafted two further petitions, to the House of Commons and House of Lords separately, and requested the assistance of William Bollan in presenting them; they also asked Bollan to become the Council's unofficial agent.[7] The councilors carefully explained to Bollan that the petitions to the king and Parliament were "expressly" praying for the repeal of the "several American revenue acts." But they were concerned that the term "drawn," used in the petition to the king, might be misinterpreted. Hillsborough's letter of 14 Sept. (**No. 679**),[8] by which the Council learned the petition to the king would be presented and considered by Parliament, had also led them to believe that FB's cover letter enclosing the petition (**No. 654**)[9] had misrepresented its intent so that it would be interpreted literally: that revenue monies ought not to be drawn from the colonies to London.[10]

In subsequent papers, the Council were obliged to clarify what they had intended. Danforth's letter to Hillsborough of 15 Apr. 1769 explained that the petition to the king argued for the repeal of all the American revenue acts in an "explicit manner" (**Appendix 4**). Part of the problem, however, was that the Council's petitions did not expressly plead for an exemption from parliamentary taxation on the basis of right, probably because that did not accord with the views of the more moderate councilors; the main thrust of the arguments was about the inexpediency of the Navigation Acts. Bowdoin, who took a lead role in drafting the petition to the king, later explained his disquiet with FB in a long letter to Hillsborough (**Appendix 3**). It is possible that this was a belated attempt to rectify an inexactitude Bowdoin supposed could damage his leadership credentials, but his letter is really a testament to how hard the "major part" of the Council had to work to preserve a united front against their governor. Nevertheless, when members of Parliament accepted the Council's petition to the Commons, they automatically concluded that a claim of right was implied (see **Appendix 2**).

---

1. **No. 679**, *Bernard Papers*, 4: 313-315.

2. **Appendix 11** enclosed in **No. 654**, ibid., 255-257.

3. Addition relocated from margin.

4. News that the Council's petition was to be presented to Parliament came by the *Thames*, Capt. Watt on 17 Nov. *Boston Weekly News-Letter*, 17 Nov. 1768.

5. Also published in *Providence Gazette*, 22 Apr. 1769; *Boston Chronicle*, 27 Apr.-1 May 1769; *New-York Gazette, and Weekly Mercury*, 29 May 1769; *Boston Gazette*, 31 Jul. 1769.

6. *HCJ*, 32: 123-124; *HLJ*, 32: 229.

7. Samuel Danforth to William Bollan, Boston, 5 Dec. 1769, *Bowdoin and Temple Papers*, 113-115. Signed by Danforth as the "president" and by the "major part of the Council," the petition to the Commons was reprinted in full in *Letters to Hillsborough* (1st ed.), 70-73. It was considered on 25 Jan. 1769 (for which see the source note to **Appendix 2**). *HCJ*, 32: 136.

8. *Bernard Papers*, 4: 313-315.

9. Ibid., 254-257.

10. FB was probably not intent on discrediting the petition, and found its moderatism encouraging. See **No. 654**, ibid., 254-257.

718 | *To the Earl of Hillsborough*

N° 35

Boston Dec. 5, 1768.

My Lord

The Council have been for a week past preparing petitions to the two Houses of parliament against the American Acts of Revenue, that is as I understand, against all the Acts imposing port duties.[1] They signified their intention to me & desired that I would either join with them, or authorise their sitting for that purpose. I reminded them that I had refused to be concerned in this business in July last, & the impropriety of this Measure was much stronger now than then. I added, that if they would be advised by me, they would not pursue this intention; which could do no good, and might turn to evil; that if the Parliament was disposed to indulge the Americans in another repeal, there were petitions enough before them to ground it upon; and their petition at best would be but a make-weight; on the other hand it might contain something that might give offence & add to the ill humour, which I feared allready prevailed against this province. But All this & more had no effect: The movers of this Business called the Council together separately from the Governor in the Council chamber,[2] according to the New Method, for which they apologise in the petition. After sevral days meeting the Petition was settled & approved: upon which there was a dispute how it should be signed, whether by evry one as private persons, as in their address to General Gage, or by the president in the name of the body; in which latter case they must be understood to act as the Legislative Council, there being no President of the Privy Council but the Governor. However It was resolved that it should be signed in the latter way.

As soon as I learned it was finished I sent for Mr Danforth the President & desired to see it: he went & procured it for me. I found it was signed "in the name and by the order of a Majority of the Council S. Danforth."[3] Mr Danforth said that he was not present when this manner of signing was resolved upon; & when he set his Name to it, He did not set the word "president" after his name: this was a poor excuse, but serves to show how little free-agency there is in a business of this kind. He also added that if he could get the Council to meet again, he was in hopes they would undo this business; for sevral of them had signified their disapprobation of it. But I had no such expectation: for the Council is brought under such an Awe of their constituents by the frequent removals of the friends of Government; that there is Very little Exercise of private Judgement in popular Questions.[4]

If by the Majority of the Council, in whose name the president is to sign, they mean a Majority of the whole board, I cannot conceive that all the persons who met at the sevral meetings upon this occasion put together could amount to the Number 12 which is the majority of the whole. But if they mean a Majority of those present when the resolution was formed, it may fall Very short of a majority of the body: 4 persons will make a majority of a quorum of the Council. In the present case I doubt whether the Number of those who really approved of this measure was much more: for it seemed to be rather submitted to than joined in. As for the petition itself, it is Very lengthy, being 6 folio pages, but has nothing new in it, nothing I beleive, but what is to be found among the writings of the House of Representatives. It differs from the petition to the King in this:[5] the latter carefully avoids all claim of right against the parliament; this is not so clear of it: it has indeed no positive assertions of right but sevral intimations of it too plain to be unnoticed. This account is taken from only once reading it & there-fore may not be free from mistakes, tho' I beleive it is right as to the general Idea.

I am with great respect, My Lord, your Lordship's
most obedient & most humble Servant,

Fra. Bernard.

The right honble the Earl of Hillsborough.

ALS, RC   CO 5/758, ff 25-26.

Endorsed: Boston Dec.ʳ 5ᵗʰ. 1768 Gov.ʳ Bernard (Nº 35) R 16 Janʳʸ 1769. B.5. Enl.ᵈ   No
enclosure has been found. Variants in CO 5/767, ff 189-192 (L, RLbC); BL: Add 35912,
ff 148-150 (L, Copy); Bowdoin and Temple Papers, Loose MSS (L, Copy); BP, 7: 111-
114 (L, LbC); *Boston Gazette*, 23 Jan. 1769;[6] *Copies of Letters from Governor Bernard to
Hillsborough*; *Letters to Hillsborough* (1st ed.), 16-17; *Letters to Hillsborough* (repr.), 30-33.
Enclosures not found. Copies of the letter were presented to Parliament on 20 Jan. 1769.[7]
FB's letterbook copy contains the following postscript on p. 114 (the original of which is
missing from the RC file).

> PS.[8] Since I wrote the foregoing I have got a List of the Gentlemen who
> passed upon the Petition Mʳ Danforth, Royal, Erving, Bowdoin, Hub-
> bard, Tyler, Pitts, Dexter. Upon Nov 30 they agreed upon the Petition
> to the Lords & Commons to be signed by Mʳ Danforth as President.[9]
> Of these 8 I have been informed of two who wanted to have it undone,
> & I can fix upon another who I dare say acquiesced rather than con-
> curred.[10]

The Council's petitions to Parliament of c.30 Nov. were the productions of a group
who styled themselves the "major part" of the Council (although they did not actually constitute a majority of members until Aug. 1769). They claimed to act "individually, and not
as a body," and convened under the presidency of Samuel Danforth. The procedure was
unconstitutional in so far as the Province Charter stated that executive meetings of the
Council were to be chaired by the governor and legislative sessions required the governor's
presence. The petitions (whose content and prayers covered the same issues) were less
strident than those adopted by the House of Representatives, the Convention of Towns, or
assemblies in other colonies. Rather than set out the constitutional bases of colonial rights
and liberties, they exhibited a conservative, economic outlook that stressed the mutual
benefits of empire.

The petition to the House of Commons began by reiterating Massachusetts's role in
extending Britain's North American empire through settlement and contributions of soldiers and money in fighting the French; shortage of specie hampered colonial economic re-
covery after the war, the petition continued, and British taxes imposed after the peace were
unnecessary when the colony was already contributing heavily to the British economy by
virtue of its increasing consumption of British manufactures. All of this probably reflected
the personal views of merchants like Royall and Erving. Only in the final paragraph did the
Council address the matter of colonial rights, by requesting "that the Charter Rights and
Privileges of the People of this Province, and their invaluable Liberties as British Subjects,
may be secured."[11] None of this would have alienated moderate or conservative Whigs. If

the petition was largely the work of James Bowdoin (as FB suspected) then it was crafted to appeal across the spectrum of opinion within the Council as well as to allay the fears of British politicians alarmed by FB's reports. The petitions were forwarded to the former province agent, William Bollan, under cover of a letter of 5 Dec., specifically requesting his assistance to lay them before Parliament.[12] Bollan's reaction is examined in the source note to **No. 765**.

---

1. Petitions of the [*major part of the*] Massachusetts Council to the House of Commons and the House of Lords, c.30 Nov. 1768. There is a signed copy of the petition to the Lords in Bowdoin and Temple Papers, Loose MSS. The petition to the Commons is in *Letters to Hillsborough* (1st. ed), 70-73.

2. These proceedings are thus not recorded in the Council's executive minutes.

3. "In the Name of the major Part of the Council aforesaid, (Signed) SAMUEL DANFORTH, President of the Council." *Letters to Hillsborough* (1st ed.), 73.

4. The Council later maintained they acted independently of popular opinion (**Appendix 5**).

5. **Appendix 11**, *Bernard Papers*, 4: 392-396.

6. Also published in *Boston Chronicle*, 27 Apr.-1 May 1769; *Boston Gazette*, 31 Jul. 1769.

7. *HCJ*, 32: 123-124; *HLJ*, 32: 229.

8. Omitted from the RC and RLbC. Supplied from the LbC.

9. Samuel Danforth (1696-1777), elected to the Council, 1739-74; Isaac Royall (1719-81), 1752-73; John Erving (1692-1786), 1754-74; James Bowdoin (1726-90), 1757-68; Thomas Hubbard (1702-73), 1759-72; Royal Tyler (1724-71), 1764-70; James Pitts (1710-76), 1766-74; Samuel Dexter (1726-1810), 1768-73.

10. The Council later contradicted this assessment, claiming that "Lincoln, Brattle Gray and Russell ought to have been inserted therein, they having also agreed to the Petitions." Thus, this would have made "a Majority of the whole" Council (**Appendix 5**). Whatever the truth in this instance, moderates who had turned against the governor remained wary of the radicals. TH later ascribed to John Erving Sr. a rather lame excuse "that until he received letters from the Lords of the Treasury to the contrary he thought he was obliged to sign every thing that was voted by the Board." To FB, 11 and 17 Aug. 1769, Mass. Archs., 26: 363. Erving was linked to FB's personal enemies (his daughter Elizabeth was James Bowdoin's wife), whence his readiness to seek accommodation with TH.

11. *Letters to Hillsborough* (1st ed.), 73.

12. Samuel Danforth to William Bollan, 5 Dec. 1768, *Bowdoin and Temple Papers*, 113-115.

719 | To the Earl of Hillsborough

N° 36

Boston Dec 12 1768

My Lord

I have wrote to your Lordship many letters upon the sevral subjects contained in your letter N° 16;[1] and yet I have not finished all I have to say. Of all the orders & injunctions contained therein there is none in which I am less able to answer expectation than in that which directs me "to set on foot an enquiry into the Causes of the riots which have disturbed the Peace of this Town & to take evry legal Method to bring to justice the most active & forward in the violences committed on the 10th of June." Your Lordship must be satisfied before now that it would be to no purpose to institute such an enquiry at the Council board. The Conduct of that board upon some late occasions sufficiently shows how little dependence I can now have upon their assistance in the prosecution of Sons of liberty, And how unable the Governor of this province is to carry on such a prosecution, against the popular cry, by the ordinary civil Magistrate, will be the subject of this letter.

I have before informed your Lordship that soon after the riot on the 10th of June, I did, with the advice of Council, order the Attorney-general to prosecute the persons concerned in that riot.[2] The Attorney-general accordingly prepared indictments & laid them before the grand Jury.[3] But when It was the business to examine Witnesses, No one person could be found who would give Evidence against any one of 3 or 400 people who committed those Outrages in the face of day. This may seem strange: but the Wonder will cease, when it is observed that 1, there is no officer within this Government whose business it is to prepare for prosecutions by procuring informations & Evidence, this seeming not to be the proper business of the Attorney general; 2, As the Attorney general has no pay from the Crown, it cannot be expected that he should go out of his Way in a Service which does not strictly belong to his Office & by being unpopular must prejudice him in his other business; 3, If he could reconcile himself to this Service he has not the means to perform it, there being no fund from which Money can be drawn to pay for private intelligence, without which prosecutions of this kind are generally defeated; 4, public offers of reward for information have so little effect, that upon the many occasions on which I have offered such rewards for the discovery of rioters &c there has not been a single instance of any intelligence being procured by these Means.

But the great difficulty which attends Crown Prosecutions arises from the Kings having really no officers for that purpose. There is indeed an Officer called the Kings Attorney; but he is really the Attorney of the People. He receives nothing from the King; what little pittance of Salary or pay he gets is from the People;[4] all the Occasional profits of his Office arise from among the people; & altho' he is appointed in the Name of the King, yet the King can't remove him, without the Council, who have been allways the political & are now the professed Creatures of the People. This is the Officer and all the Officers of the Crown, upon whom the Governor is to depend for the prosecution of offences arising from the people's disputing the rights of the Crown. I dont mean by this to charge the present Attorney-general[5] with Neglect of his Duty. He is by disposition inclined to the Service of the Crown, & if he was supported by an appointment which would counterballance his dependence upon the people, would I beleive, faithfully attach himself to its intrest. Hitherto He has been kept steady on the Side of the Crown partlly by the influence I have had on him by former services done to him, & partly by the expectation of an establishment of fixed Salaries for the Crown Officers, in which I, having seen the absolute Necessity of such a provision, & imagining that it was as well understood at Westminster as it is here, was some time ago Very sanguine. But this Expectation has of late been so dispreciated,[6] that It will not pass current Any longer: It is allready become a subject of ridicule, with the Newspaper-writers. And when there is an End of all hopes of this kind, which there is allmost now, It cannot be expected of Men in Office, however well they may be disposed to support the rights of the Crown, that they ^should^ sacrifice their intrests to that service without a prospect of being repaid even what they shall have really lost by engaging on that Side.

When An Establishment was to have been made, I should have recommended that there should have been 3 standing Council for the King in this Government namely, the Attorney general, the Sollicitor general & the Advocate general: £500 p^r an would have paid these Officers scantily 800 amply. I much doubt whether the Damage done to the Intrest of the Crown by the Want of such officers may not be rated at as many thousands. Such an appointment would have had one effect, which would have added strength to the Government; this is, it would have made the principal Lawyers look towards the Crown; whereas now they generally turn to the people. When this Business was in agitation I have had private intimations from Gentlemen of the Law of their inclination to quit the Cause of the people for that of the Crown: but now the latter is thought the losing Game & the former the Winning one. The part which the Lawyers take in disputes concerning civil rights is of no little importance to Government.

I write this, My Lord, that too much may not be expected from this distracted, debilitated Government: Evry thing that can be done, by such means as are in the hands of the Governor, will be done. At the same time I have the pleasure to inform your Lordship that the Honour of the Crown is like to be in some measure Vindicated by some prosecutions now carrying on in the Court of Admiralty by order of the Commissioners of the Customs, who wanting not money to go to work with have procured a full discovery of some of the late highhanded breaches of the Laws of trade & particularly that which occasioned the riot on the 10th of June.

I am with great respect, My Lord, Your Lordships
most obedient and most humble Servant

Fra. Bernard

The right honble the Earl of Hillsborough

ALS, RC   CO 5/758, ff 31-34.

Endorsed: [_ _ _]⁷ Govʳ. Bernard (Nᵒ. 36) R 10ᵗʰ Febʸ 1769. B.7.   Variants: CO 5/893, ff 92-94 (dupLS, RC); CO 5/767, ff 194-199 (L, RLbC); BP, 7: 115-118 (L, LbC). Considered by the Board of Trade on 1 Dec. 1769. *JBT*, 13: 125.

FB's comments on reforming the Massachusetts legal system reveal him as a benevolent imperialist, keen to Anglicize institutions and to advance the careers of colonial lawyers, notably Jonathan Sewall. He desired, in replication of the English system, three "standing Council for the King": an advocate general, an attorney general, and a solicitor general. For each he proposed annual Crown salaries of £500 plus additional funds to conduct investigations. Crown salaries would convert all three positions into royal offices. The advocate general, a position held by Jonathan Sewall since Apr. 1767, was already a Crown officer, for his appointment lay with the lords of the Admiralty. He was responsible for the enforcement of the trade laws in the Vice Admiralty courts; the prosecutor (usually the advocate general) and the governor were each entitled to a one-third share of the profits arising from the prosecution of smugglers. Sewall was expected to work closely with Judge Robert Auchmuty and the American Board of Customs.

Sewall was also province attorney general, appointed by the governor with the advice and consent of the Council. He was the government's chief legal adviser and lead prosecutor. But he soon came under pressure from Britain to institute criminal proceedings against rioters who obstructed the implementation of the Townshend Acts. Unsalaried at present, Sewall was reliant upon his income from private practice.

The position of solicitor general, however, had no meaningful portfolio in Massachusetts, yet its introduction allows some inferences to be made as to what the governor might expect of Sewall overall. In England, the solicitor general was the attorney general's deputy and expected to carry out the bulk of the court work; he was also a political appointee and traditionally the attorney general's replacement-in-waiting.

Sewall occupied all three of these offices at the end of 1768, more by accident than design. He had been appointed "special attorney general" on 25 Mar. 1767 on the understanding that he would succeed the elderly incumbent attorney general, Jeremiah Gridley. Doubts concerning the legality of Sewall's special commission prompted FB to create the new position of solicitor general, on 24 Jun.⁸ Gridley died on 7 Sept. and Sewall's commission as attorney general took effect on 18 Nov.

FB's accounts of Sewall's dispute with the Customs Board (in **Nos. 719** and **728**) hint at the probability that Sewall had other sources of information, perhaps in the Whig camp.

⇥ 136 ⇤

The most likely person was his old friend John Adams, who had acquired a reputation as a skilled lawyer (and whose recent handling of cases concerning admiralty matters had bolstered his private practice). Nowhere in his correspondence does FB mention that Sewall, acting on his behalf, approached John Adams with the offer of the advocate general's office. Adams noted the governor thought him the "best entitled" of any province lawyer to fill the position, "and he had determined Accordingly, to give it to me" pending confirmation by the king. Adams, a committed Whig, refused without hesitation.[9] The exact date when Sewall approached Adams is unknown, but it was probably in July soon after Sewall had threatened to resign (**No. 728**). Bringing in Adams as advocate general, would have freed Sewall to concentrate on his attorney general's duties, especially if FB were to give the solicitor general's office to another of their colleagues, such as Samuel Quincy or Samuel Fitch.[10]

FB's end of year review of the effectiveness of Crown law officers touched upon some of the issues and concerns raised by Jonathan Sewall in his roles as advocate general and attorney general. As advocate general, Sewall was responsible for the prosecution of John Hancock and his associates arising from the seizure of Hancock's *Liberty* on 10 Jun., a task for which he mustered little enthusiasm. (The prospect of prosecuting fellow Whig Hancock, may have played some part in Adams refusing the governor's offer to become Sewall's replacement.) FB's warning that Hillsborough should not expect "too much" from the prosecution of Hancock and his men is probably indicative that he shared Sewall's concerns about obtaining evidence to secure convictions for smuggling (see the source note **No. 678**).[11] Also, FB may have been sympathetic to Sewall's desire to preserve the independence of both his legal offices from the interference of the commissioners, yet he was more interested in obtaining a salaried law officer prepared to do the government's bidding. FB likely doubted the durability of Sewall's political loyalty. At least such might be inferred from his intriguing comment about the risk of acting on "private intimations from Gentlemen of the Law of their inclination to quit the Cause of the people for that of the Crown": this may be a reference to the failed attempt to turn John Adams.[12]

On 29 Oct., Sewall filed *in personam* actions against Hancock and five of his men. With penalties set at £9,000 per person, FB (as governor) and Sewall (as prosecutor) were entitled to one-third of the profits from a successful prosecution. The extraordinarily high penalties included a fine set at three-times the value of property seized, and reflected Hancock's enormous wealth. Hancock was bailed at £3,000 until 7 Nov. when Sewall presented informations in the New England Admiralty Court. Hancock was defended by John Adams. The trial proceedings were reported in the radical "Journal of the Times" and serialized in the New York and Boston newspapers.[13] They illuminated the glaring weaknesses of the prosecution case, above all the failure to persuade any witness to provide testimony of Hancock's criminality. On 25 Mar., the Customs Board agreed with Sewall that the prosecution should be abandoned.[14] While Hancock and Sewall appeared to settle their differences in the following years, in the aftermath of the Boston Tea Party of 1773, Attorney General Sewall was obliged to make plans to prosecute Hancock and other leading Whigs for treason.[15] By that time, after a long courtship, Hancock was engaged to be married to Sewall's wife's sister, Dorothy Quincy (1747-1830), though the marriage itself was delayed by politics and war until 1 Aug. 1775.[16]

1. **No. 661**, *Bernard Papers*, 4: 271-276.

2. **No. 660**, ibid., 266-270.

3. On 29 Jul. the Governor and Council directed the attorney general to prosecute "all persons guilty of the Riots and disorders of the 10th or that any way aided or abetted the same." CO 5/827, ff 53-56.

4. The attorney general did not receive an annual grant of salary from the General Court, but was allowed expenses. In 1772, his salary was paid by the Crown from revenue raised by the tax on tea. He was permitted to carry on his business as advocate for private individuals, as was his counterpart in England until 1895.

5. Jonathan Sewall.

6. That is "depreciated".

7. Obscured in the fold of the binding.

8. Berkin, *Jonathan Sewall*, 43.

9. Lyman H. Butterfield, ed., *The Diary and Autobiography of John Adams*, 4 vols. (Cambridge, Mass., 1961), 3: 287-288.

10. Sewall may have nominally continued to hold the solicitor general's position following his appointment as attorney general until he was replaced by Samuel Quincy (1735-89) on 21 Mar. 1771. William H. Whitmore, *The Massachusetts Civil List for the Colonial and Provincial Periods* (Albany, 1870), 125.

11. *Bernard Papers*, 4: 307-313.

12. See **No. 728**.

13. The "Journal of the Times" or "Journal of Occurrences," which first appeared in October, also detailed casual confrontations between Bostonians and soldiers and provided day-by-day commentaries on the business of the Governor and Council (see **No. 748**). Dickerson, *Boston Under Military Rule, 1768-1769, as revealed in a Journal of the Times*.

14. L. Kinvin Wroth and Hiller B. Zobel, eds., *Legal Papers of John Adams*, 3 vols. (Cambridge, Mass., 1965), 2: 181-191. The only reliable account of the trial by Hancock's several biographers is William M. Fowler, Jr., *The Baron of Beacon Hill: A Biography of John Hancock* (Boston, 1980), 100-101.

15. See John Adams to James Warren, Boston, 22 Dec. 1773, *Papers of John Adams*, 1: 2-3.

16. The Quincy-Hancock-Sewall connection is not discussed in Ellen C. D. Q. Woodbury, *Dorothy Quincy, wife of John Hancock: with events of her time* (Washington, D.C., 1901), 50-93.

720 | To the American Board of Customs

Copy.

Boston Dec[r]. 22. 1768.

Gentlemen

You have made application to each of us separately[1] and desired our answer to the following questions viz[t].

1st. Whether it is our opinion that, at the time you went on board the Romney Man of War,[2] you cou'd have remained in safety at Boston?

2. Whether if you had remained in Boston, and any violence had been offered to your persons or properties, there was a probability of your receiving protection from Government, or otherwise?

3. Whether you could have returned to town, and have executed your Commission there in safety, before the arrival of his Majestys troops?

4. Whether your retiring to the Castle as a place of Security, and remaining there in the exercise of your Commission, were not the best measures you cou'd take in the circumstances of affairs, for the service of Government, and the honor of your Commission?

We have thought to confer together, and finding that we are all of one sentiment; we think it most convenient to give you a joint answer.

And to your first question, we say.

That we are of opinion from the Spirit which had been excited in the populace against all the Commissioners of the Customs, except M[r]. Temple, you cou'd not have remained long in safety in the town of Boston after the seizure of the Sloop Liberty; but wou'd have been in great danger of violence to your persons and properties, from a mob, which at that time, it was generally expected wou'd be raised for that purpose.

To the second we say.

That it had been found by experience that the authority of Government was insufficient to restrain, suppress, or punish, the several Mobs which had been assembled since the 14.th of Aug[st] 1765, in some of which, felonious acts of violence had been commited. And we are of opinion, that at the time you retired to the Castle, there was no probability that the same authority cou'd have had any greater force in restraining, suppressing, or punishing a mob raised against the four Commissioners of the Customs, than any other mob which preceded it.

To the third, we say.

That we are of opinion, that you cou'd not have returned to town, and executed Your Commission with safety, at any time after your withdraw[al],[3] before the arrival of His Majestys troops.

To the fourth, we say.

That we know of no better measure you cou'd have taken, than your retiring to Castle William, there being no place within this Province, where your persons wou'd have been equally safe, and where the honour of His Majesty's Commission could be better maintained; and where it could be exercised with more convenience to his Subjects.

We are with great regard. Gentlemen. Your most obedient humble Servants.

Fra Bernard
Tho Hutchinson
And[w]. Oliver.
Rob[t]. Auchmuty

To the Hon[ble]. Henry Hulton. William Burch. Charles Paxton John Robinson Commissioners of His Majesty's Customs, in Boston.

L, Copy   T 1/465, ff 311-312.

Endorsed: Boston Dec[r]. 22. 1768. Copy of a letter from The Governor, L[t]. Governor, Secretary of the Province, & Judge of the Admiralty, to four of the Comm[rs]. of the Customs. Read 6th. June 1769.

Having returned to the Boston Customhouse and their private residences in the first week of November, the Customs commissioners approached FB and his "cabinet" of advisers to provide letters of reference justifying their retreat after the *Liberty* riot and their five-month sojourn at Castle William. It was probably a precautionary exercise, lest the British government mounted an investigation. The commissioners could count on the support of FB, who remained vulnerable to criticism by their disgruntled colleague John Temple.

---

1. Probably orally, for there is no extant correspondence on this matter in the papers of FB and TH.
2. Over 11 and 12 Jun. 1768.
3. Editorially supplied for purposes of clarification.

721 | To John Pownall

Private & Confidential

Boston Dec 24 1768

Dear S[r]

The inclosed Letter is the Result of divers Conferences I have had with some of the cheif Members of the Government & the principal Gentlemen of the Town, in the Course of which I have scarce ever met with a Difference to the Opinions there laid down. I have been frequently importuned to write to the Minister upon these Subjects, that the fair Opportunity which now offers to crush the Faction,[1] reform the Government, & restore Peace & Order may not be lost. I have however declined it not thinking it decent in me to appear to dictate to the Minister so far as to prescribe a Set of Measures. Besides I have thought the Subject & manner of treating it too delicate for a public Letter. However as it appears to me that the Wellfare of this Province, the Honour of the British Government & the future Connexion between them both depend upon the right Improvements[. *For*][2] the Time present I have put the Thoughts to writing in a Letter, in which I have avoided all Personalities which discover the Writer & even the signing & addressing it. If these Hints are like to be of Use communicate them in such a Manner that the Writer may not be known unless it is in Confidence. If they come too late or disagree with the present System destroy the Paper. All I can say for them is they are fully considered & are well intended.

I am &c

J Pownall Esq[r]

L, LbC BP, 7: 252.

Probably in handwriting of Thomas Bernard.

The enclosure (not found) was probably a private paper for Hillsborough on the reform of colonial government and imperial administration. FB had periodically urged reform in his correspondence with ministers and friends. This latest paper probably discussed some of the issues FB raised in **No. 719**, including the appointment of three chief legal officers. It was drafted after consultation with a hand-picked set of advisers; their identities are unknown, but from the government side could have included TH, Andrew Oliver, and Jonathan Sewall (who presently held all three positions: advocate general, attorney general, and solicitor general). The "principal Gentlemen of the Town" were unlikely to have been councilors associated with the Whig Bowdoin and may have included more conservative Whigs or merchants who had leased property to the British Army.

It is unfortunate that the group's paper has not survived for it was considered by the British cabinet. In **No. 743**, John Pownall indicated the paper "had a very considerable weight" on ministerial planning in the spring of 1769. In the context of reforming colonial government, the group recommended the "disqualification [*from office*] of persons referr'd to in that letter," a list that probably included James Bowdoin. If that were the case then this might provide a personal motive for Bowdoin secretly purloining copies of FB letters on Council business (for which see the **Introduction**, p.8).

---

1. This may be a reference to the trial of John Hancock, which had commenced on 7 Nov. and to which FB alludes in **No. 719**.

2. Editorially supplied. Text may be obscured in the gutter of the binding.

722 | *From the Earl of Hillsborough*

(Nᵒ. 22.)

Whitehall 24ᵗʰ: December 1768.

Sir,

I have received and laid before the King your dispatches, Nᵒˢ. 29, 30, and 31,[1] and as every circumstance relative to the state of your Government is now before Parliament, I shall hope to be able to send you very soon the result of their proceedings. In the mean time[2] I am to acquaint you that His Majesty approves your conduct in every part of it, and sees with concern and dissatisfaction how greatly His Service is obstructed, and the Dignity and Spirit of His Government destroyed, by the unwarrantable & unjustifiable behaviour of the Council upon many occasions, and more especially with respect to quartering His Majesty's Troops; a Service, in the facilitating of which they were called upon, by every consideration of Duty to the Crown and of regard to the Peace of the Public to exert themselves to the utmost of their power.

I am with great truth & esteem Sir, Your Most Humble and Obedient Servant

Hillsborough

Governor Bernard

LS, RC

BP, 12: 25-28.

Endorsed by FB: Earl of Hillsborough Dec 24 1768. Docket by Thomas Bernard: Approv^g his Conduct.   Variants: CO 5/757, ff 522-523 (ALS, RC); CO 5/765, ff 53-54 (L, LbC); *Letters to the Ministry* (1st ed.), 76; *Letters to the Ministry* (repr.), 102-103. Copies were laid before both houses of Parliament on 20 Jan. 1769. *HCJ*, 32: 124; *HLJ*, 32: 229.

---

1. **Nos. 703**, **706**, and **708**.
2. Left marginalia: there is a red line from here to the end the paragraph, probably added by FB.

723 | *From John Pownall*

Dear Sir

Inclosed I send you the resolutions & proceedings of the house of Lords upon the publick transactions at Boston in the Course of this Year, which trifling & ineffectual as I think them, will be rendred more so by a Spirit of procrastination that destroys the Spirit of business, & for the Commons to whom these resolutions have been communicated for concurrence have postponed the consideration of them till next month at their meeting after the holidays.

I know you will say that it would have been better to have done nothing than not to have done more — and I wish the opinion may not be justified by the Event.

I will not attempt to tell you all that passed in the House of Lords when these resolutions were agreed to but I must not deny you the satisfaction of knowing that your conduct & character was vindicated & supported in the warmest manner by our noble friend Lord Hillsborough, who upon this occasion as he has upon every other & in every place spoke of you in the fullest commendation.

I want very much to know your real sentiments upon the present very critical situation of american affairs and the more fully I hear those sentiments the greater will be the obligation conferred upon

Your most faithfull & aff^t. Humble Servt.

J Pownall

Decr. 24. 1768

Govr. Bernard.

ALS, RC   BP, 12: 29-32.

Minor emendations not shown. Endorsed by FB: Mr J Pownall Dec 24 1768.   Enclosure: resolutions of both Houses of Parliament, relative to the public transactions in His Majesty's Province of Massachusetts Bay, [*15 and 16 Dec. 1768*]. FB received Pownall's letter on 24 Mar. and replied the following day with **No. 758**.

On 28 Nov., the British government presented to the Houses of Parliament some sixty items of official correspondence concerning the American Colonies, many of them letters from FB, plus their enclosures. A second set of letters, mainly authored by Commodore Samuel Hood and Lt. Col. William Dalrymple, was presented on 7 Dec. On 15 Dec., the House of Lords adopted eight resolutions respecting Massachusetts moved by Hillsborough. (See **Introduction**, 11-14.) While the resolutions signaled the continuation of the government's tougher approach, Pownall's disappointment with their efficacy probably sprang from the failure to reform the Massachusetts Charter or act upon other suggestions of FB's, such as introducing Crown salaries or restoring the government officers to the Council.[1] Much of the criticism, as observed, focused on the absence of specific measures. The earl of Shelburne, the former secretary of state, "spoke rather darkly," thinking the resolutions "ineffectual" though "not improper" if "leveled only at Boston."[2]

Neither FB nor anyone else in or close to the provincial government was keen on apprehending the Massachusetts Whigs on charges of treason or collecting the evidence for a Crown commission. In replying to Pownall, FB stressed that the Lords' resolutions were accorded a lukewarm reception by the friends of government and were "laughed at by the Faction." (**No. 758**.) The Whigs' friends in London, meanwhile—notably, William Bollan—now fretted that if treason trials were to be averted urgent action was required to combat the negative impressions created by FB's reports in Whitehall, Westminster, and the Court at St. James's Palace. (See **No. 761** and **Introduction**, 14-21.)

The Massachusetts resolutions were received by the House of Commons on 16 Dec. and considered by the whole House on 26 Jan. 1769, along with the mass of correspondence that Lord North had presented to the House on 28 Nov. and 7 Dec. During an extended debate, FB's conduct was reviewed by speakers on both sides. The Commons finally approved the Lords' resolutions and address to the king on 8 Feb.[3]

---

1. *HLJ*, 32: 209-210. For a brief discussion of the debates see Nicolson, *The 'Infamas Govener'*, 188-190; **Introduction**, 14-20.

2. Quoted in the Hardwicke Papers, cited in Wright, *Cavendish's Debates*, 1: 193-194.

3. *HCJ*, 32: 185. The resolutions as adopted by the House of Commons were printed in the *Boston Gazette*, 17 Apr. 1769.

724 | To the Earl of Hillsborough

Nº 37

Boston Dec 26th 1768

My Lord

In my Letter Nº 33[1] I informed your Lordship that I should endeavour to reform the Bench of Justices, by appointing some new Justices, & by engaging proper Gentlemen now in the Commission to qualify themselves to act therein. In the first of these I have been able to appoint only 2 Gentlemen[2] who would undertake to act & who I thought proper for the Office; altho' I offered it to some others, who declined it upon the Terms of undertaking to act, which I made inseparable from the appointment.

In the second Method, I applied to about 12 Gentlemen at once with the privity of one another; among whom were the Secretary & Mr Flucker of the Council a Gentleman singular for his fidelity to the King, both of which & one or two others engaged to act if I could engage 4 or 5 others to join with them. For this Purpose I invited those, whom I had applied to, to dine with me, when we talked the Matter over; but I could not engage them to join in any Number for the intention proposed & was obliged to refer it to a farther time. Some time after Mr Flucker[3] who had undertook to sollicit this business with the Gentlemen separately, reported to me that He could not engage any Number of them to act. The Reason given for their refusal was that there were among the present acting Justices so many that were leaders or creatures of the faction, that if they were to associate with them, they must expect to be affronted & insulted & by all ways & means made sick of the Office; that whilst there sat upon the bench persons who had publickly avowed the principles of opposition to the Kings Government & even resistance to his legal Authority & had openly & in the day time supported & headed the mobs raised for that purpose, they could not think that Bench to be a Seat of honour; They must therefore wait, till they see what Steps will be taken for restoring the Authority of this Government; and punishing the disturbers of the peace of it: and if the Justices who have cooperated with the faction in opposition & resistance to the King, shall be removed from their Commissions, either by superseding their particular Commissions or, what would be much better, by superseding of the whole Commission & appointing a New Commission, some of them & others as good would be ready to go upon the bench.

I could not oppose the force of this reasoning, but was obliged to give up the urging this proposal for the present, even with those who had half-engaged; as they had made it a condition that others should join with them. I shall however neglect no oportunity of adding a good Man to the Bench when I can. But the friends of Government have not yet recover'd themselves: personal intimidation indeed has been a good deal removed by the arrival of the troops; but political intimidation is not much abated, nor as yet ^has^ had any proper releif. Great Pains have been taken to work up an actual Warfare between the Town & the Soldiery: but these Attempts have hitherto been defeated by the prudence of the officers & the patience of the Soldiers. In this infamous Work, some of the Justices have laboured in granting Warrants against Soldiers for obeying orders & doing their duty according to the usual discipline; And it is threatned that there will be a prosecution at the quarter Sessions against the officers & Men who releive the guards on a Sunday, which they say is a breach of the Sabbath. I shant wonder if it is so: but in such Case, I shall interpose by ordering a *Noli prosequi*.[4]

I am, with great respect, My Lord, your Lordships most obedient & most humble servant

Fra Bernard

The right honorable the Earl of Hillsborough.

ALS, RC   CO 5/758, ff 38-40.

Endorsed: Boston 26th. Decr. 1768. Governor Bernard (No. 37) R 24th: Feby 1769. B.9.   Variants: CO 5/893, ff 96-97 (dupLS, RC); CO 5/767, ff 202-204 (L, RLbC); BP, 7: 118-121 (L, LbC). Hillsborough acknowledged receipt in a letter of 1 Mar., intending to delay replying until the Parliament had completed its present deliberations on American affairs.[5] BP, 12: 61-64. FB's letter was considered by the Board of Trade on 1 Dec. 1769. *JBT*, 13: 125.

---

1. No. 711.

2. The appointments of James Murray and William Coffin Jr. were approved by the Council on 7 Dec. CO 5/827, ff 68-69.

3. Flucker would appear to have distanced himself from the Whig councilors, not having joined them in signing the address to Gen. Gage (**Appendix 1**).

4. *Nolle prosequi*, meaning not to pursue, a legal term and proceeding indicating that a prosecutor, plaintiff, or pursuer no longer wishes to pursue an action.

5. Hillsborough's next letter, of 22 Mar., was a private notification that FB had been made a baronet (**No. 755**); his next business letter, dated 24 Mar., announced FB's recall (**No. 757**).

725 | A Plan for an American Bishop

[1768?]

A Plan for appointing a Bishop to reside in America for the Purpose of Ordination, & for the Support of such Bishop in his Residence there.

By an Act of the 26 Hen 8 Ca 14.[1]

for the Nomination of Suffragans & Confirmation of them, It is enacted that every Bishop being disposed to have any Suffragan shall name two discreet spiritual Persons & present them to the King praying him to give to one of them the Dignity of a Bishop and the King shall have Power to give to one of them the Title of a Bishop of any of the Suffragan Sees within the Province whereof the Bishop presenting him is.

And the King shall present such Bishop to the Archbishop of the Province requiring him to consecrate him; who shall consecrate him accordingly.

Provided that no such Suffragan shall take or receive any Profits from their Sees nor use or exercise any Jurisdiction or episcopal Power within any Diocese or Place in this realm or elsewhere within the Kings Dominions but only such Profits Power & Authority as shall be licenced & limited to them to take & execute by any Bishop within their Diocese to whom they shall be Suffragans, by Commission under his Seal & for such time only as shall be limited in such Commission. And the Residence of such Suffragan shall serve for Residence upon any other his Benefice & such Suffragan may have two Benefices with Cure.[2]

Upon this Act this Proposal for appointing a Bishop to reside in America is founded.

The Bishop of London is generally reputed to be the Diocesan of America; and has been usually confirmed in that Office by a Commission from the King. Let that Commission if it does not subsist now, be revived with such additional Powers, if any, as may be wanted for the present Purpose.

Let this Bishop present two Divines to the King praying him to appoint one of them to be his Suffragan.

Let the Person so to be appointed be previously engaged to reside in America for a certain time and let him be provided with Benefices in England sufficient to support him in America.

It would not be amiss if some very good Benefice which did not necessarily require Residence should be appointed to this particular Service, and, as it were, annexed to it.

By the Act the Office of Suffragan will be a Dispensation of Residence upon his Benefices.

Let the Bishop of London grant to the Suffragan a Commission empowering him to ordain and confirm in America with such other Powers as shall be thought proper carefully avoiding the Exercise of any coercive Jurisdiction.

When the time limited for this Service is expired, let the Suffragan be rewarded with an English Bishoprick; and let this Service be considered as a Step to a Bishoprick.

Besides the Support which such Suffragan will derive from his Benefices in England, he will receive some Assistance from the Benefactions allready made for the Support of a Bishop in America; & there is no Doubt but many other Benefactions will be added to them when an Appointment has once taken Place.

It is not improbable that the Residence of the Bishop will be sollicited by different Provinces & Provincial Appointments will be made to engage such Residence.

If more than one Bishop shall be thought necessary to America another may be made in the like Manner; and a third also for the West Indian Islands if wanted.

At first it will be best to appoint only one and let him be settled with as little Shew & Parade as possible.

The properest Place for the first Settlement will be at Perth Amboy in New Jersey where there is a very good House built for the Governor (who at present chuses to reside at Burlington) ready to receive him; and the Inhabitants who are allmost wholly of the Church of England are well disposed to this Appointment.

After the Business is quieted the Bishop may be removed wherever it may be thought more proper viz to Philadelphia, if there is to be but one for the whole Continent, or to New York or Williamsburgh, if there are to be two. But this should wait for an Invitation.

By this Proceeding all the Difficulties which have hitherto obstructed the appointing a Bishop in America will be removed. The pretended Jealousy of the Dissenters of the Admission of a Bishop into America, which is generally artificial, will be exposed, if they should urge it against an Appointment made according to Law and granting to those of the Church of England no greater Priviledges than what the Dissenters in America of all Denominations enjoy themselves, namely a Power of continuing the Succession of their Ministry within their own Country, & of using the religious rights which belong to their Church.

The Difficulty also of providing for an American Bishop, with which this Business has hitherto laboured more than it ought to have done, will be removed by making----a Provision for him out of the Revenues of the Church of England, which by laying it upon some of the Dignities may be done without any Disservice to the Church.

As for establishing Church Discipline over the Ministers of the Church of England in America, otherwise than by a voluntary Submission (in which way it is now exercised with Effect by the dissenting Ministers of all Denominations) as it cannot be done at all without the Authority of Parliament, nor with Propriety without the Concurrence & Good Will of the Ministers of the Church & their Congregations, it would be better to postpone it to a more proper Season, which probably the Appointment before recommended will soon bring forward.

Ms, AC   BP, 12: 261-264.

In handwriting of Thomas Bernard. The "Plan for an American Bishop" is undated but may have been prepared for the Rev. Henry Caner, rector of Christ Church, when he traveled to England in the late spring of 1768 (**No. 620**).[3] Thomas Bradbury Chandler's *An Appeal to the Public in Behalf of the Church of England in America* (New York, 1767) had generated fresh controversy over the Anglicans' campaign for an American episcopate, and drew replies from spokesmen for other denominations throughout the colonies, including Massachusetts' Rev. Charles Chauncy, to which Chandler published rejoinders.[4] Equally, FB's "Plan" might have been drawn up following the death of Archbishop of Canterbury Thomas Secker on 3 Aug. and in anticipation of being able to influence his successor.[5]

The Church of England was a minority church in New England. Membership was elitist in Boston and Cambridge, but historians no longer think it so socially exclusive in the rest of the region. FB's plan sought to address one major concern of the Anglican clergy: that the ordination of priests could only be carried out in England, by the bishop of London, whose diocese extended to the American Colonies. The appointment of a "suffragan" or assistant bishop to reside in the colonies would obviate the requirement for ordinands to cross the Atlantic. Chandler had previously considered the idea but did not accord it the pride of place that FB did in his "Plan."[6] Criticism of Chandler by Congregationalists and Presbyterians, which played on colonial apprehension that taxes would be levied to support a full bishop and a new American diocese, might explain why FB proposed a suffragan bishop maintained from current church revenues and did not argue for extending ecclesiastical "Discipline." The controversy over the episcopate lacked the intensity of the early 1760s, when it sparked bitter exchanges between clergymen, but colonists alarmed by Parliamentary taxation remained apprehensive of being directed to maintain an American bishop.[7] With this "Plan" FB revealed himself to be an Imperial Anglican,[8] albeit one who better understood the extent of opposition from the Dissenters.

---

1. The Suffragan Bishops Act, 26 Hen 8, c. 14 (1534), listed those sees considered suitable for the "Nomination of Suffragans," to which FB proposed adding the diocese of the bishop of London, whose ecclesiastical jurisdiction extended to the American Colonies. The paragraphs following the citation of the act do not paraphrase or quote its provisions, and are original in construction.

2. That is, a parish in the charge of a rector, vicar, or curate.

3. The Rev. Henry Caner (1700-92) was rector of King's Chapel where FB worshipped. His journey to London was ostensibly to represent the interests of New England's Anglican clergy (of which convention he was its recognized leader) to Richard Terrick (1710-77), the bishop of London, 1764-77. Caner pressed the case for an American episcopate, of which he had been a firm advocate, and may have carried with him a copy of FB's draft plan to establish a bishop at Perth Amboy, N.J. **No. 725**. Caner returned to Boston in Apr. 1769. *Boston Chronicle*, 21-24 Aug. 1769.

4. Charles Chauncy, *The Appeal to the Public Answered in Behalf of the Non-Episcopal Churches of America* (Boston, 1768); Thomas Bradbury Chandler, *The Appeal Defended; Or the Proposed American Episcopate Vindicated* (New York, 1769). The debate can be followed in Carl Bridenbaugh, *Mitre and Sceptre: Transatlantic Faiths, Ideas, Personalities and Politics, 1689-1775* (New York, 1962), 289-292.

5. Thomas Secker, (1693-1768). FB wrote a letter of congratulation to the new archbishop, Frederick Cornwallis (1713-83), on 24 Oct. BP, 6: 148-149.

6. Thomas Bradbury Chandler, *An Appeal to the Public in Behalf of the Church of England in America* (New York, 1767), 50-51, 80-81.

7. See Jack M. Sosin, "Proposal for Establishing Anglican Bishops in the Colonies," *Journal of Ecclesiastical History* 13 (1962): 76-84; Bruce E. Steiner, "Anglican Officeholding in Pre-Revolutionary Connecticut: The Parameters of New England Community," *WMQ* 31 (1974): 369-406; John F. Woolverton, *Colonial Anglicanism in North America* (Detroit, 1984), 220-233.

8. The imperial dimensions of American Anglicanism are discussed in Peter M. Doll, *Revolution, Religion, and National Identity: Imperial Anglicanism in British North America, 1745–1795* (Madison, NJ, 2000).

726 | *From Lord Barrington*

Cavendish Square Jan: 2ᵈ. 1769.

Dear Sir,

I have received your Excellency's Letter of the 22ᵈ. Oct. and the Duplicate.[1] All your Letters convey to me very unfavourable Ideas of your part of the world. There is only one comfortable circumstance, which is that the troops are quietly lodged in Boston. This will for a time preserve the ^publick^ Peace, and secure the persons of the few who are well affected to the mother Country. I wish there were a better prospect of such measures at home, as will tend to preserve the Obedience of the Colonies, and such have been proposed; I can moreover assure you that they have been relish'd by the majority of the Cabinet; but by some fatal catastrophe, two or three men there, with less ability, less credit, less authority & less responsibility than the rest, have carry'd their point and produced that flimsey unavailing Address which has past the Lords, has been sent down for concurrence to the Commons,[2] and which will be considered by them after the Holydays. I think there is a bare possibility that it may be amended in that House of Parliament. I think however it is determin'd by all the ministers, not to repeal Mʳ. Townshends Acts till the Colonies have submitted thoroughly to them.

The Picture I have drawn of things here will not encrease your inclination to remain at Boston. I earnestly wish you were removed to some other Government; or provided for at home ^to^ which your Services abroad give you the justest claim. I have said & shall say this at all proper times & to all proper persons. I am fully instructed as to your wishes concerning other Governments, except that I am not clear whether you should like Barbadoes if it were to become vacant; and in that respect I beg full & clear information. You may be assured that I shall do you every good office in my power, according to your own Plan. As to S. Carolina it is not vacant, or likely to become so,[3] & I well remember'd your sentiments concerning that province.

I beg you will present my best Complim[ts]. to M[rs]. Bernard and to all my Cousins. I wish them & you many happy years and am with the most perfect regard Dear Sir

Your Excellency's most faithful & most obedient humble Serv[t].

Barrington.

ALS, RC BP, 12: 33-36.

Endorsed by FB: Lord Barrington d Jan 2 1769 R Mar 14.   FB replied with **No. 753**.

Barrington's intimation that the Grafton administration was not considering repealing the Townshend Revenue Act, 7 Geo. 3, c.46 (1767) was accurate. Having defended policy in parliamentary debates, ministers were determined not to back down on the question of legislative supremacy; but they were not averse to exploring options that could restore equilibrium in British-American relations. In Jan. 1769, merchants and colonial agents, ably assisted by the Rockingham Whigs, campaigned for the repeal of the Revenue Act.[4] The administration was also "under pressure" from parliamentarians (including Barrington) and governors (including FB) to strengthen imperial authority. Barrington was deeply disappointed by the lack of practical measures in the Lords' resolutions on Massachusetts, a view partly informed by the reports he had been receiving from FB.[5]

---

1. **No. 705**.

2. The House of Lords adopted eight resolutions on 15 Dec. and passed them to the House of Commons the next day. See source note to **No. 723**.

3. Lord Charles Greville Montagu (1741-84) was governor of South Carolina 1765-73.

4. See Thomas, *Townshend Duties Crisis*, 123-126.

5. See the source note to **No. 723**.

Augustus Henry FitzRoy, third Duke of Grafton. Oil on canvas, by Pompeo Batoni, 1762. © National Portrait Gallery, London.

727 | From the Earl of Hillsborough

N°. 23.

Whitehall 4th January 1769.

Sir,

I have received and laid before The King your Dispatches N[os] 32, and 33,[1] which appear to contain only further accounts of the obstruction given by the Council to Government in general, and of their determined resolution to pursue a Conduct that can have no other effect than to defeat the Measures His Majesty has thought fit to adopt for restoring peace and good order in the Town of Boston. __ As the State of the Province is still under the consideration of Parliament,[2] I have nothing to add to what I have already said to you in my Letter N°. 22, upon that Subject,[3] and have only to repeat to you that so soon as the proceedings of Parliament are brought to a conclusion, I shall not fail to transmit to you the result of their deliberations, in the meantime, I am persuaded there will be on your part, no relaxation of that Attention to the execution of your Duty which does you so much credit, and that you will steadily and firmly pursue every Constitutional measure for the support of His Majesty's Authority, and the dignity of His Government.[4]

I am with much Esteem & Regard Sir, Your Most Humble & Obedient Servant

Hillsborough

LS, RC   BP, 12: 37-40.

Annotations were probably added by FB. Endorsed by FB: Earl of Hillsborough d Jan 4 1769 r Mar. 14. Docket by Thomas Bernard: That Am Affairs are before Parliament__.   Variants: CO 5/758, ff 1-2 (L, AC); CO 5/765, ff 54-55 (L, LbC); *Letters to the Ministry* (1st ed.), 76-77; *Letters to the Ministry* (repr.), 103. Copies were laid before both houses of Parliament on 20 Jan. 1769. *HCJ*, 32: 124; *HLJ*, 32: 229.

The House of Lords' resolutions on Massachusetts and its address to the king, adopted on 15 Dec., were considered by a committee of the whole House of Commons on 26 Jan. Initiated by the Grafton administration, these proceedings constituted the most significant parliamentary debate on British colonial policy and American affairs in nearly two years. Several speakers reviewed FB's correspondence that had been presented on 28 Nov., 7 Dec., and 20 Jan.—all of them concerned to establish if the governor had presented evidence sufficient to warrant the administration's proposal to investigate treason. Opposition Rockingham Whigs instead advocated a parliamentary inquiry into the situation in Massachusetts, accusing FB of being a ministerial tool and of willfully exacerbating the crisis by his high-handed treatment of the colonists; they accepted the House of Representatives' contention that FB had misrepresented colonists' views and exaggerated their radicalism, but did not explicitly accuse FB of manufacturing a sense crisis (which he had) in order to obtain British troops.[5] Hillsborough, North, and Grafton could have chosen to make

FB a scapegoat for the administration's failure to prevent an escalation of the situation in Boston; Hillsborough had already expressed concerns to FB about the probity of his reporting. But Hillsborough pressed ahead with FB's proposals for reforming the Massachusetts government, which he laid before the cabinet on 13 Feb. (for which see the source note to **No. 740**). Only when these proposals were rejected, did Hillsborough decide to recall FB, whilst politely expressing his and the king's continued support.

1. **Nos. 709** and **711**.

2. See the summary in the source note to **No. 723**.

3. **No. 722**.

4. Left marginalia: the passage "I am . . . Government" is marked by a red line in the margin and by lines at the beginning and end of the text.

5. A close reading of the debates of 25 and 26 Jan. is provided in the **Introduction**, 15-20, and the editorial commentaries to **Appendix 2**.

728 | To the American Board of Customs

Province house, Janr 6th. 1769.

Gentlemen

In answer to your Letter of the 3[d] instant,[1] I shall endeavour to recollect the particulars of what M[r] Sewall informed me concerning the advices he had received of the Commissioners of the Customs having sent home Complaints against him for neglect of the Duties of his Office.[2]

About the beginning of July last, he came to me & desired to resign his place of Advocate General, and gave for Reason that he could not please the Commissioners of the Customs, for thô he had always done his best for the King's Service yet they had sent home Complaints against him for neglect of his Duty, in such a manner as must bring the censure of his Majesty's Ministers upon him.[3] I endeavoured to persuade him that he must have been misinformed; for that as his Office was in my Department I did not think that the Commissioners would send home a formal complaint against him without acquainting me with it, especially as some of them knew that I had recommended him to the Office; also that I was frequently in company with four of the Commissioners and should have heard of some of the particulars of the Charge against him, ^if any such had been made^; but I never heard of any articles sufficient to ground a formal Complaint upon, and therefore did not believe that there had been any such Complaint; I therefore cautioned him against giving Credit to this Information, He said that he should soon know whether it was true or not, from a Gentleman who could not be mistaken.

Some time after, about the End of July, M[r] Sewall came to me again, and told me that M[r] Lisle the Sollicitor of the Customs had according to his Promise introduced M[r] Venner Secretary of the Customs[4] to him to confirm this Information; that they both dined with him at his house in Cambridge on the 20th. of July; and that M[r] Venner in the presence of M[r] Lisle had assured him that the Commissioners had sent to the Lords of the Treasury two Memorials against him, with one letter to the Secretary;[5] that the memorials had represented him as too much attached to the people and unfaithful in his Office and prayed to be relieved;[6] from whence he (M[r] Sewall) concluded, that if these Memorials were attended to, he must expect to be dismissed from His Office with disgrace; that he was also mentioned to his disadvantage in other Memorials or public Letters, and he believed that there were private Letters sent home against him; and M[r] Sewall added, that he heard from other persons, that upon this occasion M[r] Paxton was most violent against him, and had proposed or made alterations in some of the Expressions of the memorials to make them more severe. I thereupon told him that I was convinced from the last circumstance that the Information was false: for I knew myself that M[r] Paxton when at London had done him many friendly Offices; particularly by sollicting in person with the Lords of the Admiralty his appointment to the Office of Advocate General, and by communicating a Letter which I had wrote to M[r] Paxton in favour of M[r] Sewall to a Minister of State in another Department; and, at Desire, leaving it with him.[7] It was therefore inconceivable that M[r] Paxton should be so firm a Friend to him in London, & in a few months after be so inimical to him at Boston, without any Cause appearing to account for so extraordinary a Change. Upon the whole I asked Mr Sewall if I might communicate this Information to some of the Gentlemen who were charged by it; He answered that Mr Venner had laid him under no obligation of Secrecy and that he required none of me. It may be proper to add in this place, what I have two or three Times heard Mr Sewall say, thô I am not sure that the Time now meant was one of them, thô I believe it was, that Mr Venner told him that he had often put his name to public Letters and afterwards been obliged to contradict them by private.

Some time after having satisfied myself of the Falsity of the Information, & procured some sort of proof that it was so,[8] I saw Mr Sewall again, and communicated to him what I had been made acquainted with concerning it, he seemed surprized & expressed some Resentment against those that had misinformed him, saying, that if the Comm[rs]. would show him the Memorials in Question & thereby convince him that they were not to the purpose which had been reported, he should think himself at Liberty to discover from whence he had his Information, not meaning thereby the Gentlemen who first gave him the Hint of this as his Friends, who most probably were deceived themselves, but that Gentleman (Mr Venner) who must have known the Falsity of what he related, & must have intended to deceive. Soon after which there passed some Letters between the Commissioners and Mr Sewall,[9] as I was informed, in one of which he gave the same Expectation of his making a Discovery of the misinformer, as he had verbally made to me. And I doubted not but he would have given the Commissioners the Satisfaction they had a right to expect from him. But having delayed it for some time, he at length acquainted me that he could not consent to make a formal Discovery of his informer; he has given me no Reasons for this Change of Sentiment, but has hinted that they were of a private nature, and not to be made public. At the same Time he has made no objection to my revealing what passed between us, nor has been under any Reserve in repeating such particulars as I have from Time to Time enquired about. Some of the conversations I had with Mr Sewall were in company with the Lieut. Governor, some between us alone:[10] I cannot ascertain the particular Times, nor do I pretend to repeat the exact Modes of Expression: for having for some months together Expected that Mr Sewall would give an account of this business, and not imagining that I should be called upon for that purpose, I did not charge my Memory with it, as I should otherwise have done: but I believe that I am right in the Substance of what I have now recollected

I am with great Regard Gentlemen Your most obedient humble Servant

(signed) Fra: Bernard.

To the honble The Commissioners of His Majesty's Customs.

L Copy T 1/471, ff 83-85.

Endorsed: Copy of a Letter from Governor Bernard to the Comm^{rs} dated Province house 6th Janr 1769. No. 28 Read 2^d. June 1769. The RC has not been found. This letter was the twenty-eighth enclosure in the memorial of the American Board of Customs to the lords commissioners of the Treasury, Boston, 16 Feb. 1769, pertaining to the suspension of Samuel Venner and David Lisle, T 1/471, ff 435-436.

When Advocate General Jonathan Sewall began the prosecution of John Hancock on 28 Nov. in the Vice Admiralty Court, his relationship with the American Board of Customs commissioners had not improved any. But the dispute which had undermined Sewall's morale and led FB to question his commitment to the government was drawing to a close, as the letter printed here indicates. (See also **Nos. 678**,[11] **710**, and **719**.)

FB managed to persuade the commissioners to show their memorials to himself and to Judge Robert Auchmuty and TH, who in turn assured Sewall that he had not been misrepresented. While Sewall was professionally close to Auchmuty and TH, he probably did not count them as personal friends; he did not accept unreservedly their reassurances when first proffered. FB's intimation that he would have expected the commissioners of Customs to reveal to him any concerns about Sewall—which evidently they chose not to do—also explains why Sewall could not rely solely on the word of a governor obliged to assist the Board. All of this might also explain why FB, TH, and the commissioners pinned the blame for Sewall's dysfunctional relationship with the Customs Board on the two Board officials named in this letter, Samuel Venner and David Lisle. Venner and Lisle were accused of circulating rumors about Sewall's professional abilities, for which both were subsequently suspended. The commissioners also appeased Sewall by allowing him to view the Board's memorials in which he was mentioned. Sewall no longer tried to protect Lisle and Venner, and was prepared to let them suffer humiliation as the price for viewing the documentation (even though it is probable that neither man was the original source of the information that aggrieved Sewall in the first place). To the commissioners, FB, and TH, Samuel Venner was a convenient scapegoat; he was suspended on 19 Jan. 1769 for "malicious" intent "to sow discord between the Commissioners and the Attorney General."[12] The charge asserted that the information Venner passed to Sewall about the commissioners questioning his fitness for office was simply untrue and was an act of "unfaithfulness and malfeasance." However, a close examination of the commissioners' memorial of 12 May reveals, as Sewall always maintained, that the Board had purported to undermine his authority by questioning his competency.[13]

The commissioners emerged from the affair thinking that Sewall might have been acting on information supplied by the disgruntled fifth commissioner, John Temple. Temple was certainly better placed than Venner to cause mischief for his colleagues and the governor. In their memorial reporting the affair and filing the papers, the commissioners expressly noted "Mr Sewall's reluctance to discover his authors, which he can best explain."[14] David Lisle was also suspended for his part in the affair. Both Lisle and Venner petitioned the Treasury for redress on the grounds of unfair treatment, with Venner travelling to London to present a memorial.[15] Both men were exonerated by the Treasury and positions were found for them away from Boston: Venner in London and Lisle in Piscataqua, Maine.[16]

1. T 1/471, ff 77-78.

2. "If Mr Sewall should be thought right in his opinion [*in the Lydia case*], there is a necessity that our Officers should have further powers, otherwise the service cannot, by reason of the severity of the climate in this Country, be carried into effect." American Board of Customs, memorial to the lords commissioners of the Treasury, Boston, 12 May 1768, T 1/465, ff 64-65. For an explanation see the source note to **No. 678**, *Bernard Papers*, 4: 307-313.

3. Sewall offered his resignation upon learning that the commissioners had sought the advice of the English attorney general in the proposed actions against John Hancock, effectively ignoring the opinion he tendered in the *Lydia* case. See **No. 678**, ibid., 307-313.

4. David Lisle was formerly a solicitor to the Wine Licence Office and, having successfully applied for the position of solicitor general to the American Board of Customs, arrived in Boston in May 1768 (whereupon he sent off a report complaining about the lawlessness in the town). T 1/456, ff 132-145; T 1/465, ff 77-78. Samuel Venner assumed that he would be the Board's chief secretary, in accordance with his instructions from the Treasury, though he subsequently complained that even before the Board's departure from London in 1767, the commissioners were determined to reduce his administrative authority and role. T 1/471, ff 491-502.

5. Sewall was probably not aware of the exact items, for FB, TH, and Auchmuty were not shown the full range of documentation. (See the source note to **No. 678**, *Bernard Papers*, 4: 307-313.) There were three memorials of relevance that the American Board of Customs sent to the lords commissioners

of the Treasury: those of 12 Feb. and 28 Mar. (which the provincial officials did not see) and that of 12 May 1768, which mentioned Sewall by name. T 1/465, ff 21-25, 64-65. The letter to the secretary of the Treasury noted here was probably Samuel Venner to Thomas Bradshaw, 7 Jun. 1768, enclosing several cases relating to the enforcement of the Revenue Act (7 Geo. 3, c. 46) for the opinion of the English solicitor of Customs and attorney general.

6. This is not an accurate summation of what the commissioners had written of Sewall (for which see note 2 above). But it probably reflected what FB and the commissioners were both thinking: that Sewall's opinion in the *Lydia* case and his reluctance to prosecute using informations were symptomatic of Whiggish sympathies.

7. FB's account is plausible, given that Paxton had been a firm supporter of the governor and that Sewall was FB's protégé. Paxton traveled to England in the summer of 1766, carrying letters of introduction supplied by FB, in expectation that he would give a favorable report of the governor's conduct. FB's letter to Paxton of 21 Jan. (**No. 530**) intimated that he was appointing Sewall advocate general of Vice Admiralty, his first major office, which was confirmed on 1 Jul. 1767. *Bernard Papers*, 3: 309-312; ADM 2/1057, f 251.

8. After 15 Aug., see source note to **No. 678**, *Bernard Papers*, 4: 307-313.

9. Samuel Venner to Jonathan Sewall, Castle William, 25 Aug. 1768, T 1/471, f 29; Richard Reeve to Sewall, of the same date, ibid., f 31. Sewall wrote to the Board on 5 Aug., and it is to this letter that FB is probably referring. There is an extract in **No. 678**n1, *Bernard Papers*, 4: 312.

10. One meeting is recorded for 9 Nov. **No. 710**.

11. *Bernard Papers*, 4: 307-313.

12. Minutes of the American Board of Customs of 13, 19, and 23 Jan. 1769, T 1/471, ff 14-15.

13. See source note to **No. 678**, *Bernard Papers*, 4: 307-313.

14. American Board of Customs, memorial to the lords commissioners of the Treasury, Boston, 16 Feb. 1769, T 1/471, ff 435-436.

15. Venner's memorial to the Treasury (dated Boston, 29 Apr. 1769) carefully documented his deteriorating relationship with the commissioners before he became embroiled in the Board's dispute with Sewall. T 1/471, ff 491-502.

16. Lords commissioners of the Treasury to the American Board of Customs, Treasury Chambers, 29 Jun. 1769, Customs GB II, 10: 26-31.

729 | To John Pownall

Private

Boston Jan[ry] 13 1769

Dear Sir,

Three Days ago we received a Copy of the King's Speech from New York;[1] you may imagine it has had various Effects with the People here according to their different Arrangements; but it is most apparent among the Friends of Government, who have no Reason to conceal their Joy at seeing the Time coming when this Country will be delivered from the baneful Influence of the Faction who have harrast it so long. For myself I expect the best Consequences of those spirited Measures which the Parliament will undoubtedly adopt at this critical Time. Happily it is not now too late; very soon hence it would have been, and it is hoped that the favorable Opportunity which the Madness of the Leaders of the Faction & the Folly of their followers have put into the Hands of the Government at home to enable it to reform this Government will not be neglected. Never again must be expected so happy an Occasion to do the Necessary Business.

The Assembly at New York has at length declared itself by a Set of Resolutions. As they are not published in the N York Papers, I send you a Copy of them which our Printer has struck off. I think that the second Resolution by its serious & deliberate Explicitness exceeds every Thing that has been published against the Authority of Parliament.[2] It is high Time that the Question whether the Parliament has any Authority over the American Assemblies or not should be settled.

I hinted in a former Letter that great Part of the present Troubles of this Government arose from private Animosities in another Department than mine.[3] The Explanation of this has not gone on so fast as I expected: but I beleive it will begin to be sent home about this Time. I shall give a more explicit Hint of this in a Supplement to this which you must treat confidentially. You may depend upon it, it will be agreeable to the Sentiments of all the principal Officers of the Crown and the cheif Friends of Government.

I send this with a Cover directed[4] to you inclosing a Letter to the Magistrates of Strasburg with a Letter in form desiring you to forward it; in which I hope I am right.

I am S^r &c

John Pownall Esqr

PS Jan 19th

Since I wrote this a Ship has brought in here the Duplicates of my Lord H's Letter N° 21 & the Inclosures.[5] The Addresses of the two Houses seem not to intimidate the Faction; at least they don't show it[;][6] they endeavour to counterballance them by many Extracts of Letters some wrote others only pretended to be wrote in London averring great Lies & Absurdities.[7] Mr Deberdt says that the Convention was a prudent Measure & their Friends increase.[8] I'll send you a printed Sheet as a Sample; and also a New York Newspaper with a fuller Account of their Proceedings in Assembly than I had before.[9] I can now send the Supplement proposed but will only say that the Difficulties of the Commissioners &c appear to arise from one of their own Board;[10] I will thank you for your very kind Letter in my next.[11]

J Pownall Esqr

L, LbC   BP, 7: 252-254.

In handwriting of Thomas Bernard. The RC may have enclosed an undated letter from FB to the master and council of the City of Strasbourg (not found); copies of the *Boston Post-Boy and Advertiser*, 16 Jan. 1769, and possibly the *New-York Gazette, or Weekly Post-Boy*, 9 Jan. 1769; the "supplement" enclosed was probably a paper on the American Board of Customs.

The king's speech at the opening of Parliament on 8 Nov. signaled his government's anxiety at the situation in Boston, as Hillsborough reported to FB in **No. 712**. But FB was quickly disappointed by the resolutions of the House of Lords failing to recommend "spirited Measures" for tackling opposition to the Townshend Acts.[12]

---

1. The king's speech of 8 Nov. 1768 was first reprinted in the *New-York Gazette*, 2 Jan. 1769, followed by the *Boston Chronicle*, 9-12 Jan.; the *Boston Weekly News-Letter*, 19 Jan.; the *Boston Evening-Post*, 23 Jan.; and the *Essex Gazette*, 17-24 Jan. 1769.

2. *Boston Post-Boy and Advertiser*, 16 Jan. 1769. On 31 Dec. 1768, the New York Assembly had first resolved itself into a committee before passing the following resolution:

    > *Resolved, Nemine Contradicente*, That it is the Opinion of this Committee, That no Tax under any Name of Denomination, or on any Pretence, or for any Purpose whatsoever, can, or ought to be imposed or levied upon the Persons, Estates, or Property of his Majesty's good Subjects within this Colony, but of their free Gift, by their Representatives lawfully convened in General Assembly.

    In locating the exclusive authority to tax with the colonial assemblies, the resolution *ipso facto* repudiated Parliament's authority to tax the colonists, a position more advanced than that propounded by the Massachusetts House of Representatives. See **No. 579**, **No. 581**n7-8, *Bernard Papers*, 4: 65-68, 75-76.

3. This was probably an allusion to the "divers Conferences" FB had been having recently with senior government officials and leading merchants, at which the internal affairs of the American Board of Customs would likely have been discussed. See **No. 721**.

4. FB probably did not send a separate "cover" after completing the postscript, and likely enclosed the missive to Strasbourg with this letter. FB had been trying to attract German immigrants to his Mount Desert Island estate. (*Bernard Papers*, 2: 141, 216n.) The Strasbourg authorities had contacted FB to verify the credentials of his agent, the Rev. John Martin Schaeffer, who had returned to Europe in order to procure settlers. Schaeffer was also collecting debts due him under the authority of a power of attorney granted him by a fellow German migrant, now deceased; by this document he laid claim to property and estate in the possession of the deceased man's family in Strasbourg. The Strasbourg authorities, however, accused Schaeffer of fraud, and his prosecution ended FB's interest in the emigrant scheme. The master and council of the City of Strasbourg to FB, 23 Sept. 1767 (translated from German) BP, 12: 143.

5. Hillsborough's letter (**No. 712**) enclosed copies of the addresses of the House of Lords of 15 Dec. and the House of Commons of 16 Dec. 1768.

6. Editorially supplied.

7. FB likely had in mind the "Extract of a Letter from a Gentleman in London, to his Friend in Boston," dated 4 Oct. 1768 and printed in the *Boston Gazette*, 9 Jan. 1769.

    > Your Troops you may depend upon it, will all be called away in the Spring, and the Ships too. Doctor F — [*Benjamin Franklin*] has given it as his Opinion, that the Colonies will obtain all that they can desire or wish for,

> if they behave with Firmness. — Your Commissioners [*of Customs*] stand here exactly in the Character that they have established for themselves in America; and it is the opinion of every one, that the Board will be recalled, and a new Governor appointed for your Province. Lord H — himself says, he entirely dislikes their Conduct.

8. This information was accurate. Dennys DeBerdt had informed Thomas Cushing that he would "make the best use" he could of the petition to the king prepared by the Massachusetts Convention of Towns, "as it is couched in very decent Terms." 7 Dec. 1768, in Matthews, "Letters of Dennys DeBerdt, 1757-1770," 347. FB may have learned of DeBerdt's reaction from a conversation with Cushing or another leading Whig. For the petition see the source note to **No. 698** and note 2, *Bernard Papers*, 4: 70.

9. The proceedings were extracted in the *New-York Gazette, or Weekly Post-Boy*, 9 Jan. 1769.

10. John Temple: he had been excluded from much of the business of the Board since the previous summer. One of the major flashpoints between Temple and the Board concerned the dismissal of customs collector Timothy Folger (1732-1814). Folger had been appointed by Temple when he had been surveyor general, but his appointment was revoked by the Customs Board, thus calling into question the legitimacy of Temple's other appointments. While Temple complained to the Treasury about being marginalized by the commissioners, Folger appealed unsuccessfully to the commissioners to be reinstated. Temple to Thomas Bradshaw, Boston, 10 Aug. 1769, Bowdoin and Temple Papers, Loose MSS. The papers of the American Board of Customs relating to Folger are in T 1/471, ff 177-182.

11. **No. 742** replying to **No. 714**.

12. The resolutions are summarized in the source note to **No. 723**.

730 | *To the Earl of Hillsborough*

Nº 1

Boston Jan 23 1769

My Lord

I have received your Lordships letter Nº 20[1] and the duplicate of Nº 21.[2] By the former I have the instruction I desired concerning calling the Assembly: if I receive no orders, Writs will issue of course on the 29th of April returnable on the 31st of May; for I apprehend that the Suspension of the annual Assembly can be ordered by no less Authority than that of parliament. But if it should be thought proper to prevent their proceeding to business at that time, I could prorogue the Assembly immediately after the Election of Councellors, & the signification of my Assent & Dissent: nay, I apprehend that I could suspend that signification by an adjournment; but I should not care to take such a step without orders.[3]

I foresee that I shall be under infinite difficulties at the next Election, unless I am relieved by the proceedings at home or orders in consequence of them. Heretofore I could show a sufficient resentment of the Opposition to the Kings Government by negativing 5 or 6 at a time: But the Defection of Councellors is now become so prevailing among those living within or near to Boston, that I cannot by myself withstand it: nor do I see that I can do Any effectual Service but as an Executer of Orders. Happy will it be for all persons concerned in the Government & for the people themselves, if the parliament shall take this Matter into consideration with effect.

I shall still consider myself to be under orders to call the Assembly at Salem or Cambridge;[4] as the Reasons which occasioned this order still subsist & are like to subsist I shall prefer the former, as Cambridge is too near to answer the present purposes of the Change. But if the Seat of Government was to be removed out of Boston for a continuance, I should then prefer Cambridge, which would become the Westminster of the Metropolis; but with such an interval between, as would, in some degree, put the Government out of the reach of the Seditious Spirit which prevails [at][5] Boston. But If this should be thought advisable, still it would be best to call the next Assembly at Salem.

I communicated to the Council the 2 paragraphs relating to ^not^ presenting the address;[6] tho' it was unnecessary, as it was known before that your Lordship had not seen the address at the time you was charged with suppressing it. This appeared from Mr Deberdts advertisement, which shewes that they were informed of the truth at the time that they published this infamous Lie.[7] But this is common with them; if a Lie does but answer the purpose of the day they are perfectly unconcerned at the future detection of it; & when the falsity is made apparent, they stand wholly unabashed.

I return your Lordship my most humble thanks for continuing to represent my conduct to his Majesty in so favorable a manner as to procure for me his most gracious assurance of his protection. The truth is I do the best I can; and when I appear to act otherwise, it is either thro error of judgement or want of Authority; which latter is a great impediment to my Service.

I am, with great respect, My Lord, Your Lordships most obedient & most humble Servant

Fra Bernard

The right honorable the Earl of Hillsborough

ALS, RC   CO 5/758, ff 48-49.

Endorsed: Boston Jan.[y] 23[d]. 1769 Governor Bernard. (N[o]. 1) R 29th March B.11.   Variants: CO 5/893, ff 98-99 (dupLS, RC); CO 5/767, ff 206-209 (L, RLbC); BP, 7: 121-123 (L, LbC). Considered by the Board of Trade on 1 Dec. 1769. *JBT*, 13: 125.

1. **No. 702**.

2. **No. 712**.

3. Hillsborough did not issue further instructions addressing FB's questions, expecting that FB would call the assembly together in accordance with the instructions he provided in **No. 702**. Moreover, **No. 661** allowed FB a discretionary power to convene the General Court at Salem or Cambridge. *Bernard Papers*, 4: 271-276. This measure was endorsed by the cabinet (see **No. 727**). FB was thus obliged to summon the General Court to meet in May, though he was clearly apprehensive at the prospect of meeting his enemies in the House of Representatives face-to-face. The first session of the 1769-70 legislative year ran from 31 May to 15 Jul. 1769.

4. **No. 661**, *Bernard Papers*, 4: 271-276.

5. Obscured by binding and supplied from LbC.

6. FB evidently read to the Council extracts from **No. 712** wherein Hillsborough explained why he had not yet presented the House of Representatives' petition of 20 Jan. to the king. This is not recorded in the Council's executive minutes but would have occurred shortly after FB received the duplicate of **No. 712** on c.19 Jan. 1769.

7. Dennys DeBerdt had printed advertisements in the Boston newspapers quashing rumors that Hillsborough was determined not to present the House's petition to the king.

> *August* 26, 1768.
>
> Whereas it has been publickly reported that the Earl of Hillsborough has neglected to deliver a petition from the Assembly of the Massachusetts Bay to his Majesty, at a time when his Lordship had not even seen the said petition, I think it my duty to inform the public that such insinuations are entirely groundless. My reasons for any delay and proceedings therewith, I have truly given the Assembly in my letters to them of the 12th and 18th of March, and 27th of June.
>
> Dennys De Berdt.

Hillsborough took delivery of the petition from DeBerdt's friend Stephen Sayre on 2 Jun. But Hillsborough had already indicated to FB his determination not to receive the petition since it had not been formally transmitted by the governor. **No. 603**, *Bernard Papers*, 4: 142-143. Nevertheless, DeBerdt continued to expect that Hillsborough would transmit it to the king at an opportune moment, writing Thomas Cushing on 18 Nov. that "Hillsborough had more than once or twice assured me the King has seen Your Petition & the difficiency in official forms did not in the least retard it which will with the rest of the Colonies petition* be brought before Parliament." Hillsborough's letter to FB of 15 Nov., which FB read to the Council, however, explained that the unconventional "manner" by which he received the petition rendered it "impossible" to lay the it before the king; when he did "communicat[e]" it to the king, "His Majesty not considering ^it^ as coming properly before him, did not think fit to signify to me any Commands thereupon." (**No. 712**.) The Whigs responded by publishing DeBerdt's letter to Cushing (of 18 Nov.) in the *Boston Gazette*, 23 Jan. 1769, demonstrating that Hillsborough had told DeBerdt that protocol was no barrier to the petition being considered and thus contradicting what Hillsborough had told FB. While Hillsborough's explanation may have been factually correct, there is little doubt he misled DeBerdt and, as his colonial critics anticipated, was committed to undermining the House of Representatives' case for the repeal of the Townshend Acts. Sayre to Hillsborough, [London], 2 Jun. 1768, CO 5/757, ff 458-459; Dennys DeBerdt to Thomas Cushing, London, 18 Nov. 1768, in Matthews, "Letters of Dennys DeBerdt, 1757-1770," 344;

    *DeBerdt is referring to petitions from colonies other than Massachusetts. However, only one other petition from a colonial assembly, that of the Pennsylvania, was brought before Parliament that winter, on 7 Dec., when the Commons refused to receive it.

731 | To the Earl of Hillsborough

N.º 2

Boston Jan 24th 1769

My Lord

In your Lordships Letter N.º 21[1] you signify his Majesty's Commands that I should extend my Enquiries to such illegal and unconstitutional Acts as have been committed since the Disturbances on the 10th of June. In some of my former Letters I express the Difficulties which attend the procuring Informations in Regard to Crimes of a popular Nature: but I have not in the Mean Time remitted my Endeavours to procure such Informations; and I plainly perceive that by patience and perseverance the Cabinet of the Faction may be laid open. But this is a Business which must not be precipitated; time must be given for those who can make Discoveries to reconcile themselves to doing it; and they must appear as much as possible to be volunteers in this Business. Self preservation will by and by make Informers: And where Accomplices are wanting, there are many Persons who abhor the Proceedings of the Faction and yet have been let into their Secrets.

To enable me to execute my present Orders & such of the like kind as I may hereafter receive, as I have at present no privy Council that will give me real Assistance, I have formed a Cabinet Council consisting of the 3 principal Officers of the Crown, the Lieutenant Governor, the Secretary and the Judge of Admiralty, whose Zeal Fidelity and Ability cannot be suspected.[2] To show your Lordship that we are not unemployed, I shall enclose in the Cover of this a Deposition taken before us, in which the Spirit of the Movers of the Boston Mobs will be explained & the Intention of the Faction exemplified in one [of] the principal and most desperate of the Cheifs of the Faction.[3] I shall probably accompany this with some other Proofs of the Declarations of the Faction which will fully expose their Intentions:[4] One of which I will mention now as I am fully Master of the Intelligence. A Cheif of the Faction in justifying himself to an Acquaintance who was not of the Party said that he was allways for gentle Measures, for he was only for driving the Governor and Lieut Governor out of the Province and taking the Government into their own Hands. Judge, My Lord, what must be the Measures proposed by others, when this is called a gentle Measure.[5]

The same Gentleman makes a great Merit of calling the Convention, which he say[s][6] was the Means of keeping the Country quiet. But was that their Intention? Nothing is[7] more plain than that their Design was quite the contrary; No one can read the Proceedings of the Town-Meeting and doubt of their Intention to make the Convention a Means to render the proposed Insurrection general. There is an

Expression in the circular Letter of the Selectmen, (which, by the by, is wholly their own Work and never had the Sanction of a Town-Meeting)[8] which is explicit of this Purpose, wherein they say that a Convention is necessary to prevent any sudden & *unconnected* Measures being taken for redressing themselves. What can *unconnected* be applied to but to forcible Opposition to the Kings Government. If this can be doubted it will not be difficult to prove it from some of their own Mouths, that the Plan was to remove the Kings Governor &c & reassume the old Charter.[9] And when one considers the many Means by which this was defeated, It has been a great Disappointment to some of them that it was not done.

In my Letter N° 37[10] I informed your Lordship of the Difficulties I met with in engaging Gentlemen of Figure to qualify themselves as Justices of the Peace, and the Reasons given for their Refusal. Since that I have made a Successful beginning of this Business: The Cheif Justice having made an Offer to qualify himself as a Justice of Peace if I desired it, (for which Practice his immediate Predecessor has afforded a Precedent) I made use of this to engage the Secretary, Mr Flucker and Mr Auchmuty Judge of Admiralty, to join with him in it; and I accordingly qualified them all four together.[11] This will do honor to the Bench, strengthen it on the Part of Government, and in Part remove the Objections which have prevented other Gentlemen coming upon it. Notwithstanding which the Reasons assigned in such Objections ought to be attended to upon Account of their general Weight and Consequence.

I am with great Respect My Lord, Your Lordship's most obedient and most humble Servant

Fra Bernard

The Right Honorable The Earl of Hillsborough

P.S. I send your Lordship an account of the forementioned Conversation from the principal.[12]

LS, RC   CO 5/758, ff 50-51.

In handwriting of Thomas Bernard (except where noted). Endorsed: Boston Jany 24th. 1769 Govr. Bernard (N°. 2) R 29th. March B.12.   Enclosed **Nos. 732** and **733**. Variants of the letter in: CO 5/893, ff 100-101 (dupLS, RC), with enclosures at ff 102-106; CO 5/767, ff 209-213 (L, RLbC); BP, 7: 123-126 (L, LbC). The letter and enclosures were considered by the Board of Trade on 1 Dec. 1769. *JBT*, 13: 125. The LbC contained an additional postscript (perhaps added by Thomas Bernard) marked for deletion by a cross. BP, 7: 126.

<P.S. Feb 4th

The Intelligence of the Anecdote at the end of the second Paragraph of this Letter came to me from two Different Channels, both of them from Gentlemen of undoubted Veracity who had the Account from one of the Parties to the Conversation. Since my Writing the foregoing Letter I have recieved from one of those Gentlemen a Letter giving an Account of that Conversation in precise Terms. From this it appears that this Account differs from mine in the Body of the Letter not materially but in the Inconnection of the two Parts of the Speech. On the other hand it goes further in a very material Circumstance, that there was a Motion in the Convention that they should take the Government into their Hands:[13] that it was moved by a Gentleman who has since made a Merit of the Moderation of the Convention, on Behalf of his own Party.>

---

1. **No. 712**.

2. Robert Auchmuty (c.1725-88) was judge of the Admiralty Court in Massachusetts when, on 22 Sept., he was appointed the judge of the newly established Vice Admiralty Court for New England, sitting at Boston. *Bernard Papers*, 2: 275; ADM 2/1057, ff 288-291. FB may have excluded Attorney General Jonathan Sewall from his cabinet of Crown officers because the attorney general was a provincial officer appointed with Crown approval; but Sewall was also advocate general of Vice Admiralty, a Crown position. A more plausible explanation for Sewall's exclusion is that FB had entertained doubts about his reliability under pressure, which he had previously intimated to Hillsborough in **No. 719**.

3. **No. 732**.

4. **No. 733**.

5. FB is referring to Thomas Cushing whose conversation with Nathaniel Coffin is reported in the enclosure **No. 733**.

6. Obscured by binding.

7. LbC and dupL: "was".

8. **Appendix 13**, *Bernard Papers*, 4: 400-401.

9. He is referring to the Charter of Massachusetts Bay (1629), abrogated initially under Charles I and James II and finally under William III.

10. **No. 724**.

11. Robert Auchmuty's appointment as justice was the only one of the group of four to be presented to the Council for approval on 1 Feb. The omission of the others from the record is unexplained, for justices' commissions required the Council's authorization. In April, FB obtained the Council's approval for the appointment of his son John and the friend of government Joshua Loring. William H. Whitmore, *The Massachusetts Civil List for the Colonial and Provincial Periods* (Albany, 1870), 131; CO 5/829, f 5.

12. **No. 733**. The postscript is in FB's hand.

13. Cushing did not venture an opinion on any "Motion" made in the Convention, as FB states here. Coffin reported Cushing as stating that fellow Whigs should "drive off" FB and TH: "they then should have the Council in their own Hands and could oblige them to call an Assembly" to discuss the impending arrival of the British troops.

732 | *Declaration of Richard Silvester*

Copy

Province of Massachusetts Bay

The Information of Richard Silvester of Boston in the Province aforesaid Inn-holder[1] taken before me Thomas Hutchinson Esq[r]. Chief Justice of the said Province this 23[d]. day of January in the ninth year of his Majesty's Reign.

This Informant saith, that the day after the Boat belonging to M[r] Harrison was burnt the last Summer,[2] the Informant observed several Parties of Men gathered in the Street at the South end of the Town of Boston, in the Forenoon of the day. The Informant went up to one of the Parties, and M[r]. Samuel Adams then one of the Representatives of Boston hapned to join the same party near about the same instant of time, trembling and in great agitation. The Party consisted of about seven in number, who were unknown to the Informant, he having but little acquaintance with the Inhabitants; or if any of them were known, he cannot now recollect them. The Informant heard the said Samuel Adams then say to the said Party— If you are Men, behave like men, let Us take up Arms immediately, and be free and sieze all the Kings Officers; We shall have thirty thousand men to join Us from the Country. The Informant then walkd off, believing his Company was disagreeable.

The Informant further saith, that after the burning the Boat aforesaid, and before the Arrival of the Troops, the said Samuel Adams has been divers times at the House of the Informant, and at one of those times particularly, the Informant began a discourse concerning the Times; and the said Samuel Adams said, We will not submit to any Tax nor become Slaves. We will take up Arms and spend our last drop of blood before the King and Parliament shall impose on Us or settle Crown Officers in this Country to dragoon Us. The Country was first settled by our Ancestors, therefore We are free and want no King. The times were never better in Rome than when they had no King, and were a free State, and as this is a great Empire, we shall soon have it in our power to give Laws to England. The Informant further saith, That at divers times between the burning the Boat aforesaid and the arrival of the Troops aforesaid, he has heard the said Adams express himself in words to very much the same purpose, and that the Informants Wife has Sometimes been present, and at one or more of such times, George Mason of Boston, Painter was present.

This Informant further saith that about a fortnight before the Troops arrived, the aforesaid Samuel Adams being at the House of the Informant, the Informant asked him what he thought of the times. The said Adams answered with great alertness, that on lighting the Beacon, we should be joined with thirty thousand men from the Country with their Knapsacks and Bayonets fixed: and added, We will destroy every Soldier that dare put his foot on shore: his Majesty has no right to send Troops here to invade the Country, and I look upon them as foreign Enemies.

This Informant further saith, that two or three days before the Troops arrived, the said Samuel Adams said to the Informant that Governor Bernard, M[r] Hutchinson and the Commissioners of the Customs had sent for Troops, and the said Adams made bitter exclamations against them for so doing, and also repeated most of the language about opposing the Kings Troops, where he had used as abovementioned about a fortnight before. The Informant contradicted the said Adams, and attributed the sending Troops to the Resolves of the General Court, and the proceedings of the Town meeting.

The Informant further saith that several times between the months of May & December last, Doct[r]. Benjamin Church of Boston[3] aforesaid has been at the House of the Informant, and the Informant has heard him frequently say — The King and Parliament have no right to tax Us, nor will We suffer the Kings Officers to be here to dragoon Us. We will take up Arms and maintain our Freedom. The Informant said to the said Church, that such Proceedings were Treason.

The Informant further saith, that upon its being reported that the Troops were coming, he heard the said Doctor Church say — The King has no right to send Troops to invade Us. I look upon them as foreign Enemies. Not one of them shall set his foot onshore; for on lighting the Beacon, thirty thousand men under Arms from the Country will join Us. This is a great Empire; We soon shall be able to give Laws to England. She is arrived at the height of her Glory and must soon fall, as there are divisions at home as well as here. The Informant further saith that at one of the times between the months of May & December aforesaid, he heard the said Doctor Church say, I am sure the Rascals, the Governor and Lieutenant Governor have wrote home against the People, it will be necessary to sieze them and their Papers to come at the truth, and send them home in Irons.

The Informant further saith, that after the Soldiers were landed, the said Doctor Church said to the Informant, that he the said Church had certain intelligence, that some particular persons here would be sent home prisoners. The said Church seemed to be much terrified, and said nothing could be proved against him without Edes and Gill should impeach,[4] as they knew the Authors of the different pieces in the News Papers; that he the said Church was the Author of that Letter in the News Paper which M[r]. Grenville carried into the House of Commons the last Session of Parliament and represented treasonable;[5] that he had been at the printing Office for his manuscript, but had not got it, and further said, that Doctor Warren[6] had burnt his own papers.

This Informant further saith, that a short time before the Stamp Act, so called, was repealed, he was at the Crown Coffee House in Boston where one Thomas Chase of Boston, Distiller,[7] was present in the same Room with the Informant, and several other persons, of whom the ^afore^said George Mason was one, and the Informant heard the said Thomas Chase then and there say —The King is a Fool and a Rascal, and ought to have his head cut off, and the Lord and Commons are Rogues and Scoundrels and a short time before the Troops arrived, the Informant heard the said Chase say that he would take up Arms, and oppose the Soldiers in landing: that the King had no right to send them here to invade the Country, and that he looked upon them as foreign Enemies.

Sworn to T Hutchinson

Rich^d. Silvester

Endorsed: In Govr Bernards (N° 2) of 25 Jan^ry 1769

Ms, Copy   CO 5/758, ff 54-55.

Enclosed in **No. 731**. Another copy at CO 5/893, ff 104-106.

---

1. Richard Silvester (b.1706) served in the Royal Navy for twenty-three years before becoming a land-waiter in the Boston Customhouse. Silvester became a Loyalist and, despite his advanced years, left Boston in Oct. 1776. Jones, *Loyalists of Massachusetts*, 261.

2. That is, on Saturday 11 Jun. 1768. See **No. 623**, *Bernard Papers*, 4: 185-190.

3. Benjamin Church (1734-78) was a Boston physician and one of the foremost radicals, even when he became a government spy in the early 1770s.

4. Thus in manuscript: he meant that nothing could be proven unless the printers Benjamin Edes and John Gill were "impeach[ed]".

5. It cannot be established with certainty the particular newspaper article of which Church claimed authorship. The annotated newspapers of Boston shopkeeper Harbottle Dorr—so often the only means of identifying authors of anonymous pieces—identifies two pieces in the *Boston Gazette* that prompted former prime minister George Grenville to denounce the paper: the first, by "Sui Imperator," was published on 31 Aug. 1767, the second, by "Hyperion," on 5 Oct. 1767. Dorr did not reveal the author of either essay. Dorr Collection, 1: 712, 730.

   It is not implausible that Church wrote one or both essays. They were self-evidently radical productions, urging resistance to arbitrary power, and stylistically similar, in so far as they indulged in literary references and allusions. Sui Imperator's essay has previously been discussed, in *Bernard Papers*, 3: 398-399, and it is important here to consider reasons why Grenville might have found Hyperion's so offensive. The pseudonym, the name of a Greek mythological titan, in itself would have meant little to Grenville, beyond symbolizing power. But it may also have had some currency in the politics of food, particularly with Bostonians advocating the nonconsumption of imported Bohea tea subject to the Townshend duty, in the weeks leading up to and following the adoption of the nonconsumption agreement on 28 Oct. 1767. Tea was not included in the list of goods (mainly manufactures) subject to nonconsumption, though it was in those boycotted under the nonimportation agreements adopted in Boston and elsewhere from 1768. Before then, "Hyperion tea", a native concoction of dried raspberry leaves or herbs, was being touted as a palatable substitute for dutied tea. (See the letter from Newport, R.I., printed in the *Boston Post-Boy and Advertiser*, 7 Dec. 1767). "Hyperion tea" may have paid homage to the writer Hyperion, who contributed at least five essays to the Massachusetts papers, the first on 28 Sept. 1767 (*Boston Gazette*) the last in 1771 (*Essex Gazette*). The occasional verse therein, more so than the classical and Biblical references, are redolent of Benjamin Church's satires. But the piece printed in the *Boston Gazette* on 5 Oct. was notable for its denigration of the British imperial elite as "vermin" (a brutalizing exhortation when sounded again by the Sons of Liberty in the summer of 1768, **No. 623**), and also its evocation of the Puritan mission writ large as American exceptionalism.

> Be not terrify'd by the threats and vaunting of your sworn foes: For even in our times, we have seen the finger of the Lord: And we have heard with our ears, and our fathers have told us the great things, which GOD did for them in their day; how he deliver'd them, in the howling wilderness, out of the paw of the Lion, and out of the paw of the Bear; how, with an out-stretched hand, he led them thro' the dreary desert, giving them the manna of Heaven for food, and the water out of the rock for drink; how he miraculously preserved his chosen people from tempest, fire, sword and famine, and put all their lurking and insidious enemies to flight: Surely, his ear is not heavy, that he cannot hear, nor his arm shorten'd, that he cannot save.— Did he not plant us with his own hand? Hath he not nourish'd and brought us up as children? Surely, he will not, now, altogether cast us off! If we seek him, he will be found of us; while we serve him, he will never forsake us. —And, if our GOD be for us—who shall be against us? Tho' our enemies should be as the vermin of the field, or as the insects of the air, yet will I not be dismay'd; for the breath of his mouth shall scatter them abroad, the power of his strength shall confound and overwhelm them with mighty destruction.

> HYPERION.

The citation adapted from Romans 8:31-33 ("If our God be for us, who shall be against us?") appropriated God for the Americans ("our GOD") and left any British reader (the verminous imperial elite) to mourn their nation's loss of providential favor.

"Mr. Greenville seems our most bitter enemy, and takes every opportunity to render us obnoxious," wrote Nathaniel Rogers upon hearing of Grenville's tirade in the House of Commons, and proposed "that an Enquiry should be entered into by the House upon a certain Boston paper of October 5 . . . containing the most virulent aspersions and insinuations." Rogers, moreover, reported that the advent of the nonimportation movements had convinced many Britons, Grenville included, that the Americans were intent on separation from Britain. Long smarting from opposition barbs that his American Stamp Tax had started the quarrel with the Americans in the first place, Grenville must have bridled at HYPERION's invocation that British officials were the instruments of their own destruction. It is likely that Grenville brandished the *Boston Gazette* containing HYPERION's piece when he spoke in the House of Commons' debate of 8 Nov., occasioned by the king's speech. Lord Barrington had already decried the Americans "traitors," according to Sir Henry Cavendish, when Grenville rose to condemn the Americans' resistance to Parliament's authority, expressing "surprise" at any who supposed the Bostonians were "disposed to return to their duty." Grenville spoke again on American affairs, on 7 Dec., when the Commons refused a motion to receive the petition of the Pennsylvania assembly protesting the Townshend duties (having first re-read the Declaratory Act's assertion of parliamentary supremacy over the American Colonies). Cavendish does not state that Grenville actually discussed a Boston newspaper, though such can be inferred from Rogers's report (for which source I am grateful to John W. Tyler). Nathaniel Rogers to TH, London, 30 Dec. 1767, Mass. Archs. 25: 240-241a; Wright, *Cavendish's Debates*, 1: 41-42.

Another summary of Grenville's speech of 8 Nov., contained in a letter from England printed in the *Boston Evening-Post* on 30 Jan. 1769, amplifies Cavendish's account.

> In the Course of the Debate the whole Behaviour of the People of Boston was stated . . . . Mr. Greenville agreed in imputing the present Mischiefs principally to the Countenance which the Denial of the Right had received here; he observed that the Writings and Votes in America all refer'd to that Authority; . . . he approved of the late Revenue Law, because it preserved the Principle: but join'd in censuring the Order to require the Assembly to re-

scind, and on non-compliance to dissolve: He thought that the Secretary of State should not thus take upon himself to annihilate Corporations for disobeying Mandates: that Recourse should have been first had to Parliament.

Thus, it is plausible that when denouncing the "Writings . . . in America" Grenville proceeded to make a specific proposal for punitive measures against Boston.

Boston Whigs such as Benjamin Church were not slow to appreciate the antipathy of British statesmen like Grenville. The printers of the *Boston Evening-Post* prefaced the letter from London with a revealing editorial note, based on information tendered by Capt. James Scott. It explained that a newspaper of 19 Sept. 1768 (almost certainly the *Boston Gazette* of that day), which reported the proceedings of the Boston town meeting of 12 Sept., had an immediate impact when it was received in London on 27 Oct.: "the Expectation of People in general of the Consequence of those Proceedings was much raised." This anodyne phrase referred to the manifest anxiety among British ministers that the town would resist the landing of the Regulars. It was not until 5 Nov. that colonial ships brought news of the soldiers' peaceful disembarkation. Grenville, therefore, delivered his speech of 8 Nov., at a moment when the friends of the Americans on the opposition benches were urging the Grafton administration to repeal the Townshend Acts and critics of the government like Grenville were condemning its apparent failure to take a firm line against the supposed insurrectionists in the Boston town meeting. (The extract above was subsequently cited by Boston Whigs criticizing Secretary of State Hillsborough's reliance upon FB's reports on the Massachusetts Circular Letter, see the source note to **No. 742**).

If Silvester can be believed, Church was terrified of discovery. Why he should also, in the autumn of 1768, confess to being the author of a scurrilous and seditious essay is not so clear cut, unless he anticipated that with the troops behind him, the governor was intent on arresting the leading the Whigs (which in fact he was not).

6. Joseph Warren (1741-75), the Boston physician and radical, and author of the libel signed "A True Patriot," for which see **No. 593**, *Bernard Papers*, 4: 112-118.

7. Thomas Chase (b.1737), a member of the Boston Sons of Liberty and a participant in the Boston Tea Party.

733 | *Declaration of Nathaniel Coffin*

Copy

Nathaniel Coffin Esq[r] declareth that the Day or two after the Town-meeting for calling the Convention broke up[1] this declarant understanding that it was resolved to oppose the landing of the Kings Troops, expostulated with Thomas Cushing Esq[r] upon the Misery which he and his Party were bringing upon the Town by the Opposition which they were meditating. Whereupon the said Cushing said that for his Part he had allways been for moderate Measures, and had proposed among them to drive off the Governor and Lieut Governor; they then should have the Council in their own Hands and could oblige them to call an Assembly. He added that his Moderation had made him obnoxious to his own Party and Otis had said to him that he was as great an Enemy to his Country as Frank Bernard Tom Hutchinson or the Commissioners. And he further said that he had allways behaved with

Decency towards the Governor and was dissatisfied with the Load of Calumny and Scurrility which had been flung upon his Excellency. Upon which the Declarant reminded him of his Speech at the Town-meeting, which was far from being calculated to bring about moderate Measures, and observed ^that it appeared^ that they all had their Parts to act upon this Occasion, all tending to produce the Resolves which afterwards followed: to which he answered Nothing. But after he said that he was for the Convention, expecting that it would bring together some prudent People who would be able to check the violent Designs of others. Upon which the Declarant observed that it was probable that the People who had the Lead in the Town would take the Lead in the Convention. He replied that I was mistaken; for there would be many Members in that Assembly who would not be led to those Purposes, but would be a Check upon those who were for violent Measures. And this Declarant says that the said Thomas Cushing when he mentioned the driving off the Governor and Lieut Governor he did not seem to mean that it was a desirable Act, but only to prevent more violent Measures. And this Declarant further saith that the first Part of this Conversation was between them two only but afterwards it was renewed at the Town-house in the presence of several Gentlemen; in the Course of which this Declarant said that if the Party made an Opposition to the Troops they would find it would be resented by the People of the Town when they came to feel the Effects of it; and for his Part he should make no Scruple to shoot the Man who would by such Means bring Misery upon himself & his Family. And he this Declarant further said that if he was obliged to take Arms it would be on the Side of Great Britain: and (Cushing) would find a great many more of this Town whom he little thought off would be on the same Side.

(Signed) Nath Coffin

Boston Feb^ry 6th 1769

Ms, Copy CO 5/759, ff 52-53.

In handwriting of Thomas Bernard. Enclosed in **No. 731**. Another copy in CO 5/893, ff 102-103 (Ms, Copy).

Nathaniel Coffin (1725-80) was a scion of one of Massachusetts's first families. Formerly a merchant and town tax collector, Coffin was appointed deputy cashier to the American Board of Customs on 7 Nov. 1768. Coffin was initially a Whig and his brother William a firm supporter of the Sons of Liberty. Coffin regularly attended Boston town meetings, and was well-placed to act as the government's informer, at least until his appointment to the Customs Board. Until then, Coffin may have masked whatever misgivings he felt about crowd action. But, as the declaration printed here indicates, Coffin made no secret of his distaste for radicalism on the eve of the British occupation. His report probably captured the predicament of many conservative Whigs who feared that hotheads in their ranks might resist the British troops when they landed. Coffin's candor in conversation, as much as his official duties, probably undermined his effectiveness as an informer from this point onward, although by his own account he continued to pursue his private and public business without "popular resentment."[2]

---

1. On 13 Sept. 1768.

2. Nathaniel Coffin to Charles Steuart, Boston, 14 Aug. 1770, National Library of Scotland: Charles Steuart Papers, 5026: 101-104. See Colin Nicolson, "'McIntosh, Otis & Adams are our demagogues': Nathaniel Coffin and the Loyalist Interpretation of the Origins of the American Revolution," *Proceedings of the Massachusetts Historical Society* 108 (1996): 73-114.

734 | *To the Earl of Hillsborough*

N.º 3

Boston Jan 25 1769

My Lord

It is hoped & expected that if the Government at home should proceed to censure the disturbers of the Peace of this province & the rest of the continent, that the printers of the Boston Gazette Edes & Gill will not be thought unworthy of the public Notice. They may be said to be no more than mercenary printers; but they have been & still are the trumpeters of Sedition, & have been made the apparent instruments of raising that flame in America,[1] which has given so much trouble & is still like to give more to Great Britain & her Colonies. And yet I should not be against passing them by, if their Writers could be come at any other wise than thro them. But there seems to be no other way ^so easy^ to penetrate into the Cabinetts of the Faction as to put their printer under the Necessity of discovering the Authors of the Numberless treasonable & Seditious writings published by them. And the Way to them is plain: there is no other evidence wanting against them but their own papers with some proof of their coming from their press. And the Law, well known to printers, is plain; discover the Authors or take the Authorship upon yourselves. They would do the former if the question was put to them; as I am told they keep themselves provided with these means of Defence against an evil hour. It seems therefore that the first step for calling the cheifs of this Faction to an Account would be by seizing their printers together with their papers, if it can be: I will ^not^ take upon me to pronounce any particular pieces absolutely to be treason: but there are many of them which come so near to it as to appear Very like it.

I have occasionally sent many of these papers to your Lordships office but have not continued a Series of them. I don't doubt however but there are compleat sets of them in sevral hands in London. But least they should be wanted, I will by the Conveyance which carries this, send a compleat Set of these from the 14th of August 1767, when the present troubles began, to the present time. I wish I had leisure to look them over & point out the useful places: but I have not time for it.

I am with great respect, My Lord, Your Lordships most obedient & most humble Servant

Fra Bernard

The right honble the Earl of Hillsborough.

P.S. These papers will afford numberless instances of a breach of the priviledge of parliament; and it seems to be a fair Oportunity for the House of Commons to give an instance of the extension of the power of parliament over America by punishing breaches of priviledge committed in it. But a difficulty would attend this exertion of the power of parliament, as an Order of the house could not well be executed in the same Session it was made, unless it was issued Very early. But this might be remedied by an Act of parliament: and it will be well Worth the while; for I know of nothing which would be so effectual to prevent the inflammatory Means to make a breach between Great Britain & her Colonies, as for the parliament to animadvert upon the seditious & treasonable papers published in America.

FB

ALS, RC   CO 5/758, ff 56-57.

Endorsed: Boston January 25th. 1769. Governor Bernard. (No. 3) R 29th March. B.B.   Variants: postscript omitted in the BP, 7: 126-128 (L, LbC) but included in CO 5/893, ff 108-109 (dupL, RC) and CO 5/767, ff 213-215 (L, RLbC). The "compleat Set" of the issues of the *Boston Gazette* published since 14 Aug. 1767 has not been found in the TNA. The enclosures and letter were considered by the Board of Trade on 1 Dec. 1769. *JBT*, 13: 125.

Two days before FB wrote this letter to Hillsborough, Benjamin Edes (1732-1803) and John Gill (1732-85), proprietors of the *Boston Gazette*, published a six-page "Supplement (*Extraordinary*)" comprising transcriptions of six letters that FB had previously sent Hillsborough.[2] While FB's communications with the assembly and the Boston town meeting were printed regularly in the press, this was the first occasion when full copies of his official correspondence were made public. By way of justification, the supplement printed extracts of several private letters from London and a digest of the *London Gazetteer* reporting how FB's correspondence with Hillsborough was influencing ministers' and parliamentarians' hostile perceptions of the situation in Boston.[3] The columns also noted FB had refused the request of the Massachusetts assembly to view his correspondence shortly before its dissolution, in June. Back then, FB's Whig enemies had threatened to petition the king to have him removed, and it is possible they might have commanded majority support for such a controversial maneuver when emotions were running high after the House refused to rescind its vote approving the Circular Letter. FB denied the House the opportunity of preparing a petition when he dissolved the assembly, in accordance with Hillsborough's instructions.[4] FB's correspondence was peripheral to these actual proceedings, but it was never out of mind. The Whigs never relented in their accusation that their governor had misrepresented the province in order to obtain the Regulars he had long desired. With the arrival of the Regulars in October, Whigs doubled their efforts to disgrace their governor, and acquire evidence that could justify their own position to a wider audience in America and Britain. Someone, somehow finally managed to read what FB had written Hillsborough.

How the printers acquired copies of the six letters is a mystery.[5] Judging by FB's comment in the postscript about a "breach" of parliamentary privilege, he guessed that an MP had requested copies of his letters and forwarded them to friends in Boston. But it is most unlikely that Edes and Gill were working from copies sent over from England. There was very little time for anyone with access to government files (prior to the letters' presentation to Parliament) to make copies of the letters as they arrived in England and then send them to Boston. The originals of the five letters written in November (dated 1, 5, 12, 14, and 30 Nov.) were dispatched separately to London soon after they were written: the first two (**Nos. 706** and **708**) were received on 23 Dec. and two others on 30 Dec. (**Nos**. **709** and **711**); the last letter written in November (**No. 717**) was received on 16 Jan. along with the final item in the batch, dated 5 Dec. (**No. 718**). Even allowing for a speedy four-week crossing in mid-winter, it is most unlikely that copies of the original letters could have been returned to Boston in time for publication on 23 Jan. (Of course, duplicates might have been received earlier than the originals, perhaps by a week or so, but these have not survived). Authentic transcripts were sent to Boston on 30 Jan., by William Bollan, ten days after copies of the six letters had been presented to Parliament; transcribed by the clerk of the papers of the House of Commons, these versions were published in a pamphlet in April that year, and subsequently filed in the papers of councilor James Bowdoin, who drafted his own and the Council's public commentaries on FB's six letters (**Appendices 3** and **4**).[6]

When FB wrote to Hillsborough on 25 Jan. (**No. 734**), he was still unaware that any of his correspondence had been presented to Parliament. The largest batch (his letters dated 21 Jan. to 5 Oct. 1768) were presented on 28 Nov., and the remainder on 7 Dec. and 20 Jan.[7] It was not until April that the province newspapers reported that FB's six letters (1 Nov. to 5 Dec.) had been laid before Parliament by the leader of the Commons, Lord North, on 20 Jan.[8] FB had long anticipated that ministers would use his papers to justify the deployment of Regulars to Boston. Likewise, he expected his enemies in Boston to exploit whatever official correspondence they could purloin. FB knew that James Bowdoin coordinated opposition in the Council with that of Whig colleagues in the House of Representatives and Boston town meeting. He also acquired evidence of Bowdoin colluding with Edes and Gill to publish confidential Council papers (**No. 703**). Bowdoin kept his own minutes of Council proceedings, although his access to the "Council books" was never restricted by the province secretary; it was from these official papers that Bowdoin worked, FB later noted, when he took a lead role in preparing an edition of FB's correspondence for publication. (**No. 779**.) It is plausible, therefore, that Bowdoin orchestrated publication of FB's letters in the *Boston Gazette* on 23 Jan., though how he managed it remains unclear.

We can only speculate as to the *modus operandi*. Perhaps Bowdoin or Edes and Gill bribed a clerk or domestic servant to copy the governor's letters. Perhaps someone else, close to FB, secretly aided them. Perhaps they or others hired a burglar to do the job. Whatever the scenario, the spy would have needed plenty of time to copy the letters from FB's letterbook, perhaps *in situ* but certainly unhindered. It is unlikely that anyone would have been able to remove the letterbooks undetected. FB did not always carry his letterbooks with him on business, but they would have been stored at one or more locations between 1 Nov. and 23 Jan: his farm at Jamaica Plain, the Province House in Boston, the Council Chamber, or Castle William. The Province House and Council Chamber seem the most likely locations.[9] Whoever managed to view FB's letterbooks had time to make good copies, for the published transcripts are generally accurate renditions of the letterbook versions; the differences in grammar and orthography likely reflect editorial preference, and additional words can be attributed to scribal error.

All of this indicates the spy (if there was one) was probably someone with regular access to the governor or at least working in close proximity. Only two clerks maintained the letterbooks during this period: FB's second son, Thomas (1750-1818), and the unidentified clerk no. 3. Thomas Bernard had been working regularly as a private secretary since the summer of 1767, and he was probably the only clerk FB ever fully trusted. As such, Thomas was a potential target of Whig surveillance, though it is most unlikely he was ever a willing accomplice to espionage. His first biographer considered him a deeply principled young man with a social conscience.[10] While it is conceivable that Thomas could have defied his father if he believed an injustice had been done, for Thomas to betray his father would have been devious, dishonest, and incompatible with his future philanthropic career. Clerk no. 3, who had worked for FB since the early 1760s, is a more plausible candidate for the role spy. The last evidence of clerk no. 3's employment was in copying a letter to Hillsborough dated 14 Nov. 1768, one of the six letters published in the *Gazette*. His disappearance from the scribal record is intriguing but does not on its own implicate him or her in espionage.

Publication of FB's six letters was illegal, and the governor was intent on revenge. He now moved for the British government to institute legal proceedings against the printers in the hope that they could be persuaded to divulge the identities of those who had conspired against him and authored libels in the press.

Edes and Gill had been at the forefront of opposition to FB's administration from the early days. Edes was a Son of Liberty and a member of the Loyal Nine who organized the Stamp Act riots.[11] He probably first caught FB's attention when he met with Andrew Oliver to arrange the publication of Oliver's letter of resignation as stamp distributor.[12] The printers had fallen foul of authority long before FB accused them of sedition. In Mar. 1757, the Boston selectmen censured their publication of materials that "reflect grossly" upon religion, whereupon Edes promised to "publish nothing that shall give any uneasiness to any Persons whatsoever."[13] The printers' subsequent careers made a mockery of such an undertaking. Their newspaper, the *Boston Gazette*, was by far the most partisan of Massachusetts's newspapers (whereas other proprietors tended to print letters and essays from across the political spectrum). Yet in continuing to highlight the major political issues of the day, their newspaper evinced an unwavering commitment to journalism for its own sake. From the Stamp Act Crisis onward, the *Boston Gazette*, with a weekly circulation of around two thousand copies, became a forum for the leading Whig opinion-formers, most of whom wrote anonymously or under cover of pseudonyms, including John Adams, Samuel Adams, James Otis Jr., and Dr. Joseph Warren. By 1768, the *Boston Gazette* was the voice of the protest movement (or the organ of sedition as government men put it). Between 1764 and 1776, Edes and Gill also issued sixty-two pamphlets from their press, including thirty-four original works.[14]

FB had never encountered such a level of anti-government activity in newspapers when in England. Nor could he properly appreciate the extent to which political journalism was changing the face of British politics during the 1760s and 1770s. FB's initial reaction was to consider newspaper criticism of his own administration as being largely misguided and misinformed, but by 1768 thought it wantonly seditious. On three recent occasions FB seriously considered instituting legal proceedings for sedition. FB alerted Secretary of State the earl of Shelburne to "Sui Imperator," published on 31 Aug. 1767, with Shelburne cautioning against prosecution even if FB were to discover the author's identity.[15] Next, FB was deeply offended by the attack on his reputation mounted by "A True Patriot" (Joseph Warren) on 29 Feb. 1768. But he hesitated to instruct the attorney general to prosecute Edes and Gill, mindful of Shelburne's advice to have the backing of the assembly when taking action against the printers rather than the authors.[16] Instead, Chief Justice Hutchinson presented the article to a grand jury of the Superior Court. It was the jury's responsibility to establish the facts surrounding publication and the judge's to establish seditious intent. In this instance, the jury agreed the attorney general should commence a prosecution, before changing their mind the following day, having been intimidated by Edes and Gill (**No. 596**).[17] The jury's initial response to the Warren libel indicates a general acceptance of the principle that publishers and authors were liable for their actions. (For freedom of the press expressly meant the absence of pre-publication censorship, not freedom of speech.) [18] But it might also indicate deep concern that the Chief Justice would deny the printers a fair trial. Indeed, by the time of the third alleged libel, published on 6 Jun. (and described by TH as an "infamous burlesque" on an address of the Council), FB was keen on using prosecution as a political lever; that is to say, pursuing the printers in order to get at the authors.[19]

It is doubtful if Edes and Gill would have succumbed easily to judicial pressure to name names, as FB anticipated. In **No. 734**, FB proffered an intriguing profile of two highly-committed Whigs who nevertheless maintained their own kind of insurance—a list of authors—against any polemicist ready to betray the printers' confidence or willing to testify against them. (One of them at least, Dr. Benjamin Church, FB knew was uncomfortable with this situation, see **No. 599**.)[20]

The postscript to the letter indicates that FB wished to avoid prosecutions for libel or sedition in the colonial courts by bringing publishers to trial in England under a new act of Parliament. There is no doubt that any such proceedings would have been highly controversial. Massachusetts Whigs and lawyers, versed in the language of liberty and the ins and outs of the John Wilkes trial, would have turned any sedition trial into a *cause célèbre* about liberty. In **No. 734**, FB responded to Hillsborough's instruction not to "communicate" the contents of his official correspondence to the assembly, after extracts had been printed in the *Boston Gazette* in "breach of the priviledge of parliament" (**No. 670**).[21] Hillsborough thus echoed the concerns of the British government presently facing the Wilkesite campaign to remove restrictions on the reporting of debates in Parliament. It is uncertain if FB knew much about the English polemicists (notably "Junius"), who argued the case for unfettered reporting, or the extent to which British newspapers were reporting parliamentary proceedings (before the legal prohibition was lifted in 1771).[22] Ironically, it was FB himself who became the most high profile victim of British parliamentary reporting when his enemies in London supplied his enemies in Boston with further copies of correspondence that had been presented to Parliament by Hillsborough and his ministerial colleagues. Published in pamphlet form in 1769, the Bernard Letters indubitably aided the Whigs' campaign against British colonial policy and appeared to vindicate the radicals' criticism of FB for misrepresenting the province to his superiors in London.[23]

1. Here FB conflates his own oft-used depiction of James Otis Jr.'s radicalism ("raising a flame") with a famous quotation from Thomas Hobbes: "the tongue of man is a trumpet of warre, and sedition." *Cive* (1642; English trans. ed. 1651). 5.5. The "mercenary printers" jibe was unfair and inaccurate, in so far as Edes and Gill committed their business (and Edes his person) to the colonial protest movement from the early days of the Stamp Act Crisis.

2. FB's letters to Hillsborough of 1, 5, 12, 14, and 30 Nov., and 5 Dec. 1768. **Nos. 706**, **708**, **709**, **711**, **717**, and **718**. Also printed was Thomas Gage to Hillsborough, Boston, 31 Oct. 1768. *Boston Gazette, Supplement*, 23 Jan. 1769.

3. For example, "C. L." wrote in the *London Gazetteer* of 9 Nov. that the people of Massachusetts were "subjected to the dreadful alternative of taking up arms against the King's troops, or tamely submitting to every insult and cruelty that can be offered them." *Boston Gazette, Supplement*, 23 Jan. 1769, p. 1. From letters and public prints brought in by Capt. James Scott, the paper continued, it was evident

> That the Colonies, and this Province and Town in particular, had been most grossly misrepresented from hence, but that Pens had not been wanting at home to set G. B. and the C—m—rs* characters in their true light . . . that this Town had been actually in arms, and the Province ready for settling up an independency; . . . That anonymous papers had gone from hence to L—d H—h,+ scandalizing and abusing the most respectable among us, which his L—d had sent back to G. B. to enquire into. [p. 2]

*Commissioners of Customs. + Lord Hillsborough.

Articles such as these, usually spread across the first and second pages, vindicated the editors' decision to publish as a counter-offensive against their governor's hostile accounts of the state of the province; for so long as FB had Hillsborough's backing he remained a dangerous enemy. The printers, however, did not offer an editorial rationalizing their position or explaining how they acquired FB's letters.

4. See **No. 638**, *Bernard Papers*, 4: 220-230.

5. The letters were **Nos. 706**, **708**, **709**, **711**, **717**, and **718**, dated 1, 5, 12, 14, and 30 Nov., and 5 Dec. 1768, respectively.

6. *HCJ*, 32: 123-124; *HLJ*, 32: 229; Bowdoin and Temple Papers, Loose MSS; *Letters to the Right Honourable the Earl of Hillsborough, from Governor Bernard, General Gage, and the honourable His Majesty's Council for the Province of Massachusetts-Bay. With an appendix, containing divers proceedings referred to in the said letters* (Boston: Edes and Gill, 1769). On Bollan see **Appendix 2**.

7. The correspondence is listed in the **Introduction**, 50-51n32. See also source note to **No. 735**. An extract from the House of Commons' journals listing FB's correspondence among sixty items presented to Parliament on 28 Nov. 1768 was printed in the *Boston Weekly News-Letter*, 7 Apr. 1769.

8. *Boston Chronicle*, 10-13 Apr. 2013.

9. Between 1 Nov. 1768 and 23 Jan. 1769, all bar three of FB's out-letters that were copied into his letterbooks were written at "Boston": a letter to the American Board of Customs of 12 Nov. written at Jamaica Plain, to Samuel Hood dated Province House, 18 Nov.; and to John Pownall, Jamaica Plain, 26 Nov. BP, 7: 163-173, 214-215.

10. James Baker, *Life of Sir Thomas Bernard* (London, 1791).

11. *Bernard Papers*, 2: 306; 3: 56n.

12. *Bernard Papers*, 2: 434-435.

13. *Reports of the Record Commissioners*, 10: 54-55.

14. Arthur Meier Schlesinger, *Prelude to Independence: the Newspaper War on Britain, 1764-1776* (New York, 1958), 85-109, 110; Stephen Botein, "'Meer Mechanics' and an Open Press: the Business and Political Strategies of Colonial American Printers," *Perspectives in American History* 9 (1975): 127-225; G. Thomas Tanselle, "Some Statistics on American Printing, 1764-1783," *The Press and the American Revolution*, edited by John B. Hench and Bernard Bailyn (Worcester, Mass., 1980), 315-363.

15. *Bernard Papers*, 3: 397-98.

16. "I should be led to hope that the Assembly would vindicate their own Honor, and make the Guilty feel the Displeasure of an injured Province." Shelburne to FB, 14 Nov. 1767, **No. 574**, *Bernard Papers*, 3: 423.

17. *Bernard Papers*, 4: 121-124. See also source note to **No. 593**, ibid., 112-118.

18. See Leonard W. Levy, *Legacy of Suppression Freedom of Speech and Press in Early American History* (Cambridge, Mass, 1960), 14-15, and passim.

19. TH to Thomas Pownall, Boston, 7 Jun. 1768, Mass. Archs., 25: 262, in Hutchinson Transcripts, 1: 262. The Council's address of 28 May had praised FB's "thorough Knowledge" of the boundary dispute with New York. The "burlesque" in question was a comedic verse mocking both the Council's apparent subservience and the governor's "wond'rous great . . . Knowledge" that "never will admit Debate," and his "Profundity of Wit." An anonymous piece, it nevertheless resembles Dr. Benjamin Church's satires. While of little relevance in itself, the "burlesque" is indicative of the sometimes strained relationship between the Council and Whig leaders in the House, before James Bowdoin's emergence as a dominant figure in the Council (for which see **No. 703**).

20. *Bernard Papers*, 4: 127-128.

21. *Bernard Papers*, 4: 292-293.

22. Peter D. G. Thomas, *John Wilkes: a Friend to Liberty* (Oxford, 1996), 125-140.

23. *Letters to the Right Honourable the Earl of Hillsborough, from Governor Bernard, General Gage, and the honourable His Majesty's Council for the Province of Massachusetts-Bay. With an appendix, containing divers proceedings referred to in the said letters* (Boston: Edes and Gill, 1769); *Letters to the Ministry from Governor Bernard, General Gage, and Commodore Hood. And also Memorials to the Lords of the Treasury, from the Commissioners of the Customs. With sundry letters and papers annexed to the said memorials* (Boston: Edes and Gill, 1769).

735 | *To the Earl of Hillsborough*

Duplicate

private

Boston Jan 26 1769

My Lord

I have the highest Sense of the honor your Lordship has done me by your private Letter of Nov 19[th1] and the kind Assurances of your ~~kind~~ ^favorable^ Disposition towards me. The Regret of the Disappointment of your former Intention, was little more than momentary, & soon gave Way to the Calls of my Duty at that critical Time.

I am extremely obliged to your Lordship for your Offer of freeing me from the Expence of a Baronets Patent, if his Majesty should confer it upon me. This was not a principal Objection with me tho' it had some Weight: for since I have been in America, now in the 11th Year, I have made very little Advancement in my Estate, and for near 4 Years past I have gone backward. This your Lordship will easily beleive when I assure you that my Income for some Years past has not exceeded a thousand guineas a year, and I am the first Man in a great Capital.

I have no Appetite of Honours, but as they are public testimonials of the Kings Approbation of the Conduct of his Servants. In this Sense they are allways desirable, and at some times may be of considerable Utility. At a critical time & in a peculiar Situation when an Officer has a difficult Task or arduous Undertaking upon his Hands, so high a declaration of his Majesty's Approbation and Confidence, as the conferring an Honor amounts to, may add to his importance and enlarge his authority, & thereby render his Services more effectual. I will not say that this will be the Case with myself: but if your Lordship shall see the Occasion when my receiving this Honor will probably strengthen my hands in the Service of the Government, I will not hesitate in accepting it most thankfully. At the same Time I will sincerely own to your Lordship that your intended favor of freeing me from the Expence of the Patent will at this Time be a Benefaction convenient to me. As for the Objections arising from the Number of my Children & my Inability in my present Station to add to the Family Stock, I shall ballance them with the Expectations I may justly entertain of being better provided for, when time and Opportunity shall serve.

I never expected that my Letters would not be communicated to Parliament;[2] all my hopes were that they would be put under a Restriction which would prevent Copies being taken to afford Materials for Pamphlet-Writers & News-paper-essayists. It is in the Power of each House of Parliament, and I am sure it is their Intrest to prevent Official Letters addressed to the Kings Ministers transpiring out of their house. If they will not take this Care all Confidence, which is the Spirit of Correspondence, will be destroyed; and all official Letters will be dictated with this Consideration, how they will bear printing if the Parliament should call for them. This is a Matter of no little Importance in an Empire so widely extended as Great Britain.

For my own Part I should have no Objection to my Letters being made public, if Truth was as much respected as it is respectable. I write as I speak from my own heart, & with a Strict Regard to Truth, so far as it is discernible by Means in my Power. Your Lordship has generally the original Draught of my Letters in my own hand; and indeed the inaccuracies which occur in them are Proofs that they are wrote freely. Freedom of writing like Freedom of Speech is more conducive to Truth, than Accuracy attentive more to Forms than to Matter. In my Situation a Suppression or a Perversion of Truth would have been highly criminal; and the endeavouring to avoid being a Party in these Disputes and to keep upon good Terms with the Sons of Liberty might have led me into Misprision of Treason.

I quite agree with Lord B,[3] that when I have Nothing to manage with the Faction nor any Thing to fear from them I may be indifferent about my Letters. But I know not that this is my Case at present nor how soon it will be. For whilst I continue in this Government, I shall have Business to manage, which may be rendered difficult by making my Letters public. For instance, I would not have it known that I have been an Advocate for altering the Constitution of the Government in that fundamental Error, the Appointment of the Council. and yet I have for some time past avowed my Opinion that it must be done some Time or other; and I can with the greatest Truth aver that I am convinced that it is become a necessary Measure not only to the Stability of Government but to the Peace and good Order of the Province & consequently to the general Wellfare of the People. But the Propriety of this Measure will not be judged among them by Reason but by Prejudice; and whoever shall appear to have an hand in it, will be liable to be made obnoxious to the People. So in Respect to Representations of particular Persons, which I have avoided as much as possible, but could not keep entirely clear of, I would not have those exposed, tho' I have not knowingly injured any one in any Instance. But as I do not suffer my official Conduct to be influenced by personal Animosity so it ought not to be an Object of personal Resentment. Upon the whole, my Lord, I am quite easy about my Letters, fully trusting that your Lordship will be able to prevent their being put to any Use detrimental to Government, which is all I mean by my Apprehensions for myself.

I am much favoured by your Lordship's giving me Leave to acquaint you with any Inclinations in regard to myself, and especially the very kind and polite Terms with which you assure me of your friendly Concern for my Intrest. But at a Time when the public Business requires so much Attention, I should be loth to interfere with private Concerns of my own. Nevertheless if any thing occurs to me, which will not bear Delay, I shall take the Liberty to trouble your Lordship with it. As for Governments my Lord B is well apprized of my Sentiments,[4] and can inform your Lordship that the Value I set upon an healthy Climate or the Fear I have of an unhealthy one will preclude me from the best Governments, I mean those of the Islands except Barbadoes; & that being so lately disposed of can afford no Expectation:[5] and indeed it is the same Case with the two other principal Island Governments. The Continent also seems to afford no Prospect at this Time. So that if it should be thought necessary & proper to continue me here, I have no other Prospect but from my Appointments being augmented by some Means or other. It must be done with this Government whether I keep it or leave it.

I am with the utmost Respect and Gratitude, My Lord,
your Lordships most obed[t] & most humble Servant

Fra Bernard

The Right Honourable The Earl of Hillsborough

AC, dupLS   BP 12: 41-48.

Variants: the RC has not been found, but there is no reason to doubt that FB sent an original of this fair copy to Hillsborough. There is a corrected draft among the file of "state letters" in BP, 7: 128-132 (L, LbC) and an extract in BP, 7: 216. Hillsborough did not reply directly to this letter.

Hillsborough had promised FB that if he was to lay their correspondence before Parliament, he would "cautiously keep back every thing that I find I can" (**No. 713**). In fact, on 28 Nov. Lord North, acting for the administration, presented Parliament with copies of FB's letters dated 21 Jan. to 15 Oct. 1768.[6] Hillsborough did not notify FB of the cabinet's intention to do so; nor did he let on that the correspondence had been presented in any of the out-letters he sent FB during November and December (**Nos. 712** and **713**), and which FB received on 25 Jan. (the day before he wrote **No. 735** to Hillsborough). Hillsborough's January letters, though they revealed nothing about Parliament, notified FB that the king was aware of his reports (**Nos. 722** and **727**); FB received the second of the letters several weeks after writing **No. 735**. FB's sanguine comment in **No. 735** above that he had "no Objection to my Letters being made public" implies acceptance that, for the moment, he had been outmaneuvered by enemies on both sides of the Atlantic.

FB was probably confident that his reputation would survive any political fallout from publication of the six letters in the *Boston Gazette*. (First printed in the issue of 23 Jan. they were published in a pamphlet in April; see the source note to **No. 734**.) In these letters, FB made some controversial comments favoring the appointment of a royal Council,[7] but he did not actually accuse individuals of sedition, the one issue he was most anxious to keep secret from his enemies (**No. 735**). However, FB would not have been aware just how much of his correspondence had been laid before Parliament presented—nearly three-quarters of the letters he had written to the secretaries of state during 1768. Private letters from England printed in the colonial newspapers confirmed that FB's letters had been debated in Parliament (see source note to **No. 734**). But FB was not aware of the full list of correspondence until he received notification from John Pownall on 24 Mar. 1769 (**No. 723**) and read extracts from the House of Commons' journals printed in the Boston newspapers in April.[8] By then, he no longer cared what the colonists made of his frank and self-validating reports.

Hillsborough was unaware that FB's correspondence had been published in Boston when he dispatched **No. 757** recalling FB to London. FB received **No. 757** on 10 Jun., his last important instruction as governor, requesting that he make a personal report on the state of affairs in Massachusetts.

1. **No. 713**.

2. FB's letters and their enclosures were communicated to Parliament on 28 Nov. 1768. They are listed in full in *PDBP*: 3: 19-27; *HCJ*, 32: 74-76; *HLJ*, 32: 182-185. The transcripts printed in *Bernard Papers*, vols. 4 and 5 are listed above in **Introduction**, 50-51n32 and n33.

3. See **No. 707**.

4. **No. 666**, *Bernard Papers*, 4: 285-287; **No. 705** in this volume.

5. William Spry (1729-72) had been appointed governor in 1767 and served until his death.

6. FB's correspondence was not in the public domain. Despite legal prohibitions on the reporting of parliamentary debates, the substance of the debates was discussed in the British press and mentioned in the private letters of Britons corresponding with Americans, which were printed regularly in the colonial newspapers. Thus, there was always a possibility that British or American newspapers could print extracts of FB's letters. Even so, the *Annual Register*, an organ of the opposition Rockingham Whigs (and reprinted in Murdoch below), did not publish any of FB's letters that were laid before Parliament in November. David Murdoch, *Rebellion in America: A Contemporary British Viewpoint, 1765-1783* (Santa Barbara, Calif., 1979).

7. FB discussed this matter further in his next letter to Hillsborough, **No. 736**.

8. FB's correspondence was listed in the extract from the House of Commons' journals showing sixty items presented to Parliament on 28 Nov. 1768 and printed in the *Boston Weekly News-Letter*, 7 Apr. 1769. FB's six letters to Hillsborough, dated 1 Nov. to 5 Dec. 1768, were presented to Parliament on 20 Jan. as reported in the *Boston Chronicle*, 10-13 Jan. 1769. The Commons resolutions of 8 Feb. condemning Massachusetts, were adopted after consideration of the papers presented between 28 Nov. and 20 Jan., and subsequently printed in the *Boston Gazette*, 17 Apr. 1769.

James Bowdoin II. By Robert S. Feke, 1748. Bowdoin College Museum of Art, Brunswick, Maine. Bequest of Mrs. Sarah Bowdoin Dearborn.

736 | To the Earl of Hillsborough

N.º 4

Boston Febry 4 1769

My Lord

It is generally expected here that among the measures to be taken for restoring peace & good Order to this Government, the putting the appointment of the Council in the Kings hands will be one. This is imagined not only from the necessity of the measure, which, to be sure, is very forcible, but from many advices received by private letters, that such a reform would Very soon take place. This Opinion is so sanguinely entertained, that Recommendations have been allready sent home for this purpose, and by some, if I am rightly informed, who have no pretension to recommend the appointment of the Doorkeeper of the Council chamber.

I should have waited untill this business was more ripe before I troubled your Lordship with my sentiments upon this subject. But I am called ^upon^ by some of the best men in the province to lose no time in representing the Matter to your Lordship:[1] least Importunity Misrepresentation & Want of a right knowledge of persons should lay a foundation for some appointments which had Much better be prevented than hereafter want to be corrected. When this Regulation shall be ordained, the Manner of carrying it into execution will be of the greatest importance; and unfortunately it is put under uncommon difficulty by the late conduct of some of the principal Councellors; the overlooking of which I fear it would be in vain for me to propose if I knew how to do it.

Whenever this Reformation is made (& some time or other it must be done) it will be best to carry it into Execution in a way most reconcileable to the prejudices of the people. And for this purpose, I should ^some time ago^ have recommended that the standing Council should have been taken wholly into the Kings Council, tho at the same time I must have owned that there were some among them that were by no means deserving of that honor. But the Scene in the Council is so changed within these 8 months that it is now become incompatible with the honor of the King to admit the whole of the present Council into the royal Council. Some (but few) must be positively excluded others (not many) must be shut out at present with a door left open for them when they choose to enter as the *Kings Councellors*. This Distinction makes a great difficulty: for whilst one sees the necessity of resenting some late proceedings of the Council, one cannot but be desirous that sevral respectable Men concerned in these proceedings may not [be][2] alienated from the Service of the Crown. This is a delicate business & the most difficult that I have had for some time upon my mind.

The Rules for appointing a new Council at present seem to stand thus: 1. To restore all those who have been turned out for their attachment to Government, as the Lt Gov, Secretary, Judges &c; these will amount to about 8 ~~or 10~~. 2. To take out of the present Council such persons who have not joined in the late violent measures, & some of those who have joined, who appear rather to have acquiesced than acted in it; 3. To appoint others out of some of the officers of the Government, such as the Judge of the Admiralty, Attorney general &c ^& Gentlemen^ settled & estated in the province, avoiding those who are seen as strangers here, residing on account of their offices & not considered as settled here.[3] And tho' it may be thought proper and necessary that some (one at least) of the Commissioners of the Customs should be of the Council yet the Appointment should by all means be deferred untill things are settled & all is quiet. It will be absolutely necessary that the first constitution of this board should be directed as little as possible by partial sollicitations, of which your Lordship must expect to have a great many. For my own part I shall not suffer private considerations to influence the recommendations which I may have to make to your Lordship upon this occasion

To avoid the difficulties which will attend the immediate Nomination of the entire Council, especially with relation to some of the present Council whom one can't tell in or to leave out, It may be advisable at first to name only 12 living in or near Boston & to signify (if it shall be thought proper) his Majesty's intention to fill up the whole Number of Councellors as intended by the Charter (which I call 30 reckoning the Lt Governor & Secretary as Councellors ex Officio) in time as He can inform himself of the Merit of the persons ^to be^ appointed. This would leave a door open for such ^of the present^ Councellors as cannot well be admitted now, untill they have taken some steps to reconcile themselves to Government. This method also would give time for taking due precaution to prevent improper appointments; which must happen more or less from an hasty Nomination of the whole at once.

And now I am upon this Subject I will take the liberty to mention to your Lordship some thoughts of mine upon the Functions of the American Councils, which are of some standing, as seem to deserve consideration. The Kings Councils in America have two separate functions; that of the House of Lords or middle Legislative & that of the privy Council. From this duplicity of functions arises the Objection of the Councellors holding their places at the pleasure of the King; which is true only in respect to the legislative. There indeed, if the Members of the upper house hold their Seats at the pleasure of the king, they are not a separate body, but the Kings delegates; and He may be said to have two negatives in the Provincial Legislature. This may be said to be not constitutional that is not conformable to the Sovereign Legislature. But for the privy Councellors to hold their places at the pleasure of the King is constitutional & necessary to Government. And this Necessity of keeping the privy Council dependent upon the King must make the Legislative Council also dependent, whilst they are united in one body.

But as the assimilating the American Governments to the Sovreign Government as nearly as can be consistent with their dependence must be the Means of improving them; I have often thought that when a Colony is grown to a certain degree of Maturity, The middle Legislative should be separated from the privy Council & the Members of the former appointed by the King to hold during good behavior, with a proviso that male conduct[4] so as to forfeit a seat should be adjudged, either by the upper house with the consent of the Governor & the Confirmation of the King, or by the King in his privy Council. And the provincial privy Council might be composed cheifly of Members of the upper house with some few of the lower house, & upon some occasions of Gentlemen who have seats in neither.

I am fully persuaded that a Constitution of this kind would go a great way to remedy the disorders to which the Governments of America are subject to. Evry one knows that the King being the Fountain of honor is one of the brightest jewells in his Crown, & becomes one of the principal Means of balancing the weight of the people. This power cannot be carried to great lengths in America: but it may be carried greatly farther than it is at present. If there was an Upper House, besides a privy Council, both deriving their appointments from the King, it would afford the King ^means^ to distinguish the friends of his Government & give greater Encouragement to people to desire to be reckoned in that Number. And this Method would multiply the honors conferred by his Majesty at least fivefold in evry province, without making them cheap. And to inhance the Value, it may be proper to allow a title to the Members of the Upper house such as Baron prefixed to their Name, which is no more than a Lord of a Maner in England has a right to, whose Court is now called Curia Baronis. If this should be thought advisable at least so far as to make a trial; a proper Opportunity will offer upon the change of this Government. And It will be further recommended by the consideration that the appointing many royal honours in the new form of Government, will assist the establishment of it, by engaging men who are ripe for honours to the reconciling the people to the System which introduces them.

This will probably appear a mere Reverie: but I have ^long^ thought it serious & intresting; and have heretofore wrote upon it in a fuller manner than I do now. In regard to the appointment of persons, I shall inclose a List of the present Councellors & of the former Councellors which have been ^turned out^. To enter into distinctions of persons is a difficult & disagreable task: I must do in it as well as I can. After all, possibly by anticipating this business I may have given your Lordship & myself unnecessary trouble. If this should be the Case, your Lordship will excuse your share of it: for myself trouble ^without success^ is become familiar to me.

I am, with great respect, My Lord, Your Lordships
most obedient & most humble Servant

Fra Bernard

The right honble the Earl of Hillsborough.

PS Feb 19 Supplement to N° 4 private

I have enclosed a List of the present Councellors & of the turned out Councellors who ought to be restored. I add a List of Persons fit for 12 Councellors to
be appointed in the first instance, If it should be thought proper. I have taken them
out of the List of Councellors former & present to avoid giving umbrage. This latter
I have wrote on a separate paper that your Lordship may separate it from the public
Letter if you please; tho the whole is in its nature Very confidential & should be
viewed as such. I had prepared a short Account of the political Merit, which distin-
guishes the present Council; but having allready anticipated this business I shall
reserve that for the next Ship, before which I hope to receive some advices from
England which may afford some light to me.

F.B.

ALS, RC   CO 5/758, ff 58-62, 64-65.

Endorsed: Boston Feb[y] 4th. 1769. Governor Bernard. (N° 4) R 29th March B.14.   Variants: CO 5/893, ff 110-114 (dupLS, RC); CO 5/767, ff 215-224 (L, RLbC); BP, 7: 132-138
(L, LbC). Enclosed two lists of councilors: **Nos. 737** and **738**. The letter and enclosures
were considered by the Board of Trade on 1 Dec. 1769. *JBT*, 13: 125.

FB argued that a royally-appointed Council was one way of redressing the political
balance in a legislature dominated by Whigs since 1766. The lists of councilors enclosed
with this letter identified potential appointees, all of them friends of government. British
intervention would also compensate for FB's failure to reach a compromise with his enemies to restore ousted government men.[5] Any such measure, however, would have required
parliamentary legislation to revise the Province Charter. Discussion of reforming colonial
government in this letter was triggered by news of the king's speech of 8 Nov., which
reached FB in mid-January (**No. 729**). But FB's hopes evaporated when he received news
in March of the resolutions of the House of Lords of 15 Dec., which ignored the issue of
reform (see the source note **No. 723**).

---

1. FB was probably acting at the behest of his cabinet council of TH, Oliver, and Auchmuty, and with the
    full agreement of other friends of government alluded to (though not named) in **No. 729**.

2. Omitted in error and editorially supplied from the LbC.

3. This is an allusion to the commissioners of Customs, two of whom (Henry Hulton and William Burch)
    were English sojourners, whereas the others were native New Englanders (Temple, Paxton, and Robin-
    son).

4. That is "malconduct."

5. *Bernard Papers*, 2: 157, 405; 3: 16, 182n, 364, 395n.

737 | *Lists of Councilors*

A List of the Councellors of Mass Bay elected in 1768 & consented to in order of their Seniority[1]

A List of the former Councellors turned out of the Council with the last 4 years, who ought to be Restored[2]

1. Samuel Danforth
2. John Hill
3. Isaac Royal
4. Benjamin Lincoln
5. John Erving

6. William Brattle
7. James Bowdoin
8. Gamaliel Bradford
9. Thomas Hubbard
10. Nathanael Sparhawk
11. Harrison Gray
12. James Russel
13. Thomas Flucker
14. Nathanael Ropes
15. Timothy Paine
16. John Bradbury
17. Royal Tyler
18. Samuel White
19. Jeremiah Powell
20. James Pitts
21. John Worthington
22. Samuel Dexter

Thomas Hutchinson Lt Govr

Andrew Oliver Sec^y

Benjamin Lynde

John Cushing

Peter Oliver

Edmund Trowbridge

} Judges of the Sup^r Court

Israel Williams

John Chandler

AMs, RC   CO 5/758, ff 62-65.

Enclosure to **No. 736**. Written c.19 Feb. 1769. Variant in CO 5/893, f 116 (dupMs, RC).

---

1. The following list of councilors provides life dates (in parentheses) followed by dates of election to the Council. Elections were held annually in May, and the period of service ended on the day of the subsequent election. Thus, John Hill elected each year between 1742 and 1769 served from May 1742 to May 1770. However, the Massachusetts Government Act of 1774 instituted a royally-appointed Council, which started meeting in August, thus ending the term of all councilors elected in May that year. Samuel Danforth (1696-1777), 1739-74; John Hill (1703-72), 1742-69; Isaac Royall (c.1719-81), 1752-73; Benjamin Lincoln (1699-1771), 1752-69; John Erving (c.1692-1786), 1754-74; William Brattle (1706-76), 1765-66 and 1770-73; John Cushing (1695-1778), 1737-64; Gamaliel Bradford (1704-78), 1757-69; Thomas Hubbard (1702-73), Nathaniel Sparhawk (1715-98), 1760-65 and 1767-72; Harrison Gray (1711-94), 1761-72; James Russell (1715-98), 1761-73; Thomas Flucker (1719-83), 1761-68; Nathaniel Ropes (1726-74), 1761-68; Timothy Paine, (1730-93), 1763-69; John Bradbury (1697-1778), 1763-72; Royal Tyler (1724-71), 1764-70; Samuel White (1710-20 Mar. 1769), 1766-68; Jeremiah Powell (1720-83), 1766-72 and 1774; James Pitts (1710-76), 1766-74; John Worthington (1719-1800), 1767-68; Samuel Dexter (1726-1810), 1768-73.

2. Thomas Hutchinson (1711-80), elected to the Council, 1749-65, lieutenant governor, 1758-71, governor, 1771-4, chief justice of the Superior Court, 1760-71; Andrew Oliver (1706-74), elected to the Council, 1746-65, province secretary, 1756-70, lieutenant governor, 1770-74; Benjamin Lynde (1700-81), elected to the Council, 1737-40 and 1743-65, justice of Superior Court, 1746-70, chief justice, 1770-72; John Cushing (1695-1778), elected to the Council, 1737-64, justice of the Superior Court, 1748-71; Peter Oliver (1713-91), elected to the Council, 1759-65, justice of the Superior Court, 1756-72, chief justice, 1772-74; Edmund Trowbridge (1709-93), elected to the Council, 1764-65, justice of the Superior Court, 1767-74; Israel Williams (1709-88), elected to the Council, 1760-66; John Chandler (1721-1800), elected to the Council, 1765-67.

738 | A List of Twelve Councilors

A List of 12 Persons proper to be appointed of the Council of Mass Bay in the first Instance.

Thomas Hutchinson Lieut Gov[r]

Andrew Oliver Secretary

Benjamin Lynde

John Cushing

Peter Oliver   } Judges of the superior court

Edmund Trowbridge

Benjamin Lincoln

Thomas Hubbard

James Russel

Thomas Flucker

Nathaniel Ropes

Timothy Paine

The 6 first have been turned out of the Council

The 6 last are Councellors at present

To rank according to their former Appointments.[1]

Ms, RC   CO 5/893, f 115.

In handwriting of Thomas Bernard. Written c.19 Feb. 1769. This copy was enclosed in a duplicate of **No. 736**. The manuscript has been annotated, probably by a clerk in the Plantation Office: an "x" was placed in the left margin alongside the names of Hutchinson, Lynde, Cushing, Trowbridge, and Lincoln, though its significance is unclear. This list was compiled by FB with a view to identifying suitable candidates for a royally-appointed upper chamber. When Lord North's administration established such a Council with a royal writ of mandamus in 1774, under the Massachusetts Government Act, ministers considered lists of candidates submitted by FB at the time.[2] Of those listed here five were appointed to the mandamus Council (Andrew and Peter Oliver, Russell, Flucker, and Paine), but only Flucker took the oath of office.

1. For dates of election to Council see **No. 737** notes 1 and 2.

2. American Papers, Dartmouth Papers: D(W)1778/II/314. Staffordshire Record Office, Stafford, England. See Nicolson, *The 'Infamas Govener'*, 230.

739 | *From Samuel Venner*

Boston 10th Feb[y] 1769

Sir,

Some Letters having passed from your ~~Excellency~~ to the ~~Commrs~~ of the Customs concerning some Intelligence said to be given by me to M[r] ~~Sewall~~,[1] Att[y] Gen[l] of this Province. In Consequence of which a suspension from ^the Execution of^ my Office has been given to me by the Board who are not disposed to grant me a Copy of what has been so written by you, And as these Letters have been wrote to a Public Board, and made the Grounds of accusation against an Off[r] belonging to it, And as I cannot suppose that your ~~Excellency~~ would say Any thing that may have a tendency to accuse any Man which you would not wish to furnish him with that he may have an Opportunity of making his Defence in the best Manner that truth and justice would admit of, I am therefore to request that your ~~Excy~~ will favour me with Copies of such Letter or Letters as might have been wrote by you as Evidence against Me in this Matter either to the Board, or Members of the Board as it may be of some servicer for me to be possessed of them in Boston in Order to prepare my Justification to my superiors at home

I have the Honor to be &c

SV

To his Excellency Gov[r] Bernard

N.B. An exact Copy of the above excepting the Address was sent to the L[t] G[r2]

ALS, LbC: Mass. Archs., 25: 292-293.

Endorsed: 10 Feb: 1769 Letter from M[r] Venner to Gov[r] Bernard & Chief Justice Hutchinson N[o]. 1. The canceled text indicates the alterations, *mutatis mutandis*, for the variant. It is strange why FB should have a copy of Venner's emended draft unless he assisted Venner with its preparation.

Samuel Venner was suspended on 23 Jan. 1769 from his position as secretary to the American Board of Customs. The commissioners accused Venner of malfeasance, as they did also the Board's solicitor David Lisle. Both men, the commissioners claimed, had persuaded Jonathan Sewall that the Board had questioned his competency as the province's chief law officer. There is no doubt that Venner and Lisle briefed Sewall on the Board's several memorials in which Sewall was mentioned (see **No. 728**), and that Venner (more so than Lisle) nursed his own grievances against the commissioners. But Venner was really a scapegoat in a scheme hatched by the commissioners to save further embarrassment; the tacit agreement of FB and TH can be assumed, though it is more than likely that they were willing participants in order to prevent Sewall from resigning his several offices, as he had threatened to do the previous summer (See **No. 678**). In writing FB, Venner was gathering information for his own memorial. He later accused the commissioners of incompetence and malpractice and of conspiring to replace him with Richard Reeve, the nephew of the former secretary to the Treasury, Charles Lowndes.[3] There is no evidence to suggest that FB furnished Venner with copies of the correspondence that he requested, though he might have advised him, in the process perhaps acquiring some information about his old adversary, John Temple. Temple planned on using Venner's testimony as evidence for his own complaint to the Treasury about having been excluded from the business of the Customs Board. Venner was exonerated by the Treasury on 7 Jun., with the promise of a position elsewhere in the king's service.[4]

Temple resumed his attendance at Board meetings when his fellow commissioners returned to Boston. Nevertheless, his friendly association with leading Whigs (notably his father-in-law James Bowdoin, but also Samuel Adams and John Hancock) further undermined his relations with his colleagues. Following the Boston Massacre, John Robinson made an in-person report to the Privy Council at its enquiry into the recent "Disorders," reporting on 26 Jun. 1770 of Temple's recent estrangement from the Board. Robinson's contribution helped to undermine Temple's dwindling reputation, and though Temple journeyed to England later in the year neither he nor his influential patron, George Grenville (who died on 13 Nov. 1770), were able to counteract the impact of the commissioners' negative portrayal. The Treasury relieved Temple of his commissioner's position the following year, replacing him with Benjamin Hallowell. Temple was not disgraced by the close of this life chapter and received further high-ranking appointments in the king's service, notably as British consul-general to the United States of America, in 1785.[5]

1. Venner wrote to Jonathan Sewall on 28 Jan. requesting copies of Sewall's correspondence with the Customs Board. Sewall's reply amounted to a "recital of the Facts" but he promised to provide the material requested. Sewall to Venner, Cambridge, 7 Feb. 1769, T 1/471, ff 87-88.

2. Not found.

3. Richard Reeve served as secretary to the American Board of Customs between 1769 and 1772.

4. Memorial of Samuel Venner to the lords commissioners of the Treasury, 29 Apr. 1769, T 1/471, ff 491-502; memorial of John Temple to the lords commissioners of the Treasury, Boston, 20 Feb. 1769, T 1/471, ff 303-312.

5. *APC*, 5: 252-254; Neil Longley York, *Henry Hulton and the American Revolution: An Outsider's Inside View* (Boston, 2010), 66-67.

740 | *From Lord Barrington*

Private

Cavendish Square 12th. Feby 1769.

Dear Sir,

There were no Packets on this Side the Atlantick the first Wednesday of this Month, which has retarded my writing till I could inform you that the Resolutions which so long ago came down from the House of Peers, were agreed to by the Commons:[1] I mean the Resolutions concerning America; concluding with an Address, which tho' voted by the two Houses, I believe is not approved by five Men in either: Some thinking it too much, & others too little in the present Crisis.[2] I am one of those who think the measure futile & in no respect adequate. I am convinced the Town Meeting at Boston[3] which assembled the States of the Province against the King's Authority, & armed the People to resist his forces, was guilty of high Crimes & Misdemeanors, if not of Treason; And that Mr Otis the *Moderator* (as he is improperly called) of that Meeting together with the Selectmen of Boston who signed the Letters convoking the Convention, should be impeach'd. This would convey terror to the Wicked & factious Spirits all over the Continent, & would shew that the Subjects of Great Britain must not rebel with impunity anywhere. Five or Six Examples are sufficient; and it is right they should be made in Boston, the Only place where there has been actual Crime; for as to the Opinions almost universaly held thoroughout[4] America, concerning the Claim of Taxation, I think every man has a right to judge & to speak his Judgement concerning Laws, tho' he has no right to disobey them. It also seems to me that the Council of Boston which has opposed the calling for Troops & the Quartering of them; which published their answer to the Governour before they had made it, and their proceedings without his knowlege & consent, should no longer be Democraticaly elected; but, like all other Councils be appointed by the Crown. Any measures short of these seem to me trifling and dangerous.

We have at last expelled Mr Wilkes:[5] He will be rechosen for Middlesex, and then declared incapable of sitting in this Parliament according to precedent, after which the County must elect some other person. His Cause seems however drooping very fast, and will I am persuaded be soon forgotten. Tho' he has been twice chosen Alderman of London, his Brethren will not let him sit among them, if they can help it, and I am told they can.

I am with my best Comp^s. to all my Cousins Dear Sir Your Excellency's
most faithful & most obedient Servant

Barrington

P S March. 1ˢᵗ. 1769.

There will be a Cabinet on American affairs in a few days when whatever is or is not to be done will be fixt. The Packett can be kept no longer and goes off to day.

ALS, RC   BP, 12: 49-52.

Endorsed: Lord Barrington dat feb 12 & Mar 1 1769 r May 20.   FB replied on 30 May.[6]
Barrington's mention of John Wilkes's expulsion from the House of Commons offers a clue to his hardening attitudes toward radicals in England and America. Wilkes had returned to England after a four-year exile in France, having been expelled from the House of Commons in 1764 and convicted *in absentia* of publishing libel. Although he had been outlawed, Wilkes was not pursued by the government upon his return until he stood for reelection, first in the City of London and then in Middlesex, which he won while being held in prison on account of his earlier convictions (and where he remained until Apr. 1770). As secretary at war, Barrington publicly defended the army's killing of "five or six" of Wilkes's supporters in St. George's Field on 10 May 1768, and proposed a government bill enabling the king to summon the militia to suppress rioters (in addition to thwarting rebellion or repelling invasion). The bill did not proceed beyond a first reading on 17 May.[7] Barrington also welcomed the renewed determination with which the government pursued Wilkes, who rightly accused Barrington of turning the military on his supporters.[8] On 3 Feb. 1769, Barrington proposed the House of Commons' motion intended to achieve Wilkes's expulsion; the House resolved that five of Wilkes's publications were either seditious or obscene, and on that basis voted to expel him from Parliament. Wilkes was quickly returned in a hastily organized by-election, on 16 Feb., and again on 16 Mar. after the Commons voided his election. The ministry's objections (on the grounds of Wilkes's incarceration) paved the way for the return of the defeated candidate, a government man. The whole episode provoked a storm of controversy (for Wilkes was returned four times by the Middlesex voters) and contributed to the downfall of Grafton's administration on 28 Jan. 1770.
Wilkes's reputation in America as a champion of Liberty was probably not unknown to Barrington (though he did not discuss it with FB). The government's efforts to expel Wilkes from Parliament were reported regularly in the London columns of the Massachusetts newspapers. From the summer of 1768, Wilkes was applauded by the Boston Sons of Liberty, who warmed to his dissociation from violent direct action and generally considered his tribulations indicative of a "ministerial plot" to thwart popular aspirations and undermine representative government.[9]
Barrington was equally uncompromising with the Bostonians. There were two principal aspects to the hard-line colonialist approach he laid out in his letter to FB of 12 Feb. (**No. 740**): (a) that James Otis Jr. and other Whig leaders should stand trial in Boston for high crimes and misdemeanors (and the "Five or Six Examples" he proposed may have been an unconscious acknowledgement of the dead at St. George's Field); (b) that the Crown should assume the power of appointing the Massachusetts Council. Barrington had enthusiastically welcomed the military occupation of Boston, and on supposing that the townsfolk had instituted a "Rebellion" in anticipation of the soldiers' arrival was convinced of the necessity of taking punitive action against the ringleaders (**No. 699**). But the Lords' resolutions on Massachusetts, approved by the Commons on 8 Feb., disappointed him:

after declaiming the province's several "illegal Combination[s]" and Boston's "State of great Disorder and Confusion," the resolutions avoided recommending legislation to curtail the provincial legislature and initiate legal proceedings against the town leaders. Barrington's support for punitive constitutional measures, nevertheless, continued to carry weight with the colonial secretary, the earl of Hillsborough.

1. On 8 Feb., the Commons approved the resolutions on Massachusetts and the address to the king voted by the Lords on 15 Dec. *HCJ*, 32: 185. See source note to **No. 723**.

2. While the Commons made only minor amendments to the phraseology of the Lords' resolutions, the members divided on a second reading of a resolution proposing the approval of the Lords' address to the king. Sixty-five members supported a motion to recommit the address to a House committee which had considered it earlier, while 169 opposed the motion, thus ensuring that the address passed unaltered. *HCJ*, 32: 185.

3. On 12 and 13 Sept. 1768. *Reports of the Record Commissioners of Boston*, 16: 259-264.

4. Thus in manuscript.

5. On 3 Feb 1769.

6. Transmission of the letter to Barrington was delayed, whereupon FB added a postscript, dated 17 Jun. BP, 7: 293-294, 299.

7. Wright, *Cavendish's Debates* 1: 21-23.

8. Ibid., 1: 41.

9. Excluded from the Commons, Wilkes continued to harass Lord North's administration from his position as an alderman of London, leading the successful campaign to end the prohibition on Parliamentary reporting, in 1771. In 1774, Wilkes was elected Lord Mayor and won the Middlesex seat at the general election; he remained a constant critic of the government's American policy during the early stages of the War of Independence. For his distant but profound influence on the Whig protest movement see Pauline Maier, *From Resistance to Revolution: Colonial Radicals and the Development of American Opposition to Britain, 1765-1776* (London, 1973), 161-183. On Wilkes's career see Peter D. G. Thomas, "Wilkes, John (1725–1797)," in *ODNB-e* (http://www.oxforddnb.com.ezproxy.stir.ac.uk/view/article/29410, accessed 26 Sept. 2013); Thomas, *John Wilkes: a Friend to Liberty.*

741 | *From the Selectmen of Boston*

[*16 Feb. 1769*]

May it please your Excellency

At a Time when artful & mischievous Men have so far prevail'd as to foment & spread divisions in the British Empire: When mutual confidence which had so long subsisted with mutual advantage between the Subjects in Britain & America is in a great measure broken: When Means are at length found even to excite the resentment of the Mother State against the Colonies: & they are publicly chargd with being in a state of disobedience to Law, and ready to resist the constitutional

authority of the Nation; The Selectmen of this Metropolis cannot be the unconcerned or silent spectators of the Calamaties, which in consequence thereof have
already fallen upon its inhabitants. — To behold this Town surrounded with Ships
of War; and military Troops even in a time of peace; quarterd in its very Bowels;
Exercising a Discipline with all the severity which is used in a Garrison, and in a
state of actual War, is truly alarming to a free People. And what still hightens the
misfortune is, that our gracious Sovereign & his Ministers have formed such an
Idea of the present State of the Town, as to induce a necessity of this naval and
military force, for the aid of the civil Magistrate in the preservation of its peace and
good order —

Your Excellency can witness for the Town that no such aid is necessary: Loyalty
to the Sovereign; and an inflexible Zeal for the support of his Majestys Authority
and the happy Constitution is its Just character: And we may appeal to the impartial World, that Peace and order were maintained in the Town, before it was ever
rumoured that his Majestys Troops were to be quartered among us, then they have
been since. Such a Measure then we are persuaded would never have been ordered
by the Wisdom of the British Administration, had not the necessity of it been
drawn from the Representations of some of his Majestys Servants in this Province
— Your Excellency will allow us to express our Opinion; and the behavior of some
of its Individual Inhabitants have been greatly misapprehended by his Majestys
Ministers. We therefore in duty to the Town we have the honor to serve, respect-
fully wait on your Excell^y. and pray that you would be pleased to communicate to
us such Representations of *facts only*, as you Judged proper to make since the commencement of the last Year. And as there is a prevailing Report that Depositions are
& have been taken *ex parte*[1] to the prejudice of the Town & particular persons, may
we not assure ourselves, that your Excell^y. will in Justice cause to be laid before us
such other Representations as may have come to your knowledge, that the Town
knowing clearly & precisely what has been charged against it, may have an opportunity of vindicating it self. —

transcript, PC   *Reports of the Record*
                                                      Commissioners of Boston, 23: 6-7.

This address to FB was voted unanimously by the Boston selectmen at a meeting on 16 Feb.
1769. Those present at the meeting should be considered its authors:[2] Joshua Henshaw
(1703-77), Joseph Jackson (1734-96), John Ruddock (1702-72), John Hancock (1737-93),
John Rowe (1715-87), Samuel Pemberton (1723-99), and Henderson Inches.

The address constitutes Boston's formal assessment of the governor's conduct over
the past year, following publication of FB's six letters in the *Boston Gazette* on 23 Jan. FB
mentioned the Boston selectmen in **Nos. 706** and **711,** and in the latter drew attention
to the "5 select men" who had signed the circular for summoning the Convention of Towns
(**Appendix 13**, *Bernard Papers*, 4: 400-401). While their names had been deliberately

omitted from the printed circular, the selectmen evidently suspected that the governor was aware of their identities. In fact, there were four not five selectmen who authorized the circular and four of them approved the document printed here (**No. 741**): Jackson, Ruddock, Hancock, and Pemberton. They were not aware FB advised the British that the selectmen's precept was evidence of sedition (in **No. 681**), though they remained highly distrustful of their governor.

The last paragraph of **No. 741** exhorted FB to come clean and deliver up other correspondence in which he maligned the town and the province. But that would have required him to offer a *mea culpa* and reveal plainly his part in trying to persuade Hillsborough to dispatch the soldiers and tackle allegedly seditious behavior. He remained defiant, replying

> I have no Reason to think that the public Transactions of this Town have been misapprehended by his Majesty or his Ministers, or that their Opinions thereon are founded upon other Accounts, than those published by the Town itself —

> If therefore you can vindicate your selves from such Charges as may arise from your own Publications, you will in my Opinion have nothing further to apprehend. —[3]

While the selectmen did not possess the evidence they needed to prove the governor was lying, they had enough to justify pushing him further in **No. 747**.

---

1. Trans.: by or from one party; that is (by insinuation) FB himself.

2. FB concluded that this and a subsequent address were written by Samuel Adams who "put upon the Selectmen to present, they not daring to refuse what is dictated by the Faction . . . being part of the faction themselves." FB to John Pownall, Boston, 7 Mar. 1769, BP, 7: 262-263.

3. FB to the selectmen of Boston, Province House, 18 Feb. 1769, *Reports of the Record Commissioners of Boston*, 23: 7.

742 | To John Pownall

Private

Boston Feb 18 1769

Dear S[r].

Your kind Letter of Nov 19[1] has been a great Comfort to me harrast as I am with Business of the most unpleasing kind. I have also had some other Letters which show that my late Conduct has been generally approved of.[2] I have had some Compliments here upon my Conduct at the Convention. For it is certain that the Faction here intended an Insurrection, & the Convention was called to make it more general. But it had a contrary Effect by the Diffidence of the Country People, which was much encreased & confirmed by my Message[3] which frightened them not a little. I wont say that it gave the Turn to the Business, but I am assured that it contributed greatly to it. My Friends say that it was the boldest Thing that I have done yet: for I knew that if their Deliberations had taken another Turn my Person was to have been seized: & what has been said of the Imprisonment of a King might be applied to that of a Governor; especially as we have Persons here who would have preferred extreme Violence to make the People desperate.

I consider myself as fixed here at least to next Midsummer, & how long farther I don't pretend to know. I expect to have uncommon Business committed to me; I hope I shall have full Instructions & desire to have as little left to my own Judgement as can be: I have a Set of the wickedest Fellows to deal with that ever man was concerned with. The least Error of Judgement would be improved against me to the utmost Advantage, as would have been any Act of Corruption if they could have fixed one of the most trifling Kind upon me. But I have had the Prudence to keep my hands perfectly clean & myself poor. For Notwithstanding Mr Temple in his Publications against me called me Verres,[4] It is certain that I have acquired no Money in my Government & now spend more than I receive from it.

The Anonymous Letter you sent me is of no Consequence; tho the Hand is feigned, I presently knew it to be the same in which I had formerly received anonymous Letters not worth Notice. I showed it to some Gentlemen to ask their Opinion & they agreed with me that no Notice should be taken of it. But somehow it came to Otis's Ears that I had such a Letter: & his Conscience & fears brought him to me to desire a Sight of it. As the Hand was sufficiently disguised, I let him see it: and my Condescension has been generally approved of.[5]

I have many Things to write to you about & some of Consequence; & if the Wind does not Change tomorrow I shall add some more. But I must in the Mean Time conclude this: & if it is called for tomorrow I will write again by the next Ship a week hence.[6] The News papers which I promise to my Lord H, will go in Mr Olivers Box of Papers, which probably will not be ready for this Ship.

I am &c

J Pownall Esq

P.S. Secret & confidential

I have taken the Liberty to hint to My Lord H[7] that if a Council for this Province is to be appointed from home, it would be necessary to permit as little as possible private Sollicitations to influence the Appointment; as it will be quite necessary to the well executing so important a Change that public Considerations should direct the Appointment. For the same Reason I must recommend that your nearest Relation may have no hand in the Nomination of the Persons to be appointed. He is now, with my Knowledge, carrying on a Correspondence with the Sons of Liberty, in which I fear he will go too far; and he may be more intent upon his own Scheme than the Security of the Government.[8] I am sure that none of the Friends he is now acquiring can be appointed to the new Council without Detriment to the Government. Excuse this Liberty; keep this Secret; & burn this Paper.

P.S. Secret & Confidential

M[r] Temple & the other 4 Commissioners are at length come to an absolute Rupture. They charge him with being the principal Mover of all the Difficulties & Troubles which have obstructed the Execution of their Office & the Abuses which they have received both in their official & personal Characters. There is no Doubt but this is true; tho probably it will not admit of positive Proof; but circumstantial Evidence & the general Opinion of good People are full in the affirmative. I have kept myself from being a Party in this Dispute: tho M[r] T continues to abuse me in the public Papers the last Instance of which with the internal Evidence it affords, I shall send to My Lord H in my next Packet as he has a Share in it.[9] I shall write to you more fully upon this Subject probably by my next Packet. Memorials against M[r] Temple, I understand, go ho[me] in this Ship.[10]

L, LbC   BP, 7: 255-258.

In handwriting of Thomas Bernard. Minor emendations not shown.

FB's wild allegations about the colonists plotting insurrection at the Convention of Towns echoed concerns that he had at the time. As this letter demonstrates, FB now regarded these concerns (questionable though they were when first raised) as established facts. In part that was because FB had become emotionally detached from his province. He was impatient for the leave of absence that would take him home. But his careworn recklessness betrayed deep anxiety at the sullying of his reputation, following the publication of his six letters in the *Boston Gazette* (see source note to **No. 734**). Malicious articles in the *Gazette* compared FB to the infamous Roman governor Verres,[11] a tactic employed previously by Whigs.[12] FB assumed that his old adversary John Temple was making common cause with the Whigs (see also **No. 744**). But FB was confounded. Temple was unlikely to have authored the open letter written under the pseudonym "Paoli," a nickname deriving from the Corsican independence leader Pasquale Paoli[13] and given to the Whig radical William Molineux.[14] While Molineux's authorship of the "Paoli" essay in the *Boston Gazette* on 30 Jan. 1769 cannot be established with certainty,[15] "Paoli" proffered an intelligent criticism of FB's relationship with Hillsborough in line with radical Whig thinking. It relayed a private conversation between FB and an unnamed Boston gentleman in which "Verres" (FB) declared that the Bostonians' "disobedience" of parliamentary authority was sure to provoke British retribution, probably in the form of trade sanctions. (FB would have presumed that his comments in conversation were somehow being conveyed to Temple by his father-in-law James Bowdoin.) Such hostile opinions, "Paoli" continued, could also be found in reports of Parliament's debates on Massachusetts, from which he speculated that "Verres" had "wrote or dictated . . . intelligence" in the *"Court Gazette.*"[16] "Paoli" was on surer ground in alleging that "Verres" had made "diabolical representations" to the British government. He had no firm evidence of this, but his accusation rested on the sound knowledge that (a) FB's letters had been presented to Parliament; (b) Hillsborough had been criticized by George Grenville and other MPs[17] for acting on information received from FB; and (c) FB's six letters in the *Boston Gazette* ensured common knowledge of the governor's hostility toward the province. While FB also had his admirers in the Grafton administration, "Paoli" astutely noted that Hillsborough would not hesitate to make FB a scapegoat for the failure of the government's American policy. At the same time, the use of the pseudonym "Paoli" would have conveyed that the writer wanted to lead his countrymen and women to independence from an alien maritime power by force of arms, and in Jan. 1769, with the real Paoli in exile in England following France's conquest of Corsica, everyone would have taken the meaning as intended.

---

1. **No. 714**.

2. No such private correspondence from England has survived. FB is probably referring to letters from London extracted in the province newspapers, in which his conduct as governor was said to have been widely praised in Parliament. *Boston Evening-Post* on 30 Jan. 1769. For a discussion of such letters see **No. 744**n3.

3. FB had protested that the Massachusetts Convention of Towns was an illegal assembly and instructed it to disperse. **No. 685**, *Bernard Papers*, 4: 330-331.

4. "Paoli" in the *Boston Gazette*, 30 Jan. 1769.

5. Pownall had transmitted to FB a manuscript letter originating at Boston and whose author had attempted to disguise his handwriting on account of the letter's "strong" opinions (**No. 714**). Otis was worried lest he be held accountable, though FB did not presume that he was the author.

6. FB's next letter to Pownall was dated 5 Mar. 1769. BP, 7: 262-263.

7. In **No. 736**.

8. FB was uncomfortable about discussing John Pownall's brother, Thomas, the former governor of Massachusetts. Their relationship was never close, and FB had learned that Thomas Pownall had been corresponding with Boston Whigs, including the Rev. Dr. Samuel Cooper. Copies of Pownall's letters to Cooper, c.Jan. 1769-14 Jul. 1770, are in MH-H: MS Sparks 16.

9. "Paoli," *Boston Gazette*, 30 Jan. 1769. FB immediately, and without evidence, assumed that "Paoli" was the work of his enemy John Temple. He also assumed that Temple was writing comedic essays over the pseudonym "Candidus," as part of his campaign to denigrate his fellow commissioners on the American Board of Customs. *Boston Gazette*, 5 and 12 Dec. 1768, and 13 Feb. 1769.

10. American Board of Customs to the Treasury, 20 Feb. 1769, T 1/471, ff 429-430. Temple's own memorial defending his conduct and complaining of the Board's irregularities is also dated 20 Feb. and is in T 1/471, ff 303-312.

11. Gaius Licinius Verres (c.120-43 BC) was regarded by eighteenth-century scholars as an archetypal tyrannical governor, whose self-enriching taxation, depredations, and corruption in Roman Sicily were thwarted by Marcus Tullius Cicero in 70 BC, forcing him into exile. He was ultimately killed by order of Marcus Antonius (83-30 BC), as was Cicero in 43 BC during the civil war that followed the assassination of Caius Julius Caesar. *Bernard Papers*, 3: 311.

12. *Bernard Papers*, 3: 311.

13. Filippo Antonio Pasquale di Paoli (1725-1807) was elected president of the Corsican Republic in 1755 after a successful rebellion against rule by the Republic of Genoa in which most of the Genoese were expelled from the island. But Genoa ceded Corsica to France, which conquered it by the summer of 1769. Paoli led the Corsican resistance to French occupation, but defeated in battle he fled to England,

where he found friends and sympathizers among the British literati and political elite, including the king. Paoli's fame in the American Colonies owed much to the popularity of James Boswell's *An Account of Corsica, the journal of a tour to that island and memoirs of Pascal Paoli* published in Glasgow, London, and Dublin in four editions, 1768-69. Extracts were printed in the *Pennsylvania Chronicle*, 6 Jun. 1768.

14. See John C. Miller, *Sam Adams: Pioneer in Propaganda* (Stanford, Calif., 1936), 87, 236.

15. Harbottle Dorr did not reveal his identity.

16. There was no such author in the court publications, although the historical character figured in press articles arguing for freedom to report Parliamentary proceedings, which prohibition was not lifted until 1771. *London Chronicle*, 31 Jan. 1769 and the *Public Advertiser* 1 Feb. 1769.

17. Grenville's speech of 8 Nov. 1768 was summarized in the letter from London printed in the *Boston Gazette*, 30 Jan. 1768. It is discussed in **No. 732**n5.

743 | *From John Pownall*

London-Febry. 19. 1769.

Dear Sir,

It has long been my firm & unalterable opinion upon the fullest consideration of what has passed in America that all our measures should be directed to these objects.

1. to vindicate the authority of the supreme Legislature by inflicting due punishment upon those who have been the authors & promoters of those unwarrantable Resolut[ns]. and proceedings by which it has been violated and obstructed.

2. to adopt such measures of regulation & reform as would be most likely to prevent the same things happening again.

3[d]. to seek out the ground upon which GB and her colonies may meet in a constitutional reconciliation.

How far what has been done does accord with these sentiments I leave to yourself to determine — I sincerely wish it may produce good, or rather that it may do no harm.

It is however a satisfaction to me to tell you that there is now a probability that matters will not rest where the present resolutions of Parliament have left them,[1] — the late advices from yourself and from other Governors[2] have induced propositions now under Consideration that do very much square with the Objects I have stated on the other side of the paper, and in the forming of which the copy of a Letter inclosed in yours to me of the 24 of Dec[r].[3] has had a very considerable weight and Share so far as regards your Government.

1. disqualification of persons referr'd to in that letter.

2. Reform in respect to Council.

3. Resolutions denying Rights of Parliam[t]. forfeiture of Charter.

4. Troops &c to be in part withdrawn.

5. Gov[r]. to be created a Baronet at publick expense and have leave to come home with allowances equal to Gov[r]. till otherways provided for. g. confirm[n]. of M[t]. Desart.[4]

6. removal of Councillors in NY who advised ag[t]. dissolution

7. punishm[t] and disqualificat[n] of persons who move, put, or record resolutions denying Right.

8. Act of 7. of Geo. 3[d].[5] repealed as to those Colonies when provision has been made for support of Gov[t]. upon a permanent & constitution^al^ plan continuing with respect to the others, untill they have done the same

9. Mutiny Act[6] to be altered & continue no longer than untill Colonies have made proper provision by Laws of their own.[7]

If things were as they ought to be here all might yet be well, that this disagreable business may end to your personal honour happiness and advantage is the sincere wish & will ever be the zealous endeavour of

Your most faithfull & Aff[t].

J. Pownall

RC, ALS   BP, 12: 53-56.

Minor emendations not shown. Endorsed by FB: Sec Pownall d feb 19 1769 r Ap 20.

Pownall's letter lists the several controversial punitive measures Hillsborough was pushing in cabinet discussions. Top of the list were FB's proposals to exclude his Whig enemies from office and make the Massachusetts Council a royally-appointed body. FB replied with **No. 766**. All of the proposals would have required Parliamentary legislation; any such attempt to reform or abrogate the Massachusetts Province Charter or to insist that officeholders subscribe to a test act acknowledging Parliament's supremacy in America would have outraged New Englanders—as the secretary of state ought to have realized.[8] It is not clear if Hillsborough intended keeping FB in office to impose the transformation or—more likely—if he expected to bring him home. Hillsborough presented his proposals to the cabinet on 13 Feb. Following FB, Hillsborough suggested the royal appointment of the Governor's Council; he reiterated the instruction given in **No. 661**[9] allowing the governor to call the General Court to a place outside of Boston; and, recommended that any transgression or denial of the doctrine of parliamentary supremacy by the House of Representatives would be grounds for the forfeiture of the Province Charter. On that third and most controversial point Hillsborough gave form not to FB's ideas but to his predictions, the governor having often declaimed that forfeiture would be the logical outcome of the House's protests. On the first and third points, Hillsborough's thinking was in line with Barrington's and FB's. But Hillsborough was not presently planning to bring alleged rebels to trial in England, assuming that any criminal trial of the Whig leaders could take place in Massachusetts. FB was currently obliged by Hillsborough's instructions of 15 Nov. (**No. 712**, which he had received on 25 Jan.) to extend the inquiry into the Liberty riot and investigate "illegal and unconstitutional Acts" committed since then.

Peter D. G. Thomas observed that it "is astonishing that Hillsborough does not seem to have anticipated that this projected legislation might produce any resentment or resistance." What is more likely is that Hillsborough trusted Barrington's judgment about the veracity of FB's reports. He also had resolved to bring the disputes to crisis point, fully expecting that with the troops at their back the governor and Customs Board could rebuild imperial authority. Hillsborough's proposals were sensibly rejected by the cabinet and the king, whose preference was for conciliation rather than confrontation. (That did not yet extend to repealing the Townshend duties.) Had the administration followed Hillsborough's harder line, there is little doubt, as Thomas concluded, the Sons of Liberty in Boston and elsewhere would have resisted.[10]

Pownall continued the discussion of British politics and policy in a subsequent letter dated 22 Mar. 1769, but it has not survived.[11] FB replied with **No. 771**.

---

1. On 8 Feb. the House of Commons approved with amendments eight resolutions passed by the House of Lords on 15 Dec. condemning the proceedings of the Massachusetts House of Representatives, the disorders in Boston, and the Convention of Towns, and justifying the deployment of British Regulars. The resolutions did not propose concrete reforms. However, the address to the king called for the establishment of a Crown commissioner to investigate acts of treason committed in America. *HCJ*, 32: 151.

2. Pownall is referring to the sixty items of American correspondence presented to Parliament on 28 Nov. and additional correspondence presented on 7 Dec. and 20 Jan., including FB's *Letters to Hillsborough* up to 5 Dec. 1768.

3. The enclosure to **No. 721**, which has not been found.

4. Meaning confirmation of the land grant of Mount Desert Island, which the province awarded FB in 1762. The Privy Council finally confirmed the grant on 8 Mar. 1771. *APC*, 4: 614-615.

5. The Revenue Act, 7 Geo. 3, c. 46 (1767).

6. Known as the Quartering Act, 5 Geo. 3, c. 33 (1765).

7. This could suggest that Thomas Pownall was acting at the behest of the cabinet or reflecting ministerial thinking when he made his proposal to the House of Commons on 15 Mar. See **No. 754**n3.

8. For over a year, the American Whigs had been challenging Parliament's authority to levy any tax on the colonies. Moreover, the Massachusetts Council's petition to the king (1768) in urging the repeal of *all* the American revenue acts, indicated how far moderate opinion had traveled in favor of dismantling the mercantilist system; by June, the House's resolves protesting the governor's plans to reform the Council went so far as to declare them a violation of their English constitutional rights and heritage (see the source note to **No. 792**). **Appendix 11**, *Bernard Papers*, 4: 392-396.

9. *Bernard Papers*, 4: 271-276.

10. Thomas, *Townshend Duties Crisis*, 121-129, quotation at 127; Nicolson, *The 'Infamas Govener'*, 187-191.

11. FB acknowledged receipt of this and two other letters from Pownall in **No. 771**.

744 | To Lord Barrington

Boston Feb 20 1769

My Lord

I must appear negligent in not writing to your Lordship of late but I assure you that it is not for Want of Respect or Attention to Business. I am hard worked every way; & in writing I have none but myself & my third Son, who having taken his Degree of A.B.[1] I am obliged to employ as a Copyist, not daring to trust Strangers. An Answer to your last[2] could not have gone before, if it had been immediately wrote after their Receipt.

The Affair of Virginia has long ago been settled in my Mind. As for the Title I see great Difficulties in declining it which did not attend the first Proposal. Many private Letters from London, which have been published in the Newspapers, mention an Intention to make me a Baronet,[3] so that it has generally gained Credit. And my declaring that I had no Expectation of it (I meant immediate) has been interpreted, that I have refused it. This has made my Friends blame me for neglecting to take this Opportunity to advance my Family; & my Enemies for presuming to refuse his Majesty['s][4] honours if they were really offered to me. Mr Temple has made this a Subject of Part of a Libell he has lately published against me,[5] which, as My Lord H has a little Share in it, I shall send to him by my next Packet.[6] I could bear this; but my Lord H having kindly offered to take off from me the Expence of the Patent, which I have since: freely owned will be a Benevolence convenient to me, I know not how to refuse his Favours.[7] I have therefore wrote to him[8] that if his Lordship shall think that such an Appointment will promote his Majesty's Service either in this Station or in any other to which I may be appointed, which I must own I think it may, I shall most thankfully accept of this Honor, if his Majesty shall be pleased to confer it upon me. And I have for this Purpose been forming a Scheme which with a little Help, not unreasonable to request, will provide for an Income to attend upon this Honor. I have it not ^the plan^ ready now, & If I had, I should not send it, as it it[9] would look like making Terms.

I have no Thoughts of going from hence 'till after the next Meeting of the Assembly, which will not be, without special Orders, untill the last Day of May. When the Session is over, if Things are tolerably quiet & I have no particular Commands to execute, I should be glad to go to England so as to arrive there before Winter sets in. But if the Kings Service shall require my staying here I shall chearfully comply. Your Lordship is pleased to signify your Approbation of my Conduct: it is generally allowed that my spirited Message to the Convention contributed greatly to the preventing violent Measures. My Friends here say that it was the boldest Act I have ever yet done; & indeed I knew if their Deliberations has[10] taken another Turn I was to have been seized;[11] & whether my Life would have been spared or not would have been determined by very wicked Men. But it was quite necessary to the Kings Service, & I did not ballance about the Consequences.

My Friend Mr Temple as your Lordship has been pleased to call him some Time ago, has got Business enough upon his Hands now, not to need to quarrel with me. The Disputes between him & the other 4 Commissioners, which began soon after they arrived here & have improved with their knowledge of him have ^now^ got to such a head, that it is declared on both Sides that they cannot continue together: that is that the 4 Commissioners who have endeavoured to support their Commission & the Laws by which & for which it was constituted & have acted therein in Concurrence with & with the Advice & Approbation of all the Officers of the Crown, except Mr Temple himself, must either be removed to keep Mr Temple; or the latter associated with the Party in Opposition to the Government & the Power of Parliament, & cooperating with them in endeavouring to prevent the Execution of the Commission & to oblige the Ministry & Parli^{mt} to revoke it, & thereby restore the Inactivity of the Laws of Trade which prevailed before this Appointment, must be removed, that the Commissioners may go on with the Execution of their Office without Obstruction. This is just as if a Question was put whether Mr Hutchinson or Mr Otis was the fittest Person to be Governor of this Province: The Contrast is not greater in the former Case. I have bore no Part in this Dispute, except from the Effects it had upon my own Business, as it has been the Cheif Occasion ^of all the Opposition^ I have met with from the Council within these 6 months past:[12] but I have not as yet assigned this Cause for it. As I have entered so far into this Business, your Lordship will use this Information with all due Caution & Secrecy.

I am &c

The Right honble The Lord Visc^t Barrington

L, LbC   BP 7: 258-261

In handwriting of Thomas Bernard. Barrington replied with **No. 760**, expressing an interest in undermining John Temple with information provided by FB.

---

1. Thomas Bernard graduated from Harvard in 1767, and received his MA *in absentia* in 1770. His biographer accurately depicted Thomas as his father's "confidential Secretary." His father probably paid him for his labors, as the usage of "employ" implies. Baker, *Life of Sir Thomas Bernard*, 2.

2. **No. 707**.

3. For example, the *Boston Chronicle*, 26-30 Jan. 1769 contained two items that would have caught FB's attention. One letter from London, dated 17 Nov., claimed FB was to be paid a "pension" of £2,000 from a new tax on American lawyers and clerks, while TH was to be raised to the governorship and maintained by revenues from taxes on woolen manufactures. A summary of Parliament's

debates, printed in the same newspaper, noted that members proposing trade restrictions in retaliation for Boston's defiance "also spoke with great respect of Governor Bernard, and mentioned among his difficulties" two issues that he had discussed in official correspondence: the annual election of the Council, which rendered that body subject to the influence of the lower house, and the fact that juries were "often an instrument of faction, instead of a check upon it." Hillsborough's "neglect" to present the petition of the House of Representatives to the king was also commented upon. The remainder of the article reiterated Grenville's Commons' speech of 8 Nov. and other Parliamentary proceedings, also printed in the *Boston Gazette*, 30 Jan. 1768 (for which see **No. 732**n5). Another letter from London, dated 19 Nov., was more explicit, communicating that FB was held in the "highest credit" by British ministers. It correctly predicted FB would be awarded a baronetcy and that the earl of Hillsborough would remain in office following Parliament's scrutiny of the Grafton administration's American policy. *Essex Gazette*, 24-31 Jan. 1769; a fuller version of this letter was printed in the *Boston Gazette*, 6 Feb. 1769.

4. Editorially supplied.

5. See **No. 742**n9.

6. Possibly **No. 748**.

7. In **No. 713**.

8. **No. 735**.

9. Thus in manuscript.

10. Thus in manuscript.

11. Such had been the treatment of Edmund Andros, governor of the Dominion of New England. Andros was removed by a coup in April 1689 following the deposition of King James II during the Glorious Revolution, and held captive for over a year in Boston before being allowed to return to England.

12. FB does not allude to the fact that Temple was James Bowdoin's son-in-law,* though evidently— now rather late in the day—began to suspect they had been colluding against him. There is no substantive evidence to justify such a claim, yet equally it is most unlikely that Temple and Bowdoin would not have co-operated by exchanging information if it could benefit the other in their respective quarrels with the Customs commissioners and the governor.

*Temple married Elizabeth Bowdoin (1750-1809) in 1767.

745 | From the Earl of Hillsborough

(N°. 24.)

Whitehall February 20th: 1769.

Sir,

Inclosed I send you a copy of an Address to the King from the Lords Spiritual and Temporal and Commons in Parliament assembled, presented to His Majesty the 13th, instant, together with His Majesty's most gracious Answer thereto;[1] and, in pursuance of this Address, the King has thought fit to direct me to signify to you His Majesty's Commands, that you do take the most effectual Methods for procuring the fullest information that can be obtained, touching all Treasons or misprisions of Treason[2] committed within your Government since the 30th, Day of December 1767, and transmit the same to me, together with the Names of the Persons who were most active in the Commission of such Offences.[3]

I have it further in command from His Majesty to transmit to you the inclosed Resolutions of both Houses of Parliament, upon a consideration of the Papers ordered by His Majesty to be laid before them, relative to the public proceedings in His Majesty's Province of Massachuset's Bay in the Course of the last year; and His Majesty trusts that these Resolutions and this Address will have the Effect to induce a due obedience to the Constitutional Authority of Parliament.

Your Dispatches N[s] 34, 35, & 36,[4] have been received and laid before the King; and His Majesty's Servants have now under their consideration what further Measures it may be adviseable to recommend to His Majesty, in consequence of those public transactions in the Province of Massachuset's Bay, of which intelligence has been received since the above-mentioned proceedings in Parliament. I am with great Esteem & Regard Sir

Your Most Humble & Obedient Servant

Hillsborough

Governor Bernard.

LS, RC   BP, 12: 57-60.

Left marginalia: there are virgules at the start of the first and second paragraph indicating the enclosures. Endorsed: (N[o]. 24) Earl of Hillsborough d Feb 20 1769 r Ap 20. Docket by Thomas Bernard: Inclos[g] the Address of Both House concerning America —   Variants: CO 5/758, ff 36-37 (LS, AC); CO 5/765, ff 55-57 (L, LbC). Enclosures not found (for which see *HLJ*, 32: 201, 209-210).

Hillsborough's directions to investigate treason committed since 30 Dec. 1767 followed upon instructions given earlier to pursue the *Liberty* rioters (**No. 661**).[5] While action against these rioters had been dropped,[6] FB would have assumed (correctly) that Hillsborough's advice on the mode of prosecution still stood: that any colonist charged with high crimes and misdemeanors could be tried in the court of the King's Bench in London under the Treason Act of 1543 (35 Hen. 8, c. 2), though Parliament's address to the king of 8 Feb. did not specify proceeding in that court. Hillsborough's latest instruction was the source of anxiety for it failed to clarify if any trial would be held in England. Also, FB was to undertake what he termed a "public enquiry"—by which he meant an indictment before a grand jury—to establish evidence sufficient for a treason trial. He replied with **No. 778**, setting forth the "forcible" reasons why his government was unable to proceed further.

1. The address of both Houses, calling for an investigation into treasonable activities, was presented to the king at St. James's Palace at 2 PM on 13 Feb. It had passed the House of Lords on 15 Dec. and the House of Commons on 8 Feb. On 9 Feb., the Lords approved the minor amendments voted by the House. Hillsborough's depiction of the king's answer to the address of both Houses as "gracious" was a formulaic invocation of his royal majesty's authority. The king's answer of 14 Feb. was anything but "gracious" toward the inhabitants of Massachusetts, with the king pledging he would "not fail to give those Orders which you recommend, as the most effectual Method of bringing the Authors of the late unhappy Disorders in that Province to condign Punishment." *HLJ*, 32: 251. Parliament's address was printed in the Massachusetts newspapers in April, including the *Boston Gazette*, 17 Apr. 1769.

2. Misprision of treason was a failure to report knowledge or suspicion of acts of treason, and was a punishable offence.

3. Left marginalia: a line marking the section "touching . . . Offences" was probably added by FB.

4. **Nos. 717**, **718** (received 16 Jan.), and **719** (received 10 Feb.).

5. *Bernard Papers*, 4: 271-276.

6. See **No. 719**.

746 | *To the Earl of Hillsborough*

private

Boston Feb 21 1769

My Lord

In a former Letter[1] I acquainted your Lordship of the printers of the Boston Gazette Edes & Gill & the use which might be made of calling them to an Account. I think it proper to illustrate that Letter by an Instance from that Paper just now published, which I shall inclose with Observations on it separate from this Letter.[2] In this I shall observe upon the Grounds of the Presumption with which the Author of this Peice has been generally pronounced without any Contradiction which I have heard of.

As soon as the Paper came out this Libell was generally assigned to Mr John Temple one of the Commissioners of the Customs; & that Opinion remains uncontradicted as far as I have learned. Your Lordship, if you don't know this Gentleman, will perhaps be surprised that a Gentleman in the immediate Service of the Crown & in a distinguished Station should libell one of the King's Governors who has laboured so hard & suffered so much in endeavouring to maintain the Rights of the Crown as I have done; & should carry his Abuse so far as not to spare the King's Minister for approving the Governors Service. But so it is, that I believe, its undoubted by every Man of Observation & Reason in this Town that this Gentleman has been employed in this Kind of Warfare against the Governor's Office &

Person, ever since they have been distinguished by the Support of the Rights of the Crown of Great Britain.

The ordinary Writers in the Boston Gazette & other seditious Papers are generally known by common Reputation as employed in the Part of Opposition to the Kings Government, altho' Care is taken that no legal Proof shall be produced against them. And by frequent Observations discerning Readers[3] pretend to distinguish the different Stiles of the several Writers, & do it with great Exactness. In this List of Writers, M[r] Temple has for 3 Years at least been reckoned, & his Pieces have been distinguished by an uncommon Rancour & Malice against the Person of the Governor, which in other Writers is carried No farther than their Purpose to get him removed requires; which being done they desires no further Hurt to him; But M[r] Temple's Intention towards the Governor has been professed both to ruin him & *his Family* to effect which he has frequently declared to a Gentleman[x4] who will attest the same when called upon, that "he would go to the Gates of Hell".

But this Kind of Proof is not the only one which will show M[r] Temple to be a Writer against Government: positive Proofs are not wanting; one of which I will now mention. About 2 Years ago, when no man could appear on the Behalf of Government, but was sure to be attacked in his Person and Character[,][5] M[r] Temple prepared a Libell for the Boston Gazette in which the Abuse was directed against the Governor, the Secretary, M[r] Flucker a Gentleman of the Council distinguished for his Fidelity to Government, & M[r] Trowbridge then Attorney general & now one of the Judges of the superior Court.[6] These 3 Gentlemen were abused for having done something or other for the Support of Government or the Defence of the Governor: it being an usual & Successful Practice with the Faction to pelt the Friends of the Government with illiberal & dirty Abuse; & this is one of the Kinds of Intimidation with which they have kept the Province in Awe, people being no more inclined to fight for their Characters than they are for their Persons.

This Libell M[r] Temple inclosed in a Cover to the Printers of the Boston Gazette with a Letter wrote wholly by himself & signed by his Name desiring them to print it. But before he sent it to the Printers he happened to send the Coat ^in a pocket of which the Letter was^[7] to the Taylors, where it was taken out of the Pocket & went thro several Hands till it came to M[r] Gray the Province Treasurer and one of the Council: The Letter was soon missed pursued & recovered. At that Time I had no Encouragement to multiply Complaints, & therefore took no Notice of it but kept it in my Mind for a proper Time. When the present Libell came out M[r] Flucker, at my Desire, talked with the Treasurer about the former Libell, expressing a Curiosity to know what was said of him. He, M[r] Gray, said that it was all in M[r] Temple's hand writing, & the Letter was signed by his Name; that it was very abusive, but he could not recollect particulars at that Time. M[r] Hallowell who is now in London knows the whole Affair: I have never attempted to get an Account of this Affair from the Treasurer; as I should expect at this Time to be refused. But if he was required to answer by Authority, so as to have Necessity to plead, he would not decline it, as his Office being elective is annually at the Mercy of the Governor.

I come now to point out the distinguishing Passage in this Libell which has convinced every knowing Reader that it is the Production of Mr Temple: & indeed it affords as Strong a Proof as the Nature of internal Evidence will admit. Every one, who is acquainted with the Writings of the Americans in opposition to the Power of Parliament, knows that Mr Greenville[8] has been a principal Object of their Resentment & Subject of their Abuse: this is stronger at Boston if possible that [than] at New York &c. And one may be positive that among all the Writers against Government at Boston there is but one who would sho[w?] a Desire of his Return to Power; as such an Expectation is directly opposite to the fundamental Principles and Views of the Faction. But as Mr Temple professes to have family-Connections w[ith] Mr Greenville such an Expectation is cons[istent] with His Views, tho inconsistent with his Proceedings: for a little Consideration might shew him that he is not like to recommend himself to Mr Greenville by abetting the Opposers of the Power of Parliament & the Persecutors of those who endeavour to maintain it. However he has so far laid his Account in this Expectation as to feed his Friends with it, even so far, as it is said, as the Disposal of the Government itself. Be this as it will, it is certain that this Dependence of Mr Temple makes him a distinguished Character in the Party he is connected with so as to form an uncommon Contrast in their Writings. For whilst all the other Writers against Government have for 3 Years together been uniformly charging the Governor, with being the Tool & Creature of Mr Greenville & in Support of this Charge have quoted the public testimonials which that Gentleman has given of his Approbation of the Gov^{rs} Conduct, One Writer only threatens him with the Vengeance of the same Gentleman when he shall come into Power. This is unaccountable in any other way than the foregoing. After this I will refer your Lordship to Note 14 of the inclosed Paper.

There are other internal Marks of this coming from Mr Temple, particularly from his using the Name of Verres (a strange Appellation to a Governor who is diminishing his Estate instead of augmenting it) which was first applied in a virulent & flagitious Libell of the Governor which had strong internal Proofs of its coming from Mr Temple, & being since preserved in his Writings,[9] & the name Palinurus used ^in^ a Libell which the Printers indirectly owned to have come from him.[10] But the first mentioned Characteristical Mark [needs?] no Confirmation. I should here mention that when I call Mr Temple the Writer of these Pieces I mean in Conjunction with Mr Fenton[11] a Lieutenant on half pay & Brother in Law to Mr Temple who is supposed to be sometimes the whole composer & generally the Corrector & finisher of the Pieces: But Mr Temple furnishes the Materials & points the

Abuse, & especially brings all the Malice; For Mr Fenton never pretended to have received any Offence from the Govr. However when the Authorship of a Piece is talked of, the two Names are quite convertible.

I cannot pass unnoticed the wicked Insinuation at the End of the Libell concerning the Baronettage, which is as false as it is envious & Malicious. The Truth is that the Report of my being to be made a Baronet is of an old standing & came here before I knew any thing of it; & has since been repeated in many private Letters. This has subjected me to many Questions to which I answered at first that I knew Nothing of it & since that I had a hint from a Friend that if I would apply for it, I might probably succeed; But so far from saying that the Title was offered me by his Majesty I never went so far as to say that it was offered me by his Minister, as in Truth I could not. As for the Letter in Question (which is but one of several with this Article in it which have reached the Press) I never saw it but in Print nor can I guess now whom it came from or to. All I shall say to it is that the Enviousness & Maliciousness of this Note is so Characteristical, that I would venture my Life on naming the Author, if I had no other Proof of it but this Paragraph. If I had not allready submitted this Matter to your Lordship with an Assurance of the high Sense I shall have of any Honor his Majesty shall be graciously pleased to confer upon me, I might enforce my Sollicitation with a Reason which Martial somewhere gives for his wanting to be rich: *Pendentem volo Zoilum videre.*[12]

I am &c.

The Right Honble The Earl of Hillsborough.

P.S.

I have taken the Liberty to entitle the enclosed Letter *private*, that it may be entirely at your Lordship's Command, & you may be under no Necessity of communicating it to any one or in any Manner but as You shall judge for the best. For tho I thought it best that Your Lordship should be cautioned against the Wickedness of this Libell, yet I by no means desire that this Letter should be made a Subject of Public Animadversion. And indeed it is made unfit for it by the Freedom with which I have made use of Mr Greeville's[13] Name, for whom I have allways expressed a great Respect & to whom for some Time past I have thought myself much obliged: but it was quite necessary to the Explication of the Case. I also think that it is not fair that Business of a private & personal Nature (by which I do not mean the Affront to your Lordship or anything but what relates to myself in [_])[14] should interfere with the great & important Affairs in which Your Lordship is now engaged.

P.S. Feb 28

I have communicated this Letter & also the Observations upon the Libell to the Lieut Govr & I have his Authority to say that he agrees with my Sentiments in general, excepting what is said of himself & the Account of Mr Gray of which he had his Knowledge from me. I have acquainted Mr Paxton & Mr Flucker of what I have wrote of them & they have again acknowledged the Truth of what they have before told me.

L, LbC   BP, 7: 141-148.

In handwriting of Thomas Bernard, except where noted. Probably enclosed a copy of the *Boston Gazette*, 30 Jan. 1769.

FB imagined John Temple to have been complicit in the Whigs' newspaper campaign against him, from the time of the Stamp Act Crisis. But he had no proof that Temple had authored scurrilous articles comparing him to the tyrant "Verres." The anecdote provided by Harrison Gray, the province treasurer, was unsupported by any documentary evidence, while the "internal Evidence" provided by the reference to George Grenville, a distant relative to Temple, is unconvincing (see the source note to **No. 742**). The double postscript could indicate that FB not only delayed dispatching the letter but hesitated, unsure of his case, after consulting with TH. The absence of a RC and enclosure could also suggest that FB never sent the letter.

---

1. **No. 734**.

2. The "Observations" have not been found. It is possible that FB is referring to an anonymous piece in the *Boston Gazette*, 20 Feb. 1769, discussing the depositions lately taken by FB "that have induced his Majesty to think we are in a State of Rebellion." The article did not name the deponents, but urged them to make copies of their depositions public (for which see **Nos. 732** and **733**). However, FB's mention of "Verres" and George Grenville suggests that he was in fact referring to the "Paoli" letter published in the 30 Jan. issue of the *Gazette*, and discussed in the source note to **No. 742**.

3. The Boston shopkeeper Harbottle Dorr was one such "discerning reader," though he did not reveal "Paoli's" identity in any of his annotated newspapers.

4. Left marginalia: "^xM^r Paxton".

5. Obscured in the gutter of the binding, here and below.

6. FB may have been thinking of the articles by "Paskalos" (Dr. Joseph Warren), one of the first polemicists to compare FB to Gaius Licinius Verres, the tyrannical Roman governor, in the *Boston Gazette*, 10 Nov. 1766. But in this letter he is not referring to a specific article but to the propaganda war that raged in the province newspapers during 1766 and 1767. See *Bernard Papers*, 3: 311.

7. Interlineation by FB.

8. Thus continually in manuscript.

9. FB meant that Temple had reused the "Appellation" "Verres," not that he had managed to spy on the commissioner's private papers.

10. "Palinurus" was mentioned in a witty article titled "The Critical Review-Makers impartially Reviewed." The "Critical Review maker" was likened to a "Butcher, Manger, and Retailer of other Men's Works, without understanding one Word of them." By "Palinurus," the anonymous author may have meant

Richard Draper, the printer of the government news-sheet the *Massachusetts Gazette*, whose columns were "*stamped . . . with an Oxonian Imprimatur*" supplied by the governor himself. Alternatively, Harbottle Dorr assumed that "Palinurus" equated with FB, as an unoriginal author and purveyor of other people's ideas. *Boston Gazette*, 10 Mar. 1766; Dorr Collection, 1: 359. Palinurus himself was the Trojan refugees' steersman, drowned but for some time refused Hades until he won funeral rites. Virgil, *Aeneid,* books V and VI. If the intention was to accuse FB of being Palinurus, the most it would mean was that he had fallen asleep while steering the ship of state, and in fact Palinurus fell asleep and drowned by a dirty trick from a god.

11. Probably James Fenton, commissioned a lieutenant in the 1st Regiment of Foot on 15 Feb. 1756.

12. Trans. "I wish to see Zoilus hanging by the neck." FB is quoting M. Valerii Martialis, *Epigrammaton libri,* IV.77.5. The epigram read in full would have alerted Hillsborough to FB's hatred of Temple, here represented by the character Zoilus, subjected to Martial's libidinous invective and personal loathing throughout the *Epigrammaton.* One modern English translation rendered the passage as "I have never asked the gods for riches, content as I am with moderate means, and pleased with what is mine. Poverty—I ask your pardon!—depart. What is the reason of this sudden and strange prayer? I wish to see Zoilus hanging by the neck." Walter C. A. Ker, ed. *Martial: Epigrams,* 2 vols. (London: 1925), 1: 285. Martial's epigrams were employed by government critics in England to parody the foibles of contemporary English aristocrats, male and female, and leading politicians. William Scott, ed. *Epigrams of Martial, &c, with Mottos from Horace, &c* ([London] 1773).

13. Thus in manuscript. A scribal error for "Greenville", a continual misspelling of "Grenville".

14. Closing parenthesis supplied. The scribe may have written "in this letter" or "in here".

747 | *From the Selectmen of Boston*

[*22 Feb. 1769*]

May it please your Excellency

The Selectmen of the Town of Boston, beg leave once more, to wait on your Excellency, hoping you will excuse this further trouble, as it is upon a matter of the greatest importance to the Town.

In your Answer to our late humble Request[1] your Excellency was pleased to say, that you have no Reason to think that the publick Transactions of this Town have been misapprehended by his Majesty or his Ministers; or that their Opinions thereon are founded upon any other Accounts than those published by the Town itself. "And that if we can vindicate ourselves from such Charges as may arise from our own Publications, we shall have nothing further to apprehend."

As the Town has published nothing but its own transactions in Town Meeting legally assembled, it gives us the greatest Pleasure to find your Excellency in your reply to us, thus vindicating it from any Just cause of apprehension from the General Character of its Inhabitants, considered as Individuals; If therefore the Town has suffered an Account of the Disorders which happened on the 18' March or the 10' June last, by Persons unknown, (the only Disorders that have taken place in this Town within the Year past) we take your Excellencys Declaration to us, to be a full Testimony, that in your Opinion, it must be in consequence of some partial or false Representations of those Disorders to his Majestys Ministers. And we rejoice to find your Excellencys Sentiments as expressed in your Reply, so far harmonizing with those of his Majestys Council not long published.[2] We have in this Case the most authentick Evidence that can possibly be had, the Joint Testimony of the Governor and Council of the Province, that the Town has not been *in a State of Opposition to Order and Government*, and such *as required a Military Force to support civil Authority.*

With Regard to the public Transactions of the Town, when legally assembled, from which alone in your Excellencys declared Opinion, the Town could have any thing to apprehend; we beg leave to say, that after the most careful retrospect, and the best inquiry we could make into the nature and Import of those Transactions, we are utterly at a loss in what view they can appear to have militated with any Law, or the British Constitution of Government. And we entreat your Excellency would condescend, to point out to us, in what particular respect they either have been, or may be view'd in such a Light, that either the Town may be made sensible of the illegality of its proceedings, or, that upon the most critical Examination its Innocence may appear in a still clearer Light.

Your Excellencys high Station in the Province; and the regard you have professed for the Interest of the Town, we humbly apprehend, must give *Propriety* to this as well as our former Address.

transcript, PC   *Reports of the Record*
                                                       Commissioners of Boston, 23: 8-9.

This address was a rejoinder to FB's letter of 18 Feb. (see source note to **No. 741**). Voted unanimously at a meeting of the selectmen on 22 Feb.: present were John Hancock, Joshua Henshaw, Henderson Inches, Joseph Jackson, Samuel Pemberton, and John Ruddock. FB replied on 24 Feb., with a brief note asserting that his comments in the letter of 18 Feb. concerned the proceedings of the town meeting and selectmen and not the "disorder[s]" of 18 Mar. or 10 Jun. 1768. *Reports of the Record Commissioners of Boston*, 23: 9.

FB revealed his "Contempt" for the selectmen's proceedings in a letter to John Pownall of 5 Mar.

> These are of no other Use but to show the Impudence Folly & Invidiousness of the Faction & the Compliance of their Tools. These were wrote by Adams & put upon the Selectmen to present, they not daring to refuse what is dictated by the Faction ^or rather being part of the faction themselves.^ Some would have had me to ^have^ refused the receiving these Addresses or giving an Answer to them: but it was much better to give Answers which not only should not answer their Purpose, but bring Contempt upon them as this has done.[3]

1. **No. 741**.

2. This is an ironic allusion to the Council's positive answer to FB's question as to whether or not the commissioners of Customs could return to Boston in safety, as discussed in **No. 708** and published in the *Boston Gazette*, 23 Jan. 1769.

3. FB to John Pownall, Boston, 5 Mar. 1769, BP, 7: 263.

748 | To the Earl of Hillsborough

(Duplicate)

N°. 5

Boston Feb: 25 1769

My Lord

In packing up the Boston Gazette, which I promised your Lordship by my Letter N° 3,[1] I have thought proper to add a Series of Evening Posts published here by J and T Fleet,[2] for the Sake of a periodical Paper published in it and continued. It was first published at New York where it is continued. It has been also, as I understand, regularily[3] sent to London and published there. It is composed by Adams and his Assistants, among whom there must be some, one at least, of the Council; as every thing that is done or said in Council which can be made use of is constantly perverted misrepresented and falsified in this Paper.[4] But if the Devil himself was of the Party, as he virtually is, there could not have been got together a greater Collection of impudent virulent and seditious Lies Perversions of Truth and Misrepresentations than are to be found in this Publication. Some are entirely invented and are first heard of from the printed Papers; others are founded on Fact but so perverted as to be the direct contrary of the Truth; other Part of the abuse consists of Reflections of the Writer which pretend to no other Authority but his own Word. To set about answering these Falsities would be a Work like that of cleansing Augeas's Stable, which is to be done only by bringing in a Stream strong enough to sweep away the Dirt and the Collectors of it alltogether.[5]

The Intention of this Journal appears as well from the Composition itself as from the Manner of publishing it at three different Presses at once, to raise a general Clamour against his Majesty's Government in England and throughout America, as well as in Massachusets Bay. And from thence they still flatter themselves that they shall get the Navy and Army removed and again have the Government and the Custom house and the Laws in their own hands. Altho' it is needless to observe upon such an heap of Falsehood, yet I will make a faithful Report of my own Opinion of the Behaviour of the Troops in general, in Contrast of the Accounts of them in this Paper. I dont beleive there ever was an Instance of so large a Body of Troops (3 Regiments) quartered in a Town so licentious as this is, behaving so orderly decently and quietly as these have done. On the other hand all Kinds of means have been used to provoke them to Violence, Not only small Parties and Centinels have been insulted, but the Main Guard upon their releiving or other parading have been surrounded by Numbers of People and abused with the most gross and scurrilous Language; all which has been taken with a Patience which affords a very exemplary Proof of the Care of the commanding Officers and the orderly Obedience of the Men. Meanwhile some of the Justices have been continually harassing the Offi-cers as well as the Men with Warrants upon every trivial Occasion and preferring Indictments against them at the Quarter Sessions. All which has been born with uncommon Patience and entire Submission to the Law. So they seem to have given up their Attempts to make a Disturbance & all Things are now quiet. This being the Truth how wicked and abandoned must be the Author of the Journal? The Vindica-tion of the Troops from these scandalous and false Imputations has been the cheif Occasion of my troubling your Lordship with this Letter.

> I am with great Respect, My Lord, Your Lordships most obedient
> & most humble Servant

> Fra Bernard

The Right Honorable The Earl of Hillsborough

dupLS, RC   CO 5/758, ff 72-73.

Endorsed: Boston 25th. Feb[y]. 1769. Governor Bernard (N[o]. 5). R 15th. May. Orig[l]. R 17 April mislaid. B. 18. Enl[d].   Enclosures: a supplement, dated 28 Feb. 1768, CO 5/758, f 74;[6] copies of newspapers (not found), including the *Boston Evening-Post* from c.19 Dec. 1768 to Feb. 1769,[7] and the *Boston Gazette*. Variants of letter in CO 5/767, ff 232-235 (L, RLbC) and BP, 7: 148-150 (L, LbC).

---

1. **No. 734**.

2. John Fleet (1734-1806) and Thomas Fleet Jr. (1732-97), publishers of the *Boston Evening-Post*.

3. Thus in manuscript.

4. The "Journal of the Times" or "Journal of Occurrences" was produced by an editorial team including Samuel Adams and was first published outside of Boston, in the *New York Journal* on 13 Oct. The ven-ture's principal aim was to raise aware of Boston's plight and garner support in other colonies. To that end the contributors examined FB's dispute with the Council over the quartering of British soldiers and documented confrontations between citizens and soldiers, all in weekly installments. The "Journal" was also reprinted in the *Boston Evening-Post* and *Essex Gazette*. Dickerson, *Boston under military rule, 1768-1769, as revealed in a Journal of the times*; Alexander, *Samuel Adams*, 87.

5. In Greek mythology, the fifth labor of Hercules (Heracles) was to sweep clean in a single day the expansive stables of King Augeas, which he managed by diverting two river courses.

6. This was an "anecdote" of Andrew Oliver's concerning a private conversation following a meeting of the proprietors of a township, who included Samuel Adams and Thomas Cushing. Adams remarked that "Things will never be properly settled in America untill the Parliament has repealed all the Acts affecting the American Trade for the 15th of Cha. 2. to the present time." FB's comment that "Here is a Proposal of Terms of Conciliation," was naively optimistic in supposing that Adams would defer to the doctrine of parliamentary supremacy, though Cushing and other moderates might have accepted such a proposal had it ever been made by Grafton or North. CO 5/758, f 74.

7. The reprints in the *Boston Evening-Post* continued until 18 Dec. 1769. FB dispatched more copies in a package of documents sent to John Pownall, c.7 Mar. 1769. BP, 7: 262-263.

749 | *To the Rev. Samuel Seabury*

Boston Feb 27 1769

Sr

I have just received your Letter of Feb 13.[1] Above a fortnight ago I signed a Paper declaring that I had no Knowledge of the Letter signed B.W. till after I saw it in Print.[2] Mr. Harrison the Collector & Mr John Apthorp signed it at the same Time; I have since heard that it has been signed by Mr James Apthorp & Mr Hall.[3] I suppose you will hear of it from Dr Caner[4] in whose Hands I put it after the three first had signed. I shall be allways ready to do any Thing in my Power to vindicate the Honor of the Society & the Reputation of its Missionaries.

I am Sr &c

The Reverend Mr Seabury[5]

L, LbC   BP, 7: 216.

In handwriting of Thomas Bernard.

FB's letter to the Rev. Seabury was occasioned by the long-running disagreements between New York Anglicans and Presbyterians over the former's support for an American episcopate. Both factions published under collective pseudonyms. The Presbyterians contributed "The American Whig" to the *New-York Gazette, or the Weekly Post Boy*, printed by James Parker. The Anglicans wrote under the pseudonym "Timothy Tickle Esqr.," whose "Whip for the American Whig" columns were printed in the *New-York Gazette, and Weekly Mercury*. When, on 4 Jul., the "Whip for the American Whig" accused the Boston Congregational pastor, the Rev. Dr. Charles Chauncy (1705-87) of willfully misleading colonists about the high costs of seeking ordination in England, Chauncy was defended by the anonymous "B. W." who accused the Rev. Seabury of being the author of this particular, malicious piece.[6] "B. W." purported to be a staunch Boston Anglican and prominent member of the Church of England's missionary organization, the Society for the Propagation of the Gospel in Foreign Parts. Seabury vociferously denied the allegation, and suspicion as to "B. W.'s" identity immediately fell upon Benning Wentworth (1696-1770), the former governor of New Hampshire. When Wentworth claimed the letter a forgery Seabury followed up the leads provided by James Parker, initially supposing that Chauncy had fabricated the letter. Chauncy's denial of authorship prompted Seabury to challenge him publicly to reveal the author's identity and listed the possible sources[7]—all of whom are named in FB's letter printed here, plus John Temple. Seabury was trying to flush out Chauncy rather than embarrass FB and the others. FB co-operated to the extent of signing a paper repudiating any involvement. In fact, Chauncy did not write the "B. W." letter, which was the work of a Boston Anglican, Thomas Brown, but he did append the initials to the letter Brown sent him, probably in ignorance of the likely consequences, before sending it to the printer James Parker.[8]

---

1. Not found.

2. "B. W", *New-York Gazette and Weekly Post-Boy*, 29 Aug. 1768.

3. John Apthorp, a Boston merchant, and son of the wealthy merchant Charles Apthorp (1698–1758). James Apthorp (1731–1799) was another merchant son of Charles Apthorp and a resident of Braintree. Hugh Hall (c.1693-1773).

4. Rev. Dr. Henry Caner (1700-92), rector of King's Chapel, Boston.

5. Samuel Seabury (1729-96) of Westchester, N.Y., was a leading proponent of an American episcopate and prominent leader among American Anglicans. He wrote a series of influential pamphlets attacking the Continental Congress (1774-75), which helped shape the Loyalists' ideological responses to the incipient revolutionary movement. He became the first Episcopalian bishop after the Revolution (1784).

6. "B. W.," *New-York Gazette, or the Weekly Post-Boy*, 29 Aug. 1768.

7. In "The Whip for the American Whig," *New-York Gazette and the Mercury*, 19 and 26 Dec., 1768. The Boston Anglicans are named in the issue of 26 Dec. Seabury's preface, dated 9 Dec. 1768, was reprinted in the *Boston Gazette*, 23 Feb. 1769.

8. "The B. W. Controversy. 1768-1769," *Memoir of Bishop Seabury*, ed., William Jones Seabury, (New York, 1908; http://anglicanhistory.org/usa/seabury/bio1908/08.html, accessed 8 Oct. 2013).

750 | *To Thomas Gage*

Boston March 2 1769

S^r

Mr Bowdoin wrote to you some time ago[1] upon a Proposal made to Mr Winthrop our Mathematical Professor for him to go or send a Disciple of his to Lake superior to observe the transit of Venus, at which Place it is to be seen from Beginning to End. To this he received from you a favorable Answer, which he communicated to me in Council.[2] We have been for a Week past considering of this, desirous if possible to find Ways & Means to fit out this Expedition. But after all we are obliged to give it up not being able to satisfy ourselves that we can constitutionally issue Money out of the Treasury for a Purpose not immediately relative to the Province: It is with great Regret that we decline this Business.

We are obliged to turn our Eyes towards you, hoping that you will see this Business in the important Light it deserves, and find it within Your Power to expedite it at the Expence of the Crown. Besides the observing the Transit of Venus, an Opportunity which if now neglected will never return, It will also afford an Occasion to take the Longitudes of different Stations upon the Lakes even to the West ^end^ of Lake superior & the Variations of the compass and the exact Latitudes, Observations, which when we consider their Importance to Great Britain, It is a Wonder they have not been taken long ago. And these Observations may be particularily[3] serviceable at this Time if any Attention should be given to Captn Carver's Travels.[4]

As Mr Winthrop cannot go himself, he has proposed Mr Danforth & Mr Willard, the one lately the other now a Tutor of the College; whom he has engaged to instruct so as to make them quite capable of the Business. We think we can fit out proper Instruments here: they are willing to undertake this without any Pay; so that the Expence of transporting them & their Subsistence will be all. The transporting them may be done with the Kings Sloops & Batteaus and may be brought into the ordinary Expence of the Garrison on the Lakes; ~~the Subsistence of them & two attend[ants]~~ ~~tho' it should be plentiful would come to no great Matter & may be brought into the ordinary Expence of the Garrison on the Lakes~~; the subsistence of them & two attendants tho it should be plentiful would come to no great Matter & might be made extra Charge; And Sr William Johnson[5] I doubt not, would so far assist this Expedition as to furnish it with Indians & Belts necessary for their Protection & ~~for~~ ^with^ some small Presents for the most distant Nations. It would also be of great Service if you could engage an Officer who is a Mathematician & would take a Pleasure in such an Expedition to accompany them.

Upon a Review of this Plan I flatter myself that it will meet with your Approbation; your carrying it into Execution will intitle you to the Thanks of the learned

World. If you should determine upon it, no time should be lost in sending Orders to the the[6] several Posts & making Provision. Our Mathematicians shall be kept in Readiness to march immediately upon receiving Orders to join Your Party at Albany; which we think will save Time. They should make the best of their Way untill they have got to the Station where they are to make their Observation of the Transit. We reckon, that if they are well attended with Sloops & Batteaus, they may get from Albany to Lake Superior in 40 Days: but 60 should be allowed for fear of Accidents; or more if they can be got. The Transit is on the 3[d] of June; when that is over they may make their other Observations at Leisure.

I am &c

General Gage

L, LbC   BP, 7: 217-219.

In handwriting of Thomas Bernard. A reply from Gen. Gage has not been found in MiU-C: Gage Papers.

---

1. James Bowdoin to Thomas Gage, Boston, 26 Feb. 1769, *Bowdoin and Temple Papers* 129-130. Bowdoin was a keen patron of the sciences.

2. While FB's support for the expedition was genuine he was not party to Bowdoin's private discussions with "some Gentlemen here"—notably Prof. John Winthrop (1714-79)—about the suggestion of the Astronomer Royal at Greenwich* that the colonies should equip an expedition to Lake Superior to observe the transit of Venus due in June. Winthrop had observed the transit in 1761 at St. John's, Nfld. Gen. Gage had already pledged his support for the venture when, on 22 Feb., Bowdoin asked the Governor and Council to fund the expedition. They did so on the understanding that Bowdoin would try to persuade Prof. Winthrop to lead the expedition in person. But Winthrop (as Bowdoin reported on 1 Mar.) excused himself on the grounds of ill health and extensive commitments as acting president of Harvard College (though FB suspected he was unwilling to undertake a risky journey deep into the wilderness). The Council adjourned further consideration, although its minute book does not record the concerns FB mentions in this letter over the province's authority to fund the expedition. In the end, neither the Governor and Council nor Gage was able to fund it. CO 5/829, ff 2-3. See Frederick Brasch, "The Royal Society of London and Its Influence upon Scientific Thought in the American Colonies," *Scientific Monthly* 33 (1931): 336-355; Harry Woolf, *The Transits of Venus: A Study of Eighteenth-Century Science* (Princeton, N.J., 1959), 170-173.

   * The Rev. Dr. Nevil Maskelyne (1732-1811).

3. Thus in manuscript.

4. Jonathan Carver (1710-80) was a native of Massachusetts and a veteran of the French and Indian War; in 1766 he led an expedition ostensibly in search of the famed Northwest Passage, in the course of which he explored the upper Mississippi River in what is now modern-day Minnesota and Wisconsin. His *Travels Through the Interior Parts of North America in the Years 1766, 1767, and 1768* was not published until 1778. Jonathan Carver, James Stanley Goddard, and John Parker, *The Journals of Jonathan Carver and related documents* (St. Paul, MN, 1976).

5. Sir William Johnson (c.1715-74), superintendent of Indian Affairs for the northern colonies.

6. Thus in manuscript.

751 | To Lord Barrington

Dup.

Boston March 15 1769

My Lord

By a Letter from a Gentleman in London to his Friend here I have learnt that my Lord Hillsborough has expressed a Concern at some disagreeable Reports of me; one only of which I have any Knowledge of, which is that I left the Town on the Arrival of the Troops. And by another Letter I understand that this Complaint has been made against me by L.ᵗ Colonell Dalrymple who commanded the Forces from Halifax.[1]

If I had not lived long enough to wonder at Nothing, I should be surprised to find myself charged with so groundless an Accusation from one who as a private Gentleman I treated with the most friendly Regard; and as a commanding Officer I waited upon with a Sedulity more inforced by my Attention to the Kings Service than reconcileable to the Dignity of my own Station. Tho I might leave such a trivial Charge to be refuted by my general Conduct; yet least it should have made an Impression to my Disadvantage, I have thought proper to give your Lordship a true state of the Fact.

When I am charged with leaving the Town[2] on the Arrival of the Troops, would not any one imagine that the ~~Place~~ Town was then the Place of my Residence? But the Truth is that ^I^ at that Time & for several Months before resided at my House at Roxbury, 4 miles from Boston, a Retreat so necessary for preserving my Health & affording me Leisure for writing, that I could not have gone thro my Business without it. From hence I have, during the Summer, attended my Business in Town with as much Punctuality as I could have done if I had resided in it.

When the Troops were expected I had left Orders at the Castle that a Messenger should be sent to me as soon as the Ships appeared. This was so punctually executed, that I was at the Castle before the Ships had all come to Anchor & above an Hour before the commanding Officers got to the Castle_ From this Day[3] to the Time that the Troops landed[4] I was at the Castle every Morning before 10 o clock & staid there till afternoon or Evening as I was wanted. At one of our Consultations there it was determined to land the Troops at Boston: immediately after this Resolution was taken I went to the Sherriff of the County[5] & gave him Orders to provide Horses & Carriages for the Baggage & Artillery which was punctually done. After Provision was made for every thing requireable of the civil Power, & the Sherriff of the County was ordered to wait on these Gentlemen I did not imagine that the personal Attendance of the Governor was either necessary or decent.

Your Lordship must know that at the Time of the landing there was not the least Apprehension of Resistance, as a Proof of which the commanding Officer went into ^the^ Town an hour before any Body of Troops landed. Every thing was done in good Order & all Provisions which could be expected were made. I was therefore at a Loss to know how I came to be blamed for not attending this Parade; till I learned it was thought that I ought to have provided a Dinner for the Officers upon this Occasion. I own it never entered into my Head to make an Entertainment at a Time of so much Hurry & Confusion: I could not have done it at my own House;[6] & I could not think it proper for me to open a Tavern upon the Occasion:[7] And this is my only Neglect of Duty.

This my Lord is the plain Narrative of Facts, upon which I shall make no Comment: But I shall only desire ^that^ if there is any Remembrance of this Charge to my Disadvantage, Your Lordship will use this Letter to my Vindication; if there is not, that you will excuse this Trouble.

I am &c

The R[t] Honble The Lord Viscount Barrington

P.S.[8] I enclose Copies of the letters which passed between me and L[t] Col Dalrymple before & after the Debarkation;[9] from which it will appear that at the time when my Absence from Town was complained of I really was in Town & made an order for the accommodation of the troops being all I could then do; and the day after[10] I was in Town & in Council upon this business. My attending in person the debarkation was not only unnecessary but highly improper.

dupL, LbC   BP 7: 267-270.

In handwriting of Thomas Bernard, except where noted. Enclosures (not found) were probably copies of the correspondence listed in n9.

What FB's letter does not reveal is that Lt. Col. Dalrymple was probably aware that FB had planned to leave Massachusetts altogether prior to the regiments' arrival the previous October, and head to England. FB had intimated his intentions to Gen. Gage before receiving further instructions from Hillsborough that obliged him to remain (**No. 680**).[11] Gage may have said something to Dalrymple about this, though if it undermined the colonel's personal respect for the governor it did not initially appear to mar their working relationship. FB did not accompany the troops ashore on 1 Oct., though he came into town shortly afterward. He remained until sometime after 4 PM, when he left for Jamaica Plain, leaving the colonel to negotiate suitable accommodation for the soldiers (see the source note to **No. 694**).

1. The recipients of the letters probably conveyed their contents privately to FB, for extracts were not printed in the Boston newspapers. Criticism of FB by "some of the [*British*] Officers" was noted by TH during the struggle to clear the Manufactory House, the previous October; nevertheless TH asserted "they blame him without cause." TH to Richard Jackson, Boston, 19 Oct. 1768, Mass. Archs., 25: 283-284, in Hutchinson Transcripts, 1: 286.

2. The phrase "leaving the Town" is underlined in the manuscript, but probably not by the author.

3. Wednesday, 28 Sept.

4. Saturday, 1 Oct. The landing is described in the source note to **No. 694**.

5. Stephen Greenleaf, sheriff of Suffolk County.

6. He meant his estate at Jamaica Plain rather than the Province House, which was used for formal dinners.

7. It is most unlikely that the town authorities would have funded a reception at Faneuil Hall.

8. Annotated "no dup". Postscript in FB's hand.

9. FB's letter to Dalrymple of 30 Sept., **No. 692**, and Dalrymple's reply of the same day (not found), *Bernard Papers*, 4: 353-355; Dalrymple to FB, 2 Oct. (not found); FB to Dalrymple of the same date; and **No. 696** replying to Dalrymple's letter of 2 Oct.

10. 2 Oct.

11. *Bernard Papers*, 4: 316-318.

752 | To Philip Stephens

Boston March 15 1769

S^r

I desire you will inform the Lords Commissioners of the Admiralty that at the time of the Appointment of Jonathan Sewell Esqr to the Office of Judge of the Admiralty at Halifax; He was the Attorney general of this Province & Advocate general of the Court of Admiralty here:[1] He held these two Offices not with an Intention of keeping them together in one Person, which I should not have thought proper, but with a View that if Establishments were made for the Support of these Offices, he might have his Option which he would continue in; & also for this further Purpose that I might have time to look out for a fit Person to recommend to the other Office.[2]

And now he is called upon to go to Halifax to open his Judge's Commission, He is engaging as Advocate general in some Crown Causes of great Consequence[3] which will be in Danger of failing, if they are not continued under his Conduct till they are concluded. And I must say, that at present I am not ready to name fit Persons for either of the Offices: such has been the prevalence of the popular Party in this Government, that some of the Lawyers, whom I should have been glad to have engaged in his Majesty's Service, have by their abetting the Factious party rendered themselves unfit Objects of the favor of Government. And as it is very expedient that these Offices should be filled with the most able Men that can be had I find it necessary to take more Time to look out for fit Persons.

For these Reasons it will be most advisable that M[r] Sewall should continue to act in these Offices till the Causes in which he is now engaged shall be concluded & his Places can be properly filled. I must therefore humbly recommend to their Lordships that after M[r] Sewall has opened his Commission at Halifax, he may have leave of Absence for one Year he appointing a proper & sufficient Deputy. For this Purpose there is at Halifax a Gentlemen (M[r] Gerrish)[4] who has for many Years acted a Deputy Judge of the Admiralty & is well versed in the Business; and he may in any Cases of Difficulty with great Ease have the Advice & Assistance of M[r] Sewall.

I am with great Respect to their Lordships & Regard to yourself S[r] &c

Philip Stephens Esq Sec[ry] of the Admiralty.

L, LbC   BP, 7: 153-155.

In handwriting of Thomas Bernard.

FB's promotion of Jonathan Sewall was not uncomplicated. While FB valued Sewall's talents as a lawyer, he entertained serious questions about Sewall's political commitment to the government side (**No. 719**). Sewall was appointed judge of the new Vice Admiralty Court at Halifax, on 22 Sept. 1768. It was one of four regional courts established by the British that year. Sewall would have preferred remaining in Boston, but the New England district court based there was headed by his associate Robert Auchmuty, whose commitment FB never questioned. Halifax was Sewall's only avenue of advancement, yet it is possible that FB and TH were pleased to push Sewall further from the center of the Massachusetts government. Sewall's involvement in the Hancock trial necessarily delayed him fulfilling the requirement that he relocate to Halifax in order to take up his judge's commission (and receive his £600 annual salary payable from seizures). Sewall did not set out for Halifax until 24 Jun. 1769 (three months after the Hancock trial ended), and conducted court business for six weeks, his jurisdiction covering Nova Scotia, Quebec, and Newfoundland. By the time Sewall returned to Boston, FB had left the province.[5]

---

1. Sewall's appointment as advocate general of the Vice Admiralty in Massachusetts was confirmed by the Admiralty Board on 1 Jul. 1767. ADM 2/1057, f 251. This office and court were unaffected by the reforms that replaced the colonial Vice Admiralty Court at Halifax with four regional courts, including that headed by Sewall.

2. Samuel Fitch (1724-99) replaced Sewall as advocate general, on 24 Nov. 1769, ADM 2/1057, f 330.

3. That is, *Sewall v. Hancock*. See the source notes to **Nos. 710** and **719**.

4. Joseph Gerrish (1709-74), a member of the Nova Scotia Council, was deputized as a judge of Vice Admiralty.

5. Carol Berkin, *Jonathan Sewall: Odyssey of an American Loyalist* (New York, 1974), 76-79; Carl Ubbelohde, *The Vice-Admiralty Courts and the American Revolution* (Chapel Hill, N.C., 1960), 130-135, 150-151.

753 | *To Lord Barrington*

Dup:

Boston March 18, 1769

My Lord

I am favoured with Your Lordship's Letter of Jan 2nd;[1] and am much obliged to you for the Hints it has conveyed of the Measures pursuing in Parliament, from which I know not how to expect that effectual Means will be used to restore the Kings Authority in this Province. I am sure that the Conclusion of the Address of the Lords[2] will have no such Effect: for a simple Order to me to make Enquiry into the Proceedings,[3] which have incurred the Penalties of Treason or Misprision of Treason, will have no other Consequence that [*than*] to show the Impotency of Government; unless I am armed with some extraordinary Power to oblige Persons, whom I shall require to undergo an Examination, to submit to it.[4] But I have no such Power at present; otherwise I should have exercised it long ago. And if I was to call before me, even by special Orders from the King, ever so many Persons knowing of the seditious & treasonable Practices of the Faction here, & was to beg Leave[5] to ask them a few Questions, I should be answered, as it is said the Secretaries of State were by Wilkes, "You have leave to ask as many Questions as you please, but I beg leave[6] to give no Answer to any of them."

In short, my Lord, this Government is now brought to this State, that if the Cheifs of the Faction are not punished or at least so far censured as to be disqualified from holding Offices; if the Appointment of the Council is not put into the Hands of the King; if the Governor & principal Crown Officers are not provided with adequate Salaries independent of the People, It signifies little who is Governor. Whoever he is, he must either live in perpetual Contention in vainly endeavouring to support the royal Rights, or he must purchase Peace by a prudential Sacrifice of them. If any one by a Comparison of former Times should doubt of this being a true State of the present, let him consider that untill the 4 or 5 Years last past, the Power of Parliament was thought omnipotent, the Authority of the King was revered, the Governor & the Council his Assistants were respected, & the

People in whom, by the Constitution, the cheif Weight of Power was lodged, were kept in awe by the Consideration that the Abuse of their Charter priviledges might occasion the Forfeiture of them. But for these 4 Years past so uniform a System of bringing all Power into the Hands of the People has been prosecuted without Interruption & with such Success, that all that Fear Reverence, Respect & Awe which before formed a tolerable Ballance against the real Power of the People, are annihilated & the artificial Weights being removed, the royal Scale mounts up & kicks the Beam. And I do assure your Lordship if I was to answer ^to^ his Majesty himself on this Subject, I would give it as my Opinion that if He cannot secure to himself the Appointment of the Council, it is not worth while to keep that of the Governor. For it would be better that Mass Bay should be a complete Republic like Connecticut than to remain with so few Ingredients of royalty in it as shall be insufficient to maintain the real royal Char^ac^ter.

For my own Part I have gone too far, to think now of purchasing my Peace by giving up what I have thought my Duty to maintain; even if I could be permitted to do it without being blamed. And as M^r· Townsends Acts, among which is that of Providing adequate Pay for the Governors &c,[7] are condemned, altho' their Execution ^of the Sentence^ is respected, I can form no Prospect in this Country; notwithstanding ^from^ my liking the Climate & loving the People I had formed Connections here, in parting with which I shall have some Loss, as well as pain. It is therefore extremely agreeable to me to see your Lordship's Concern to get me removed to some other Government or a Provision at Home tho I have no Hopes of the latter, as I am sensible how many Expectants there are for every Vacancy that happens.

It is a long Time since I first mentioned my Desire of having Barbadoes. In my Letter of Sep: 1. 1766[8] to your Lordship I mention the Governments then vacant & having declined Jamaica & the leeward Islands I add that I should most thankfully accept Barbadoes. In Jan 1767 I was advised by Mr Jackson that I might very possibly change my Government if I wished for it.[9] In Answer to this I informed him of what I had wrote to your Lordship on this Subject, & desired him to talk with You upon it; & I accepted his Offer of representing my Case to Lord Shelburne. And I wrote to your Lordship informing you of what passed between me & Mr Jackson by my Letter of Jan^ry 20.[10] About a Year after this Dr Spry was appointed to Barbadoes: I cant say but that I was mortified at this; & thought my Services & Sufferings much overlooked in seeing myself postponed to a Gentleman whose public Merit seemed to consist in his having lived 2 Years in a disagreeable Place with little to do & nothing to suffer or to fear.[11] This is the State of my thoughts on Barbadoes concerning which my Opinion is not changed. For tho I would avoid a hot Climate in general Yet I have had such favorable Accounts of the temperature of this Island, that I would venture upon it; especially as all other Considerations make the Appointment very desirable. Mrs Bernard joins with me in these Sentiments, as she does in that perpetual Respect & Gratitude which I have so frequent Occasion to express for your Lordship: with which I am My Lord &c.

The Right Honble The Lord Viscount Barrington

L, LbC   BP, 7: 263-264.

In handwriting of Thomas Bernard.

    FB's anxiety over Hillsborough's instruction that the provincial government should investigate treasonable activities in Massachusetts was shared by his chief law officer, Jonathan Sewall, and probably most officials. While some senior officers, including FB (as he reveals in this letter) were convinced that the radical Whigs harbored seditious elements, it is likely that others, including Sewall, doubted that any action was overtly treasonable or an investigation warranted. Everyone was convinced that the provincial government, given its meager administrative resources and the manifest hostility of juries, would be unable to bring cases to trial in the colony. And no one was keen to test how the colonists would react.

1. **No. 726**.

2. On 8 Feb., the House of Commons approved an address to the king and a set of resolutions that passed the House of Lords on 15 Dec. *HCJ*, 32: 185. For a discussion see the source note to **No. 723**.

3. This was communicated to FB by **No. 745**, which he received on 24 Feb.

4. See also FB's later comments in **No. 778**.

5. It cannot be established if the underlining of "beg Leave" was the work of Thomas Bernard or a non-contemporaneous reader.

6. Ditto.

7. The Townshend Revenue Act (7 Geo. 3, c. 46), which received royal assent on 26 Jun. 1767, taxed colonial imports of paper, painter's colors, lead, glass, and tea, and proposed using the revenue to pay salaries of Crown officials in America.

8. **No. 497,** *Bernard Papers*, 3: 213-216.

9. In a letter of 22 Jan. 1767 (not found), noted in BP, 6: 17.

10. **No 529**, *Bernard Papers*, 3: 306-308.

11. William Spry (1729-72), governor of Barbados, 1767-72, and judge of the Vice Admiralty Court at Halifax, 1764-67.

754 | *From Lord Barrington*

Cavendish Square 21ˢᵗ March 1769.

Private.

Dear Sir

I am very sorry to inform your Excellency that there is no hope that any thing more effectual in regard to North America will be done in Parliament this Session: Vigorous and proper measures have been propos'd to the Cabinet, but it is understood they have met with Negatives[1] there. I was directed to bring in the Short Act of last Year for continuing the American Mutiny Act without alteration or addition:[2] I propos'd in the Committee a Clause, of which I send you a Copy: Court & Opposition who have never agreed in any thing else, joined in rejecting my Proposal. The duty I owe to the Crown, the State, the Parliament & the Army, required me to endeavour that the Mutiny Act in America should be executed; the conduct of the Justices and the Council of Boston has shewn it may be evaded. I am as little desirous as any man, that Troops should be quartered in private houses; nor was that the intention of my Clause, but to engage the Americans to Quarter them according to the Act, by shewing that if they did not, worse inconveniences would happen to themselves than hireing empty houses and furnishing Bedding &cᵃ. I confess I do not see how the Troops will in several places be put under cover after this tame acquiescence of Parliament in the disobedience of the Town of Boston, in respect to Quartering those which are there: Nothing but the happy expedient of appointing Commissaries, which occurred to You last Autumn could have procured legal Cover for them even at the expence of Great Britain.

Mʳ. Pownal formerly Governeur of the Massachussets Bay, and Mʳ Garth who is Agent for one of the Colonies, (both Members of Parliament) propos'd two Clauses which you will see in the Copy of the New American Mutiny Acts, just pass'd, which I herewith enclose: I like them very well, & I think they would have produced good effects, if my Clause had been accepted likewise; but I have no conception, as things now stand, that any Man in America will take one Voluntary Step towards Quartering the Troops at the expence of the Colonies. I trouble your Excellency with these matters the more readily, as the being early apprised of them will enable you the better to give that assistance to the Troops ^at Boston^ which the present Circumstances will allow.[3]

I was acquainted two or three days ago with the opinion of Government that the next Pacquet ought not to sail for America without carrying out to You some mark of the King's favour that might shew his approbation of your conduct; and that it was therefore determined to create You a Baronet immediately. I well remember your indifference, to say the least, in respect to Honours of that kind; as likewise the peculiar delicacy of your Situation which you sometime since communicated to me:[4] but I thought on the whole such a Spontaneous mark of Royal favour bestowed at this juncture should not meet with obstruction from your friends. I was then asked how you were to be described in the Patent. I had recourse to M[r] Blackborne, by whose advice I gave the following description, *Francis Bernard of Nettleham in the County of Lincoln Esquire:* This Patent is passing, and is already so far advanced, that I may safely wish you & Lady Bernard joy.[5] I hope this will soon be followed by somewhat of a more solid Nature. You are entitled to a great deal, and the worthy intelligent part of Mankind will not think your Services overpaid by any rewards you may receive. I have taken care that the whole of this matter shall be fully explained to M[rs]. Berresford[6] by M[r]. Jackson and M[r]. Blackborne.[7] I had almost forgot to add that the expence of your Patent will be paid by the Crown; a thing very unusual, and therefore[8] the more honourable. I am told it amounts to upwards of £300. I am with great truth & regard

D[r] Sir Your Excellency's most faithful & obedient humble Servant

Barrington.

ALS, RC   BP, 12: 65-68.

Enclosures (not found): The Mutiny Act, 9 Geo. 3, c. 9 (1769); the American Quartering or Mutiny Act, 9 Geo. 3, c. 18 (1769); Barrington delayed posting this letter until FB's letter of patent for the baronetcy was issued, and enclosed it in **No. 760**, dated 5 Apr. FB acknowledged the letter with **No. 794**.

---

1. Barrington's disappointment reflected the cabinet's rejection of a series of proposals made by Hillsborough, including the reform of the Massachusetts Council which Barrington and FB had been discussing (see the source notes to **Nos. 740** and **743**). Barrington's proposed amendment to the Quartering Act, mentioned in this letter, was in tune with Hillsborough's hard-line stance. The ministry envisioned altering the act to make it easier for military commanders to quarter soldiers in public houses first, thus preventing the confusion surrounding the procedure that the Massachusetts Council and Boston selectmen had exploited in order to frustrate Lt. Col. William Dalrymple and FB. Once public houses were full, then officers would be able to quarter soldiers in private houses unless the province provided barracks. TH, on the other hand, was more concerned that the act should be more explicit in directing that barracks be utilized whenever possible. Thomas Pownall's amendment, discussed in note 3, ameliorated the act's punitive clauses by delaying implementation on condition that the province made its own provision first. Even so, Peter D. G. Thomas has concluded, "all of this was no more than a programme for the punishment and prevention of colonial defiance," though Hillsborough was not averse to agreeing to Pownall's concessions if it might dampen American criticism. *Townshend Duties Crisis*, 128; TH to Richard Jackson, 5 Oct. 1768, Mass. Archs., 25: 283, in Hutchinson Transcripts, 1: 283-284.

2. The American Quartering or Mutiny Act, 8 Geo. 3, c. 19 (1768).

3. The recommended procedures for quartering British Regulars in America are briefly described in **No. 686**n4, *Bernard Papers*, 4: 329. The House of Commons debated the issue on 15 Mar. when Barrington indicates that amendments to the Quartering Act were proposed by former colonial governor Thomas Pownall and Charles Garth (c.1734-84), agent for South Carolina, 1763-75. Thomas Pownall's amendments were intended to take some heat out of the controversy, which, as Pownall acknowledged, FB and Gage had both reported upon. His first proposal aimed to allow the provincial assemblies to make their own provision for British soldiers, without recourse to current procedures: "that this Quartering Act should not be of force in any province that had by an act (which received the approbation of the crown) made provisions for this purpose." Pownall's second proposal was to allow British commanders and municipal authorities to agree the "manner" of accommodation suitable to the circumstances and contingent upon "mutual agreement." It was reported that "His first proposal was accepted with some amendments in the draughting it, as exceptions were taken to some expressions, which seemed to derogate from the authority and competency of parliament; the clause containing his second proposal was accepted without amendment." Barrington's proposal was that if the municipal authorities refused or neglected to quarter troops according to existing procedure, then "the commanders should have orders to quarter them in private houses." It was this scenario that the American Colonists feared most, and which subsequently prompted accusations of tyranny, though the law was never changed to allow British commanders to billet soldiers on the populace. In the first instance, Barrington's proposal drew the "highest indignation" from Isaac Barré and was not adopted by the Commons. Cobbett, *Parliamentary History of England*, 16: 205-206. The Quartering Act was continued by 9 Geo. 3, c. 18 (1769), which received its final reading in the House of Lords on 22 Mar. before receiving the royal assent. *HLJ*, 32: 308.

4. In **No. 666**, *Bernard Papers*, 4: 285-287. FB's principal concern was the cost of the patent. See source note to **No. 610**, ibid., 155-157.

5. The baronetcy of Nettleham (the Lincolnshire manor where FB had acquired property) was created on 5 Apr. 1769.

6. Jane Beresford (c.1702-Nov. 1771), a cousin and close friend of FB. She was the dower proprietor of Nether Winchendon House, Bucks., her deceased husband's family home. Her only son died in 1740 and she bequeathed Nether Winchendon to FB, her executor, in 1762. Mrs. Sophie Elizabeth Napier Higgins, *The Bernards of Abington and Nether Winchendon: A Family History*, 4 vols. (London, 1904), 1: 208; Nicolson, *The 'Infamas Govener'*, 18, 22-23.

7. Leverett Blackborne, FB's business agent.

8. Annotation: vertical line from "Blackborne" to "therefore". This may be contemporaneous.

755 | *From the Earl of Hillsborough*

Whitehall 22nd. March 1769

Private

Sir

I have very great Satisfaction in making your Excellency my Compliments of Congratulation upon the honourable Mark of Favour which the King has been pleased to conferr upon you, by which His Majesty means to demonstrate to you, & to His Subjects of Massachuset's Bay his gracious Approbation of your Services in your Government of that Province. His Majesty, is farther pleased to take upon himself the whole Expence of passing your Patent, which tho' in itself no great matter, yet adds greatly to the Honour done you, as it is a favour which ^has^ seldom if ever been granted.[1] I take no merit to myself from His Majesty's Goodness to Your Excellency, as I have only done my Duty by laying your Conduct before His Majesty in it's just & true light, and I have the pleasure to assure your Excellency that notwithstanding the foul Efforts of Malevolence & Misrepresentation, the King does Justice to your Merit; & has seen with satisfaction your repeated Endeavours to promote his Service, as well as that of the Colony you preside over.

I have the honour to be with true Esteem Sir Your Excellencys
Most Obedient and Most Humble Servant

Hillsborough

LS, RC   BP, 12: 69-72.

Endorsed by FB: private Earl of Hillsborough d Mar 22 1769. r Apr 27.   The RC of **No. 755** was "brought by a Ship from London in 30 Days," FB noted in his reply (**No. 768**).

FB accepted the dignity proffered without any hesitation. The letters patent creating FB a baronet are dated 5 Apr. 1769 and filed at TNA: EXT 6/92. It was, as Hillsborough, stressed, a signal honor in recognition of FB's contribution as colonial governor during troubled times.[2] While FB considered the title a warning shot to his enemies in Boston, it had greater political significance in Britain as a public validation of the Grafton administration's American policy. Also, Hillsborough probably hoped that FB would be encouraged to resign upon returning home, leaving the stage clear for TH to succeed him[3] (he was appointed governor on 28 Nov. 1770).

---

1. The decision was made by His Majesty in Council and announced in the *London Gazette* on 22 Mar. 1769.

2. That reflected the view of King George III (**No. 760**). Baronetcies were "normally reserved for political notables possessed of English estates or considerable fortunes." Nicolson, *The 'Infamas Govener'*, 171-172. Twenty-one baronets were constituted or reconstituted between 1766 and 1770, to add to the 138 of the previous sixty years. J. V. Beckett, *The Aristocracy in England, 1660-1914* (Oxford 1986), 116-117, 489.

3. One letter printed in London hoped that FB, "a sworn Enemy to the Mode of Proceedings by SWORD AND BAYONET . . . will soon be recalled and take his place even in the Cabinet Council." *St. James's Chronicle or the British Evening Post*, 25-28 Mar. 1769.

756 | To Thomas Gage

Boston March 23 1769

S^r

I am favoured with your Letter of March 13, & am much obliged to you for your Readiness in assisting our Scheme for making the Observation on Lake Superior. I had prepared for opening a Subscription here, which would easily have raised Money enough for extraordinary Expences. But all our Plans have been defeated by the Irresolution of the principal Undertaker who has been list'ning unto Stories concerning the Dangers of the Voyage; & whilst we have been concerting means to make it practicable, has been intimidating himself against the Pursuit of it: So that upon the Receipt of your Letter I found nothing had been done in providing Instruments & learning the practical Use of them. I have therefore been obliged to give it over, & have only to return you thanks for your kind Entertainment of our Scheme, & to lament the Defeat of it.

I am &c

Genl Gage

L, LbC   BP, 7: 221.

FB's enthusiasm for the venture proposed by James Bowdoin was laced with pride at the possibility of Massachusetts being able to make a major contribution to astronomy. But FB's rather harsh judgment of Prof. Winthrop's decision to withdraw underestimated the scale of the enterprise and the dangers facing the proposed expedition to the Great Lakes to observe the transit of Venus in June that year. Having already participated in several well-supplied voyages along the Penobscot coast, FB ought to have been more understanding of the limited timescale available to Winthrop to plan and resource the expedition. Neither did FB appreciate that the observations could actually be undertaken within built-up areas (as Winthrop proceeded to demonstrate, at Cambridge). As it was, the Pennsylvania scientist David Rittenhouse (1732-96), with backing from the American Philosophical Society, undertook a series of observations in Philadelphia which confirmed Winthrop's 1761 calculations about the mean distance from Earth of the Sun's parallax and enabled him to estimate the Sun's distance from Earth at 93 million miles.[1]

---

1. For a history of the British, American, and European expeditions of 1761 and 1769 see Woolf, *Transits of Venus*. On American celebrations of Rittenhouse's achievements see William Hunting Howell, "A More Perfect Copy: David Rittenhouse and the Reproduction of Republican Virtue," *WMQ* 64 (2007): 757-790.

757 | *From the Earl of Hillsborough*

Whitehall, March 24.th 1769.

(N°. 26.)

Duplicate.

Sir,

His Majesty having thought fit, upon a consideration of the present state of affairs in the Province of Massachuset's Bay, that you should return to this Kingdom, in order to make a full Report thereof to His Majesty, I herewith inclose to you the King's Royal Licence for that purpose;[1] and have the satisfaction at the same time to acquaint you,[2] that His Majesty has been pleased to direct a Patent to be passed for conferring upon you the Dignity of a Baronet, as a Testimony of His Majesty's Royal Favour and gracious Approbation of your Services.

As it is necessary, that His Majesty's Lieutenant Governor,[3] upon whom the Government will devolve, should be fully informed of the actual State of the public Affairs of the Province, and of such Orders as have any Reference to future Measures, you will not fail to communicate all such to him, and to give your advice and opinion, with regard to such steps as it shall appear expedient to pursue in your absence,[4] for supporting the Dignity of Government and inducing such a Conduct on the part of all His Majesty's Subjects under your Government, as may testify their Affection to the Parent-Kingdom, and a due submission to it's Laws.[5]

In my Letter[6] of the 30th. of July last[7] I signified to you the King's Commands, that the next General Court should be summoned to meet either at Salem or Cambridge, as you should think most convenient;[8] but, as the circumstances, which occasioned that Resolution, have been since considerably changed, it is His Majesty's Pleasure that you (or the Lieut. Governor in case you leave the Province before the Meeting of the General Court) should use your discretion in this matter, according to the situation of affairs, and that the General Court should be assembled at either of those places or at Boston, as shall be judged most adviseable. I am, Sir,

Your Most Humble and Obedient Servant

Hillsborough

Sir Francis Bernard Bart.

P.S. You will observe that the Command I have signified, at the beginning of this Letter, does not direct that you should not hold the next General Court, if you should think it for His Majesty's Service that you should.

H.

dupLS, RC   BP, 12: 77-80.

Endorsed by FB: N° 26 Earl of Hillsborough d Mar 24 1769 r June 10 Inclos^g Leave of Absence The Dupl. rec^d Ap. 29.   The endorsement provides the dates of receipt for both the original (10 Jun.), which has not been found, and the duplicate (29 Apr.), to which FB replied with **No. 767**. Annotations probably added by FB are noted. Enclosed a royal instruction for FB's recall signed by Hillsborough and dated Court at St. James's, 23 Mar. 1769, BP, 12: 73-76. There is a variant of the letter in CO 5/765, ff 64-66 (L, LbC).

    The Privy Council meetings of 22 and 23 Mar. 1769 signaled the beginning of the end of FB's administration as governor of Massachusetts, by recalling him to London and conferring the reward of a baronetcy. Through Barrington, Hillsborough advised that FB was not to leave with "inconvenient haste" (**No. 760**); upon returning to England, FB was expected to continue as a nominal governor, with TH taking over as acting governor until a replacement was formally installed.

---

1. Left marginalia: virgule; "enclose" also underlined and "purpose" marked with a vertical line, probably by the recipient. The enclosure was a sign manual granting FB leave of absence, Court at St. James's, 23 Mar. 1769, BP, 12: 73-76.

2. Left marginalia: virgule highlighting this particular point.

3. Left marginalia: virgule.

4. While FB probably had no intention of returning to Massachusetts, he took this instruction seriously and on reaching England maintained a lengthy correspondence with acting governor TH. FB wrote c.58 letters to TH following his departure on 2 Aug. 1769 through 1770. During this same period, TH sent FB c.81 letters, and continued to write FB after FB suffered a stroke and was obliged to cease writing.

5. Annotation: "Laws" marked by a vertical line following the word.

6. Left marginalia: virgule.

7. **No. 661**, *Bernard Papers*, 4: 271-276.

8. Annotation: the passage from "convenient . . . Court)" marked by a vertical line in the left margin. The General Court met at the Town House in Boston on 31 May 1769. But after protesting the continued presence of British soldiers in the town, the House suspended normal business other than to appoint committees to prepare messages to the governor. After two weeks of inactivity, FB removed the General Court to Cambridge, meeting at Harvard College on 16 Jun. *JHRM*, 45: 115, 132-133.

758 | To John Pownall

Boston March 25 1769

Dear Sir

Your Letter of December 24[1] came to me but yesterday, the Schooner which brought it having above 11 Weeks Passage & her sailing from England being ten Days after the Date of your Letter.

You ask me my Sentiments upon the present very critical Situation of American Affairs: at present they are so full of Despondency that I know not how to own them to my most intimate Friend, unless I had an Opportunity in Person to vindicate them. I am not naturally given to Despair; I think that I have shown that I am not: but it appears to me that the British Empire was never in so immediate Danger of Dissolution as it is at present; for a Separation of the Colonies from its sovereign Power I call a Dissolution. The Disorder which is like to produce this Effect is now of near 4 Years standing & has ^been^ encreasing very rapidly; as it has been opposed by Remedies which have served to palliate the Disease rather than to check it.

It is not now a Secret that the extravagant Demands of the American Legislatures &c have been cheifly founded upon what has been said upon their Behalf in Parliament. I, who have cultivated a Reverence for my Superiors, & a high Opinion of their public Virtues & Abilities, concluded that in this Manner of vindicating the Resistance of the Americans there was some refined Policy at the Bottom; I concluded that the Argument of Representation being necessary to *precede* Taxation (*consequentially due* I think it must be allowed) was intended to introduce the Necessity of an American Representation; & I therefore made myself easy about the Consequences, which this Doctrine would introduce by reflecting that it would allways be in the Power of Parliament to apply an effectual Remedy to them that is an American Representation. But, Good God! What must be the Consequence if after a Representation is become a necessary Remedy for the Disorders of America, there should be no Disposition in Parliament to apply it. It should have been applied 3 Years ago; it is full late now; it will soon become ineffectual; & no other Means left for a Reconciliation upon general Principles admitted on both Sides.

I know not how to argue upon the Resolutions of the House of Lords: the Deference I pay to the Authority of Parliament & the Consideration of their being at present an unfinished Work make it an improper Subject of Animadversion. All I can say is that these Resolutions serve here to elate the Faction & depress the Friends of Government not so much, perhaps, on Account of the Terms in which they are conceived, as for their being Resolutions without Activity; a form of Proceedings, ^which^ considering how much the American Parliaments (as they are called here) have dealt in them, are[2] not in much Credit here & are supposed not to promise Activity, And the Conclusion of them "that the Gov[r] be directed to procure the fullest Information &c" is laughed at by the Faction, who know very well that the Governor can do nothing in such a Business with Effect unless he is armed with Powers, which he has not at present; particularly with a Power to oblige People to answer to Questions which dont affect themselves, & are of Importance to Government. In short the Contest between Great Britain & America is got far out of the Reach of the common Law of America &, as it seems, of that of England also; & is remediable only by Parliament in the plenitude of its Power.

To conclude this diagreeable[3] Subject, I shall enclose a Paper just come to Hand being cut out of the last Providence Gazette. I will venture to say there is not a sovereign State in Europe (unless it is Great Britain) by which a Paper so directly aiming at the sovereign Power would not be treated as treasonable; and Yet it will here pass unnoticed, except by the Applauses it receives from the Sons of Liberty.[4] It seems wonderful to me that the Parliament should think it worth their while to send for my M[r] Baldwyn[5] to answer for half a dozen lines (wicked & imprudent enough to be sure) relative to particular Transactions only, & take no Notice of Mess Edes & Gill, T & J Fleet, J Carter & Holt[6] &c who are continually directing Daggers to the Heart of their Mother Country & sovereign State. The Fable of the Trumpeter being told, when he was taken Prisoner that he was answerable for all the Mischeifs done by the Soldiers of his Party is very applicable to such Printers. But besides the Demerit of the Printers, this is the best & perhaps the only Way to get at their Leaders.[7]

I have ^here^ given you an Effusion of my Head & Heart, which are indeed brim full; & will not be eased to purpose on this Side the Water.[8] I have long thought & have often said that I may be made more useful at this Conjuncture at home than I can be here. The Necessity of my staying here last fall was very urgent & indeed alarming. I see it also to be unavoidable that I should continue here to open the new Assembly & untill I can receive all the Dispatches which shall arise from the Proceedings in Parliament, which will include all material Orders to the Time. After this I hope there will be no Objection to my availing myself of my Leave of Absence heretofore obtained for me.

I am ^with the truest Regard^ &c

J Pownall Esq

dupL, LbC   BP, 7: 270-274.

In handwriting of Thomas Bernard. Enclosed an extract from the *Providence Gazette*, 19 Mar. 1769. A duplicate of the letter was sent under cover of **No. 762**, along with more newspaper extracts.

THE PAPERS OF GOVERNOR FRANCIS BERNARD

1. **No. 723**, enclosing the resolutions of the House of Lords respecting Massachusetts, passed on 15 Dec. They were not approved by the House of Commons until 8 Feb. For a summary see the source note to **No. 723**. The resolutions were not printed in the colonial newspapers until mid-April (and in the form adopted by the Commons). *Boston Gazette*, 17 Apr. 1769.

2. Scribal correction, silently emended.

3. Thus in manuscript: a scribal error for "disagreeable".

4. This was probably a front page essay on "The Advantage of Independence," *Providence Gazette*, 18 Mar. 1769. The author purported to offer a thoughtful theoretical discussion on the happiness to be found in political and economic independence. He was probably following Seneca (Lucius Annaeus Seneca), *De Vita Beata* (c.58 AD). "A Good Man is Happy within himself, and Independent upon Fortune: Kind to his Friend; Temperate to his Enemy." Translated by Roger L'Estrange, *Seneca's Morals by Way of Abstract to which is added, a discourse under the title of an after-thought: adorned with cuts* (London, 1764). Classical analogy, like scripture, provided convenient code for expressing radical sentiments and airing controversial hypotheses, as FB acknowledged when he condemned the piece as treasonable. The essay's last three sentences, FB doubtless read as a personal attack upon himself.

   > The truth is, a life of independence is generally a life of virtue. It is that which fits the soul for every generous flight of humanity, freedom, and friendship. To give should be our pleasure, but to receive our shame. Serenity, health and affluence, attend the desire of rising by labour; misery, repentance and disrespect, that of succeeding by extorted benevolence. The man who can thank himself alone for the happiness he enjoys, is truly blessed; and lovely, far more lovely, the sturdy gloom of laborious indigence, than the fawning simper of adulation.

   Providence Gazette, 18 Mar. 1769. Roger L'Estrange (1616-1704), a Tory journalist and pamphleteer, was deprived of his office of surveyor and licenser of the press when William III took power and was imprisoned, 1688, 1691, and 1695-96. This increased the mockery of the citation.

5. Henry Baldwin (1734-1813), the printer of the *St. James's Chronicle* and other weekly newspapers, was called before the House of Lords on 19 Dec. to explain why he had printed a libelous commentary on a letter written by Lord Weymouth, secretary of state for the Northern Department. The letter, Baldwin admitted, had been supplied by John Wilkes. Noted in the *Boston Chronicle*, 16-20 Mar. 1769; Wright, *Cavendish's Debates*, 1: 106, 111, 113-115. Baldwin had previously published anti-governmental material but in this case his summons was part of the government's attempt to expel Wilkes from the Commons. Baldwin was later charged with reprinting (on 21 Dec. 1769) the anti-government "Junius" letters, but was acquitted of libel.

6. Benjamin Edes (1732-1803) and John Gill (1732-85), proprietors and printers of the *Boston Gazette* since 1755; they dissolved their partnership in 1776, though Edes (a Son of Liberty) continued to publish the *Gazette*. The brothers Thomas Fleet Jr. (1732-97) and John Fleet (1734-1806) published the *Boston Evening-Post*, a newspaper with less overtly Whiggish leanings and whose columns were open to writers and contributors from across the political spectrum. John Carter (1746-1814) had purchased the *Providence Gazette* in Nov. 1768 and continued the practice of the previous owner, Sarah Updike Goddard (c.1701-70), of publishing radical essays and letters. John Holt (1721-84) edited James Parker's *New-York Gazette and Post Boy* from 1760 to 1766, before starting his own newspaper, the *New-York Journal* in competition with Parker's *Gazette*. Unlike Parker (1715-70), Holt was strongly supportive of the Whig cause.

7. In **No. 734**, FB had recommended to Hillsborough that the printers of the *Boston Gazette*, Benjamin Edes and John Gill—those "trumpeters of Sedition"—be prosecuted, if only to obtain evidence about the authors of seditious writings. Like the trumpeter in Aesop's fable, "The Trumpeter Taken Prisoner," they would be held guilty for inciting their comrades (in this case to sedition rather than war) even if they were to plead innocence of personally committing any crime.

8. Thus in manuscript.

759 | *To the Earl of Hillsborough*

N.º 6

Boston Mar 27 1769

My Lord

In the Boston Gazette appears a Paper so malevolent to Great Britain & so shocking to a British Ear, that I have thought proper to send it to your Lordship together ^with^ the Providence Gazette from which it is pretended to be taken. But notwithstanding it was first printed at Providence, (a common trick with the writers here) It is undoubted that it originated here: this appears not only from the subject Matter which is applicable to no other Town but this, but also from the stile which to discerning readers evidently points out the Author. I suppose that it was designed for ^the^ liberty Tree at Boston; but their hearts failing them. It was sent to Providence in order to to [*be*] reechoed here. The Boston Gazette which I send is that which was sent by the printers to the Council chamber for my use; the Providence Gazette is one which was sent by the printer ^to a printer^ here from who I had it.[1]

> I am with great regard My Lord, your Lordships most obedient
> & most humble Servant

Fra Bernard

The right honble The Earl of Hillsborough

ALS, RC   CO 5/758, f 76.

Endorsed: Boston March 27. 1769. Gov.ʳ. Bernard. (N.º 6) R 15.ᵗʰ: May.   Enclosed copies of the *Boston Gazette*, 27 Mar. 1769 and the *Providence Gazette*, 18 Mar. 1769. CO 5/758, ff 78-81. Variants of letter in: CO 5/893, f 118 (dupLS, RC); CO 5/767, f 236 (L, RLbC); BP, 7: 155-156 (dupL, LbC).

---

1. FB marked with a black line both copies of the printed "Paper" that he enclosed. Dated Providence, 18 Mar., and addressed "To the Sons of Liberty," the letter was a mock sermon marking the anniversary of the Stamp Act's repeal with a retrospective appraisal of the state of Massachusetts under British rule. While not challenging imperial supremacy, the jeremiad nonetheless by implication questioned the morality of British rule when British statesmen appeared to have abandoned constitutional principles.

> Although the People of Great-Britain be only Fellow Subjects, they have (of late) assumed such a Power to compel us to buy at their Market such Things we want of European Produce and Manufacture. . . . and, for the Collection of the Duties, have sent Fleets, Armies, Commissioners, Guarda

Costas, Judges of Admiralty . . . Our cities are garrisoned— . . . Our Trade is obstructed. . . . every Species of Injustice that a wicked and debauched Ministry could invent, is now practiced against the most sober, industrious and loyal People that ever lived in Society. . . . When I consider the Corruption of Great-Britain—their Load of Debt—their intestine Divisions, Tumults and Riots . . . I cannot but think that the Conduct of Old-England towards us may be permitted by Divine Wisdom, and ordained by the unsearchable Providence of the Almighty, for hastening a Period dreadful to Great-Britain.

A SON OF LIBERTY.

Providence Gazette, 18 Mar. and *Boston Gazette*, 27 Mar. 1769.

760 | *From Lord Barrington*

Cav: Square Ap. 5. 1769.

Dear Sir,

Since my former Letter began in March & herewith inclosed, I have reced your's dated feb 20th.[1] I am happy to find by it that you wish to have the honour which has been confer'd upon you. I can also give you the pleasure of knowing that last Sunday the King spoke with the highest approbation of your conduct & Services in his Closet to me.[2] I am perswaded any proposal you ~~can~~ ^shall^ make for the advantage of your family will be kindly consider'd by his Majesty and his Servants. I shall make the proper use of the Particulars you send me concerning Mr. Temple.[3] I am in great haste the Packett being to be dispatch'd this Evening but I am not with less truth

Dear Sir Your Excellencys most faithful & obedt. humble Servt.

Barrington.

Your Patent is passed.

I understand you are directed to come hither, but Lord Hillsborough authorises me to say you need not be in any inconvenient haste to obey that instruction.[4]

ALS, RC   BP, 12: 81-82.

Enclosed **No. 754**.

1. **No. 744**.

2. This may have been after one of the king's regular Sunday afternoon receptions in the drawing rooms of St. James's Palace.

3. Of specific interest was FB's speculation in **No. 744** that John Temple had been conspiring with a member of the Council to leak information to the press damaging to FB; Barrington may have surmised that the councilor was Temple's father-in-law, James Bowdoin, though FB did not name him.

4. **No. 757**.

761 | To Richard Jackson

Boston April 8th 1769

Dear Sir,

The disagreeable State of the public Affair both ^at^ home & here makes them a very unpleasant Subject to write upon. And this has contributed to make our Correspondence less frequent & full than it used to be;[1] tho with Regard to myself, the Voluminous Correspondence which I am obliged by Order & Necessity to keep up with the Secretary of State has unavoidably contracted my private Letters of all kinds.

We are now waiting to know what the House Will determine upon the American Affairs now before them, our Advices having not as yet reached so far. For my own Part I give up all Thoughts of staying here. the publishing my Letters wrote in Confidence & in Obedience of strict Orders will make it necessary for the Minister to provide for me else where: and I believe the Intention is more determined upon than the Means. Lord Barrington in a late Letter[2] asks my thoughts concerning Barbados: I remind him that about 2 ^½^ Years ago I informed him & You that I should thankfully accept Barbados;[3] & I was much mortified, when about a Year after it was given to a Gentleman who had not acquired a public Character.[4] I know not how to expect its being made vacant so soon after it has been filled. But to be sure under the present Circumstances, it would suit me better than anything else I can think of.

I have often wished that M[r] Blackbourne either by his own hand or yours would have sent me a Copy of my Leave of Absence. For there may be in it Conditions & Restrictions, which I may break thro Ignorance, & yet not be allowed that Plea. If it is sent away immediately after you receive this, it may & most probably will find me here.[5] At present my Plan is to call the Assembly at Concord on May 31st; and as soon as the Session is over which if they do Nothing to hasten the Determination of it, will last at least a Month, I shall look towards England: & about that Time I may expect to receive all the Orders which will be issued in Pursuance of what will be done in Parliament. But this must be a precarious ~~threatning~~ Reckoning untill I know what Part the Parliament takes. Even now whilst I am writing this, I have received a Note advising that a Letter from New-York just arrived informs that the House of Commons have among other Things, resolved that the Constitution of this Government should be altered:[6] which shows how much too early it is for me to form a Scheme ^for disposing of myself^ half a Year hence.

I shall be glad to hear from ^you^ as often as Your Leisure will permit, & to know your Sentiments on the Public Proceedings. The Censure of Wilkes is considered here as a good Assurance of the firmness of Government.[7]

I am &c.

R Jackson Esq[r]:

L, LbC   BP, 7: 274-276.

Minor emendations not shown. In handwriting of Thomas Bernard.

1. FB's last letter to Jackson was dated 21 Jun. 1768, BP, 6: 135.

2. **No. 726**, to which FB replied with **No. 753**.

3. **No. 497**, *Bernard Papers*, 3: 213-216.

4. William Spry (1734-1802), appointed governor of Barbados in 1767, which position he held until 1772.

5. Enclosed in **No. 757**, received on 10 Jun.

6. This was a rumor, for the resolutions of the House of Lords, adopted by the Commons on 8 Feb., did not propose any constitutional reform or amendment. The resolutions were not printed in the Massachusetts press until 17 Apr. See the source note to **No. 723**. Yet, FB's supposition that Hillsborough would push for such measures in response to FB's reports was correct, although the cabinet rejected them after Parliament approved the resolutions. See the source note to **No. 743**.

7. See the source note to **No. 740**.

762 | To John Pownall

Dupl:

Private

Boston April 8 1769

Dear Sir

The Cover of this incloses a duplicate of a former Letter which went in ~~the~~ ^a^ Packet sent to New York for the Mail.[1] I have not inclosed another of the printed Papers, as there will be two of them [to] go with this in a Cover to Lord Hillsborough.[2] The Boston Gazette is marked with the initial Letters of the Person who had it from the Printer.[3] I keep another of the same by me.

It is most apparent this Paper [that?][4] comes out of the Mint of the Boston Gazette, notwithstanding it was at first printed at Providence. A Partisan of the Boston Gazette was boasting the other Day of the Correspondence with & Influence over the rest of the Printers in America which the Printers of the Boston Gazette had acquired; and added that they often furnished the other Printers with original Papers, when it was thought best they should make their first Appearance at a Distance from Boston. But without this Testimony the Papers themselves frequently show that the Copies came from Hence; as in the present Case.

In this Gazette are two Pieces of M^r^ T marked with black Lead: the first is the Abuse of an unknown Writer on the Side of Parliament, the Govr, Judge Auchmuty or Judge Sewall & Mr Paxton; the other is at the Governor only.[5] His Writings are distinguishable by Pertness, Personality & Malice;[6] He is also generally so unfortunate as to fling in some Peculiarity which necessarily points him out as the Author: as in the present Case, there is not among all the reputed Writers in the Boston Gazette a single Person who can be supposed to talk so familiarly of Kitty Fisher[7] & Haddocks[8] Bagnio but himself; unless it is his Brother Fenton,[9] and that is the same.

We have just received the Account of the Parliaments Censure of Wilks;[10] which encourages the Friends of Government to assure themselves that the same firmness will be exerted in vindicating the Honor of Government in America. It is now reported that the House of Commons has among other Things resolved that the Constitution of this Government should be altered: but it is not authentic enough to be depended upon as yet.

I am &c

J Pownall Esq

dupL, LbC   BP, 7: 266-267.

Minor emendations omitted. In handwriting of Thomas Bernard. The RC (not found) enclosed a duplicate of **No. 758** and an annotated copy of the *Boston Gazette*, 27 Mar. 1768.

FB's suspicion that John Temple was conspiring with Whigs prompted him to send Pownall what he considered evidence of Temple's duplicity in employing the pseudonym "Philanthrop," made famous by Jonathan Sewall. FB suspected Temple of trying to bluff readers of the *Boston Gazette* that Sewall was openly critical of FB's administration. Referring to FB as "Verres," "Philanthrop" proceeded to disparage as FB's "poor creature" the recently appointed judge of the New England Vice Admiralty Court, Robert Auchmuty; with a £600 salary the "creature" was now "prostituting" his pen with attacks on the "Pennsylvania Farmer" and defending the "notorious" customs officer "Charley Froth" (a Whig nickname for Charles Paxton).[11] The characterizations in "Philanthrop's" piece were consistent with recent articles by "Candidus" and "Paoli" attacking the governor and the American Board of Customs.[12] While Temple was probably not the author of any of these essays (**No. 742**), it is not surprising FB should presume his old enemy capable of such.

But it is intriguing why FB should continue to protest publicly his ignorance of "Philanthrop's" true identity, when acknowledging the connection between the latest manifestation (that he believed was Temple's appropriation) and "Philanthrop's" reputation. FB knew Jonathan Sewall's previous writings defending his administration in 1766 and 1767.[13] It may be the governor was simply protecting Sewall, whom he had once regarded as his protégé. Yet recent doubts as to Sewall's loyalty (**Nos. 719** and **728**) could also implicate Sewall as the author of the recent "Philanthrop" letter, in a double-bluff intended to curry favor with the governor. For good measure, Sewall did have motives for denigrating Paxton (because of his purported "violent" criticism of Sewall, **No. 728**) and Auchmuty (because he was Sewall's main professional rival, **No. 752**). Moreover, the satirical role-playing of the 1769 "Philanthrop" was reminiscent of "Philanthrop's" 1767 series.

If Sewall was the author of "Philanthrop's" latest incarnation then it further complicates the situation that FB tried to depict. First, it could be that Sewall was the author of the "Candidus" series, in a calculated maneuver to undermine the Customs commissioners as Sewall's dispute with the Board reached a climax. FB recognized that the stylized invention of the 1769 piece—its "Pertness, Personality & Malice"— echoed "Candidus's" approach. If Sewall was "Candidus" then we must discount Samuel Adams, a more convincing candidate for authorship (see source note to **No. 715**n2).

But the article's allusion to "Kitty Fisher," FB presumed was an unmistakable sign of Temple's authorship. The notoriety of "Froth" (Paxton) for *Venality and Corruption*, "Philanthrop" had written, was comparable to Fisher's reputation for *Prostitution and the venerial Taint*, and, like Fisher herself, "Froth" had risen from poverty and obscurity to luxury and prominence. FB wanted to believe the reference to a fêted courtesan was evidence of a past liaison. Mention of Haddock's Bagnio might also have led FB to connect Temple with Fisher, if he recollected Temple previously disclosing or revealing he had visited one of London's most popular bathhouses and brothels.

1. Probably **No. 758**.

2. **No. 759**.

3. FB is referring to the initialled copy of the *Boston Gazette*, 27 Mar. 1769, enclosed with the RC of this letter, neither of which is extant. The same person also annotated the copy sent with **No. 759**, adding the phrase "For the Governor." Whoever this person was, he had some previous connection with both the printers and the governor, and suspected that John Temple was the author of recent libels on the government. Such a slender sample does not allow for authoritative handwriting analysis.

4. Word obscured by tight binding.

5. The annotations in the newspaper enclosed with **No. 759** do not match those enclosed with **No. 762**. However, the items marked with "black Lead" would have been (a) the piece signed "Philanthrop" and (b) an anonymous attack on "Verres" addressed to "Messieurs Edes & Gill" and dated "Cranbourn Alley, 24th March 1769." *Boston Gazette*, 27 Mar. 1769, CO 5/758, f 78.

6. FB supposed both pieces were the work of John Temple.

7. Kitty Fisher (1741?-67) was a well-known courtesan, painted by Sir Joshua Reynolds and others. Cindy McCreery, "Fischer, Catherine Maria [Kitty Fisher] (1741?–1767)," *ODNB-e* (http://www.oxforddnb.com/view/article/9489, accessed 24 Dec. 2013).

8. Haddock's Bagnio was a bathhouse and brothel in Charing Cross, London, run until 1792 and originally taken over in 1742 by Richard Haddock (d.1748).

9. This is not a reference to John Temple's brother, Robert, but to his brother-in-law Lt. James Fenton. See **No. 746**.

10. On 3 Feb. 1769.

11. "Philanthrop," *Boston Gazette*, 27 Mar. 1768.

12. "Candidus," *Boston Gazette*, 5 and 12 Dec. 1768, and 13 Feb. 1769; "Paoli," *Boston Gazette*, 30 Jan. 1769.

13. See *Bernard Papers*, 3: 271, 310–12, 315.

763 | To Lord Barrington

Private

Boston April 12 1769

My Lord

Your Lordship has foreseen the Necessity of my being removed from hence: it is become very apparent; for we have just now learned that any one who will pay for them may have Copies of the ^Letters^ & Papers laid before the Parliament. There are just now arrived 6 of my Letters & 1 of General Gage's attested by the Clerk of the Papers;[1] & M[r] Bollan who has sent them hither promises the rest as soon as they can be copied. The Councellors to whom they were sent immediately met, & ordered these Papers to be printed; but the Publication of them is deferred untill Observations can be finished to accompany them, which a Gentleman has been hard at Work upon & will have completed in a Day or two.[2] They are then to be sent about the Province in order to inflame the People against the Election in May next, which they will effectually do. In the Mean time they have been read by the whole Town at the Printers.[3]

This puts an End to all my Hopes of doing any good here & necessarily turns all my future Views out of this Province. For it is impossible for a Governor who has been engaged in such Contests as I have been, & has ^as well^ by special Orders as by his own Sense of His Duty, given free & full Information of the Proceedings of the factious Party, to think of staying in the Province, after his most confidential Letters are put in the Hands of the Faction and printed & dispersed among the People. For tho the Letters may be very justifiable with indifferent & impartial Persons, yet it cannot be expected that they will be treated with any Degree of Candour by those ^whom^ they affect.

I have thought proper to give your Lordship this Account that you may see ^that^ the Question of providing for me elsewhere is determined. I have before signified my Thoughts of going to England after I have held the next Session: but it is now made a Question whether I shall be able to hold the next Session at All ~~or not~~; Some of the Council having insinuated that I shall not. However I shall make the Trial; & shall do every thing I can to defeat the Intention of the Councellors & to weather this fresh Storm. As soon as these Papers are published I will write to your Lordship again.

I am &c

The R^t Honble The Lord Visc^t Barrington.

L, LbC BP, 7: 278-279.

In handwriting of Thomas Bernard.

FB continued his account of the publication of his letters in **Nos. 764** and **765**, without adding anything substantially new. See **Introduction**, 24-28. Barrington replied with **No. 781**.

---

1. The clerk of the papers of the House of Commons, George White, countersigned the transcripts on 27 Jan. William Bollan enclosed them in a letter to Samuel Danforth dated 30 Jan. (**Appendix 2**). For an explanation of how and why Bollan obtained these six letters and others written by FB see the **Introduction**, 14-22.

2. James Bowdoin.

3. *Copies of Letters from Governor Bernard to Hillsborough.* For details of the publishing history see **List of Abbreviations**, xxiii-xxivn3 and the **Introduction**, 21, 24-27.

764 | To Richard Jackson

Boston April 12 1769

Dear Sir.

Since the coming of the Brig Last Attempt Captn Lyde[1] there has been much talk of some Letters sent by her having miscarried; four I have particularly heard of sent by Mr Hallowell to different Persons. What Truth there is in this I know not; I have talked with the Captain & he is very positive he has no Letters for me. However I think proper to mention it to you least there should be some Mistake. It is a long while ago since I heard from Mrs Beresford that I am uneasy about her.[2]

This Brig brought Copies of several of my Letters to the Secretary of State & one of Genl Gages.[3] They were sent by Mr Bollan to some of the Councillors with a Promise of sending the others as soon as they can be copied.[4] I am amazed at the ill Policy of this Proceeding [,] the permitting Confidential Letters wrote to the Secretary of State to be returned in Authentic Copies to the Province from whence they were sent & there to be published & dispersed among the People, as they are now to be, must not only be of a great Detriment to his Majesty's Service for the present, but must effectually prevent all confidential Writing to Ministers of State for the future. I am not much concerned for myself, being not at all sorry at the Determination of my Relation to this Government; as I think I must have a Compensation. When these Papers are published I will write ^to^ you again.[5]

I am D^r S^r &c.

R Jackson Esqr:

L, LbC   BP, 7: 279-280.

In handwriting of clerk no. 9.

---

1. Nathaniel Byfield Lyde, captain of the *Last Attempt*. "Capt. Lyde's" vessel is the only one listed in the shipping news to have arrived on Saturday 8 Apr., having left London on 4 Feb. *Boston Post-Boy and Advertiser*, 10 Apr. 1769.

2. Jane Beresford (c.1702-Nov. 1771), FB's cousin and the dowager of Nether Winchendon House, Bucks., her husband's family home. She had willed the manor and house to FB in 1762, and he inherited both upon her death.

3. **Nos. 706, 708, 709, 711, 717**, and **718**; a copy of Thomas Gage to the earl of Hillsborough, Boston, 31 Oct. 1768, CO 5/86, ff 214-220. All were authentic copies countersigned by George White, the clerk of the papers of the House of Commons, and dated 27 Jan. 1769. They are filed in Bowdoin and Temple Papers, Loose MSS. Versions of these letters had already been published in the *Boston Gazette*, 23 Jan. 1769. FB and his enemies did not know until 10 Apr. that these particular letters had been presented to Parliament on 20 Jan. and debated on 26 Jan. *The Boston Chronicle*, 10-13 Apr. 1769.

Other letters were presented to Parliament on 28 Nov. and 7 Dec. The list of American correspondence presented to Parliament on 28 Nov. was printed in the *Boston Gazette*, 3 Apr. 1769. The history of the six letters is discussed in the **Introduction**, 21,24-27.

4.   Enclosed in William Bollan to Samuel Danforth, Henrietta Street [*London*], 30 Jan. 1769 (**Appendix 2**).

5.   **No. 772**.

765 | To John Pownall

Dup

Private

Boston April 12 1769

Dear Sir,

Last Saturday a Ship arrived from London[1] which brought Copies of 6 of my Letters to the Earl of Hillsborough from Nov 1st to Dec 5th,[2] & also a Letter of Genl Gage to Lord H dated from Boston all attested by Clerk of the House of Commons.[3] They are sent to Mr Danforth the President of the Council by Mr Bollan their Agent, who writes that he shall send the Copies of the rest as fast as he can get them Copied.[4] The Council met on Sunday Morning (except Mr Flucker who was not asked) and sat all Day at the End of which they sent the Copies to the Printers of the Boston Gazette, with Directions to print them off directly but not to part with any Copies except three to each Councellor; but they were at Liberty to show them to whom they pleased; and there have been many Hundreds of People at the Printers to read them. This has caused a great Ferment; a great Resentment against the Governor is exprest by some of the Council & the Leaders of the Faction; the generality of People treat it as they are disposed, some justifying others condemning the Letters according to the Part they take. The Publication is deferred untill Observations upon them can be drawn up, is[5] [*in*] which Mr Bowdoin is very busy.[6] When this is done they are to be send all round the Province in order to inflame the People against the next election; & I fear it will have the worst Effects.

I must not conceal from you that amongst the Talkers upon this Occasion the Officers of the Crown & the Friends of Government are very loud: it is said that Administration is ^must^ never more expect faithful Accounts of the Proceedings of popular Assemblies for [*from*] Governors & Commanders in America. Governor Bernards Letters will be made an Example; & Governors for the future will write under a Caution how their Letters will bear being printed & returned back to their Province. I myself think that this will give a fatal Blow to American Government. I wrote to my Lord H to this Purpose & earnestly recommended that Care should be had that no Copies of Letters should be permitted to be taken out of the Offices of the two Houses.[7] I suppose some Necessity prevented this Injunction taking Place: whatever it was, it was a fatal Necessity.

For my own Part I assure myself that I shall not be left to suffer by the Consequences of these Communications. What I am most concerned at is that it cuts off all hopes of a Change of Measures in the next Assembly[.][8] For the Publication which the Councellors are now making[9] will produce a Ferment which will probably fill the Assembly House with Sons of Liberty, & make it very unfit to consent to the Necessary Amendments of Government. However I will do all I can to counterwork the Intention of the Councellors. I have wrote to you before that I should be glad to go to England after the next Session is over: but now I may be earlier; for I hear that it has been said among the Councellors that I shan't be able to stay any longer in the Province: However I shall try.

I am &c.

J Pownall Esq[r]

L, LbC   BP, 7: 280-282.

In handwriting of Thomas Bernard.

FB sent Richard Jackson a similar but less fulsome commentary upon the arrival of the "first parcel" of the Bernard Letters (**No. 764**).

---

1. Saturday 8 Apr.

2. **Nos. 706**, **708**, **709**, **711**, **717**, and **718**.

3. A copy of Thomas Gage to the earl of Hillsborough, Boston, 31 Oct. 1768, CO 5/86, ff 214-220.

4. Copies of the six letters were enclosed in William Bollan to Samuel Danforth, Henrietta Street [*London*], 30 Jan. 1769 (**Appendix 2**).

5. A scribal error.

6. A group of councilors eventually responded with a letter to Hillsborough, dated 15 Apr. (**Appendix 4**).

7. **No. 735**.

8. Editorially supplied to aid understanding.

9. *Copies of Letters from Governor Bernard to Hillsborough*. For details of the publishing history see **List of Abbreviations**, xxiii-xxivn3, and the **Introduction**, 21, 24-27.

766 | To John Pownall

private dupl

Boston April 23^{th1} 1769

Dear Sir,

I received your Letter of feb[ry]19^{th2} on April 20 & am extremely obliged to you for it, not only for the Communication it dispenses but also for the Consolation it affords; for I assure you that the Friends of Government are not as yet the triumphant Party.

The Articles you mention as under present Consideration are all of them in my Opinion relevant & unexceptionable upon this present Occasion. That of repealing the 7th of George 3rd, which I call the Salary Act ~~is~~ in ~~my Opinion relevant & unexceptionable~~ the Colonies where a civil List is allready established & continuing it in those who~~re~~ have not made such Establishment ~~is in~~ untill they make it is wise constitutional & provisional.[3] And Nothwithstanding it has become fashionable to condemn Mr Townsend's American Acts in general, yet I have allways thought that he evidenced his Knowledge of America by striking at the Root of the American Disorders, the Want of a certain & adequate civil List to each Colony.

And tho I think he did not take the best Steps for this Purpose; as it seems to me that a Requisition to the Colonies & a Refusal from them ought to have preceded this Parliamentary Provision; yet it is no little Merit to have pointed out to Administration the Necessity of this Measure & prepared the Way for effecting it. And time has been thereby given for avoiding an obvious Inequity in that Act, which struck me at the first View, that the Colonies who had established permanent civil Lists, should be taxed to make good the civil Lists of other Colonies. If this Objection is removed, & the Repeal of the Act is left to the Colonies themselves upon the Condition (which, by the by, is the Condition upon which they have received the Power of Legislation) of their establishing certain adequate civil Lists, the Sovreign Power & the Colonies themselves will be obliged to Mr Townsend for the Foundation he has laid for this necessary Regulation.

For my own Part I am very far from being sanguine in my Expectation of what will be done to retrieve the Affairs of America. But whatever the Defects in this Business are & wherever they ^shall^ lie I will acquit the Administration of them. I am fully satisfied of the Difficulties they lie under from the turbulent State of the Environs of Government & Parliament; which must in some degree defeat their Intentions for the Public Good.

The Honor proposed for me I have allready said may be of Public Service; and if it should be so expedited as to arrive here before the Meeting of the Assembly on the last Day of May (which indeed I can't expect) it might have very good Effects. I find there is to be a violent Affair made upon me by Mr Bowdoin &C^o at the opening of the new Assembly: and the Question will be whether their Proceedings for these 8 Months past, or my Reports of them are the Cause of showing the Impropriety of the popular Appointment ~~of the Cause of showing the Impropriety of the popular appointment~~ of Council. I should be ready to argue this Point with them before any adequate Judges: but the Misfortune is that they will by anonymous Libells in the Newpapers appeal to a Tribunal to whose Judicature I cannot submit, especially with anonymous Prosecutors. However I shall take Care to defeat their Intentions as well as I can; tho to be sure they have a great Advantage over me by the Possession of Letters wrote in Confidence without Expectation of their being published.

I have observed that the Orders I have received for procuring Information &c are confined to Treason & Misprision of Treason.[4] This will make my Work short: for tho their Practices were treasonable yet I cannot fix upon any Act that seems to me to be actual Treason. The Conspiracy to take the Castle, if we could get at the Bottom of it seems to me to come the nearest to it;[5] but that seems to want an ouvert Act to make it compleat Treason. And there can be no Misprision of Treason, where there is no actual Treason. I am to have a Consultation tomorrow[6] upon this Subject & then shall judge with more certainty.

I shall issue the Writs for the new Assembly next Saturday & shall call it at Cambridge.[7] This would be too near Boston if any good was to be expected from the Assembly: but Matters are in such a State of Desperation & Suspension that it signifies Nothing where the Court meets. It will be of no Use to make any more Negatives: for now the Delinquency is become so general, that there is more exception to be taken to Persons within the Council than out of it.

I am &c

J Pownall Esqr

dupL, LbC   BP, 7: 282-285.

In handwriting of Thomas Bernard.

The "relevant & unexceptionable" proposals that Pownall listed in **No. 743** may have reflected ministerial thinking in effecting compromise with the Americans, most notably an interest in repealing Townshend's Revenue Act. But the other proposals were punitive rather than conciliatory, and likely to precipitate further opposition; they were rejected by Grafton's cabinet, including an American civil list.

Charles Townshend originally intended that the Revenue Act be used to pay the salaries of Crown officers and senior provincial officials in key colonies, thus freeing officials from dependency upon assembly grants. But such a program was never implemented by the Chatham or Grafton administrations on the understanding that the colonies would make permanent arrangements to pay the salaries. Beginning in the summer of 1768, however, the British effected an "important" policy change, using the tea duty revenue to pay salary grants to the Massachusetts chief justice and the New York attorney general. The North administration extended the scheme in Jun. 1770 in respect of new appointments. Following his appointment as governor in succession to FB, TH was awarded an annual salary of £1,500 payable from the tea duty, and his deputy Andrew Oliver, a salary of £300. TH subsequently refused to accept the annual salary grant awarded by the Massachusetts General Court (in line with his instructions). In Jul. 1771, the British provided Crown salaries to the Massachusetts chief justice (£400) and Superior Court justices (£200), the attorney general (£150), and the solicitor general (£50), all payable from the tea duty. The colonial reaction helped to reignite the Imperial Crisis in 1772.[8]

---

1. Thus in manuscript.

2. **No. 743**.

3. The Revenue Act, 7 Geo. 3, c. 46 (1767), intended that Crown officers in the colonies should be paid from the trade duties, but the British government first allowed colonial legislatures the opportunity of establishing a civil list for senior officers. Massachusetts never did. See *Bernard Papers*, 3: 298, 386.

4. **No. 745**.

5. See **Nos. 644**, **646**, and **Appendix 10**, *Bernard Papers*, 4: 240-246, 390-391.

6. Probably with the chief justice and attorney general.

7. In fact the General Court met at Boston on 31 May, for reasons FB explained in **No. 767**. *JHRM*, 45:113.

8. Thomas, *Townshend Duties Crisis*, 212, 232, 234-235.

767 | To the Earl of Hillsborough

Nº 8

Boston Ap 29 1769

My Lord

I am honoured with your Lordship's Letter No 26,[1] which arrived 3 days ago in 30 days from London. I have the highest sense of his Majesty's favour in conferring on me the Dignity of a Baronet: I beg that your Lordship would be pleased to make my most humble duty acceptable to his Majesty and to assure him of the entire dedication of myself to his Service.

I was so fully persuaded that it would be expected of me that I should open the new Assembly & continue to the end of the Session, that I have ^made^ no preparation for my Voyage, & could not get away before the Assembly meets; & when I have once opened it, it will be best that I should go through the whole business. I therefore do not expect to be able to embark till towards the end of July.

As I have generally acted in concert with the Lieut Governor, acquainted him with the Motives of my conduct, & frequently advised with him in matters wherein I had doubts, He well understands my System. However, I shall still give him my Opinion in regard to those matters which I think ought to be uniformly pursued in my absence.

As your Lordships Letter arrived 3 days before the issuing the Writts, & I was thereby at liberty to call the Assembly at what place I pleased, I took the matter into full consideration with the best advice I could get: and the general Opinion was that I had best make the returns at Boston. The Reason on both sides were so weighty as to make it a Matter of doubt. What turned me in favor of Boston cheifly was, that as ^I knew that^ it was intended to promote ill humour at the opening the new Assembly, I was desirous of not giving any Cause for it myself; and therefore thought is best to steer the business in the old Channel. It is Very probable that the Boston party may abuse this indulgence: if they do, they will be answerable for it. If the next Session is to be a Term probation, let them have all possible fair play.

I have the honour to be with great respect, My Lord, your Lordships most obedient & most humble Servant,

Fra Bernard

The right honble the Earl of Hillsborough

ALS, RC   CO 5/758, ff 114-115.

Endorsed: Boston 29th April 1769. Govr. Bernard (N°. 8) R 23^d June   By Capt Bryan[2] of The Wolf B. 26. Enclosures not found. Variants: CO 5/893, ff 126-127 (dupLS, RC); CO 5/767, ff 315-317 (L, RLbC); BP, 7: 160-161 (L, LbC). The letter and enclosures were considered by the Board of Trade on 1 Dec. 1769. *JBT*, 13: 125.

---

1. **No. 757**.

2. Probably Capt. John Bryant.

768 | To the Earl of Hillsborough

Dupl Private

Boston May 1ˢᵗ 1769

My Lord

I am honoured with your Lordship's private Letter dated March 22,[1] which was brought by a Ship from London in 30 Days. Your Lordship's Favours come so fast upon me that my Gratitude can scarce keep pace with your Benevolence. The high Sense I have of the Honor done me so fills me that I can only express it by a repeated Dedication of myself & all my Faculties to his Majesty's Service. Permit me also to add that the Honor conferred upon me has received an Additional Value by the kind & polite Manner in which Your Lordship has signified it to me.

The Assurance that you give me that his Majesty has not been influenced by the Malevolence & Misrepresentation which has been used against me, is very seasonable at a Time when my Enemies are encreased by many of the Council, who are offended at the honest & just Resentment which I have expressed at their late undutiful & unconstitutional Proceedings. But I persuade myself that I am out of the Reach of their Malice.

I think it lucky that the Notice of the Honor conferred upon me arrived so early as to be inserted in the Writs for calling the Assembly: It may possibly have some good Effects; but I do not expect much Advantage to it myself; as Envy when added to Malice serves to encrease its force. However I hope it will have so much Effect as to justify my Observations, in a former Letter,[2] of the political Use of Honors. I have lately met with so strong a Confirmation of those Sentiments in an elegant modern Writer, that I beg Leave to subjoin it without applying it to myself.

"Un Altro Mezzo di prevenire i delitti e quello di recompensare la Virtu'. Sopra questo3 proposito osservo un Silenzio universale nelle leggi di tutte le Nazioni d'oggidi. Se i premi proposti dalle Academie ai discopritori delle utile Verita' hanno multiplicato e le cognizioni, e i boni libri; perche' non i premi distributi della benifica Mano del Sov'rano non multiplecherrebbero4 altresi le Azioni Virtuosi? La Moneta dell' Onore e' sempre inesausta e fruttifera nelle mani del saggio distributore."

Beccaria dei delitti & delle pene.[5]

I have the honour to be with the great Gratitude & Respect My Lord &c

The Right honble The Earl of Hillsborough

dupL, LbC   BP, 7: 156-157.

In handwriting of Thomas Bernard. Scribal copying errors are noted below.

---

1. **No. 755**.

2. Probably **No. 736**.

3. Beccaria: "*Su di questo*" meaning "About this". The transcription "*Sopra questo*" means "Above this".

4. Usu. "*multiplicherebbero*".

5. Cesare Bonesana di Beccaria (1738-94), the marchese of Beccaria-Bonesana. His *Dei delitti e delle pene* (Milan, 1764), prefaced with a commentary by Voltaire, was widely celebrated throughout Europe and America (with John Adams among his admirers). Also known by its English title, *An Essay on Crime and Punishments,* it was a pioneering treatise on penal systems which, *inter alia*, argued for the abolition of the death penalty.

   The quotation is from the penultimate paragraph of chapter xliv ("*Ricompense*"; trans. "Of Rewards") in the original 1764 Italian edition. The passage, given in modern translation below, served several purposes: to esteem Hillsborough, to praise the king's munificence, to express FB's personal satisfaction with the baronetcy, and perhaps also to remind the British that insufficient Crown patronage in the American Colonies had manifestly weakened imperial power there.

   > *Un altro mezzo di prevenire I delitti è quello di ricompensare la virtù. Su di questo proposito osservo un silenzio universale nelle leggi di tutte le nazioni del dì d' oggi. Se i premj* proposti dalle Accademie ai discuopritori* delle utili verità hanno moltiplicato e le cognizioni e i buoni libri; perchè i premj distribuiti dalla benefica mano del sovrano non moltiplicherebbero altresì le azioni virtuose? La moneta dell' onore è sempre inesausta, e fruttifera nelle mani del saggio distributore.*

   Dei delitti e delle pene (Milan, 1764; new ed. Harlem, NL, 1780), from the John Adams Library in the Boston Public Library. *Typographical errors for "*premi*" and "*discopritori*".

   > Yet another method of preventing crimes is, to reward virtue. Upon this subject the laws of all nations are silent.* If the rewards, proposed by *academies* for the discovery of useful truths, have increased our knowledge, and multiplied good books, is it not probable that rewards, distributed by the beneficent hand of a sovereign, would also multiply virtuous actions? The coin of honour† is inexhaustible, and is abundantly fruitful in the hands of a prince who distributes it wisely.

   Cesare Bonesana di Beccaria, *An Essay on Crimes and Punishments. By the Marquis Beccaria of Milan. With a Commentary by M. de Voltaire. A New Edition Corrected.* (Albany, 1872), accessed from http://oll.libertyfund.org/title/2193/202780/3339562 on 9 Feb. 2014. *A more accurate translation of this sentence would be "I note a universal silence among the nations of today." †"The currency of honour" would be more appropriate. I am grateful to my colleague Mauro Di Lullo for his assistance and advice on the transcription and translation of these passages.

769 | To the Earl of Hillsborough

N° 9

Boston May 8 1769

My Lord

Within these few days there have been 2 meetings of the subscribers against the importation of British goods to inforce the observation of their agreement. At the first meeting[1] they appointed a Committee to enquire who had imported British goods contrary to their agreement, & to engage those who had ^not^ entered into it to do it now. In the enquiry they found that sevral subscribers, some of them violent sons of liberty, had imported goods contrary to the agreement. These excused themselves by the pretence of their orders having been mistaken or miscarryed; and offered to deliver up the goods into the Custody of other Subscribers. This will be done one week,[2] untill the talk is over; and the goods will be returned in another.

In the other business they had no success, not one person, that I can learn, having added a name to the Subscription. Among the non subscribers are several of the first merchants of the Town. Some of these expostulated with the Committee upon the ruin they were bringing upon the Town; & observed to them that the Rhode Island Merchants were now importing great quantities of goods beyond what was ever known before; that 2 rich Ships were lately come into Salem & Marblehead; that others were expected at Newbury, Falmouth &c; by which means the Trade which used to go thro' Boston would get into other channels & would not be recovered. Some of the younger traders pointed to the main guard, and reminded them that the Town was not now under the Dominion of the Mob; but they were all free men. It is remarkable that the Scotch Merchants, who are a considerable Body, are all, to a Man, importers; & two ships laden with Scotch & North Country goods are just now come in.[3]

As the party cannot now exercise mob Law, upon which I verily beleive they had great dependence when they first set about this subscription, they now threaten the importers with publishing their names as Enemies to their Country.[4] To this it is answered, that if they do so, they should take care to indemnify the printers; for evry person whose name was so published would bring a separate Action against the printers. This therefore was declined; & they contented themselves with publishing an Advertisement wherein they endeavour to palliate their disappointment & make one more dying effort, before it is over with them.[5] But the general Opinion is, that the combination has allready received its deaths wound; and as soon as an Advance upon goods takes place, as it has begun to do allready, the Mask of patriotism will drop off, & the Selfishness of the engrossers will appear; and then those traders, who have been drawn into this Scheme without having made ^provision^ to prevent the effects of it upon themselves, will strive who shall stock their stores first.

A Gentleman from N York tells me that the Merchants there continue Very stout in non-exportation.[6] But if Exportation should become general at Boston, as it still continues to be at Philadelphia, the New Yorkers will find themselves between two fires, & will see their trade to New Jersey invaded on the one side & that to Connecticut on the other: and then self defence will oblige them to import also. This, in my Opinion, will be the End of this Combination before the year's out.

I have the honour to be with great respect, My Lord, Your Lordship's most obedient and most humble Servant

Fra Bernard

The right honble the Earl of Hillsborough

ALS, RC CO 5/758, ff 116-117.

Endorsed: [_ _ _][7] Gov.r Bernard (N.o 9) R 23.d June — By Capt. Bryan of the Wolf. B.27. Enld.[8] Enclosed the *Massachusetts Gazette*, 11 May 1769; a printed handbill "To Fellow Citizens and Countrymen," c. May 1769; and a [report of a meeting of the Boston merchants and traders, May 1769] extracted from the *Boston Weekly News-Letter*, 4 May 1769, CO 5/758, ff 118-121. Variants of letter: CO 5/893, ff 128-129 (dupLS, RC); CO 5/767 ff 317-320 (L, RLbC); BP, 7: 161-163 (L, LbC).

1. On 11 Apr.

2. Thus in manuscript.

3. The divisions within the Whig merchants precipitated by Boston's nonimportation agreement can be followed in John W. Tyler, *Smugglers & Patriots: Boston Merchants and the Advent of the Revolution* (Boston, 1986), 109-138; the May meetings are at 116-118. For the Scottish merchants see Colin Nicolson, "A Plan 'to banish all the Scotchmen': Victimization and Political Mobilization in Pre-Revolutionary Boston," *Massachusetts Historical Review* 9 (2007): 55-102.

4. A handbill enclosed named eight firms (none of whom had subscribed to the nonimportation agreement): Samuel Fletcher, Thomas and Elisha Hutchinson, William Jackson, Theophilus Lillie, Nathaniel Rogers, James and Robert Selkrig, Jonathan Simpson, and John Taylor. Printers were enjoined to "insert these Names in their next Paper, except [*if*] the Persons above-mentioned apply and promise Reformation." Citizens were urged to boycott the traders' shops and ostracise them socially. "When their guilty Consciences have rendered this Life insupportable; may they seriously attend to the Concerns of another: And altho' they must suffer the Punishment due to their Parricide in this World, may a humble and sincere Repentance open the Way to their Forgiveness in the next." CO 5/758, f 120.

5. The "Advertisement" enclosed with this letter noted that only six of the two hundred and eleven subscribers to the Boston nonimportation agreement had imported British goods in breach of the embargo. CO 5/758, f 121.

6. Also, FB underlined a printed extract of a letter from New York, dated 29 Apr., reporting the views of one enthusiast for nonimportation upon hearing the Bostonians had received "so many Goods." The writer confessed to his correspondent in Boston that he was "afraid you will not take the necessary Steps as the Soldiery is among you, but if you are dragooned by them you are forever undone." *Massachusetts Gazette*, 11 May 1769, CO 5/758, f 118.

7. Obscured in the binding.

8. The RC was carried by a brig departing 10 May 1769, according to **No. 770**. But Capt. Bryant's vessel must have delayed sailing until at least the following day to receive the package containing a newspaper printed that day.

770 | *To John Pownall*

Boston May 9 1769

Dear Sir

Having prepared some letters to my Lord Hillsborough[1] & expecting that a Brig will be ready to sail with them tomorrow I can only add a few Lines to you.

The Order for my going to England[2] came too late for my embarking before the Assembly met & therefore I find it proper not to let my Intention be known ~~bef~~ till the Assembly meets. At that time I shall find it necessary to profess it; & it is very apropos that my going home is now founded ^up^ on the King's Order rather than his Licence. This will be of considerable Use in the passing the Act for the Support of the Government: for it will assist me in defeating the Scheme, which, I understand is formed, to disappoint that Act. I don't think that I have any Intrest in the Event of the Act myself, as I doubt not but the Differences by its failing would be made good to me: but it seems to me to be of great Consequence ^to Government^ that this Act should not be discontinued or that the Reasons for discontinuing it should be known & avowed. If any Dispute upon this Subject should happen, it will be farther explained; if not, a farther Explanation will be unnecessary.

The Fury occasioned by the Arrival of the Copies of my Letters is something abated: but there is some great Mischeif intended which I must wait for the Breaking out ^of^.[3] One thing is remarkable that since the Arrival of the Advice of the honour conferred upon me, out of 10 Councellors whom I have been in Company with only 4 have congratulated me. The other six are indeed the cheifs of the Party in the Council; & it is obvious that they have entered into an Engagement for that Purpose; for t'other Day I was in Company with several of the Council for some Hours, & one of them distinguished himself by uncommon Civility to me, but was quite silent as to Congratulation. The next Day being Council Day[4] I mentioned the Affair myself & read to them My Lord Hillsboroughs kind & polite Letter[5] upon the Occasion: a total Silence ensued; & even they who had before congratulated me privately, durst not repeat it in Public. This shows to what a Degree of Servility the Annual Election has reduced these People.

I have wrote to my Lord H that I don't expect to embark from hence till towards the End of July.[6] Disagreeable as it is I had rather attend the Assembly than appear to run away from them. I desire, for the last Thing I do in this Province, to hear all they have to say against me. In the Assembly near 12 Months ago In the Articles of Impeachment preferred against me which, tho rejected by the House were nevertheless printed, all that had any Foundation were charges against me for doing my Duty. They have Nothing now to charge me with, but that I have made a faithful & impartial Account of their Proceedings accompanied with such Observation as occurred to every Man of Sense who was acquainted with the Subject.

I am D[r] Sir Your &c

John Pownall Esq

L, LbC   BP, 7: 286-297.

Minor emendations not shown. In handwriting of Thomas Bernard.

1. **Nos. 767** and **768**.
2. **No. 757**.
3. He may have heard rumors that the Whigs were intending that the House should petition the king for his removal and impeachment.
4. 3 May.
5. **No. 755**. The reading was not recorded in the executive minutes. CO 5/829, f 6.
6. **No. 767**.

771 | To Thomas Pownall

Boston May the 11th 1769

Dear Sir

I am obliged to you for 3 letters. feb. 3 feb. 12 & Mar. 22.[1] As I expect to see you in a few Months[,][2] I shall not enquire deeply into the Subjects of them.

I am obliged to you for your friendly Caution concerning the Orders enquiring into Treason but I don't apprehend I shall be under any Difficulty about them. For nothing has appeared to me as yet which upon a legal scrutiny will quite amount to treason. Intentions have wanted Overt Acts and Overt Acts have wanted Intentions. I know of no Instance where there has been a sufficient Connexion of both.[3] However I have not determined upon this Business.

I have not as yet seen the Mutiny Act:[4] There is one in Town, but it has not come to my Hands. I have seen a written Copy of the American Provisos: they will be of no use at present; For the Rumour now is to have nothing to do with quartering Troops. Endeavours to make it convenient or agreable are all flung away.

I received a printed Copy of a Speech, which I cant thank you for as you dont own it.[5] It is not printed for Sale with your Name prefixed to it; and wh[at][6] is surprising, the Party is greatly pleased with it, tho' it cuts up by the Roots all the Principles upon which they had raised all the late Disturbances. But principles have nothing to do with them. Nor they with Principles.[7]

If the late Resolutions and Address[8] were intended to frighten the Bostonians they will have a very contrary Effect: the Sons of Liberty here since they have received Assurances that nothing more will be done this Session,[9] are as highly elevated as ^ever they were;^ and you must expect as much Folly and Madness as ever; I send you a Specimen of it for the Present. Great ill humour is expected next Session, I shall keep clear of Giving Cause for it; but shall be firm in all necessary Duties.

You are talked of to be Agent; and so is Mr Bollan, who has greatly ingratiated himself by his volunteer Petition.[10] You are also designed to be Governor by Report: but it is no great compliment to you: since the same Authority has conferred it on Mr Wilkes on a general Plan of Conciliation.

I find myself obliged to stay here to the End of next Session: It will be an extreme disagreable Business; but on some Accounts it is proper. If I had known my Liberty, I should have embarked some Months ago; tho' there is no knowing which would be for the best. As soon as the Session is over I shall set about fixing the Time & means of my departure, which I suppose will not exceed July. Lady Bernard joins in compliments &c to ~~you &~~ Lady F.[11]

I am &c,

Thomas Pownall Esq:

L, LbC   BP, 7: 288-289.

Enclosure not found.

---

1. Not found.

2. Editorially supplied, replacing a period.

3. While this passage expressed FB's personal views on the matter, he could not, of course, reveal that he had formed a cabinet to investigate instances of treason in response to Hillsborough's instructions in **No. 731**.

4. 9 Geo. 3, c. 18 (1769), which continued the Quartering Act of 1765. Thomas Pownall successfully moved the reform of the Quartering Act in the House of Commons on 15 Mar., proposing that the act should not be enforced in provinces where quarters were specifically set aside and maintained for soldiers. See **No. 754**n3.

5. *The Speech of Th-m-s P-wn-ll, Esq; late g-v-rn-r of this province, in the H--se of C-m--ns, in favor of America* ([Boston, 1769]), *Early American Imprints, Series 1*, no. 11423.

6. Obscured by the binding.

7. The sixteen-page pamphlet cited in note 5 printed Pownall's lengthy speech to the House of Commons of 26 Jan. when the members debated the American correspondence that had been read the previous day. It is highly probable that Pownall himself supplied the Bostonians with a transcription of the speech (that he had likely read from a prepared paper). FB's reaction was polite, for there was much in the speech that would have irritated and angered him, not least Pownall's firm opposition to the proposed treason commission at this "very dangerous and perilous" juncture in British-colonial relations. Notwithstanding FB shared Pownall's concerns about the legal impracticalities of conducting treason trials, he would have doubted that Pownall favoured any kind of punitive measure to bring the colonists in line. For in addressing the Lords' resolutions of 15 Dec., Pownall urged the Commons to avoid any pronouncement on alleged "illegal and unconstitutional" proceedings in Boston without first "having thoroughly examined the case and circumstances under which these people were to act" together with a "sufficient examination of the state of the evidence" against them. In short, as FB would have realized, Pownall had urged a fuller investigation into FB's correspondence with Hillsborough. Pownall did not impugn FB's accounts, and indeed cited the governor's letters as valuable sources of information, if only to excuse the House of Representatives and Bostonians from some of the accusations that FB himself had levied. The pamphlet concluded with a six-page section (pp. 11-16) detailing Pownall's proposals for settling the taxation issue: that the British government and Parliament, in short, accept the distinction between "internal" and "external" taxation and repeal the Townshend Revenue Act. Set in a smaller type than the preceding pages it is possible that this section related the speech that Pownall delivered on 8 Feb., when he first urged repeal. On taxation, FB now evidently agreed with Pownall, albeit that, as he stated, if the Americans were to accept Pownall's proposition it would mean them surrendering the principle of Parliament's legislative supremacy in the colonies. Since he was still waiting upon some signal measure to redress royal authority in Massachusetts, FB would have been less enthusiastic about Pownall's Burkean advice to the British. "Do nothing which may bring into discussion *questions of right, which must become mere articles of faith.*" Ibid. See also in **Introduction**, 29.

8. The eight resolutions on Massachusetts and the address to the king passed the House of Lords on 15 Dec. and were approved by the House of Commons on 8 Feb. *HCJ*, 32: 151.

9. Enclosing the Lords' resolutions, House agent Dennys DeBerdt advised Speaker Thomas Cushing that "'tis believed the Ministry do not intend to put them into execution, the chief unhappiness arises from the Ministry giving entire credit to everything wrote by Gov'. Bernard. Which no reasoning can stand against altho we have all the best speakers in the House on our side of the question, who are true friends to Liberty." London, 1 Feb. 1769, Albert Matthews, "Letters of Dennys DeBerdt, 1757-1770," 355.

10. William Bollans petition to the House of Commons, 26 Jan. 1769, was printed in the *Boston Post-Boy and Advertiser*, 17 Apr. and the *Essex Gazette*, 18-25 Apr. 1769; and later in *Letters to Hillsborough* (1st ed.), 75-82.

11. Harriet Fawkener (1725-77) was Pownall's wife. They married on 3 Aug. 1765. She was the widow of Sir Everhard Fawkener (1694–1758), a merchant and diplomat, and always referred to as Lady Fawkener even after marrying Pownall. She was the daughter of Lt.-Gen. Charles Churchill (1656–1714), brother of John Churchill, first duke of Marlborough, (1650–1722).

772 | To Richard Jackson

Boston May 11 1769

Dear Sir

You are not fond of writing upon American affairs; no more am I: and that is the Cause why our Letters have not been so long or so frequent as they used to be. Whilst we thought we could do any Good, our corespondence was closely kept up: and tho' we differed about the Means, Our End was the same, the Conecting Great Britain and America upon a permanent System. It gives me great Pleasure to reflect that our Correspondence upon this important Subject, [which]¹ has been concluded with our joining of our own Accord, and without any Influence, one over the other in an uniform Opinion of the only Measure that was left to preserve the Connexion of Great Britain with America. In other ~~Difficulties~~ Particulars our differences of opinion has arose in a good Measure from the difference of our Situation. A good Friend of yours observed t'other day upon your still being an Advocate for the Constitution of this Government, that if you had seen the Effects of it upon the Spot, for these last 3 Years you would be of the same Opinion with us.

The Sons of Liberty at Boston are as [high] as ever: and indeed if nothing more is done in Parliament after the resolutions and the address, as they are assured there is not, they have good reason. I now send you a Specimen of the Fear & Reverence they have for the King and Parliament, which will show how much they have been intimidated by the late Proceedings in Westminster. If I am informed right, much more than this is to be expected; And madness and Folly will be as triumphant as ever. I am [doomed?] to stand this Session; w^h^ether it will be for the best or not I cannot now say. I shall endeavour to give as little Offence as possible: but I apprehend that the Publication of my Letters will render all Prudence and Caution of little Effect. All that I depend upon [is?] that I think I know my Business, and I beleive they do not theirs.

Heretofore I have had only leave to go home. I have now received an Order to attend the King to report to him the State of the Province. This was acompanied with a Signification of the honour being confer^r^ed, which has been long talked of. It was, I suppose, thus times to show the People that I was not called home in the Way of Disgrace. My Lord Hillsborough in this as in all other Things has acted with the utmost Kindess, and Politeness. As soon as the Session, which may last 6 Weeks [&?] not 6 Days, is over; I shall set about settling of the means of my Departure: the Latter I believe wont exceed all July.

I am Sr Your &c

Richard Jackson Esq.

L, LbC   BP, 7: 289-291.

In the handwriting of clerk no. 9. Minor emendations not shown. The enclosure, which FB described ironically as exhibiting "Fear & Reverence" for the King and Parliament, has not been found, but was evidently another copy of the newspaper cutting enclosed with **No. 771**.

---

1. Obscured in the binding here and below.

773 | Circular From the Earl of Hillsborough

Circular

(Nº. 27)

Whitehall May 13. 1769

Sir,

Inclosed[1] I send you the gracious speech made by the King to His Parliament at the close of the Session on Tuesday last.

What His Majesty is pleased to say, in relation to the Measures which have been pursued in North America, will not escape your notice, as the satisfaction His Majesty expresses in the approbation His Parliament has given to them, and the assurances of their firm support in the prosecution of them, together with His Royal opinion of the great advantages that will probably accrue from the concurrence of every branch of the Legislature in the Resolution of maintaing[2] a due execution of the Laws, cannot fail to produce the most salutary effects.[3]

From hence it will be understood that the whole Legislature concur in the opinion adopted by His Majesty's Servants, that no measure ought to be taken which can in any way derogate from the Legislative authority of Great Britain over the Colonies; but I can take upon me to assure you, notwithstanding insinuations to the contrary, from Men with factious and seditious Views, that His Majesty's present Administration have at no time entertained a Design to propose to Parliament to lay any further Taxes upon America for the purpose of raising a Revenue, and that it is at present their intention to propose in the next Session of Parliament, to take off the duties upon Glass, Paper and Colours, upon consideration of such Duties having been laid contrary to the true principles of commerce.[4]

These Sir, have always been and still are the sentiments of His Majesty's present Servants, and the principles by which their conduct in respect to America has been governed; and His Majesty relies upon your Prudence and Fidelity, for such an explanation of His Measures as may tend to remove the prejudices which have been excited by the misrepresentations of those who are Enemies to the Peace and Prosperity of Great Britain and Her Colonies, and to re-establish that mutual confidence, and Affection upon which the Glory and Safety of the British Empire depend. I am, Sir,

Your Most Obedient Humble Servant

Hillsborough

LS, RC   BP, 12: 87-90.

Endorsed by FB: No 27 Earl of Hillsborough Circular d May 13 1769. Variant in CO 5/241, f 94 (L, LbC).

Hillsborough's circular to the colonial governors was the first formal intimation that the Grafton administration was intent on repealing the Townshend duties, excepting that on tea, in the next session of Parliament. It was a turning point in colonial policy, with the government moving toward conciliation in the hope of mollifying criticism in the colonies. Hillsborough's attitude toward the Americans may have softened, for privately he professed the desirability of placating the colonists. Perhaps also he might have assumed that having recalled FB (**No. 757**), the prospects of reaching a *modus vivendi* with the Americans were more promising than they had been in the past two years. Even so, Hillsborough's "highly suspicious" conduct in preparing the circular printed here suggests that amity was grudgingly proffered. Lord Chancellor Camden complained that the circular did not properly convey the cabinet's sentiments. The final version printed here omitted key phrases (whether by accident or design is uncertain), agreed in cabinet and intended (as Grafton wrote) to "be soothing to the colonies." In the end, Peter D. G. Thomas concludes, "Hillsborough's behaviour had greatly weakened the gesture of goodwill that had been intended by way of the circular letter."[5]

---

1. Left marginalia: virgule acknowledging the enclosure.

2. Thus in manuscript.

3. The paragraph relevant to American affairs was as follows:

> The Measures which I had taken regarding the late unhappy Disturbances in *North America*, have been already laid before you. They have received your Approbation; and you have assured Me of your firm Support in the Prosecution of them. Nothing in My Opinion could be more likely to enable the well-disposed among My Subjects in that Part of the World, effectually to discourage and defeat the Designs of the Factious and Seditious, than the hearty Concurrence of every Branch of the Legislature in the Resolu-

tion of maintaining the Execution of the Laws in every Part of My Dominions; and there is nothing I more ardently wish for, than to see it produce that good Effect.

9 May 1769. *HCJ*, 32: 453.

4. An act to repeal so much of . . . an act for granting certain duties in the British Colonies and Plantations in America . . ., 10 Geo. 3, c. 17 (1770).

5. Thomas, *Townshend Duties Crisis*, 140-141.

774 | To Thomas Gage

Boston May 15 1769

S[r].

I hereby transmit to you a Copy of an Address to me signed by 10 Gentlemen of the Council, which was sent to me at my Country house early Yesterday morning in a Cover with a Letter signed by M[r] Bowdoin & M[r] Pitts signifying that they were desired to present this Address to me, & that I not being in Town, they begged Leave to inclose it to me that I might have it as soon as may be, upon Account of my Writing to you by the Post.

As this Business has been transacted at a Business[1] appointed by themselves without my Privity or Presence, I am quite unacquainted with the Motives of this Application: I know not upon what Grounds they found their Apprehensions of great Inconveniences arising from Troops being in the Town upon the Day of General Election; nor how their remaining in the Town will have any Tendency to interrupt a quiet & peaceable Election or why the removing of them is like to make the Election more free & uninterrupted than it would be otherwise. As the Gentlemen have thought proper to keep me in Ignorance in regard to these particulars, I can only transmit their Request to your Excellency & leave it to you to act therein as you shall think proper.

I am &c.

Gen[l] Gage

L, LbC   BP, 7: 233.

In handwriting of Thomas Bernard. Variants: CO 5/87, ff 115-116 (L, Copy); CO 5/893, f 134 (L, Copy); CO 5/758, f 126 (L, Copy); CO 5/767, ff 326-328 (L, LbC). Enclosed a copy of the address of the Massachusetts Council to FB, 14 May 1769 (not found, but for which see CO 5/758, f 125).

In his reply of 22 May, Gage might have discussed the logistical problems and cost of extracting the troops from Boston just for election day (31 May), but instead echoed the imperialistic tenor of FB's letter dismissing the notion. "No Inconvenience has ever been found from the King's Troops being in other Places in his Majesty's Dominions on similar Occasions, and I flatter myself, none will be found in Boston."[2]

---

1. Copies: "Meeting".
2. Gage to FB, New York, 22 May 1769, BP, 12: 95-98.

775 | To the Earl of Hillsborough

(Duplicate)

(N° 10)

Boston May 15 1769

My Lord

Yesterday Morning being Sunday, at my Country house 4 Miles from Boston, I received from the Doorkeeper of the Council-chamber a Letter signed by Mr Bowdoin and Mr Pitts two of the Council,[1] signifying that they were desired to wait upon me with an Address, which was signed by ten of the Council and contains a Desire that I would write to General Gage to order the troops to be removed out of Boston upon the Day of the Election of Councellors; and adding that I being out of Town, they begged Leave to inclose it to me that I might have it as soon as may be on Account of writing to the General by the Post.[2]

This Address was prepared, as Business of this Kind has usually been done of late, at a Meeting of the Council appointed by themselves without my Privity or knowledge; and from thence handed about to others not present, to be signed. So that I am by no means acquainted with any of the Reasons upon which this extraordinary Request is founded: however I have sent a Copy of this Address to the General as desired. I hereby inclose a Copy of the Address & also of my Letter to the General inclosing a Copy of it:[3] and I shall now make a few Observations upon this uncommon Transaction.

This is, as far as I can learn, quite a new Motion; the like never having been made by any other Assembly upon the Continent. And yet New York has never been without Troops since the End of the War; Philadelphia has seldom been without them, has a Regiment now and has lately built Barracks for their Accommodation;[4]

Charlestown has also generally had Troops in the Town; & yet none of the Assemblys of those Provinces ever suggested that Troops being in their Towns had a tendency to interrupt the Quiet & Peace of their Proceedings or that the Removal of the Troops would make them more quiet or uninterrupted than they would be otherwise. As for the General Election of Councellors, it is a Proceeding transacted within the Walls of the general Court and differs in Noways from the passing a Bill or any other Business which requires the Concurrence of the three Bodies.[5] It is plain therefore that this Transaction is an Echo to the Proceedings of the Select-men & the Town Meeting; with whom the Leaders of the Council have a more intimate Connection than is suitable with their own honor or the Wellfare of the Province.[6]

Let us now ask for what Purpose is this Application made; certainly not for that which is expressed in it. They cannot expect that the Troops will be removed, or that such Removal would promote peace and quiet. They cannot suppose that General Gage having stationed the Troops here by order of the King can remove them from hence without the like Order; or that, if he had a discretionary Power, he would make himself answerable for the Mischeifs which might be done in 24 hours Absence of the Troops only. But where are they to be quartered if they are to be removed out of Boston for a Day and a Night only?[7] in public houses near Boston? I suppose it would require a Circle of 40 Miles diameter to quarter 1500 Men in the public houses out of Boston. But who shall quarter them? the Justices in the Country certainly would not. they would say that they had no Right to demand Quarters in public Houses, when they had Barracks fitted up in the Town where they were stationed: and with much more Reason than the Town Justices refused Quarters in the Town where the Troops were ordered because there were Barracks in another Place where they were not ordered. If it should be said that the Troops might go out of Town in the Morning and return in the Evening, that wont answer the Purpose; for the Election of Councellors is seldom over till after it is dark. What then is the Intent of this Proposal? It must be one of these: either to create an Uneasiness in the General Court, because the General has not done what is impracticable; or Disorders in the Country by his attempting to do it. I acquit them of the latter, because they have not the least Expectation that the General will comply with their Request. The first therefore is the true Intent, the very contrary to their professed Purpose of preventing the Interruption of the Peace and Quiet of the General Court.

I now repent that I did not call the General Court at Cambridge;[8] & am now considering whether I cannot yet order their Meeting there. I know I can by Law but yet is quite without a Precedent in this Province, it would probably create a Dispute of which I would avoid the Trouble, tho' I should be ever so much in the right. But if the Seeds of Discord, which the Councellors are now sowing, should take Root in the General Court & produce Disorder I will remove the Court to Cambridge.[9] I am very desirous that no Cause of Offence should proceed from me: but if they will not submit to let me pursue my pacifick Intention, I must submit to the Necessity.

I have the honor to be with great Respect, My Lord, Your Lordships
most obedient and Most humble Serv.ᵗ:

Fra Bernard

The Right Honble The Earl of Hillsborough.

dupLS, RC   CO 5/758, ff 122-124.

Interlineations in FB's hand. Endorsed: Boston May 15ᵗʰ. 1769 Govʳ: Bernard. (Nᵒ. 10) R 30 June (Dupˡᵉ._ origˡ. not reced). B.28.   Enclosed copies of the address of the Massachusetts Council, 14 May 1769, CO 5/758, f 125; **No. 774** at ibid., ff. 126-127. FB's original letter to Hillsborough must have arrived after the duplicate and is filed in CO 5/893, ff 130-131 (ALS, RC); other variants in CO 5/767, ff 320-325 (L, RLbC); BP, 7: 163-166 (L, LbC). The duplicate letter and enclosures were considered by the Board of Trade on 1 Dec. 1769. *JBT*, 13: 125.

1. This letter has not been found.

2. The address, prepared by the out-going Council, requested that FB write Gen. Thomas Gage asking for the British soldiers to be withdrawn from Boston on election day, 31 May. The document was signed by ten councilors who had sustained opposition to FB since the autumn of 1768 (listed in given order): Samuel Danforth, Isaac Royall, John Erving, William Brattle, James Bowdoin, Thomas Hubbard, Harrison Gray, James Russell, Royal Tyler, and James Pitts. 14 May 1769, CO 5/758, f 125.

3. **No. 774**.

4. The barracks were erected with monies appropriated by the provincial assembly in 1768.

5. That is, the General Court, comprising the Governor, the Council, and the House of Representatives.

6. On 5 May, the Boston town meeting approved a detailed set of instructions for its four representatives in the House, enjoining them to procure the removal of the cannon stationed at the entrances to the Town House, where the assembly met, and to mount an enquiry into "all the Grievances we have suffered from the Millitary Power." This was to encompass the governor's decision to billet the troops "in contradiction" to the wording of Quartering Act, "repeated offences and Violences" perpetrated by the British soldiers, and the refusal of the attorney general to prosecute in such cases. The remainder of the instructions reiterated the town's desire for the repeal of the Townshend Revenue Act, and disquiet at the "formidable power" of the reformed Vice Admiralty Courts. *Reports of the Record Commissioners of Boston*, 16: 286-288.

7. That is, for the duration of election day, 31 May.

8. The General Court convened at the Town House in Boston on 31 May.

9. He moved the General Court to Harvard College, Cambridge, on 15 Jun., and held the first meeting on the following day. *JHRM*, 45: 132-133.

776 | To John Pownall

private

Boston May 15 1769

Dear Sir

I herewith transmit to My Lord Hillsborough an Address of the Council to me and my Observations upon it: from whence you will see that the Sons of Liberty are not dispirited:[1] I wish I could say the same of the Friends of Government.

If I thought it proper to act as freely now as I have done heretofore I would Negative 3 of the cheif Managers of the late & present Proceedings of the Council,[2] since their separating themselves from the Governor. But I must now leave the Reform of that Body to greater & abler Men than myself: and I would not negative a single Person at the next Election, if I was not apprehensive that so abrupt a Departure from my former Practice might be considered as the Effect of my being out of humour; whereas I should be sorry to have that thought of me, under an Administration from whom I have received such extraordinary Favours.

I know not how to reconcile it to myself to exclude Persons from the Council whose cheif Demerit has consisted in their single Votes, & to accept others ^who^ have been for some time ~~past~~ & are now contriving to distress & embarras ^the^ Government by all means in their Power. The Delinquency in the Council is become so general, that it is not in power of the Governor to correct it by Negatives. If therefore I shall consent to the whole of the next Council, it must not be understood as an Approbation of ~~the whole~~ all the Persons elected, but because the exceptional Part of them is too large for the Negative of a Governor.[3] The Reformation of the Council must now be made in the Body & not in the Members; it must be done at Westminster & can't be done here.

When I consider that Councellors in Character, must be supposed to be prudent Men & in some Degree politicians, I am quite at a loss to know upon what Principles these Councellors act & what is the End which they pursue. The Security of their Election which they have allways at Heart, might have been effected with much Less Desertion of Character & Duty than they have used. According to refined Policy their Actions may be fully accounted for by a Design to destroy the annual Election of Councellors, & in Consequence thereof their continual Dependence upon the People; & to effect this they have endeavoured to set in its strongest Light the Insufficiency & Unconstitutionality of a Kings Court so constituted. This would be a full Solution of their unaccountable Proceedings if it was not for one Difficulty, which is this; that by the means by which they show the Impropriety of the Constitution of the Council, ~~they also shew the impropriety of the Consti-~~

~~tution of the Council,~~ they also shew themselves to be improper Persons to be the King's Councellors. If it was not for this I should not doubt but that the Alteration of the Mode of the Appointment was the final Cause of their late Proceedings: & it is not impossible but that if that Effect should be produced, they may be allowed to apologise for their former Conduct by the Necessity they have acted under; but at present they show no Disposition to avail themselves of such an Apology, as they act with much more violence than ^there^ can be any Pretence of Necessity for.

I am S^r &c

John Pownall Esqr

L, LbC   BP, 7: 291-293.

Minor emendations not shown. In handwriting of Thomas Bernard.   Enclosed a copy of the Massachusetts Council's address to the governor, 14 May 1769. (Another copy of the enclosure was sent with **No. 775.**) No reply has been found.

---

1.   The address was enclosed in **No. 775**.

2.   He doubtless meant James Bowdoin; the other two were probably James Pitts (who was reelected on 31 May) and William Brattle (whose election FB vetoed).

3.   FB changed his mind and proceeded to negative the election of eleven, eight of whom he had rejected previously (William Brattle, James Bowdoin, Jerathmeel Bowers, Joseph Gerrish, John Hancock, James Otis Sr., Thomas Saunders, and Artemas Ward), plus Benjamin Greenleaf and Walter Spooner. Joseph Hawley declined to accept his election.

777 | *From Thomas Gage*

New York 15th: May 1769.

Sir,

   Being informed, that the King's Writs have been issued for the Calling of a new General Assembly, of his Majesty's Province of Massachusett's Bay, to meet at Boston the End of this Month; I have ordered an Account of all the Expenditures, incurred in quartering his Majesty's Forces at Boston, to be prepared.¹ Colonel Robertson,² who setts out from this Place for Boston this Day, will lay the same before you immediately, that you may have Time, to order a thorough Inspection, and Examination of the said Accounts, which when properly authenticated, you will be so good to lay before the General Assembly, that Funds may be provided to discharge the same.³

I am likewise to beg of you, that, you will be pleased to make a Requisition, that Provision may be made for the further quartering of his Majesty's Forces, in the Town of Boston, and Castle Island, according to Act of Parliament.

I take this Opportunity, to offer my Congratulations on the Dignity, his Majesty has been pleased lately to conferr upon you, which is a signal Mark of his Royal Approbation of your Conduct.

> I have the Honor to be, with great Regard, Sir, Your
> most obedient, humble Servant,

> Thos. Gage.

His Excellency Sir Francis Bernard B^t:

LS, RC   BP, 12: 91-94.

Endorsed by FB: Genl Gage d May 15 1769 conc^g the Troops at Boston —.

---

1. The actual account has not been located. Gen. Thomas Gage's papers were being catalogued when this volume was in preparation. The relevant document is likely to be in Account Book 8, 1767-1770. MiU-C: Gage Papers.

2. James Robertson (1717-88) was appointed lieutenant colonel of the 16th Regiment of Foot on 17 Aug. 1768. Robertson sent the accounts to FB under cover of a letter dated 13 Jun. 1769, Mass. Archs., 56: 559-560 (ALS, RC).

3. Gage's letter was read to the House of Representatives on 6 Jul. but the province refused to make any appropriation for the expenses incurred by the regiments in Boston. *JHRM*, 45: 164, 168-172.

778 | To the Earl of Hillsborough

N° 7.

Boston May 25 1769

My Lord

I have received your Lordships letter N° 24,[1] & observe his Majesty's orders that I take the most effectual methods of procuring the fullest information touching all treasons and misprisions of Treasons committed here since the 30th of Decr 1767. I have since had a consultation with the Cheif Justice the Secretary & the Judge of the Admiralty, in which We have taken into consideration the sevral proceedings of the Faction which may be supposed to be treasonable; & cannot fix upon any that amount to actual treason, tho' many of them approach very near to it.[2]

The cheif Distinctions which our deliberations have turned upon have been these; 1. As to the public transactions of which there is no doubt, such as the Resolutions of the Town meeting in Sept[r], the circular Letter of the Select men, & the Convention,[3] We cannot take these into consideration, because they having been fully certified & not noticed at Westminster for treason, We cannot enter into an enquiry about the nature of those offences, which have been allready before the whole legislature;[4] 2. Of the private transactions of the faction, some of which have been evidenced only by reports generally credited, there are these difficulties; where there have been consultations of a treasonable nature, they have wanted overt acts to make the crime compleat; and where there have been Overt acts apparently treasonable, they have wanted a connection with treasonable consultations. For instance, the Consultation to seize the Castle was treasonable; but it was not followed by an Overt act.[5] Again, The putting up a Beacon to alarm the Country was an Overt Act apparently treasonable, but it cannot be traced to a consultation so as to evidence the intention.[6] 3. We have not entered into the consideration of the publications in the Boston Gazette & other papers because, as they have been transmitted & are well known at Westminster, the pointing out passages which amounted to treason, (as some of them come Very near to it) should come from thence, where the precise distinctions of Law are much better understood than they can be here.

But the great Difficulty of procuring information is that the Faction is not so broke, as to make them Witness one against another, or to make voluntary informations safe. Some time ago, they were very much frightened; and if those fears had been realised, it might have ~~been~~ induced some of the lesser offenders to have consulted their safety at the expense of their leaders. But they have lately received such assurances from their correspondents that they have nothing more to fear from this Session of parliament, that they are got as high as ever; of which I shall have occasion very soon to give your Lordship most pregnant proofs.[7]

I cannot suppose that it will answer his Majesty's intention or be agreeable to your Lordships judgement, for me to institute a public enquiry without a great probability of success. The Reasons against it are Very forcible; & there is one which has great weight with me at present. All the friends and Correspondents of the party exhort them to behave very cautiously & inoffensively at the next Assembly. I do not expect that they will follow this advice; I have great reason to be assured that they will not. But I would have them have fair play; and therefore I would avoid doing any thing that should alarm or offend them at this time; as I am desirous that the ill humour which I foresee will be introduced in the General Court next Session may in no instance proceed from me. In the mean time I shall keep his Majesty's commands in my Mind, that if any means should occur to execute them, I may avail myself of them.

I have the honour to be wth great respect, My Lord, Your Lordships
most obedient & most humble Servant

Fra Bernard

The right honble the Earl of Hillsborough

ALS, RC   CO 5/758, ff 112-113.

Minor emendations not shown. Endorsed: Boston 25th. May 1769. Govr. Bernard. (N° 7)
R 23^d: June _ By Capt Bryan of the Wolf. B.25. Enl^d   Enclosures not found. Variants
of letter in CO 5/893, ff 124-125 (dupLS, RC); CO 5/767, ff 314-315 (L, RLbC); BP, 7:
157-159 (dupL, LbC). The letter and enclosures were considered by the Board of Trade on
1 Dec. 1769. *JBT*, 13: 125.

---

1. **No. 745**, received on 20 May.

2. FB and his cabinet council (of TH, Andrew Oliver, and Robert Auchmuty) had met at the turn of the
    year to review acts of treason arising from the *Liberty* riot of 10 Jun. FB convened the group to review
    the instructions arising from Parliament's address to the king, approved on 8 Feb. Once again the prov-
    ince's chief law officer, Jonathan Sewall, was omitted from the discussions, perhaps on account of FB's
    lingering doubts about the attorney general's loyalty. See **Nos. 719** and **731**n2.

3. The resolutions of the Boston town meeting, 13 Sept 1768; *Reports of the Record Commissioners*, 16:
    261-263; circular of the Boston selectmen to the Massachusetts towns, 14 Sept. 1768, **Appendix 13**,
    Bernard Papers, 4: 400-401. For a discussion of the meeting of 12 Sept. see **No. 681**, ibid., 318-324.
    The Convention of Towns met in Boston between 22 and 29 Sept. 1768, for which see the source note
    to **No. 688**, ibid., 362-365. Boston's resolutions and the selectmen's circular letter were included in
    the long list of American correspondence presented to Parliament on 28 Nov. 1768. Lord North, leader
    of the House of Commons, observed Boston's proceedings were "near to treason" when the Commons
    debated the correspondence on 26 Jan. 1769. *PDBP*, 3: 22, 27, 75-76.

4. On this point, FB and his advisers appear to have constructed a convenient explanation for their reluc-
    tance to investigate further, and an exculpation against any subsequent accusation of misprision of trea-
    son on their part. According to the Grafton administration, there was no legal impediment to bringing
    colonists to trial in England under 35 Hen. 8, c. 2 (1543), though such a rationale had already been
    strongly criticized in Parliament. See **Introduction,** 18-20.

5. Reported in **No. 646**, *Bernard Papers*, 4: 242-246.

6. Reported in **No. 681**, ibid., 318-324.

7. The point that FB was making was that the proposed treason commission was an empty threat which
    had conspired to encourage the radicals rather than scare them. One letter from London extracted in
    the newspapers declared on 3 Feb. (before the address to the king was adopted by the Commons) "you
    may rely upon it, they will never venture to execute any thing of this nature" Another wrote on 4 Feb.
    that "this seems all that will be done for America, till some fresh matters are furnished from thence."
    Boston Chronicle, 7-10 Apr. 1769. Many of the news reports from England concerned John Wilkes's
    expulsion from the Commons.

779 | *To the Earl of Hillsborough*

N.º 11

Boston June 1 1769

My Lord

Yesterday the General Court in Assembly met in the Court house here according to his Majesty's Writs. Upon perusing the returns It appeared that ^there were^ Very few of the friends of Government in this Assembly. Of the 17 rescinders only 5 were chose[1] & but 2 of them attended; Of other friends to Government, who voted against rescinding very few were chosen; the greatest part declined standing a poll, some refused serving after they were elected, & some others lost their Election. By these Means out of that party which ^heretofore^ used to keep the Opposition to Government under, there were reckoned to be not above 10 Men in an House consisting of above 120. So general is now become the Despondency of those who have endeavoured to maintain the Authority of the King & Parliament in this province.

As the Faction was so apparently possessed of the House, evry Violent Measure that could be devised was to be expected. In the Morning, before they had chose a Speaker, they sent me a Message, as inclosed,[2] the insolent Terms of which will speak for themselves. I asked the Messengers if they had chose a Speaker; they answered that they had not. I told them that I could take no notice of any Message from them untill they had chose a Speaker. However, if they would choose a Speaker to save time I would consider the Message as coming from the House & give an Answer to it. Upon this being reported they passed the resolves as inclosed & chose a Speaker, who being presented & consented to,[3] I sent them an Answer as inclosed.

In the afternoon they proceeded to the Election of Councellors. The Faction had previously declared that they would clear the Council of Tories: by this denomination they signify all those who are disposed to support the Kings Government, to acknowledge the Authority of parliament, & to preserve the people from a democratical despotism. Accordingly they turned out M.ʳ Flucker, M.ʳ Ropes, M.ʳ Paine & M.ʳ Worthington,[4] 4 Gentlemen so distinguished by their integrity ability & other qualities which form a respectable Character, that I could scarce add a fifth to them out of what is left. These Gentlemen were flung out by such large Majorities & the others, excepting the new ones & 1 or 2 more, elected so nearly unanimously, that it afforded a strong instance of the absoluteness of the Faction as well as of ^their^ disposition to abuse their power.

Before the meeting of the Assembly I had formed a great desire to lay a foundation for conciliatory Measures; it was for this purpose that I called the Assembly at Boston against my own Judgement, that all Cause of ill temper might be avoided. I was desirous, if any means could be found to justify it, to contract my negatives, or, if possible, to remove them entirely. But this could not be done without some concession from the faction, which upon their late Elevation was not likely to be obtained. I could indeed with propriety have given up the exercise of the Negative; as no longer of any use: but I did not care to give so public a testimony of despondency. But when I saw the Faction pick & cull out evry Man of the Council that pretended to any independency of them, It appeared to me that My Duty to the King, my Regard for his honour, my Concern for the Gentlemen who were thus injured for their fidelity to him, & many other Motives required of me to resent this proceeding by a retaliation. I therefore negatived the 6 negatived last year,[5] 3 of those who came in the room of those who were turned out ^now^,[6] (the 4th having desired my leave to refuse a seat at the board)[7] and 2 of the old Councellors, being the cheif Managers in the Unnatural part which the Council has acted of late.[8] Upon a reflexion upon what I have done, I can only blame myself for not having carried my negative a little farther, tho' I could not well carry it so far as it deserved.

When I had qualified the Council, I sent up for the House & made the Speech which is inclosed. Your Lordship may have observed that for some time past my Speeches have been meer Matter of form, & have had nothing in them that could afford a Subject for disputation. I cant allways avoid Altercation; but I take care to avoid giving Cause for it. The House resolved to do no Business, till the Committee appointed to take into consideration their Message to me[9] concerning removing the Troops & my Answer. As I understand that they are greatly puzzled about this business & are resolved not to give up this pretension, altho' it is really insupportable, I expect that these Debates will take up some time and must therefore suspend my Letter for a full Account of them.[10]

June 8

It is now a Week since the date of the first part of this Letter; during which The House has done nothing but debate about ^their^ requisition for removing the troops without coming to a conclusion, and another business which I shall mention hereafter not to interrupt the present Narrative.__ To explain the following Detail, I must premise that one of Otis's cheif Allies (Mr Hawley who refused to take his Seat in the Council) is gone off from him & opposes him in evry thing. This Gentleman who is of great ability & has hitherto been of the popular side is well heard in the House & has had power to controll Otis in evry thing he has undertaken; so that he has not been able to this time to get another Message to me concerning the removing the troops through the House; & yet all other Business stands still.[11]

June 10

The Debate concerning the Reply to my Answer has still continued to be the only Business of the House: yesterday it was debated for the whole day; at the close of which it was thought to be finished, the whole having been transcribed & a Committee appointed to present it. But then the Faction found out something else that was wanting, & the Business was postponed to this Morning; when a New Clause was added; & then it was referred to next Tuesday.[12] Thus the first fortnight has been entirely consumed in this fruitless dispute, & no real Business has been done. I should upon this occasion have removed them to Cambridge where their Difficulty would cease. But upon consulting the Lieut Governor upon this, He was of opinion, that as the House in general was tired of these proceedings & began to complain of the despotism of the Faction which they had set over themselves, which the Secession of those Gentlemen who on the part of Government had heretofore combated that Faction had made to be ^more^ severely felt, It would be better to let them alone & leave them to themselves till their Eyes were throughly open. And this proceeding could do no harm, as there was no prospect of any business being done, whilst the Faction continues in their present triumphant state.

And indeed there appears to be a Disposition in the Faction to put a stop to all business in order to bring difficulties upon the people & from thence raise a clamour against the Government. They have now spent near a fortnight in disputes concerning Troops being in the Town without coming to any conclusion. When this Obstacle is removed, they have another ready, which is the Salary bill; this they have declared against passing, at least in such a way as I can consent to it. The pretence is that I am going away, as they say, to quit the Government; Whereas my orders are so far from signifying an intention of superseding me, that they intimate the very contrary. I am ordered to attend his Majesty, as Governor, to report to him the state of the province; and I am directed to advise with the Lieut Govr concerning the Administration of the Government *in my absence*.[13] Upon applying these circumstances to the instruction concerning the Salary Act,[14] & the instruction for the distribution of the Salary when the Governor is absent,[15] I have no doubt but that it is as much my Duty to insist upon the Salary Act being the first that is passed at this time, as it has been at any other Time; & the Lieut Govr is of the same Opinion. I consider this only in regard to his Majesty's Service; without any respect to my own intrest, which is not concerned in the question; as I doubt not but that I shall be paid whilst I continue in his Majesty's Service by some means or other. But It is absolutely expedient that the ruling party should be obliged to grant or refuse the usual Salary according to the Stipulation entered into by their predecessors 37 years ago & observed ever since.[16] Besides, It would be hard upon the Lieut Govr to leave him at the mercy of these people; which he must be, unless a moiety of the usual Salary is secured to him by these means.[17]

The other Business which may break up the Assembly suddenly is in their own hands: The Speaker has just now received a Letter from the Speaker of Virginia inclosing a Copy of their late resolutions & desiring the Concurrence of this House.

I make no doubt but that they will concur: but they must be sensible that when they do declare their concurrence, I must immediately, at least, put an End to the Session, if not to the Assembly. If therefore they should really desire that the Business of the province should be done, they will after the late Example at New York, pass all the necessary business first, and then enter upon the resolves.[18] But if they desire to break up the Assembly without doing any business, & should fail in making the Salary Act subservient to this purpose, they will then enter upon the Virginia resolves & do it that way. There was another Business which if carried to extremity was likely to break up the Assembly, which is what I just mentioned at the bottom of the fourth page of this Letter.[19] But as this has been defeated by a large Majority in a full house, & this present Letter is allready got to a great length, I shall postpone the report of it untill there shall be more occasion for it than there appears to be at present.[20]

June 17

On Tuesday last June 13 The House sent me a Message a printed Copy whereof is herewith inclosed: on the next ^day^ I sent them the Answer as inclosed; but the House having adjourned themselves to the next day immediately upon their Meeting, the Secretary could not deliver the answer; and as by means of this early adjournment the House & Council were not sitting at the same time. He could not according to the usual form adjourn the general Court: But both these were done effectually the next Morning. When the Court met at Cambridge they both soon adjourned to the Monday following; the Council being now entirely under the Direction of the Boston party. Before this adjournment The House appointed a Committee to prepare an Answer to My Message: this will afford Matter of dispute for another Week. This is the indirect Way of stopping Business; but the Heads of the Faction declare publickly that they will do no business untill the Troops are removed out of the Province. All I want is a public declaration of such an intention ^from the House^, and then It seems to me that all Business should stand still till his Majesty can signify his Commands on this great Emergency after which It will deserve consideration how far their refusing to do the business of the province, of which there is a large arrear, when they are called together by the Kings Writs is consistent with their Charter. Your Lordship will observe that in these Messages they make the King & the Governor of Mass Bay so distinct in Authority that the latter can controll the Appointments & Orders of the former.

In this time of inactivity of the general Court The Council has not been idle: they have passed a letter to your Lordship, [21] which is generally beleived to be the Manufacture of Mr Bowdoin, as he has been known to be hard at work with the Council books before him. This Business has been carried on by the Council, notwithstanding their public legislative Character, in a private manner, without the admission of the Secretary, who is by the Kings appointment the official Clerk

& Registrar of all their proceedings. Nevertheless, I am told, their whole Business was kept from him, until it was finished & a Copy of the letter to your Lordship was ^ready to be^ sent away; after which they gave him the papers containing little more than a Copy of the present letter, but without the former letter which they have referred to by a Vote of approbation, but which they have not thought proper to leave in the Secretarys office tho' they were reminded by him, that it ought to be filed in the office as it was referred to by a Vote of their House. I have not had time to peruse this Letter &c having been for some days past by an accidental concurrence of unavoidable ^business^ worked above my strength. I shall at a proper time make my observations upon this letter,[22] which I am told is nothing but an asseveration[23] against undoubted faith without any proof to invalidate them & amounts in the whole only to a complaint that I have not joined with them in the part which they have thought proper to take.[24]

As there is a Ship ready to take this I must conclude this journal by assuring Your Lordship that I am with the greatest respect,

My Lord Your Lordships most obedient & most humble Servant

Fra Bernard

The right honorable The Earl of Hillsborough.

ALS, RC CO 5/758, ff 128-133.

Minor emendations not shown. Endorsed: Boston June 1st: 8th: 10th: 17th: 1769 Governor Bernard. (No. 11). R 24 July. B.29. Enl^d   Enclosed a copy of the *Massachusetts Gazette*, 1 Jun. 1769, containing the message from the House of Representatives to FB, 31 May 1769, and FB's answer of the same date; FB's speech to the Council and the House of Representatives, Council Chamber, 1 Jun. This item was marked as enclosure "1", CO 5/758, f 135. Also enclosed a newspaper extract containing FB's message to the House of Representatives of 14 Jun., and the message composed in reply by the House of Representatives on 15 Jun., marked as enclosure "2"; the resolutions of the House of Representatives, 31 May, marked as "3". CO 5/758, f 135. Variants of the letter in: CO 5/893, ff 136-141 (dupLS, RC); CO 5/767, ff 328-340 (L, RLbC); BP, 7: 166-175 (L, LbC). The autograph original was considered by the Board of Trade on 1 Dec. 1769, *JBT* 13: 126.

1. The five rescinders reelected in 1769 were John Ashley (1709-1802) for Sheffield; Jonathan Bliss (1742-1822), Springfield; Chillingworth Foster (1707- 79) Harwich; Timothy Ruggles, (1711-95), Hardwick; Israel Williams (1709-88), Hatfield.

2. On 31 May 1769. *JHRM*, 45: 118-120.

3. Thomas Cushing (1725-88).

4. Thomas Flucker (1719-83), elected to the Council 1761-68; Nathaniel Ropes (1726-74), elected 1761-68; Timothy Paine (1730-93), elected 1763-68; John Worthington (1719-1800), elected 1767 and 1768.

5. Jerathmeel Bowers, Joseph Gerrish, John Hancock, James Otis Sr., Thomas Saunders, and Artemas Ward.

6. Benjamin Greenleaf, John Hancock, and Joshua Henshaw.

7. Joseph Hawley (1723-88) continued as the representative for Northampton until 1780.

8. James Bowdoin and William Brattle.

9. Of 31 May.

10. The proceedings of 31 May can be followed in *JHRM*, 45: 115-121.

11. Hawley's refusal of the Council seat was typical of "conscience patriots" like James Otis Jr. and John Adams who eschewed preferment and any provincial position that carried a stipend; anything other than town representative they deemed incompatible with their commitment to the Whig cause. "But whereas his colleagues needed to convince themselves that they served the public strictly out of a sense of duty, Hawley's self-doubt could be assuaged only by self-denial." Peter Shaw, *American Patriots and the Rituals of Revolution* (Cambridge, Mass., 1981), 147.

12. The House's reply is dated Monday 13 Jun. *JHRM*, 45: 130-132.

13. Set out in **No. 757**. However, FB's personal views on the matter, which he did not make clear to Hillsborough (or Barrington or Pownall) were such that he probably had no desire to return to Massachusetts.

14. Article 60 of FB's general instructions (18 Mar. 1760) stated that the governor should "recommend it in the most pressing and effectual Manner" to the assembly that it should settle a "fixed [*i.e. permanent*] Salary" of £1,000 sterling for the governor. If the assembly refused, the governor was entitled to accept an annual salary grant, "Provided such Act be the first that shall be passed by the Assembly of the said Province before they proceed upon the Other Business of that Session, wherein such Act shall be proposed." *Bernard Papers*, 1: 470. This was article 49 in the general instructions issued FB on 27 May 1761. Nether Winchendon House, Bucks., Eng.

15. By article 64, the lieutenant governor was to receive one-half of the governor's salary, fees, and emoluments during the governor's absence. *Bernard Papers*, 1: 471-472. Article 53 in the general instructions of 27 May 1761.

16. The royal instructions issued Gov. Jonathan Belcher in 1732 recommended the assembly enact a permanent salary for the governor, which recommendation was written into article 60 of FB's own instructions (see note 14 above).

17. For a summary of the House's response see **No. 792**n24.

18. The House of Burgesses of Virginia adopted four resolves on 16 May 1769, and distributed copies to the speakers of all the colonial assemblies. The first resolve asserted that the "sole right" of levying taxes in Virginia rested with the provincial legislature; the second stated that it was "lawful" for the colony to "procure the concurrence" of other colonies when petitioning the king; the third held that treason trials should take place in the colony not in England; the fourth proposed a loyal address to the king. *Boston Chronicle*, 5-8 Jun. 1769. The New York Assembly did not approve the Virginia resolves until November. *Journal of the Votes and Proceedings of the General Assembly of the colony of New York, from 1766 to 1776* (New York, 1820), 16.

19. That is, the debate on the removal of the troops.

20. The brief proceedings of 8-10 Jun. are in *JHRM*, 45: 126-127.

21. **Appendix 5**.

22. FB never found the time to do this.

23. *OED*: "solemn affirmation, emphatic assertion, positive declaration."

24. For the proceedings of 14-17 Jun. see *JHRM*, 45: 132-133.

780 | To John Pownall

Boston June 1 1769

Dear Sir

There being a Snow ready to sail for Glascow, I take the Opportunity of sending you the printed Account of the Election & other Proceedings on yesterday & today: from which you will perceive that every thing goes as bad as could be expected. The Boston Faction has taken Possession of the two houses in such a Manner that there are not 10 Men in both who dare contradict them. They have turned out of the Council 4 Gentlemen of the very first Reputation in the Country & the only Men remaining of Disposition & Ability to serve the Kings Cause.[1] I have negatived 11 among which are 2 old Councellors Brattle & Bowdoin, the Managers of all the late Opposition in the Council to the Kings Government.[2] There is not now one Man in the Council who has either Spirit or Power to oppose the Faction; & the Friends of Government are so thin in the House, that they won't attempt to make any Opposition: so that Otis Adams &c are now in full Possession ^of this Government^ & will treat it accordingly. This is no more than was expected; I will write more particularly in a few days.[3]

I am Sr Your &c

John Pownall Esqr

L, LbC   BP, 7: 295-296.

In handwriting of Thomas Bernard. Enclosed a printed copy of the proceedings of the House of Representatives of 31 May and 1 Jun. 1769 (not found), probably extracted from the *Boston Chronicle*, 25 May-1 Jun. 1769.

The friends of government never recovered their position in the Council or the House after the 1769 elections.[4]

---

1. Thomas Flucker, Timothy Paine, Nathaniel Ropes, and John Worthington.

2. James Bowdoin, Jerathmeel Bowers, William Brattle, Joseph Gerrish, Benjamin Greenleaf, John Hancock, Joshua Henshaw, Col. James Otis Sr., Thomas Saunders, Walter Spooner, and Artemas Ward.

3. His next letter to Pownall is dated 12 Jun. **No. 784**.

4. The political realignments of 1765-69 can be followed in Colin Nicolson, "Governor Francis Bernard, the Massachusetts Friends of Government, and the Advent of the Revolution," *Proceedings of the Massachusetts Historical Society* 103 (1991): 24-113.

781 | From Lord Barrington

Cavendish Square June 4. 1769

Dear Sir,

I have communicated to Lord Hillsborough your Letter of the 15th of March[1] concerning a Complaint made by Colonel Dalrymple, whose representations have done you no harm except among those who were before very ill inclined towards you. His Lordship is not one of this number, and agrees with me that your whole conduct in respect to the Troops has been not only innocent, but highly meritorious. Whoever had a doubt before, must be clear in respect to that matter after reading your Letter which I am now answering, and the Papers by which it is accompany'd.

I have also shewn to Lord Hillsborough your Letter of the 18.th[2] the opinions of which he entirely approves. as to that part of it which concerns your self, he would most undoubtedly offer you Barbadoes if it were vacant. I have never forgotten your determination concerning that Government; but as I never lived in any sort of intimacy with Lord Shelburne I did not mention it to him: You have lost nothing by my Silence.

I am now come to your Letter of the 12th of April[3] the last I have received from you. When it became necessary to Communicate the Situation of America to Parliament, none of the material lights received from thence could be retain'd, I mean those which came in an official Way. Every Paper laid before either House is immediately known to the whole world, a very inconvenient Circumstance in our Government: I do not however see how the knowlege of your Correspondence can do you any harm in the Massachusets, for there is not one expression in it which goes injuriously to the Colony, quite otherwise. It is true you do not spare the factions, and it is your merit to have attack'd and resisted them in every possible way, by which you were as obnoxious to them before your Letters were seen, as since: Besides you are on the point of leaving your Government, and I have even doubts whether this Letter will reach you. I shall not write any more unless I find you continue on the other side of the Water longer than I expect. I wish you, Lady Bernard and all my Cousins a safe & happy passage, and I am to them all as well as to your Excellency,

A most faithful & obedient humble Servant

Barrington.

ALS, RC   BP, 12: 99-102.

Endorsed: Lord Barrington d. June 4 1769 r in London Nov 17.

Barrington's peremptory observation that FB was just as unpopular before his letters were published as he was afterward was not far wrong, though he betrayed his ignorance of colonial politics with the assertion that FB's letters had not intended or caused "harm." He also assumed that Amelia Bernard and the rest of the family would return with FB, which they did not.

---

1. **No. 751**.

2. **No. 753**.

3. **No. 763**.

782 | From Thomas Gage

New York June 5th: 1769.

Sir,

I am to acquaint you that I have sent Orders by this Occasion to Major General Mackay[1] to embark the 64th: and 65th: Regiments, as likewise the Detachment of the Royal Regiment of Artillery, now at Boston, with all convenient Speed for Halifax. I have wrote to the General to conferr with you relative to a further Disposition of the Troops that will be left at Boston, after this Embarkation takes Place, and flatter myself to have soon thro' that Channell, your Sentiments and Opinion upon that Head

I have the Honor to be Sir, your most obedient humble Servant,

Tho[s]. Gage

His Excellency Sir Francis Bernard.

ALS, RC   BP, 12: 103-106.

Endorsed: N[o]. 5 Gen[l] Gage d June 5 1769 a June 10.[2] It probably enclosed a copy of Gage's orders to Mackay. FB replied with **No. 785**.

Gage was acting at the suggestion of Hillsborough, who in March had raised the possibility of withdrawing two regiments from Boston. He "left it to the general's discretion" to decide how many regiments and soldiers should be removed. Gage initially favored withdrawing all four regiments (two stationed at the Castle and two in the town), having concluded that the troops were no longer required to protect government officials.[3] By ordering two regiments to Halifax, Gage denied FB the opportunity of any say in whether the troops should be withdrawn at all and sought his views only on how many ought to be retained.[4] FB was taken aback by Maj. Gen. Mackay's rather abrupt request (as he noted in **No. 790**):

> I receiv'd on my return to town this evening a letter from Generall Gage, wherein he says as follows The Detachment of Artillery with their Field Train must be sent back to Hallifax as fast as you can, And immediately after you have reviewd the Troops, you will likewise send the 64th & 65th Regts to Hallifax. You will receive further orders about the distribution of the 14th & 29th Regts, one of which you will quarter in the Barracks at Castle Island when the 65th is removed.

Mackay was to consult with the governor about "the necessity of continuing any of the Troops any longer at Boston" and to obtain his views in writing.[5]

1. Thomas Gage to Alexander Mackay, New York, 4 Jun. 1769, MiU-C: Gage, vol. 86. Alexander Mackay (1717-89) was the fourth son of the third Lord Reay and a career soldier, following his capture by the Jacobites at the battle of Prestonpans in 1745. He entered Parliament in 1761, representing the Scottish county of Sutherland until 1768 and the Tain (Northern) burghs between 1768 and 1773. Between 1764 and 1770 he was colonel of the 65th Regiment of Foot and his promotion to major general was confirmed in 1770; upon leaving America he commanded various military installations in Britain.

2. This is probably an error for 12 Jun. No letter dated 10 Jun. has been found, and it is unlikely that FB dashed off a written response to Gen. Gage that evening at Mackay's request.

3. There is a copy of Hillsborough's letter to Gage of 24 Mar. 1769 in CO 5/87, ff 72-76; Archer, *As If an Enemy's Country*, 140-141.

4. Richard Archer offers a different interpretation suggesting Gage effectively gave FB the authority to determine if any troops were to be withdrawn. Ibid. While Gage did not do so initially, he did (as Archer rightly assumes) subsequently offer to suspend the withdrawal of the troops pending receipt of FB's views. **No. 785**.

5. Alexander Mackay to FB, Boston, Saturday night, 10 Jun. 1769, BP, 12: 108-110.

783 | *To Samuel Hood*

Province house June 8 1769

Sr

I am favoured with your Letter of May 29th[1] informing me that you propose to order the Rippon to proceed to England very shortly.[2] I am much obliged to you for this Intimation, as it is probable this Ship may be very convenient to me without hurting the public Service. I have received His Majesty's Command to attend & Report to him the State of this Province. Nothing hinders me from obeying this Order but my Attendance upon this Session of the General Court: as soon as that is over I shall immediately set about preparing for Embarkation. I shall most probably be ready about the End of July: if that time can be made suitable to the Departure of the Rippon it will be very agreeable as otherwise I may possibly be delayed for Want of a ship.

I am &c.

Commodore Hood

L, LbC   BP, 7: 225.

In handwriting of Thomas Bernard.

---

1. Not found.

2. HMS *Rippon* was a sixty-gun fourth-rate ship of the line in the Royal Navy, captained by Samuel Thompson. She had come to the American Colonies in 1768, bringing Lord Botetourt to Virginia. She arrived in Boston harbor at the end of Apr. 1769, but was currently at Halifax when FB wrote Commodore Hood. *Connecticut Gazette*, 14 Jul. 1769.

784 | To John Pownall

private

Boston June 12 1769

Dear Sir

All the Letters I have lately received from Westminster have been extremely agreeable to me so far as they relate to myself only. But in Regard to those with whom I am connected, they afford the most gloomy Prospect. To see that Faction which has occasioned all the Troubles in this Province & I may add in America too & has quite overturned this Government, now triumphant & driving ^over^ every one who has loyalty & Resolution enough to stand up in Defence of the Rights of the King & the Parliament gives me great Concern, notwithstanding I am so near getting out of this unpleasant Scene myself. It gives me great Pain to hear the Friends of Government complain that they are sacrificed for their Fidelity to Great Britain, when I myself must be conscious that I have been a principal in engaging them to persist in that Fidelity.[1]

Some days before the Assembly met, the Factions cheifs had a Meeting wherein ~~it was~~ after a little Debate, it was determined to turn out every Councellor who had not given Testimony of their Submission to them. These were reduced to 4, all the others having made their Terms. On the Day of the Election a Member pressed Mr Otis to declare whether Col Worthington a most valuable & respectable Man living 100 Miles from Boston, was to be turned out of the Council. Otis answered that Worthington was a good Man, & he had all Respect for him; but added, He is a Tory (a term here signifying a maintainer of the Authority of the King, the Parliament & the Government) and he shall not continue in the Council.

Among the Exulters upon this Occasion none is louder that [*than*] Mr Temple. Last Saturday[2] it was circulated as from him that he had a Letter from Mr GG that assured him that the Governor would be immediately removed with Disgrace, that 3 of the Commissioners would be turned out directly & the whole Board dissolved next Winter &c. Upon his being challenged to produce a Letter signed by that Gentleman, It has turned out only that his Letter came from Mr Trecothick, & the other Gentleman was only quoted as Authority.[3]

Temple has this Day libelled me by publishing an Affidavit which he made use of in his Accusation against me some Years ago; the Contents of which I never knew before.[4] It was very unfortunate for me that I had not an Opportunity of defending myself from that Charge against me. If I had, I should have long ago put a Stop to his Wickedness by exposing the Malice & Falsehood of it. I shall not miss the Opportunity which this Publication which can come from no one else, gives me of demanding Justice against him.

The present Distress of the Friends of Government is greatly increased by Letters just now arrived from Genl Gage ordering two Regts to Halifax[5] & directing Genl Mackay to require of me an Answer in writing whether any Troops & what would be wanted in Boston. Nothing could be more Mal a propos to the Business of the Government or more hard upon me. And to add to the Difficulty it brings upon me, This Advice was spread all over the Town before I had a Opportunity of talking with Genl Mackay or writing to Genl Gage upon the Subject. I had thought that the Embarrasment I was under ~~for~~ ^by^ my Connection with the Council 12 Months ago upon Account of sending for Troops would prevent my being again distressed upon that of their being continued here. I could indeed ease myself as I did before by leaving this Business to the Council & having no will of my own. But then I must sacrifice the Officers of the Crown & the Friends of Government, many of whom declare they cannot stay in the Town; if all the Troops are removed from it. I must do the best I can; but it is a cruel Business to be thrown upon me at this time, & in this Manner. What adds to my Uncertainty is that I have no Advice of this Business from your Office.

You will observe that this Letter is entirely confidential & will use it accordingly. I shall write to My Lord Hillsborough upon this Subject as soon as I can.

I am &c

John Pownall Esq

L, LbC   BP, 7: 296-299.

In handwriting of Thomas Bernard.

---

1. This is one of the few instances where FB directly reduced the contests of the Imperial Crisis to questions of loyalty. While it reflected what he thought about his own service there is no doubt that he was speaking about the friends of government and moderate Whigs whose political decline raised for him genuine concerns about the future loyalty of the province. Although such views were decidedly antirevolutionary in conception, the reductionism of FB's analyses invited his reader—in this case a trusted friend—to consider the further prospect of enabling counter-revolutionary action of one kind or another by so-called "Tories".

2. 10 Jun.

3. Barlow Trecothick (?1718-75), an alderman of London and MP (1768-74), was a leader of the Rock-ingham faction in the House of Commons. Trecothick's letter to Temple has not been found. "GG" was George Grenville, the former prime minister and a distant relative of Temple.

4. The deposition of Sampson Toovey, Salem, 27 Sept. 1764. *Boston Gazette*, 12 Jun. 1769. Toovey had been clerk to the Salem collector, James Cockle, who Temple had accused of fraud and corruption, and for which Cockle was dismissed from the service. Toovey's deposition claimed that Cockle used to share with FB boxes of fruit and wine offered by merchants as a "Gratuity" for entering false informa-tion in the Customhouse records in order that they might escaping paying duties in full. FB claimed that such gifts were commonplace but Temple alleged the governor was complicit in a scheme to defraud the Crown by threatening smugglers with seizures and encouraging them to compound for part payment of the duties. See *Bernard Papers*, 2: 125, 486, 498-499.

5. **No. 782**.

785 | To Thomas Gage

Copy/.

Boston June 12th: 1769.

Sir,

I have recieved your Letter of the 5th: Instant,[1] and have had a Letter from Major General Mackay[2] wherein he signifys your desire that he would ask my Opinion in Writing whether His Majesty's Service requires Troops to remain here, and what Number. You know the Difficulties I lye under in regard to my Connexion with the Council, and you must be sensible that this is a question of great impor-tance to his Majesty's Service. I must therefore take time to consider of it and to know the Opinion of a Number of Gentlemen who will be affected by the deter-mination of this question, who have already expressed a great alarm at hearing that it is proposed. In the mean time I must recommend that the removal of the two remaining Regiments may be suspended, till this measure can be fully considered.

I am, with great Regard, Sir, &ca.

(Signed) Fra Bernard.

His Excellency Major General Gage.

L, Copy   CO 5/87, ff 128-130.

This copy of the RC was made by Gage's clerk and enclosed in the general's letter to the earl of Hillsborough, New York, 22 Jul. 1769, CO 5/87, ff 124-128. There is a copy in BP, 7: 226 (LbC, Copy).

Gage's reply of 2 Jul. drew a line under his disagreement with FB over the troop withdrawal, but not before mildly rebuking the governor, in a colonialist fashion, for having discussed imperial policy with leading colonists.

> I . . . wish a little more Secrecy had been observed, upon your Account, there was no occasion to divulge anything I wrote concerning an opinion, except only to those concerned. What I have lately said to Major General Mackay seems to coincide with your Ideas, and from thence I hope all Matters will be fixed to your Satisfaction.[3]

1. **No. 782**.
2. Dated 10 Jun. 1769, in BP, 12: 108-110.
3. BP, 12: 115-118.

786 | *From Thomas Gage*

New=York June 18th. 1769.

Sir,

I am sorry to find by your Letter of the 12th. June,[1] that the Question Major General MacKay was desired to ask of you about keeping Troops longer at Boston, has thrown you into any Difficulties. It was your own Opinion on this head, not the Opinion of your Council, that I am desirous to be informed of, as you must from your Situation be able to Judge what is best to be done for the King's Service, much better than I can do at this Distance: and I mean to act for his Majesty's Service as far as my Powers and Judgement will let me; which Inclination induced me to ask your opinion, for my own satisfaction; not to publish it or even make it known; at least on this side of the Atlantick. The Removal of the two Regiments shall be suspended, I know of no occasion there is to hurry them away, or can I see any Reason why other Provinces should quarter those Regiments, more than the Province of Massachusetts Bay. I hope soon to have your sentiments on this head in a plain and open manner, you must yourself be the properest Judge of it, without that the necessity of consulting other People.

I am with great Regard, Sir, Your most obedient humble Servant,

Tho⁵. Gage

His Excellency Sir Francis Bernard,

ALS, RC   BP, 12: 111-114.

Endorsed by FB: Genᴵ. Gage d June 18 1769 r June 23.

Gage had not requested FB's opinion on the withdrawal of the troops *per se*, only how many should remain after issuing orders relocating two regiments to Halifax (**No. 782**). This letter now conceded that the withdrawal ought to wait upon FB's views. Gage's barbed comment about FB needlessly seeking the Council's advice probably reflected anxieties arising from FB's prolonged negotiations with the Council over the quartering of the regiments the previous autumn. FB replied with **No. 791**, clarifying the situation.

1. **No. 785**.

787 | To Thomas Gage

Boston June 19 1769

Sʳ

Upon a full Consideration of the Question you have directed Genᴵ Mackay to put to me, whether His Majesty's Service does require that Troops should remain at Boston & what Number, whether one or two Regiments, I am of Opinion that as the Troops were sent here by the immediate Order of the King, & I have received no Orders from the Secretary of State concerning their further Disposition, it is not my Business to interupt a Question about their Removal. And I am the more confirmed in this, as I don't see that there is any Abatement of that Spirit which occasioned the sending the Troops hither, altho it has been controlled by their Presence. I therefore do not think it proper to put this Question to the Council.

Nevertheless I have according to my former Letter enquired into the Sentiments of others upon this Measure: and I find it to be the Opinion of *all* the principal Officers of the Crown & Government that the Removal of the Troops at this time would probably have very dangerous Consequences, & that I could not answer it to the King to have any hand in it. I also understand that the Report of this Intention has caused a great Alarm among those who consider themselves obnoxious to the popular Party, the Number of which is greatly increased by the Inclusion of all those who have imported Goods contrary to the Combination. This Report has also given great Encouragement to the popular Party, which among the lowest of them has been carried so far as to produce Threats against some of the Officers of the Crown, as they have gone thro the Streets. Upon a full Consideration of these Circumstances I cannot think it proper for me to concern myself in the Removal of the 2 remaining Regiments or any Part thereof.

Col Robertson has put into my hands the Accounts of the Expenditures for providing Barracks & other Necessaries for the Troops in this Town.[1] The Assembly has hitherto done no Business: they insisted upon the Troops being removed out of the Town of Boston Before they entered upon Business. I have therefore removed the Assembly to Cambridge[:][2] it is now said that they will do no Business till the Troops are removed out of the Province;[3] if that is the Case, Nothing will be done. If they proceed to Business, I will lay these Accounts before them. But I do not expect that they will discharge any Part thereof, not even such Part thereof as relates to the Parliamentary Allowances only.

I have the Honor &c.

Gen[l] Gage.

L, LbC   BP, 7: 226-228.

In handwriting of Thomas Bernard. Gage extracted the first and second paragraphs in a copy for Hillsborough, sent under cover of a letter 22 Jul. 1769, CO 5/87, ff 124-128, and filed at CO 5/87, ff 130-132.

While FB was excusing himself in the decision to withdraw the troops, Gage had written asking his views on the matter and suspended the withdrawal until he had heard from him (**No. 786**). The accounts for the quartering of the British soldiers were never settled by the General Court.

1. James Robertson to FB, Boston, 13 Jun. 1769, Mass. Archs., 56: 599-600.

2. Obscured in the fold of the binding.

3.   The General Court met at Harvard College, Cambridge on 16 Jun., having been moved there by an order of the governor issued the previous day. *JHRM,* 45: 132-133. The protest in refusing to do business outside of Boston ran for over two years and "forced" Gov. Hutchinson "to justify the crown's authority to dictate the location of the Court and to explain the obligations which a Massachusetts royal governor owed to the crown and to the province." The dispute can be followed in Donald C. Lord and Robert M. Calhoon, "The Removal of the Massachusetts General Court from Boston, 1769-1772," *The Journal of American History* 55 (1969): 735-755 quotation at 736.

788 | To Thomas Hutchinson

Jamaica farm June 19 1769

S[r]

I have been desirous of acting in Concert with you ~~with~~ in the Business of this Session but since it cannot be done I must do as well as I can. I was endeavouring that a Union of Sentiments & Coalition of Interests between us two should appear at this time, as I think it necessary to his Majesty's Service that there should not only be but appear to be a perfect good Understanding between us in our Ideas of the Exigences of this Government: if the contrary should hereafter be made apparent by your Disavowal of the Measures which I have thought fit to pursue, it must weaken your Administration as well as reflect upon mine. I was therefore willing to consult you in every Step I took in this Session.

As to the Salary Act I have hitherto understood that you quite agreed with me in Opinion that it was proper to insist upon its being passed in Conformity to the Instructions. I have wrote so to My Lord Hillsborough:[1] I must now let him know that you have changed your Opinion; & therefore I must change my Intention: I had your Intrest full as ~~much~~ ^well^ as my own in the proposing this Method but the Service of the King more than either. And if you think that a Contrast of your Administration with mine will be for the best, I shall sincerely wish you Success in it.[2]

I shall write to you by the Portsmouth Carrier if there shall ^be^ any thing occur to require it: if you receive no Letter from me you must conclude there is no Occasion for one. I wish you a good Journey[3] & shall be glad to see you at the earliest day of your Return.

I am S[r] &c.

The honble L[t]. Gov[r].

L, LbC   BP, 7: 228-229.

In handwriting of Thomas Bernard.

This letter briefly indicates a difference of opinion between FB and TH over Britain's insistence that the General Court should enact a permanent salary for the governor and appropriate funds for the acting governor, upon FB's departure. The "Contrast" that FB mentions here and in **No. 789** suggests that TH wanted a fresh start with the assembly—to the extent that such were possible. He might have intended letting the salary lapse (perhaps expecting the British to make provision), though later changed his mind and complained to Britain about the assembly's neglect.[4] TH replied to FB the same day, but the letter has not been found.

---

1. **No. 779**.

2. FB did not revisit the issue of the governor's salary in his next letter to Hillsborough (**No. 790**), while his comments in the letter following (**No. 792**) did not address TH's entitlement as acting governor.

3. TH was probably preparing for the Superior Court circuit.

4. Bailyn, *Ordeal of Thomas Hutchinson*, 205.

789 | *To Thomas Hutchinson*

Jamaica Farm June 21 1769

S[r]

A Letter containing such important Matters as yours of the 19th sent by a Servant[1] who is to wait for an Answer may easily receive so hasty a one, as to be liable to be misunderstood: this has been the Case with my Letter. And now I cannot undertake to explain myself by a Letter which is to go by so uncertain a Conveyance as this. All I can say at present is that the Contrast was not mentioned as supposed to be purposely designed but as probably consequential to a Want of Communication. However I shall endeavour to steer this Business, which I can consider of great Importance *in such a Manner* as to present such Effects.

I am &c.

Lieut Governor

L, LbC   BP, 7: 229.

In handwriting of Thomas Bernard.

---

1. Letter not found.

790 | To the Earl of Hillsborough

[N°. 12][1]

Boston June 25 1769

My Lord

On the 10th of June I received a letter from Gen¹ Gage acquainting me that He had ordered the 64th & 65th regiments and the train of Artillery to Halifax & had directed Gen¹ Mackay to confer with me about the disposition of the rest of the troops.[2] I had a letter the next day from Gen¹ Mackay informing[3] that Gen¹ Gage had desired him to consult with me concerning the *Necessity* of continuing *any* of the troops *any longer* at Boston, and to have *my opinion in writing* whether his Majesty's Service does *require* that Troops should remain there any longer & what Number of troops, whether one or two regiments.

It is impossible to express my surprise at this proposition or my embarrasment upon account of the requisition of an Answer in writing; which was greatly encreased by the report of it being spread all over the Town immediately, with the addition of its being to be[4] referred to the Council. However I saw Gen¹ Mackay & for the present declined giving any Answer to the question except that I would write to Gen¹ Gage upon the Subject. I wrote accordingly[5] & having Mentioned to him the difficulties of my connection with the Council & the importance of the question I desired time to consider of it & to know the Opinion of those who would be affected by it.

In the Mean time there arose a general Consternation among the civil Officers of Government, the friends of it & the importers of goods contrary to the combination, who are Many; And there was a proportional triumph among the Sons of liberty, which in some of the lowest of them produced threats of what would be done when the troops were gone. After a Weeks observation I wrote ^again^ to Gen¹ Gage[6] & having given him the reasons why I did not think it proper to put this Question to the Council, I told him that I had enquired into the Sentiments of others & found it to be the Opinion of *All* the principal Officers of the Crown & Government that the removal of the troops at this time would probably have very dangerous Consequences. I added that the Report of it had caused a great alarm among those who were obnoxious to the popular party, & had given great encouragement to that party so as to produce threats. I therefore could not think it proper to concern myself in the removal of any of the troops.

Soon after I sent away this Letter I received Another from Gen¹ Gage,[7] wherein after expressing a concern for having thrown me into difficulties by his former letter He adds that He desired my Opinion & not that of the Council; and that it might be free & open, He assured that He should not publish it or make it known on this side of the Atlantick. I immediately returned for answer[8] that in confidence of that assurance, I had no Hesitation to declare my Opinion that it would be detrimental to his Majesty's Service to remove any of the two regiments remaining; and that it would be quite ruinous to the Cause of the Crown to draw all the troops out of Boston. Nevertheless I was enclined to think that a Regiment in Town ^& another at the Castle^ might be sufficient.

Thus, I hope, is ended this Business, which has given much trouble to me & has caused great uneasiness among many people, who declared they must quit the Town if the troops were removed.

I have the honour to be with great respect, My Lord, Your Lordship's
most obedient & most humble Servant

Fra Bernard

The right honble the Earl of Hillsborough.

ALS, RC   CO 5/758, ff 152-153.

Endorsed: Boston June 25th. 1769 Sir Fras. Bernard (No. 11) R 3d: August. B.33. Enld.   May have enclosed copies of FB's correspondence with generals Gage and Mackay (which he also sent John Pownall) but these particular items have not been found.[9] Variants of letter in: CO 5/893, ff 142-143 (dupLS, RC); CO 5/767, ff 353-356 (L, RLbC); BP, 7: 175-177 (L, LbC). The letter and enclosures were considered by the Board of Trade on 1 Dec. 1769. *JBT*, 13: 126.

1. Editorially supplied. First written as "No 11" and annotated "x/12" probably by the receiver's clerk. No. 11 in the sequence of FB's out-letters was **No. 779**, dated 1 Jun. 1769.
2. **No. 782**.
3. Alexander Mackay to FB, Boston, 10 Jun. 1769. See the extract in the source note to **No. 782**.
4. Thus in manuscript.
5. **No. 785**.
6. **No. 787**.
7. **No. 786**.
8. **No. 791**.
9. These would have included copies of **Nos. 782**, and **785** to **787**; Alexander Mackay to FB, Boston, 10 Jun. 1769, BP, 12: 108-110; James Robertson to FB, Boston, 13 Jun. 1769 (of which the RC is in Mass. Archs. 56: 559-560); FB to John Pownall, Boston, 25 Jun. 1769, BP, 7: 300.

791 | To Thomas Gage

Copy./

Boston June 26th: 1769.

Sir,

I wrote to you by Colonel Robertson who set out for New York on Thursday last. I have now the favor of your Letter of June 18th:[1] The Reason why I have declined giving an Answer as Governor of the Province to the question of continuing or removing the remaining Troops arises from a Clause in the Order of Council, for the Command of the Troops quartered in the several Governments whereby the Governor's are directed to take the Advice of their Council's in the moving of Troops. And tho' the Constitution of the Council here and their known disposition make them very unfit Advisers in such a question, yet I still remain under an Obligation to consult the Council according to the strict Letter of that Order.

However as you ask my Advice seperately from that of the Council, and in confidence that it shall not be made known on this Side of the Atlantic, I have no hesitation to declare my Opinion, that it will be detrimental to His Majesty's Service to remove any part of the Two Regiments remaining here, and that it would be quite ruinous to the cause of the Crown to draw all the Troops out of the Town of Boston. On the other hand, I am inclined to think that Two Regiments, One in the Town, and the other at the Castle Island may be sufficient. For tho' the latter will be of no use in quelling a Sudden disorder in the Town, yet it will serve to keep them in Awe, and will afford an actual relief, when there is time for Notice. I have long ago wondered why Boston has not been thought as proper a Town to quarter Two Regiments in, as New York Philadelphia &ca, and have often thought that it would be best to make the Stationing of them here merely of Business of cantonment, without making a Question whether they were or were not wanted for the support of Government.

I have the honor to be with great Regard Sir, &ca

/Signed Fra Bernard,

His Excellency General Gage

L, Copy   CO 5/87, ff 132-134

There is a variant in BP, 7: 230-231 (L, LbC). Gage's clerk copied the RC of **No. 791** for dispatch as an enclosure under cover of Gage's letter to Hillsborough of 22 Jul. 1769, at CO 5/87, ff 124-128.

1. **No. 786**.

792 | To the Earl of Hillsborough

Nº 12[1]

Boston July 1 1769

My Lord

As evry thing which passes the House is printed & in general designed for the press & for that purpose only, I shall have little else to do but to send your Lordship the printed Copies, as their writings at present want Very little Comment. I now send your Lordship four of those Copies: Nº **I** is a Message to me which rests all its complaints upon this fallacy. They had required of me that I would *order* the *King's* Ships out of the Port & his Troops out of the Town.[2] To this I answered that I had no power to make such order. They now complain that I did not use my influence to remove the Main guard which was kept in an house hired for that purpose & had as usual two pieces of small Cannon before it, near the Town house. This was no part of their request, that being wholly confined to the whole body of the Troops & urged in the way of demand. They knew that if they had applied for the removing the Main Guard it would have been done; & therefore they would not ask for it & declared that they would not. As to the removing the two pieces of cannon after the adjournment, they were removed in pursuance of an order from Genˡ Gage, which did not arrive till the third Evening after the adjournment; to send the train of artillery to Halifax. These are trifling Matters, but serve to show the *falsehood* & prevarication of these people.

Nº **II** is a Message I sent to them on the 6th day after their meeting at Cambridge upon learning that no Business had been done in all that time, which had finished the third Week. The Articles enumerated there are the ordinary Businesses of the province, of which I have seldom or never had occasion to take notice of in any of my Speeches, as they must occur to ev'ry one & come in of Course. And Yet your Lordship will by & by find that this Omission which has been Constantly practised for many Years past will be seriously urged as an Excuse for their inactivity.[3]

Nº **III** is a Message I found it necessary to send to them upon their having entered into their 5th week without having done any thing towards the support of Government. I have never had occasion before to mention a Word about my Salary: it has been usually granted the first week of the Session according to the Kings instructions. I dont conceive myself to be interested in this question: but I think it my duty to state the Circumstances of the present Case to them, & to require a positive Answer. It has been generally thought that they will not grant a Salary, or do it in such a Manner that I can't accept it. Possibly their Refusal may be of more Service than their Compliance.[4]

N° **IV** is a preamble & a resolve which will Speak for themselves: the cheif use of these are to induce the printing these Letters of the Council, some of which are now upon the Sea in their passage,[5] the publishing here being the cheif End of these Writings. I will make only one Remark upon this resolve: The Governor's dissolving the Assembly in Obedience to his Majesty's ^positive^ Order signified by a Letter from his Secretary of State[6] is called a Wanton Act; & his declining to call another Assembly until he had orders therefor, in obedience to an implied order in the same letter, is said to be arbitrary.

July 7

On Monday the 3[d] inst came out in three of the public papers, one of which is published by the printer of the Journal of the House,[7] a Set of Resolves said to be the Substance of the Resolves passed unanimously by the House, a Copy of which N° **V** is herewith inclosed.[8] I immediately sent 2 of these papers in a cover to New York to go by the packet.[9] In the Evning I met Commodore ^Hood^ & Gen[l] Mackay at their desire. They expressed their surprise at these resolves & *other dangerous reports which had come to their knowledge* & said they had been considering whether it would not be best to stop the 64th regiment which was ready to embark for Halifax, the 65th having been sent thither before. I said that tho' I had never had any question put to me concerning the removing those 2 regiments[,][10] I had in a letter to Gen[l] Gage sent by the post that day, expressed my Sense that the tendency of those resolves was such that it seemed rather to require a Reinforcement of the Kings Forces at Boston than a weakening of them.[11] I therefore readily agreed with them in the propriety of suspending the embarkation of that regiment for the present. It was thereupon concluded that Gen[l] Mackay should give present orders for suspending the embarkation, & send an express to Gen[l] Gage[12] the next morning informing him of it with the reasons for it: which was accordingly done.

The next morning[13] I went to Cambridge & sent the Secretary to the Speaker to demand an Attested Copy of the resolves. He answerd that the publication was not authentick; that the House had indeed passed some resolves, but they had ^not^ completed them; that there were among the printed resolves some which had not passed the House; as there were also some which had passed the House & were not printed. That the House was now going to proceed upon the Resolves & when they had finished them, I should have a Copy. Notwithstanding what the Speaker has said, M[r] Adams the Clerk of the House has declared, both out of & in the house too, as I am told, that the publication is from a Copy of the Minutes of the House, which he gave or suffered to be taken; that it is a true Copy, & that the resolves, as printed, did pass the House; that they may alter them if they please; but that they were for the present entered as having passed the House. To reconcile this difference, It has been an Usage in the House, as I am told, when a Vote has been passed & entered so, upon a motion for a reconsideration, to order it to lye on the table, but not to rescind the Vote, which should be done only in a fuller House than that which passed it, otherwise it remains good. According to this practice the Speaker & the Clerk may differ only in their Conception of it, & both may agree in the same fact.

In the Evning I met the Commodore & the General. They had also informed themselves that the Authenticity of the printed resolves was denied; and the Reports of the Designs of the party had been softened. They therefore thought there was no Necessity for detaining the 64th regiment unless I should desire it. I said that I did not apprehend any danger at present; & that to provide for the future was more the Lieut Governor's business than mine: that he was just come to Town from his Circuit, & I would advise with him. The next Morning[14] I saw the L[t] Gov[r] in the presence of the General & the Commodore at different times.[15] His Opinion was that as there was no prospect at present of a forcible opposition to Government there was no occasion to detain the 64th regiment. I could not but accede to this Opinion, & accordingly wrote the same day to Gen[l] Gage[16] to give him an Account of it & at the same time to signify that it was the same person's Opinion that the other two Regiments must remain here.

The House has proceeded farther in the consideration of the resolves; but they had not concluded the business yesterday morning (July 5) time enough for the printer of the paper of that day to insert them. They have, I am told, made a material alteration in the resolve the second of the present publication. That Resolve, tho seemingly referring only to the resolutions in 1765 goes much farther than they did: for this includes all Acts of parliament of what kind soever; whereas they were confined to Acts of Taxation only. I am told that this is now amended so as to be referred to Acts of Taxation only.[17] But this is but procrastinating: All Acts must come in by, ^& by^ especially the Navigation Act,[18] which has been declared to be a principal Object.

On Tuesday July 4 The Committee of the ^two^ Houses presented a joint Answer to my Speech at the opening the Session.[19] For some years past I have made my opening Speeches mere form avoiding all subjects of dispute & giving only a few harmless periods. For 3 years past I've never mentioned any business at all in an opening Speech & I never have at any time made the ordinary businesses of the province the subjects of such Speech, as I have left them to occur, as they have hitherto done, to the Houses. And yet in this Answer they wrote that I had pointed out what was expected from them. And this they deliver to me on July 4, notwithstanding I had on June 21 pointed out all the public business to them foreseeing that this subterfuge would be made use of. The Barefaced Chicanery & Falsity of this writing as well as the Stile, which is well known, make it evident that it was wrote by Adams; and yet It was sent to the Council to originate with them.[20] Upon receiving this I exprest my concern to the Council, that their board should be brought so low as to be obliged to adopt so notorious a piece of prevarication, which not a Word was their own. No Answer was given: and enough has been said to show how this once respectable Body is humbled.

July 11

Last Saturday, July 8, the House finished their resolves which were printed in all the Newspapers yesterday.[21] The most material Alteration is in the second resolve, which in the first Set comprehends all Acts of parliament whatsoever,[22] in the second set is confined to Acts of Taxation only. Another Distinction may also be drawn from the Word *Taxes* in the latter, that they intended only internal Taxes & not port duties; but when it is considered that all the late disputes have arose from port duties only it cannot be supposed to be their intention to make a distinction in favour of them. And indeed the Resolve, as it now stands, does not imply an admission of port duties or of Acts of parliament in general; but still leaves them at liberty to bring within their claims an Exemption from all Acts of parliament, when it shall be a convenient time to urge it. And It is extremely plain from their common conversation, their speeches in public, & the general tenor of their writings that they do not intend to stop at internal taxes, or at port duties, in their pretensions against the power of parliament. I now send your Lordship an attested Copy of these resolves, upon which I shall at present make no other remarks. I also add a printed Copy marked Nᵒ **VII**. If your Lordship will look into the Message of the House of the 13ᵗʰ of June, about the middle of the last paragraph, you will find an Exemption from Laws which they do not consent to asserted as fully & pretty near in the same words as the second of the first set of resolves.[23]

July 13.

I have now an Opportunity of adding some more printed papers: Nᵒ **VIII** is an Answer to my message concerning the Salary, conceived in that illiberal style which is so familiar to these Writers. I shall not observe upon it now, as it deserves a Separate letter,[24] being in my Opinion a Matter of great importance to Government and for that reason I found it necessary to push it to the Issue, in which I know it would end. The other papers[25] are Messages which I have sent on the Subject of making provision for the Soldiers: they are determined to do nothing in this, & I suppose would avoid giving ^an^ Answer. If I cant get a positive one, I must take their

Silence as a refusal. Yesterday I gave notice in Council[26] that I should put an End to the Session next Saturday, & desired that evry thing which was to be laid before me might be ready at that time. As there is a Ship ready now to sail for London, I shall conclude this long letter or rather Journal. Yesterday the Rippon Man of War which is to carry me to England came into the harbour: I shall endeavour to embark in her before the end of this Month. My Attendance on this Session has much delayed me: but it was quite necessary.

> I have the honour to be, with great respect, My Lord, Your Lordships
> most obedient & most humble Servant

> Fra Bernard

The right honble the Earl of Hillsborough.

ALS, RC   CO 5/758, ff 154-159.

Minor emendations not shown. Endorsed: Boston July 1st. 7th. 11th. 13th. 1769. Sir Francis Bernard (N°. 12) R 20 Aug. B.34.   Enclosed a printed page with copies of the following: message of the House of Representatives to FB, 13 Jun. 1769, marked "**I**" by FB; messages from FB to House of Representatives, 21 Jun., marked "**II**", and 28 Jun., "**III**"; a single resolve of the House of Representatives, 22 Jun., approving the Council's "Remarks" on FB's letters to Hillsborough, "**IV**". CO 5/758, f 160; the resolutions of the House of Representatives of 29 Jun., printed in the *Boston Post-Boy and Advertiser*, 3 Jul. 1769, marked "**V**" on the verso page, CO 5/758, f 161. Also enclosed another printed sheet containing: the answer of the Council and the House of Representatives to FB's speech of 1 Jun., dated 4 Jul., and the votes of the Boston town meeting, 4 Jul., marked "**VI**", CO 5/758, f 162; a printed copy of the resolves of the House of Representatives of 7 Jul. (extracted from one of the newspapers published on 10 Jul.) was **VII** in the sequence, but is missing from the file; FB also enclosed a manuscript copy of the resolves written out by Thomas Cushing and attested by Samuel Adams on 8 Jul. ibid, ff 164-167. A third printed sheet[27] contained: the answer of the House of Representatives to FB's speech of 28 Jun., dated 4 Jul., marked "**VIII**"; FB's message to the House of 6 Jul., "**IX**"; FB's message to the House of 12 Jul., "**X**", ibid., f 163.

Variants of letter in: CO 5/893, ff 144-149 (dupLS, RC), with enclosures at ff 150-154; CO 5/768, ff 1-13 (L, RLbC); BP, 7: 177-185 (L, LbC). The original letter and enclosures were considered by the Board of Trade on 1 Dec. 1769. *JBT*, 13: 126.

Like many of the later legislative pronouncements of colonial assemblies, the resolves of the Massachusetts House of Representatives of 7 Jul. 1769 in their entirety anticipated the accusatory style of the American Declaration of Independence's enumeration of the king's "abuses and usurpations." But on this occasion it was the king's representative, the governor of Massachusetts, who was being symbolically tried by the people's representatives.

The first resolve pledged allegiance to the king, but the second asserted that the right of taxation lay solely with the provincial assembly, and the third reiterated the "indubitable Right" of the king's subjects to petition for redress of grievances.

Resolves four to seven, however, directly concerned FB. The fourth accused the governor of wielding an "absolute" power to dissolve the assembly. (FB had proclaimed the dissolution of the assembly in Jun. 1768 in accordance with Hillsborough's instructions following the House's refusal to rescind the vote approving the Circular Letter.) The fifth resolve justified the convening of "Committees" to consider the several American revenue acts by reason of the dissolution of the assembly and obstructions preventing the assembly's petition (of Jan. 1768) reaching the "Royal Ear" in timely fashion. (The committee intended was the Convention of Towns, which met in Boston in Sept. 1768.) The sixth resolve accused FB of providing "false and highly injurious Representation[s]" of the Council, Boston's magistrates, municipal officials, inhabitants, and "some individuals" in his several letters to Hillsborough. (The evidence for this comprised the copies of the governor's letters published in the *Boston Gazette* on 23 Jan. and the first batch of authentic copies acquired from William Bollan in London and published in Boston in April.) From these letters, it was deduced that the governor aimed to introduce "a Military Government and to mislead . . . Parliament into such severe Resolutions, as a true, just and candid State of Facts must have prevented." (FB, therefore, was being blamed for bringing the British Army to Boston in Oct. 1768 and providing Parliament with justification to pass its resolutions on Massachusetts, 15 Dec. 1768 and 8 Feb. 1769.) The seventh resolve accused FB of striking at the "Root" of the "Constitutional and Charter Rights" of the province by suggesting in a letter to Hillsborough (**No. 709**) that the Council should be appointed by the Crown.

The eighth, ninth, and tenth resolves protested the presence of the "Standing Army" that FB had visited upon Boston in contravention of the constitutional principles of Magna Carta, the English Bill of Rights, and the Province Charter. The eleventh warned that "whoever" misrepresented the province to the king's ministers as being in a "State of Disobedience and Disorder" was an "avowed Enemy" to the province. By implication, the House meant FB. For in the twelfth resolve FB was accused of persuading ministers to dispatch the troops. (The documentary evidence supporting this accusation was not received until Bollan's second batch of the governor's letters arrived in Boston on 19 Aug., for which see **Introduction**, 35.) The thirteenth resolve condemned FB and Gen. Thomas Gage for quartering the soldiers and placing canon and guards at the Court House doors to intimidate the legislators.

The remaining resolves targeted the imperial elite: Thomas Gage for meddling in the "internal Police" of the province; and the attorney general and advocate general, Jonathan Sewall, for refusing to prosecute "in Cases favorable to the Liberty of the Subject" (by which was meant that he refused to prosecute British soldiers). Also condemned were the Vice Admiralty Courts for imposing a "System of insupportable Tyranny" on America; and the American Board of Customs for funding a horde of placemen from the king's revenue. The last resolve concluded by asserting that any treason trial should take place in the colony where the crime was committed and not in Britain, as Parliament (poisoned by FB) now wished.

1. First written as "11".

2. The House's message was a stentorian challenge for FB to exercise or abdicate his royal authority.

> We clearly hold, that the King's most excellent Majesty, to whom we have, and ever shall bear, and since convening of this present Assembly we have sworn, true and faithful Allegiance, is the supreme executive Power through

all the Parts of the British Empire: And we are humbly of Opinion, that within the Limits of this Colony and Jurisdiction, your Excellency is the King's Lieutenant, Captain-General and Commander in Chief, in as full and ample a Manner, as is the Lord Lieutenant of *Ireland*; or any other His Majesty's Lieutenants in the Dominions to the Realm of *Great-Britain* appertaining.

From hence we think it indubitably follows, that all Officers, civil and military, within this Colony, are subject to the Order, Direction and Controul of your Excellency . . .

13 Jun. 1769, *JHRM*, 45: 18. The first article of FB's instructions gave him authority as commander in chief of the militia and "all Our Forces . . . within" Massachusetts and Rhode Island, but he did not exercise authority over Gen. Gage, commander in chief of the British Army in North America. The governor did not possess the requisite authority to order the withdrawal or removal of the troops for that would have usurped the general's authority and contravened Hillsborough's instructions to Gage, which gave the general a discretionary power to remove all or some of the regiments. But the Whigs were probably aware that Gage and FB had been discussing their options for withdrawing the troops, and on this point tried to push their advantage.

3. FB's message of 21 Jun. contained the following injunction.

I shall now capitulate the principal Articles of the public Business, which have hitherto waited for your Notice.

They are, 1. The Support of the Government; 2. The Supply of the Treasury; 3. The providing for the Payment of the provincial Debt, which now amounts to One hundred and five Thousand Pounds; 4. The Tax-Bill; 5. The Impost-Bill; 6. The Excise-Bill, if thought proper; 7. The Establishment for Forts and Garrisons; 8. The Continuation of the Truck Trade: 9. The Continuation or Revival of expiring or expired Laws, &c.

JHRM, 45: 139.

4. FB's message to the House of 28 Jun. *JHRM*, 45: 38-39.

5. **Appendix 4**, commenting upon the six Bernard Letters of 1 Nov. to 5 Dec. 1768; **Nos. 706**, **708**, **709**, **711**, **717**, and **718**. The resolve of 22 Jun. expressed approval for the Council's "Zeal" and "Attention . . . to the public Interest . . . not only in thus vindicating their own Character, but guarding their Country from meditated Ruin, by truly stating Facts and justly representing the Duty and Loyalty of this People at so critical a Time when the Governor of the Province had wantonly dissolved the General Assembly . . ." *JHRM*, 45: 29.

6. **No. 730**.

7. Benjamin Edes and John Gill.

8. FB enclosed the copy printed in Richard Draper's *Boston Post-Boy and Advertiser*, 3 Jul. 1769. The resolves of 29 Jun. were also published in Edes and Gill's *Boston Gazette* and the Fleets' *Boston Evening-Post* of the same date. The newspaper version purported to provide the "substance" of the resolves but the "corrected" final version entered into the journals of the House on 7 Jul. (discussed in the notes below) contained substantive differences. The former reported fifteen resolves, the latter nineteen. While the printers did not claim to be working from an authentic copy they were certainly acting upon information supplied by the clerk of the House, Samuel Adams. The variations were amendments and revisions added after further debate, as mentioned in this letter (though the debate is not recorded in the House journals). The comments pertaining to FB in resolves four to eleven echoed the accusations made by the House's petition to the king of 27 Jun. praying for FB's removal. On that day, the House did not approve resolves condemning the governor before or after approving the petition. Thus it is probable that the entry in the House journals for 7 Jul. provided *ex post facto* justification for the petition.

9. Under cover of a letter to John Pownall, Boston 3 Jul. 1769, BP, 7: 300.

10. Obscured by tight binding.

11. The resolves revealed a "Tendency . . . so dangerous that it seems to require the strengthening rather than the weakning the Forces now at Boston." FB to Thomas Gage, Boston 3 Jul. 1769, BP, 7: 231.

12. Alexander Mackay to Thomas Gage, 4 Jul. 1769, MiU-C: Gage, vol. 86.

13. 4 Jul.

14. 5 Jul.

15. This is the only reference in FB's papers to the controversial case of *Rex v. Corbet*, 1769.* FB and Hood were members of a panel of eleven commissioned judges (including customs officers and judges of Vice Admiralty) that formed a special court of Vice Admiralty to try Michael Corbet (or Corbit) and other colonial seamen accused of murdering Lt. Henry Panton of HMS *Rose* on 22 Apr. in the course of resisting impressment. The Panton trial was potentially explosive, not only because of colonial anger over impressment, but because Corbet et al. faced the death penalty. Under civil law proceedings in an admiralty court manslaughter could not be returned as a verdict, and the defendants stood trial accused of murder. A second issue concerned the mode of proceeding. When the trial opened on 23 May, the defense team of John Adams and James Otis Jr. pressed the court to hold a jury trial, allowed under a statute of Henry VIII (28 Hen. 8, c. 15) and confirmed by the Piracy Act, 4 Geo. 1, c. 11 (1717). The legal argument was seemingly convincing, and obliged the judges to consider a jury trial, despite their considerable misgivings about the integrity of Boston juries. To Adams's consternation, "The Govr . . . . talked that they [*the defendants*] might be sent to England for Tryal, &c." This was probably a provocative comment rather than a serious proposal, even though it echoed the spirit of Parliament's recent endorsement of bringing colonists to trial in England. TH, as presiding judge, however, accepted that a jury trial was permissible at the court's discretion. But the defense counsel did not win the pretrial argument, and *Rex v. Corbet* proceeded on 14 Jun. without a jury. The defence case rested upon justifying the killing of Panton as an act of self-defense: that the defendants were resisting an impressment in violation of 6 Anne, c. 37 (1707). Adams skilfully connected the defense to the broader ideological issue of arbitrary infringements to colonists' natural rights and liberties, but a short adjournment by TH denied Adams the opportunity of developing the argument fully. The court found in favor of Corbet and the others, with FB delivering the judges' verdict of justifiable homicide on 29 May. The verdict, according to Hiller Zobel, was properly cognizant of the "reasonable doubt" surrounding the evidence of the defendants' actions. Wroth and Zobel, eds., *Legal Papers of John Adams*, 2: 276-288, with FB's quotation at 288. See also Hiller B. Zobel, *The Boston Massacre* (New York, 1970), 113-131.

    *This absence from official correspondence can be explained by the pressure of other business, notably the meeting of assembly, discussions to withdraw the troops, and making preparations for his departure.

16. **No. 793**.

17. The second resolve: "That the sole Right of imposing Taxes on the Inhabitants of this his Majesty's Colony of the Massachusetts-Bay, is now, and ever hath been legally and constitutionally vested in the House of Representatives, lawfully convened according to the antient and established Practice, with the Consent of the Council, and of his Majesty, the King of Great-Britain, or his Governor for the Time being." 7 Jul. 1769. *JHRM*, 45: 168. The version in the newspaper read: "Resolved, That this House do concur in and adhere to the Resolutions of the House of Representatives in the Year One Thousand seven Hundred and sixty-five, and particularly in that essential Principle, that no Man can be justly taxed by, or bound in conscience to obey, any Law to which he has not given his Consent in Person, or by his Representative." CO 5/758, f 161.

18. By this term he probably meant all the American revenue acts and trade laws.

19. This was added to the House journals on 14 Jul. having being "by mistake omitted." *JHRM*, 45: 189-190.

20. The answer contained the caustic retort that "had your Excellency in humble Intimation of your Royal Master during your Administration acted from such noble Principles, many of the Disputes between your Excellency and former Assemblies would have had no Existence." 4 Jul. *JHRM*, 45: 159-160.

21. The *Boston Post-Boy and Advertiser*, the *Boston Gazette*, and the *Boston Evening-Post* of 10 Jul. 1769.

22. That is the enclosure marked "**V**". For the differences see note 17 above.

23. Resolves eight and nine did not repeat the message of 13 Jun. verbatim but in citing Magna Carta, the Bill of Rights, and the Province Charter reiterated the spirit of the message, which pledged the "Preservation of the Rights derived from the British Constitution" and urged "securing . . . true old English Liberty." *JHRM*, 45: 130-131.

24. FB's next missive, **No. 797**, did not discuss the House's refusal (on 22 Jun.) to make provision for the acting governor, as FB had requested in his message of 13 Jun. On 14 Jul., the House of Representatives promised to "make the necessary provision" for the governor's salary after FB's departure from the province (on the grounds that he was salaried until then). But the House never made any provision for TH during his time as acting governor; TH complained to them on 11 Apr. 1770 about their studied inattentiveness. *JHRM*, 45: 189-190; 46: 149-150. Upon his appointment as governor in 1771, TH was awarded an annual salary of £1,500 from the Crown, payable from the tea duty.

25. Left marginalia: "**IX X**".

26. 12 Jul. CO 5/828, ff 11-12.

27. All three sheets were probably printed by Edes and Gill.

793 | *To Thomas Gage*

Boston July 5 1769

S[r]

As Col Gubbat[1] is going immediately to New York I think it proper to inform you that upon my sending the Secretary Yesterday to the Speaker for a Copy of the Resolves printed in the last Monday's Paper, He told him that Publication was not authentick; for some of the Resolves which were printed, had not passed the House, & others which had passed the House were not printed. But the Clerk of the House M[r] Adams averrs that what is printed is extracted from the Minutes of the House in his Custody. However the House has appointed the Day to consider the whole, & may & probably will make Alterations; tho they will come very awkwardly after this Publication.

I find that Gen[l] MacKay & Commodore Hood have alterd their Minds concerning the Necessity of suspending Embarkation of the 64th Reg[t]: ~~As~~ ^I must therefore beg leave to change mine.^[2] I am the more induced to this, as I have taken the Opinion of the Lieut Governor, who thinks that as there is no Appearance of an Intention make a forceable Resistance at present there is no Occasion for detaining the 64th Regiment. But he continues fully persuaded that the two other Regiments may be kept here one of which at least must remain in the Town.

I expect to embark for England in about 3 Weeks time, & desire that if your Excellency has any particular Services that I can do for you there, you will favour me with them, & you may depend upon an exact Observance of your Commands.

I am &c.

Gen[l] Gage

P. S. I shall send you an Account of what the House determines upon these resolves as soon as I can.[3]

L, LbC   BP, 7: 232-233.

In handwriting of Thomas Bernard. Gage replied on 19 Jul. to wish FB a safe journey and to confirm that it was now appropriate to commence the relocation of the 64th Regiment to Halifax which began on 11 Jul. and was completed by 25 Jul.; the 65th had already left for Halifax, on 24 Jun. The 14th and 29th Regiments of Foot remained at Boston and Castle William.[4]

---

1. Joseph Gabbett, lieutenant colonel of the 16th Regiment of Foot.
2. Interlineation in FB's hand.
3. Postscript in FB's hand.
4. Archer, *As If an Enemy's Country*, 141. After the Boston Massacre of 5 Mar. 1770, the 29th Regiment was sent to New Jersey and the 14th Regiment removed from the town and put into the barracks at Castle William; two years later the 14th was deployed to the West Indies.

794 | *To Lord Barrington*

Boston July 8 1769

My Lord

I had but just time in my last Packet to acknowledge ~~the Receipt of~~ your Lordship's Letter of March 21-April 1.[1] Since this no Ship has sailed from hence to London; & I have been fully employed as your Lordship will see by the inclosed papers.

If there has been a Difference of Opinion in the Administration about American Measures, as we learn by wofull Experience there has,[2] It can not continue a Year longer; for the Americans will make them open their Eyes in Spight of their Teeth, & tell them in Words of Scripture "you are careful about many Things but one Thing is needful."[3] There is but one Way now of dealing with America: Lenitives have brought the Disease to its present Height & will if continued make it incurable.

A Member of Parliament (a friend of your Lordships & a protestee against the late inactive Proceedings) writes to his friends here, that he does not see that any thing will rouse the Government, but the Americans attacking the Navigation Act. If that is wanting it will not be so long: for I can assure you the Navigation Act is a principal Object with them. Some Months ago one of the Cheifs of the Faction here said in a Company consisting cheifly of his own Party, that things would never be properly settled in America till the Parliament had repealed all the Acts affecting the American Trade from the 15th of Charles 2 to the present time. This I took down from a Gentleman who heard it spoke; & you may tell it to Mr Stanley as a Fact.[4]

Your Lordship will judge of the temper & disposition of the Faction & its Creatures who are no less than the whole Council & the whole House (excepting some few Members of the latter who never come near it) from the Papers I send you with this, which are a Continuation of the Papers published by the House.[5] I have no time to animadvert upon these; but must observe that upon the Publication of the Resolves on July 3, The Speaker denied that those Resolves had *all* passed the House; The Clerk of the House insisted that they had passed the House; & that it was a true Copy. However the House has again taken them into ^Re-^Consideration, & has, as I understand, qualified the second, in this Edition, so that it shall refer to Acts of Taxation only, whereas at present it extends to ^all^ ~~Acts of Taxation~~ whatsoever. But this is only procrastinating: for both their Arguments and their Intentions lead equally to all Acts of Parliament.

Your Lordship judges right of the Efficacy of the Additional Clauses in the Mutiny Act: they will have no Effect in this Country. I am assured for certain, that the House will make no Provision for the Expence of hiring Barracks here, nor for the Parliamentary Provisions in such Barracks; neither will they provide any Funds for making any further Provisions for the Troops in the Provincial Barracks at Castle Island. I expect to be able to inclose in the Cover of this an Account of a positive Refusal of this Demand: So that you must not depend upon the Mutiny Act for quartering Soldiers in this Country. The inclosed Papers will show you what you have to expect: but that is of another Kind than Obedience to Acts of Parliament. __ I expect to have an Opportunity of adding another short Letter to this; so will conclude this with assuring you that I am with a most perfect Respect

My Lord &c __

The Rt Honble The L Visct Barrington

L. LbC   BP, 8: 1-3.

In handwriting of Thomas Bernard. Enclosure not found.

1. He probably meant 5 Apr., the date on which **No. 754** was posted.

2. Thus in manuscript.

3. FB used the same scriptural reference in a letter to John Pownall of 25 Nov. 1768. For an explanation see **No. 715**n4.

4. Hans Stanley (1721-80), MP for Southampton, was a Grenvillite and strong supporter of the Chatham and Grafton administrations. Stanley had seconded the Commons motion for an address to the king, in early January, acting on behalf of the ministry. A letter from London extracted in the newspaper (in which Stanley was mentioned) rightly claimed that the administration was determined not to repeal the Townshend Revenue Act, in order to uphold the principle of Parliament's legislative supremacy in the American Colonies. But the piece also asserted that British Regulars stationed in Boston would be used to enforce obedience to the act, and claimed ministers had "a settled plan . . . for absolutely and permanently enslaving" the Americans. *Boston Evening-Post*, 26 Jun. 1769.

5. Probably a copy of the final set of resolves approved on 7 Jul. but not published in the *Boston Evening-Post* until 10 Jul. For a summary the source note to **No. 792**.

795 | *From Thomas Gage*

New York July 9th: 1769.

Sir,

I have received your's of the 3d. Inst:,[1] with a Letter inclosed for Mr: Pownall, which shall be forwarded to England by the first opportunity. General Mackay has wrote to me concerning your opinion,[2] in which both he and the Commodore have joined, upon the present Situation of Affairs. I answer the General by this opportunity in a manner I hope agreeable to your Sentiments respecting the dangerous Appearance Affairs wear at present, and have recommended Secrecy to him respecting his orders.

I am with great Regard, Sir, your most obedient humble Servant,

Thos. Gage

His Excy: Sr: Francis Bernard,

ALS, RC   BP, 12: 119-122.

Endorsed by FB: Genl Gage d July 9. 1769.

1. The letter to Gage is at BP, 7: 231. The letter to Pownall of the same date is at ibid., 300.

2. Mackay to Gage, Boston, 4 Jul. 1769, MiU-C: Gage, vol. 86.

796 | From Thomas Gage

New York July 10th 1769

Sir,

Colonel Gabbitt arrived last night, by whom I had the honour to receive your Letter of the 5th Ins[t].[1] I find your Assembly is going to change their Resolves, in consequence of which the Intention of detaining the 64th; Regiment is also changed. As for the Destination of the two Regiments remaining in Boston, that stands fixed at least for some time. The altercation between the speaker and the Clerk may possibly produce some Discoverys or create Dissentions between themselves. They have handled us pretty roughly but as they have put us in such good Company as the Lords & Commons of Great Britain, whom they seem to have treated with the same ill manners, are may I think, be much obliged to them. I sincerely wish you a safe voyage to England, where you will enjoy more Peace and Tranquility than have fallen to your Lot for some years past, and I doubt not meet with as Reception and Reward due to your Services.

I am with very great Regards, Sir, your most obedient humble servant

Tho⁵ Gage

Sir Francis Bernard

ALS, RC   BP, 12: 123-126.

Endorsed: Gen Gage d July 10 1769.

---

1. **No. 793**.

797 | To the Earl of Hillsborough

(Duplicate)

(N° 13)

Boston July 17 1769

My Lord

On Saturday last July 15 I dismissed the General Court by a long Prorogation to January the 10th, after a Session of 46 Days,[1] the longest that has been known at this time of the Year. And yet there never was so little real Business done as at this Session: the cheif Part of the Time has been employed in denying the Power of the Parliament, arraigning and condemning its Acts, abusing the King's Ministers at home and his principal Officers in America, reproaching the whole British Nation, & declaring in plain if not direct Terms their Right and Intention to separate themselves from its Government. Every thing bad was expected from them; But their Acts have exceeded all Expectation and have been carried to a greater Length than ever have been known before. Their last Message in Answer to my Requisition of Provisions for the Troops exceeds every thing: it was delivered to me on Saturday last a little time before I prorogued them;[2] and I now send your Lordship the first Copy of it.

As I am apprehensive that I may be censured for suffering the House to sit after they had published Assertions and Resolutions so derogatory to the Sovereignty of Great Britain, I think it proper to explain the Motives of my Conduct, and to show as well as I can, that what I have done is for the best.[3] I had no special Instruction or Order to direct me upon the Occasion, nor any other Rule to go by, but Similarity of Circumstances; and they seldom happen so as not to leave a material Difference between the two Cases compared together. I had no other Way to direct my Judgement, but by considering what would be best for His Majesty's Service: and I assure your Lordship that in my own Opinion, I never judged better in any Business than in this.

It was plain to me from the Beginning that the Intention of the Faction was to provoke me to dissolve or prorogue the General Court before the public Business was done: and they did enough to justify such a Proceedure if I had not been guarded against it. If they had succeeded in this Scheme they would have made the following Uses of it: they would have raised a general Clamour throughout the Country founded upon the Distresses which would be brought upon the People for Want of the Supply Bill, which would have been real. In Case of a Dissolution immediately upon my Departure they would have obliged the Lieutenant Governor to have called a new Assembly, and it seldom happens but the dissolving an Assembly, in the Way of Censure, and calling another immediately after does more Harm than Good. In Case of a Prorogation, which must have been long to have had the Effect of a Censure, they would have obliged the Lieut^t Governor to have called the Assembly anew in the Way of Convention, as it has been upon an extraordinary Occasion once practised pending a Prorogation.[4] The Necessities of the Government for Want of Money in the Treasury, and the Distresses of the People upon raising the whole Provincial Debt within the Year according to Law, or, what would have been more probable, the Destruction of the public Credit, by the People refusing to submit to that Law, would have obliged the Lieutenant Governor to have acceded to one of the two Measures above mentioned; altho' he must have foreseen that his Compliance therewith would have given the Faction great Advantages both against him and the Government. I therefore could see Nothing but evil Consequences like to follow the resenting the Proceedings of the House by breaking up the Assembly before the public Business was done. In this Opinion I was confirmed by the Lieutenant Governor who was very anxious that the Session should not be ended before the Supply Bill and Tax Bill should be passed.[5]

On the other hand by my Patience and Perseverance in continuing the Session till the public Bills were passed I have gained this Advantage, that if a public Censure by Way of Dissolution should be thought proper, there is Nothing in the Way to hinder it: the public Business is provided for for a Year; and there are no Exigencies of State or Necessities of the People to prevent a long Intermission of the Assembly if it should be thought advisable. In this Proceeding I have lost Nothing but the inflicting the Censure myself, which, as it would have been known that it came from me only without any special Order from above would have had no great Efficacy. All Censures of this Kind should come from the Government at home to have their due Weight: tho' at this time even that Authority has not the Weight it should have. I would not be understood to recommend such a Censure or any Censure: that should be considered by the Government at home; and as the Facts are plain and undoubted, should be adjudged there. I cannot judge for my Superiors; I can feel for myself in the Business committed to me by them: but perhaps my feelings may not produce the same Ideas as theirs.

Another Advantage gained by this Conduct is, that it will give the Lieutenant Governor fair Play in the Opening of his Administration.[6] If I had abruptly broke up the Session I should have greatly distressed him: The Faction was so sensible of this that they could not conceal their Exultations upon the Prospect. In particular it was said that they would proceed to a new Election of Councellors and make him accept those whom I had rejected; and at different times it has been frequently talked of how soon they would make him sick of his Seat. They have allready begun with him with Libells preparatory to his taking the Chair; some of which I shall lay before your Lordship; as they are by Universal Report, supposed to have come from those whose Duty ought to have employed them in another Way.[7] But by my getting the public Business done and proroguing the Assembly to a long day I have put it in his Power to postpone the Days of his Trouble, till he can be strengthened with your Lordship's Opinion and where there shall be Occasion, with his Majesty's Instructions: and it will be in the Power of the King to put off the Day of his Trial to a still farther time. This Acquisition I consider to be of great Consequence to Government in its present State.

I have thought it proper to give your Lordship this Explanation of my Proceedings, the Substance of which is contained in my Speech at the closing the Session;[8] For I would not have my Conduct misunderstood even for a few Days: and I think it cannot be many between your receiving this and my waiting on you in Person. I hope to embark about the End of next Week.

I have the Honor to be, with a most perfect Respect, My Lord, Your Lordships most obedient & most humble Serv[t]

Fra Bernard

The Right Honorable The Earl of Hillsborough

dupLS, RC   CO 5/758, ff 175-178.

Endorsed: Boston July 17. 1769 Sir Fra[s]. Bernard (N[o]. 13) R 5th Sept[r]. (Dup[ce]: orig[l]: not reced) B.36.   Enclosed a page extracted from the *Boston Post-Boy and Advertiser*, 17 Jul. 1769 containing the House of Representatives' message to FB of 14 Jul. and FB's reply of 15 Jul. These were marked "**XIV**" and "**XV**", continuing the series from **No. 792**, and were probably extracts from the newspapers that he deemed "Libells" on TH. Variants of letter in: CO 5/893, ff 155-157 (dupALS, RC); CO 5/768, ff 13-19 (L, RLbC); BP, 7: 185-190 (L, LbC). The letter and enclosures were considered by the Board of Trade on 1 Dec. 1769. *JBT*, 13: 126-127.

1. The assembly did not meet again until 15 Mar. 1770. *JHRM*, 46: 89.

2. On 15 Jul.

3. In refusing to settle the accounts of the British soldiers quartered in Boston, the House challenged the legality of the Governor and Council making such an application under the Quartering Act. But the remainder of the message likened the Townshend Revenue Act and other revenue acts to "*Acts for raising a Tribute in America for the further Purposes of Dissipation among Placemen and Pensioners.*" The colonists' predicament was akin to those who suffered "under the Administration of the most oppressive of the Governors of the Roman Provinces," a clear allusion to the tyranny of Verres and his self-enrichment through taxation and oft-used by Whigs to ridicule FB. *Boston Post-Boy and Advertiser*, 17 Jul. 1769. Also recorded on 14 Jul. in *JHRM*, 45: 189-190.

4. Following the coup against Gov. Edmund Andros in 1689, the king's government in Massachusetts (within the Dominion of New England) was "dissolved." The following month the colony's Council summoned a convention of delegates from the towns; sixty-six met in Boston with the majority favoring restoring the colonial government under the terms of the original Province Charter of 1629. FB and

TH could not have warmed to such a mode of proceeding given the 1689 convention's association with revolutionary action, and their having accused the 1768 Convention of Towns of sedition. On the former see John Gorham Palfrey and Francis Winthrop Palfrey, *History of New England*, 3 vols. (Boston, 1858), 3: 588.

5. An act for apportioning and assessing a tax of thirty thousand pounds, 31 May 1769; an act for supplying the treasury with eighty-thousand one hundred and fifty-eight pounds, 15 Jul. 1769. *Acts and Resolves*, 5: 5-20, 28-30.

6. TH had known from at least Nov. 1768 that Hillsborough was likely to "nominate" him as FB's successor, based, he said, on information received from "sevral of my friends." TH to William Palmer, 23 Nov. 1768, Hutchinson Transcripts, 2: 686.

7. This intriguingly suggests that the author may have been a provincial office holder.

8. On 15 Jul., *JHRM*, 45: 196-197; also printed in the *Boston Post-Boy and Advertiser*, 17 Jul. 1769.

798 | To Thomas Hutchinson

Boston July 29th 1769

S^r

As I am going to leave the Province I think it proper to inform you that after the Death of the late King, the Council advised me to appoint Mr John Cotton & Mr William Cooper to be joint Registrars of the Court of Probates in the County of Suffolk they being then in the same Office: but that upon some Doubts of the form of such Appointment it was deferred for some time.[1] In this Interval I discovered ^that^ Mr Cooper was so unfit to bear any Commission under the King, that I determined not to compleat this Appointment in Regard to him: but having no Objection to the Nomination of Mr Cotton, I should have made out a Commission to him, if I had not doubted of the Propriety of separating Persons named by a Joint Vote of Approbation: but I intended to have settled this Matter with the Council by the first Opportunity. In the mean Time the Faction which has harrast this Country by setting them in Opposition to the King and Parliament (in which Faction Mr Cooper was known to bear a principal Part) had gained so much Ground and created a general Intimidation amongst good Men who desired to be quiet, that I could not find a proper Opportunity to propose this Matter to the Council. I therefore left the Office to be executed under the former Commission, which appointment must be understood to continue while it was acquiesced in by the Judge. But being now leaving the Province I think it necessary to inform your Honour that there is no Commission of the Office of Registrar of the Court of Probates for the County of Suffolk granted by me since the Death of the late King; and therefore the Place, as I understand, is still vacant and remains to be filled up; and I must add that Mr William Cooper is (in my Opinion) a most unfit Man to serve the King in any Office whatsoever.

I am with great Regard Sr Your most obedient humble Servant,

Fra Bernard

The Honorable Lieut Govr Huchinson

LS, RC Mass. Archs., 25: 321-322.

In handwriting of Thomas Bernard. This was probably the last letter FB wrote in America, before boarding HMS *Rippon* on 1 Aug.

---

1. John Cotton and William Cooper (1720-1809) were appointed joint registers of probate for Suffolk County on 19 Dec. 1759, under a commission of George II. The king's death on 23 Oct. 1760 necessitated the renewal of all provincial commissions. The continuation was immediately authorized by an order-in-council issued by the Privy Council, and a six-month period was advertised by governor's proclamation on 16 Oct. 1761. The joint appointment of Cotton and Cooper was approved by the Governor and Council on 5 Nov. 1761. Whitmore, *Massachusetts Civil List*, 81; *Bernard Papers*, 1: 59; CO 5/823, ff 103, 105. However, in this letter FB is suggesting that he never expressly confirmed the joint commission under the new provincial seal effective upon George III's accession. He thus thought he had found a means of checking the advancement of one Whig. Cooper, the older brother of the Rev. Samuel Cooper (the minister of the Brattle Street Church) had been town clerk of Boston since 1761, and in which capacity emerged as a local leader of the opposition. He held this office until his death in 1809.

APPENDICES

Appendix 1

ADDRESS OF MEMBERS OF THE
MASSACHUSETTS COUNCIL TO THOMAS GAGE

To his Excellency General Gage Commander in Chief of his
Majesty's Forces in America

The Address of the Subscribers Members of his Majesty's
Council of the Province of Massachusetts Bay

Sir,

A General Council being held yesterday gives the distant members of it, together with the members in the Town and neighbourhood, the pleasure of Addressing you.

We take this first opportunity of doing it; and at the same time to pay our Compliments to your Excellency.

In this time of Public distress, when the General Court of the Province is in a state of dissolution; when the Metropolis is possessed by Troops, and surrounded by Ships of War; and when more troops are daily expected, it affords a general Satisfaction that your Excellency has visited the Province, and has now an opportunity of knowing the state of it by your own observation and enquiry.

Your own observation will give you the fullest evidence that the Town and Province, are in a peaceful state: your own enquiry will satisfy you, that tho': there have been disorders in the Town of Boston, some of them did not merit notice; and that such as did, have been magnified beyond the truth.

Those of the 18th: of March and 10th: of June are said to have occasioned the abovementioned Armament to be ordered hither.

The first was trivial, and could not have been noticed to the disadvantage of the Town, but by persons inimical to it: especially as it happened in the Evening of a day of recreation.

The other was Criminal, and the Actors in it were guilty of a riot: but we are obliged to say it had it's rise from those persons who were loudest in their Complaints about it, and who by their overcharged representations of it have been the occasion of so great an armament ^being^ ordered hither.— We cannot persuade ourselves to believe they have sufficient evidence to support such representations: which have most unjustly brought into question the Loyalty of as Loyal a People as any in his Majesty's Dominions.

This misfortune has arisen from the accusation of interested Men, whose Avarice having Smothered in their breasts every Sentiment of humanity towards this Province, has impelled them to oppress it to the utmost of their Power; and by the consequences of that oppression essentially to injure Great Britain.

From the Candor of your Excellency's Sentiments we assure ourselves you will not entertain any apprehension, that we mean to justify the disorders and riotous proceedings that have taken place in the Town of Boston. We detest them, and have repeatedly and publicly expressed that detestation; and the Council have advised Governor Bernard to order the Attorney General to prosecute the perpetrators of them: but at the same time we are obliged to declare in justice to the Town, that the disorders of the 10th: of June last, occasioned by a Seizure made by the Officers of the Customs, appear to have originated with those, who ordered the Seizure to be made. The hour of making the Seizure (at or near Sun Set) the Threats and Armed Force used in it, the forcibly carrying the Vessel away and all in a manner unprecedented, and calculated to irritate, justify the apprehension that the Seizure was accompanied with those extraordinary Circumstances in order to excite a riot and furnish a plausible pretence for requesting Troops. A day or two after the ^Riot^ and as if in prosecution of the last mentioned purpose, notwithstanding there was not the least insult offered to the Commissioners of the Customs either in their persons or property, they thought fit to retire, on the pretence of Security to themselves, on board the Romney Man of War, and afterwards to Castle William: And when there, to keep up the idea of their being still in great hazard procured the Romney and several other Vessels of War to be stationed as to prevent an Attack upon the Castle: which they affected to be afraid of.

These proceedings have doubtless taken place to induce a belief among the Officers of the Navy and Army, as they occasionally came hither, that the Commissioners were in danger of being Attacked; and to procure from those Officers representations co-incident with their own, that they really were So. But their frequent landing on the Main, and making excursions into the Country, where it would have been easy to have Seized, if any injury had been intended them, demonstrates the insincerity of their declarations, that they immured themselves at the Castle for Safety.

This is rather to be accounted for, as being an essential part of the Concerted plan for procuring Troops to be quartered here: in which they and their Coadjutors have succeeded to their wish: but unhappily, to the mutual detriment and uneasiness of both Countries.

We thought it absolutely necessary, and our duty to the Town and Province required us, to give your Excellency this detail, that you might know the Sentiments of this People; and that they think themselves injured: and injured by men to whom they have done no injury. — From the justice of your Excellency we assure ourselves your mind will not admit of impressions to their disadvantages from persons who have done the injury.

Your Excellency in your Letter to Governor Bernard of the 12th: of September[1] gave Notice, that one of the Regiments from Halifax was ordered for the present to Castle William, and the other to the Town: but you was pleased afterwards to order both of them into the Town.

If your Excellency when you know the true State of the Town, which we can assure you is quite peaceable, shall think his Majesty's Service does not require those Regiments to continue in the Town, it will be a great ease and Satisfaction to the Inhabitants, if you will please to order them to Castle William, where Commodious barracks are provided for their reception, or to Point Shirley, in the neighbourhood of it: in either of which or in both they can be well accommodated. As to the two Regiments expected here from Ireland, it appears by Lord Hillsborough's Letter of the 30th: of July, [2] they were intended for a different part of North America.

If your Excellency shall think it not inconsistent with his Majesty's Service, that they should be sent to the place of their first destination, it will contribute to the ease and happiness of the Town and Province, if they might be ordered thither.

As we are true and faithful Subjects of his Majesty, have an affectionate regard for the Mother Country, and a tender feeling for our own, our duty to each of them makes us wish, and we earnestly beg your Excellency to make a full enquiry into the disorders abovementioned; into the cause of them and the representations that have been made about them: in doing which your Excellency will easily discover who are the persons that from lucrative views have combined against the Peace of this Town and Province: Some of whom it is probable have discovered themselves already by their own letters to your Excellency.

In making the Enquiry, tho' many imprudences and some criminal proceedings may be found to have taken place we are persuaded from the Candor, Generosity and Justice that distinguish your Character, your Excellency will not charge the doings of a few individuals, and those of an Inferior Sort upon the Town or Province: and with regard to those individuals, if any circumstances shall appear justly to extenuate the Criminality of their proceedings your Excellency will let them have their Effect.

On the same Candor Generosity and Justice we can rely, that your Excellency's representations of this Affair to his Majesty's Ministers will be such as even the Criminals themselves shall allow to be just.

S. Dexter[3]	N Sparhawk	Samuel Danforth
		John Hill
	Harrison Gray	Isaac Royall
	James Russel	John Erving
	John Bradbury	
	Royal Tyler	James Bowdoin
	Samuel White	Gam[l] Bradford
	James Pitts	Tho[s]: Hubbard

Boston Octo[r]: 27: 1768

Ms, RC   CO 5/86, ff 220-222.

Endorsed: In Major Gen[l]. Gage's (N[o] 18) of 31. Oct[r]. 1768.   Enclosed in Thomas Gage to the earl of Hillsborough, Boston, 31 Oct. 1768, CO 5/86, ff 214-219. The signatures are autographs; dates of Council membership are given in the notes. Variants: Bowdoin and Temple Papers, Loose MSS (AMs, AC); Add 35912, ff 126-129 (Ms, LbC); M-Ar.: Council Executive Records, GC3-327, 16: 369-370 (transcript, RbC); CO 5/757, f 519 (newspaper, PC). Printed in the province newspapers: *Boston Post-Boy and Advertiser*[4] and *Boston Evening-Post*, 31 Oct. 1768; *Massachusetts Gazette and Boston News-Letter*, 3 Nov. 1768; *Letters to Hillsborough* (1st ed.), 66-68; *Letters to Hillsborough* (repr.), 129-134. Copies of the address and letter were presented to Parliament on 20 Jan. 1769.

FB discussed the Council's address in **No. 706**, having been left in no doubt that the majority of councilors blamed him personally for joining with the commissioners of Customs in a "Concerted plan" to bring British troops to Boston.

> This misfortune has arisen from the accusation of interested Men, whose Avarice having Smothered in their breasts every Sentiment of humanity towards this Province, has impelled them to oppress it to the utmost of their Power; and by the consequences of that oppression essentially to injure Great Britain.

The address to Gage encapsulated the Whig councilors' attempts to distance their cause from disorderly crowd action and was consistent with their having advised that the commissioners of Customs could return safely to Boston. The address was also the finale to FB's attempts to win over the Council, for in accusing FB of conspiring with the commissioners the councilors (intentionally or otherwise) averted public condemnation of facilitating the return of the Customs Board. Gage's prompt and brief reply made no mention of the accusations against FB and the commissioners or the Council's proposal for an inquiry into the riots, and advised "that the future Behavior of the People, will justify the best Construction of their past Actions."[5]

1. **No. 675**, *Bernard Papers*, 4: 304.

2. **No. 661**, ibid., 271-276.

3. Signatories with dates of election to the Council:* James Bowdoin (1726-90), 1757-68, 1770-73; John Bradbury (1697-1778), 1763-72; Gamaliel Bradford (1704-78), 1757-69; Samuel Danforth (1696-1777), 1739-74; Samuel Dexter (1726-1810), 1768-73; John Erving (c.1692-1786), 1754-74; Harrison Gray (1711-94), 1761-72; John Hill (1703-72), 1742-69; Thomas Hubbard (1702-73), 1759-72; James Pitts (1710-76), 1766-74; Isaac Royall (c.1719-81), 1752-73; James Russell (1715-98), 1761-73; Nathaniel Sparhawk (1715-76), 1760-65, 1767-72; Royal Tyler (1724-71), 1764-70; Samuel White (1710-20 Mar. 1769), 1766-68.

   *Elections were conducted at the beginning of the assembly's legislative year, in May, votes being cast by the new House of Representatives and the outgoing Council. Appointments to the mandamus Council in Aug. 1774 have been excluded.

4. FB enclosed a copy of this newspaper in **No. 708**.

5. Gage to the Council, Boston, 28 Oct. 1768. CO 5/86, f 222.

Appendix 2

WILLIAM BOLLAN TO SAMUEL DANFORTH.

Henrietta Street Jan^ry. 30th. 1769

Sir,

Having on the 16th inst^t. received your favour, inclosing petitions of the major part of the council of the province, to the Lords & Commons,[1] desiring their presentation, with my endeavours for their success, I have applied myself with diligence to this hard service. In order to a right[2] understanding of the present state of your affairs, I must observe that on the 15th. day of last month the lords came to certain resolutions, whereby they censured the council & representatives of the province, and the civil magistrates & inhabitants of Boston for several causes, and grafted thereon[3] an address to the king, which supposes that the subjects in the colonies are liable to be taken from their proper domicil, & brought into England, & there tried for treason, or misprision of treason. The resolutions & address were afterwards sent down to the comons[4] for their concurrence.[5] Being at this time closely engaged in a difficult & laborious work, I had no knowledge of this business til some days after its transaction. On being inform'd of it, as the resolutions & address were not inserted in the votes of the house of comons, and copies of them cou'd not be had otherwise than by or under the authority of a member, I desired the favour of a principal member, & one of your best friends,[6] with whom I had before concerted measures for your service, to get me proper office copies. He bespoke them with intent that I shou'd have them before he went out of town, upon the recess of both houses;[7] but he did no[t][8] receive them til they came to hand at his seat in the country, whence he sent them, desiring me to consider them well, & send him my thoughts upon them, which I did accordingly.[9] The reading of them gave me great surprise & concern, and the more I considered them, together with the temper of the times, the more my concern encreased. I was a long time much at a loss what to do for the advancement of the comon cause; at lenghth, as no man loses his domicil by going abroad in public service, I determined by petition, as an inhabitant of Boston, tho' residing here, to prevent, if possible, the concurrence of the house of comons, and was busy in preparations relative to this petition when I had the honour to receive your letter. That House was adjourned to the l9^th. inst^t., & American affairs stood appointed for consideration on the 23^d., when your petition was intended to have been presented by M^r. Beckford; but by a singular event he was prevented. On the 25th., after gov^r. Bernards, gen^l. Gages & commodore Hoods letters, which on motion made on behalf of the colonies had been on the 20th. brought in & laid upon the table,[10] were read, he presented it; and on his behalf M[r]. Ald[n]. Trecothick[11] read it, with such an audible voice that it is supposed every member in the house clearly understood it; and being objected to a debate ensued, wherein the petition was nobly supported by divers worthy members.[12] The chief objections, I am told; for I was not, as formerly, admited into any part of the house, were that no council could be convened without the governours order, and that by the constitution of the colony there cou'd be no president of the council, unless when there was no governour, or lieut[t] govern[r].: in answer whereto, I am inform'd, it was said, that in the present great distress of the province no assembly was called, & no council convened from time to time with liberty to defend upon the present great occasion the rights & interest of the province;[13] and that the objections to your petition, instead of being founded on the principles of natural justice, equity, & the constitution of the kingdom,[14] rested in a good measure on the representations of gov[r]. Bernard,[15] the copies of whose letters I have so lately received that I know not their contents,[16] but without opening send them to you as I received them, in order to your receiving further information for your future guideance than I can otherwise give you. Upon a large debate, I understand, several ministerial persons were enclined to admit your petition, & it was at last without any division received & laid upon the table; whereupon a motion was made that it shou'd be refered, together with the other papers[17] to a comittee of the whole house.[18] Upon this a new debate ensued, with a consequent division, whereon, I am told, the number for refering it was 70, & the number against it 133. On the next day[19] my own petition, a copy whereof you have inclosed, after my waiting on the speaker, & his reading, & comending it in some respects, was presented by Sir George Saville,[20] who in the opening read the whole of it, and which in the course of the ensuing debates was well supported by several intelligent, respectable & public spirited persons, insomuch that altho' I believe this petition was more disliked by the adminis[n]. than yours, because it more directly opposed their present measures,[21] after a sharp debate, upon a division, a greater minority, as I am informed, appeared in my favour than has appear'd at any time in the present parliam[t]. against the adminis[n]., to wit, 105, or, as more accurate persons say, 107 (two who came out of the house with the others coming in after the numbers were declared) against 136.[22] Pray don't mistake me; this advance was owing to the goodness of your cause, rather than to my abilities. After rejecting my petition the house was resolved into a comittee,[23] and the debate at large coming on, your cause was defended with arguments so forcible, & a spirit so noble, that it is impossible for me in my present[24] hurry to do justice in any tolerable degree to the parties concern'd; but at 4 o'clock in the morning, the admint[n]. carried their point, by 150 against 90, upon a division.[25] The report is to be made four days hence,[26] when another great debate will come on, & new matter be advanced, and tomorrow, when a full house is expected, a motion will be made respecting the accompts of the revenue raised in America, at so great expense various ways, which have not yet been brought in, according to order given upon motion made some time past.

Your petition is the first that has been received since introducing the new system of governm^t for America. One that came from Philadelphia, I am told, was offer'd some time ago, but withdrawn, at the proposal of the chan^r. of the excheq^r. to be presented some other time, & I have since heard nothing of it. Having this moment received a copy of gen^l. Gage's letter, which a principal member tells me contains some important matter, I send it inclosed.

I am, with the greatest respect for all the members of the council, Sir,
Your most obed^t humble serv^t.

W. Bollan.

The Honble. Saml. Danforth, Esqr.

ALS, RC   Bowdoin and Temple
                                              Papers, Loose MSS.

Endorsed: M^r. Bollans Letter Jany 30. 1769. Printed in *Bowdoin and Temple Papers*, 121-125. The numerous differences between the previously published version and the transcript printed here concern punctuation, spelling, and capitalization; the original forms have been restored where possible; substantive differences are noted below. An extract of the RC was included in *Letters to Hillsborough* (1st ed.), 83, and *Letters to Hillsborough* (repr.), 164-165. The RC enclosed authentic copies of the first six items in the series of Bernard Letters that the governor's enemies subsequently published (**Nos. 706, 708, 709, 711, 717, and 718**)[27] plus Thomas Gage to the earl of Hillsborough, Boston, 31 Oct. 1768; and William Bollan, petition to the House of Commons, 26 Jan. 1769. Filed in Bowdoin and Temple Papers, Loose MSS. Bollan's part in the procurement of the Bernard Letters is discussed at length in the **Introduction**, 14-22, 35-36.

1. The "major part of the Council," petitions to the House of Lords and the House of Commons, c.30 Nov. 1768, enclosed in Samuel Danforth to William Bollan, 5 Dec. 1768, Bowdoin and Temple Papers, Loose MSS.

2. Thus in manuscript, but Bollan may have intended to use the adverb "aright".

3. *Bowdoin and Temple Papers*: "them on".

4. The manuscript renders the "m" in "comons" with a tilde, here and below.

5. The Lords' resolutions and the address to the king were received by the House of Commons on 16 Dec. and approved with minor amendments on 8 Feb. 1769.

6. Probably William Beckford. See note 11 below.

7. On 22 Dec., the House of Commons adjourned to 19 Jan. 1769.

8. Editorially supplied to aid understanding.

9. The acquisition of authentic copies of the six Bernard Letters is discussed in the **Introduction**, 14-22.

10. *HCJ*, 32: 123-124; *HLJ*, 32: 229. The first order of the day was to read the American correspondence presented to Parliament on on 28 Nov., 7 Dec., and 20 Jan., including all of FB's official letters to Hillsborough. The House resolved to consider the material at noon the following day, 26 Jan. *HCJ*, 32: 136.

11. William Beckford (bap.1709-70), a former West India sugar planter and a wealthy merchant, was the City of London's MP, 1754-70, and its mayor, 1762 and 1769-70. Barlow Trecothick (?1718-75), an alderman of London and MP, 1768-74, was a leader of the Rockingham faction in the House of Commons.

12. Other speakers on Beckford's motion to accept the petition were Isaac Barré and Lord North (both in favor) and Hans Stanley and Lord Strange (both against). The principal difficulty, as Bollan rightly pointed out, was whether or not the House could admit the petition as if coming from the Council (as Lord North initially wished to do, particularly since he thought the petition "cautiously and properly drawn" and whose "little insinuations" in matters of right the House could "pass . . . over".). Wright, *Cavendish's Debates*, 1: 184-190.

13. By Cavendish's account, Trecothick's emotive plea persuaded North and others to seek a form of words to facilitate acceptance of the petition:

> The practice of refusing to receive petitions from America is, it seems, to be continued. Small things ought to give way to great. Shall we stickle at a little want of form, in a matter where substance is so materially concerned? You throw out of doors the first movement made towards a reconciliation with our colonies. I will meet the noble Lord [*North, who had withdrawn his support for the motion*] half-way.

Isaac Barré (1726-82), the MP for Chipping Wycombe, 1761-74, and a veteran of the French and Indian War, was equally forthright: "I tremble at the possibility of our treating this petition with neglect; a petition in words stronger than any lately presented. These poor people have been trampled on." Barré was also a Chathamite Whig who, like many staunch friends of the Americans, openly criticized the administration's American policy after the earl of Chatham left control to Grafton's leadership in 1767 and resigned in Oct. 1768. Wright, *Cavendish's Debates*, 1: 185-186.

14. An indecipherable word, scored out by the author, has been omitted.

15. After Barré had spoken, Hans Stanley (1721-80), MP for Southampton, 1754-80, arose to remind the House that having read the papers before them members would "find" the "whole transaction" described in one of FB's letters (**No. 718**).

16. *Bowdoin and Temple Papers*: "of their contents".

17. That is, the American correspondence previously read.

18. The formulation agreed upon was prompted by Thomas Pownall's brief intervention to confirm that the "president" (as the petition designated Danforth) had no constitutional role and thus the petition was the work of a majority of members acting in a private capacity. Wright, *Cavendish's Debates,* 1: 186. The petition was ordered to "be brought up, not as a Petition of the major part of the Council," but as a petition coming from Samuel Danforth "on the Behalf of the several individual Members of the said Council at whose Request he signed the same." *HCJ*, 32: 136. The petition is printed in ibid., 136-137.

19. 26 Jan.

20. Sir George Savile (1726-84), MP for Yorkshire, 1759-83, was a respected independent keen to encourage the Rockinghamites and the Grafton administration to effect reconciliation with the colonists.

21. Specifically, Bollan challenged the legal basis of the presumption in the Lords' address to the king that treason trials should proceed under 35 Hen. 8, c. 2. *Letters to the Ministry* (1st ed.), 148-164. Several speakers commented upon Bollan's reasoning, while government men questioned Bollan's right to petition against the proceedings of the Houses of Parliament. Edmund Burke conveyed the sense of

urgency pervasive among opposition Whigs that colonial grievances were being dismissed too readily. "In these times, and upon these great occasions, when so many perilous questions are depending, we ought to let the Americans know that they are fully heard." Wright, *Cavendish's Debates*, 1: 191.

22. Bollan's figures are accurate, here and above. *HCJ*, 32: 151.

23. The House debated the wealth of papers presented to Parliament on 28 Nov., 7 Dec., and 20 Jan., prior to considering the Lords' resolutions of 15 Dec. Afterward, the chairman of the committee responsible for drafting a response to the Lords announced that he was ready to present the report, which the House agreed to receive one week later (2 Feb.). *HCJ*, 32: 151.

24. *Bowdoin and Temple Papers*: "great".

25. For a summary see **Introduction,** 14-20. The debates are reported in detail in Wright, *Cavendish's Debates*, 1: 191-207.

26. 2 Feb. But the debate on American affairs was delayed by proceedings on the libels of John Wilkes, who was expelled from the Commons on 3 Feb. The resolutions and address were approved with minor amendments on 8 Feb. For reports see Wright, *Cavendish's Debates*, 1: 207-225.

27. The copies were scribed by four different hands, and each bears the attestation and signature of George White,* the clerk of the papers of the House of Commons, dated 27 Jan. 1769. They were filed in James Bowdoin's personal papers after Bowdoin and his colleagues subsequently published a pamphlet edition. Bowdoin's papers do not hold copies of the other letters from FB to Hillsborough, again supplied by Bollan and published later in the year. *HCJ*, 32: 123-124; *HLJ*, 32: 229; Bowdoin and Temple Papers, Loose MSS; *Letters to Hillsborough* (1st ed.)**,** 3-33.

* On White see Williams, *Clerical Organization of the House of Commons*, 143, 182-183.

Appendix 3

JAMES BOWDOIN TO THE EARL OF HILLSBOROUGH

Boston April 15. 1769

My Lord

The occasion of my addressing your Lordship proceeds from a Letter of Govr Bernard to your Lordship dated the 30th. Novemb.^r last:[1] a copy of which, with copies of other Letters of the Governor have been sent to the Council of this Province.

This Letter my Lord, as it wholly relates to a conversation between the Governor & myself, and to what happened in consequence of it, the Council have taken no further ^notice^ of in their Letter to your Lordship than to refer to what I have now the honor of writing to you on the subject of that Conversation.

The Council's Petition to his majesty, which the Govr enclosed to you in his Letter of the 16th. of July,[2] was the Subject of it: and what passed upon it I beg leave, at the desire of the Council, to inform you. But to make it intelligible, it is necessary to quote part of the prayer of the Petition: which follows—

"and if it should appear to y.^r Majesty, that it is not for the benefit of Great Britain & her Colonies, that any revenue should be *drawn* from the Colonies, we humbly implore your Majesty's gracious recommendation to Parliament that your American subjects may be relieved from the operation of the several acts made for that purpose, in such manner as to the wisdom of your Majesty & Parliament may seem proper."

The design of the Council my Lord, and it appears by the general tenor of the Petition, & by the above-cited clause their design was, to implore his Majesty's recommendation to Parliament, that his American Subjects might be ^wholly^ relieved from the several acts of Parliament made for the purpose of raising a revenue from them: ^or that the said acts might be repealed.^

That this design might be more effectually answer'd, the Council, confiding in the Governor, desired him to transmit to your Lordship this petition; and to use his influence that the prayer of it might be granted. He transmitted it accordingly, together with a Letter to you, in which from the Conversation refer'd to, I was induced to think the Governor had endeavor'd to give a sense to the above-cited clause, very different from what he knew was the intention of the Council, and from the sense, which the words themselves taken altogether, in common construction convey.

From the word *drawn* in the said clause, I was led to think he had drawn this construction of it — that it meant nothing more than to desire that whatever money might be raised in the Colonies by virtue of the said acts of Parliament, might not be *drawn* from or sent out of the Colonies: but that the whole of ~~them~~ ^it^ might be expended in them. "You meant said the Governor (speaking to me at the College where the conversation was had) by revenue *drawn* from the Colonies, revenue *raised* in them. But however, said he, I have taken your meaning to be, that you desire that none of the revenue ~~shall~~ ^money may^ be sent away out of America: and accordingly I have wrote to the Secretary of State, representing the inexpediency or ordering any of the American Revenue to be sent out of America; and you may ^depend^ it will not be done: for his Majesty's Service in America will require more money than that revenue can Supply." — Thus far my Lord, the Subject could give ^me^ no occasion to suppose, that what the Governor said was in joke__ "There is money in the Revenue Chest, continued the Governor, and I hope it will be ordered out soon, and that I shall have some of it." __ Here indeed there might have been room for some pleasantry: but the Governor appeared to mean what he said.

This, my Lord, is the Substance of what passed. I was astonished at his endeavouring to pervert the intention and meaning of the petition: and several Gentlemen of the Council, to whom I mentioned this conversation on the same day, were no less astonished at it too: and it was thought, if he had done so, he had not only betrayed the trust reposed in him by the Council; and by so doing abused the Province: but at the same time had endeavoured to impose upon your lordship; and [_]³ through your Lordship, upon his majesty.

Soon after the Commencement (July 20ᵗʰ) on which day the conversation happened, a number of the Council met together to consider about petitioning the two Houses of Parliament: principally with a view of preventing the Council's petition to his majesty being misunderstood. But as there was time enough before them, they postponed it, and afterward in november proceeded upon it, and forwarded to Mʳ. Bollan two Petitions to the Lords & Commons for that purpose.

I will now proceed with the leave of your Lordship to take notice of the Governor's Letter:⁴ in which informing you of the conversation with him, whereby I justified what he is pleased to call my charge against him, he says I mentioned "something which explained the whole, and shewed that what he said upon that occasion was intirely in joke: and this was confirmed by a Councellor."

What the Governor did say, my Lord, I have represented above: to the truth of which I shall be ready to testify, whenever your Lordship, or the Governor shall desire it. In the mean time, as I would not trouble you with any unnecessary observations, I shall leave to your Lordship to determine, whether it can be inferred from the account above given, that what was said, was said in joke.

But "this was confirmed, says the Governor, by a Councellor."—^What passed my Lord, was between the Governor and myself; and could not be heard by anyone else.^ What this Gentleman said was, that the Governor talked very faceciously, or joked about a large Salary he expected to receive out of the American Revenue. But even this was on a different part of the day, and at this Gentleman's house, where I was not present; and no way related to the Governor's Conversation with me: nor to his giving to your Lordship a meaning to the Council's petition different from their own.

The Governor says, his Letter in question ^dated July 16th.^ he had copied; and that the three or four Gentlemen, to whom he communicated it, were greatly Surprized to find it so clear of my charge." __ This charge my Lord, whether true or false, was not my charge: it was the Governor's against himself; and was ^only^ related by me, as I had it from his own mouth. _ I was obliged to believe it, or call in question his veracity. I wish the account he has given to your Lordship, relative to our conversation, had helped me out of this disagreable dilemma. The Governor informs your Lordship, he produced the letter at Council, and read the whole passage refer'd to: from whence it appeared he says, "that in mentioning the prayer of their petition he used their own words, without adding a single word of his own._ this appeared satisfactory to the whole Council, except Mr. Bowdoin."

The Governor, my Lord, read a Paper, which he did not deliver out of his hand; and which, not having an opportunity of reading it myself, I might misapprehend. But from my remembrance of it, if the words of the prayer were used in it, they were introduced with so much address, as to give me a very different idea, from that which the same words, as introduced and used in the prayer itself, do convey. It was not therefore (as the Governor justly observes) satisfactory to me: nor was it satisfactory to the whole Council beside, notwithstanding he is pleased to declare so.

There is one passage more I beg leave to remark on. The Governor informs your Lordship, that I have "all along taken the Lead of the Council in their late extraordinary proceedings."

The Council my Lord, see and act for themselves: they have no Leader — no Guide but Law, reason and the Constitution. As they acknowlege no Leader, So neither have they any fondness for a Dictator: in which character, my Lord, Governor Bernard seems lately to have been endeavouring to establish himself.

As the Governor has unjustly represented me the Leader of the Council, I beg leave to assure your Lordship, it is a character that does not belong to me: and I take this occasion wholly to disclaim it. — In regard to the late extraordinary Proceedings (as the Governor is pleased to call them) the Council have wrote your Lordship a full account concerning them. In those and all their other Proceedings they have been actuated by the Principles of duty and loyalty to his Majesty, and by a regard to his Honor, and the welfare of his faithful Subjects of this Province: and with respect to myself in particular, I humbly hope, my Lord, that I have been at least in some measure under the influence of the same principles. I have the Honor to be with the most perfect Regard

My Lord Your Lordship's most obed[t].[5] & most hble Servant

James Bowdoin

The Right hon[ble]. the Earl of Hillsborough.

ALS, RC   CO 5/758, ff 86-89.

Minor emendations not shown. Endorsed: Boston 15th April 1769. M[r]. Bowdoin. R 29 May
– from M[r]. Bollan B. 21.   Variants: CO 5/767, ff 238-246 (L, RLbC); Bowdoin and
Temple Papers, Loose MSS (LS, AC); *Letters to Hillsborough* (1st ed.), 44-47; *Letters to
Hillsborough* (repr.), 86-93.

---

1. **No. 717**.

2. **No. 654**, *Bernard Papers*, 4: 255-257.

3. Obscured by the binding.

4. **No. 717**.

5. Smudged.

Appendix 4

MEMBERS OF THE MASSACHUSETTS COUNCIL
TO THE EARL OF HILLSBOROUGH

Boston April 15th: 1769

My Lord

The Council having received from M[r]: Bollan authenticated Copies of six Letters from Governor Bernard to your Lordship,[1] containing many unjust reflections upon the Council, and divers misrepresentations of their Conduct, and also manifesting his earnest wish and Endeavours to bring about an alteration in the civil Government of the Province,[2] We are obliged in justice to ourselves and the Province, to address your Lordship on the Subject matter of those Letters, and pray your candid attention to what we have now the honor to write to your Lordship.

In the first of the said Letters dated Nov[r]: 1: 1768,[3] Governor Bernard informs your Lordship "he now proceeds to conclude his narrative of his endeavours to get quarters for the King's Troops."

The preceeding part of this narrative we have not seen;[4] but if there be in it the same want of candor as is discoverable in the concluding part, contained in the said Letter, it is necessary for your Lordship's right information to give you our narrative on the same subject, which we shall do as summarily as may be.

On the 19th: of September, the Governor called the Council, and communicated to them a part of your Lordships Letter of the 30th: of July,[5] informing of two Regiments being ordered to Boston, from Ireland; and also communicated a Letter from General Gage, of the 12th: of September,[6] informing of two other Regiments being ordered from Halifax, one of them to Castle William, and the other to the Town; both Letters requiring that quarters be prepared for their reception.

The Halifax Regiments being first expected, the Council immediately Advised, that the Barracks at Castle William should be prepared for the Regiment ordered there. And with regard to the other, as it was an affair that more immediately concerned the Town of Boston, they thought it advisable to appoint a Committee to confer on it with the Selectmen;[7] who on the Conference very justly observed, that by Act of Parliament[8] it was made unlawful to take any measures for Quartering troops till the said Barracks provided by the Province were full: and they said they could do nothing in the Affair.[9] This being reported to the Governor in Council, on the 22[d]:[10] he proposed to the Council that a house in the Town, called the Manufactory house, should be fitted up for the reception of the Troops: but it was objected that the Act of Parliament had in a very particular manner directed the process in Quartering; and that it was not in the Power of the Council to do any thing contrary to that direction.__ The Governor however strongly urged them to it; and was very angry because they declined acting contrary to Act of Parliament:[11] The Council desired an adjournment, that they might give him a written answer to his proposal; which, after repeated refusals, he at length granted.__ On the 24th: they waited on the Governor, and delivered to him their Answer.__ He proposed an alteration in it, which they were then for considering; but he said, they might do it on Monday Morning the 26th: and without the formality of another meeting with him, deliver the answer to the Secretary.__ It was done accordingly, and the answer delivered at that time to the Deputy Secretary, the Secretary himself not being at his Office.[12]

These Circumstances are so minutely mentioned because the Governor took great offence at the Council's ordering their said answer to be published in one of the News Papers of that day; and said he should represent to your Lordship the indignity offered him, by the Councils publishing their answer before it was presented to him. But your Lordship will perceive from the foregoing account, which contains the true state of the fact, that the answer was presented to the Governor, two days before the Publishing of it; and that the Circumstances posterior to it's being presented were quite immaterial, even in the Estimation of the Governor himself.[13]

In the debate on the forementioned proposal it was said by one Gentleman, that Castle William being part of the Town of Boston, it would comport with the requisition for Quartering, to quarter both the Regiments at the Castle. Tho': this was casually said, and no stress laid upon it, and was not adopted by the Council, the Governor notwithstanding represented it to the Commanding Officer of the Regiments as the reason of the Councils not agreeing to his proposal: and it is possible he may have made the same representation to your Lordship. But your Lordship will please to judge of the reasons the Council proceeded upon, by what is contained in their answer aforesaid, and by nothing else; which answer it appears by the printed Votes of the House of Commons[14] was, with other papers, laid before that house the 27th: of November last;[15] it being there called "minutes of Council the 26th: September 1768, extracted from the Boston Gazette", and was inclosed in Governor Bernards Letter to your Lordship of that date;[16] as may be seen in the Votes page 79. N°: 54 of the said papers. __

These minutes are mentioned as extracted from the Boston Gazette: by which it seems the Governor represented to your Lordship that the said answer was published before it was presented to him: and it being said to be extracted from the Boston Gazette, which the Governor stiles a most infamous paper, seems intended to reflect some Infamy on the answer. But the truth is, it was first published in the Massachusetts Gazette (authorized by the Governor and Council) and from thence taken into all the other Boston news Papers.[17]

On the 29th: of September a Council was held at Castle William,[18] Captain Smith Commanding Officer of the Sea Armament, and Lieu[t]: Col[o]: Dalrimple of the Troops, being desired by the Governor to attend.__ The Governor informed those Gentlemen what had been the Resolutions of the Council with regard to Quartering the said Troops, and what he was pleased to call the reason of the resolutions, viz[t]; that the Castle being in the Town of Boston, the Council declined providing quarters for the Troops, before the Barracks at the Castle were full. __

It appears above that the Governor had no foundation for saying the proceeding of the Council was grounded on the reason he mentioned:[19] and he had not the Candor and Justice to inform the said Gentlemen of the written answer aforesaid, containing the true reason of the Proceeding, and of which the Council informed them.

Col[o]: Dalrimple acquainted the Board that his orders from the Commander in Chief were, that one of the Regiments now arrived should be quartered in the Town of Boston, and that he could not consider Castle Island to be in the Town of Boston, within the intention of his orders, that he could not himself depart from the said orders, and that he now made a requisition for quarters accordingly. Whereupon (after the said Gentlemen had retired) his Excellency desired that the Board would reconsider the proposal he had before made to them of fitting up the Manufactory House as a Barracks for the reception of Col[o]: Dalrimple's Regiment, which is the Regiment destined for the Town, in case it can be done at the expence of the Crown; and in Case they should adhere to their former resolution, that they would assign their Reasons therefor.

The Governor was immediately told the Act of Parliament obliged them to adhere to their former resolutions. Whereupon, with such as spoke on the occasion, he entered into an angry dispute, and began to take minutes of what they said in answer to him, in order that he might represent it to administration at home.__[20]

This was objected to as an unfair way of proceeding, and he was told if he wanted a fuller answer than what had already been given, He should have it in writing, if he would give opportunity for it. But this was refused, and he insisted on our immediate Answer. Accordingly an Answer was agreed on, and given to him, and was inclosed in the Governors Letter to your Lordship dated October 1.1768,[21] as your Lordship may see in the printed Votes N[o]: 56 of the said Papers. __

We are very sorry to have reason to complain that in the whole of this affair the Conduct of the Governor was arbitrary and unbecoming the dignity of his Station. __

October 3. Col[o]: Dalrimple being admitted with Cap[t]: Smith before the Board,[22] took occasion to explain the intention of his requisition by Letter viz[t]: That as the Board could not think themselves authorized to provide Barracks in the Town, inasmuch as Barracks had already been provided by the Government at Castle William, he had encamped some of his Troops, and was providing Barracks for the rest in the Town; so that he considered all as in Barracks, and demanded Barrack provisions, agreeable to Act of Parliament. Whereupon his Excellency moved to the Board that they would appoint some suitable Person to make such provision. __

The Council desired time to consider, and give an Answer to his motion; but the Governor refused it, insisting on the Answer immediately. __

However after repeated solicitations, and much altercation, the Governor adjourned the Board to Wednesday October 5th,[23] when they gave him an answer; Copy whereof (as appears by the forementioned printed Votes) was inclosed to your Lordship in the Governors Letter of that date.[24]

Part of the said Answer runs thus, "Advised that agreeable to his Excellency's motion, one or more person or Persons be authorized and appointed, to furnish and supply the Officers and Soldiers, put and placed in the Barracks, with Fire, Candles &c[a]: as particularly mentioned in the Act of Parliament:[25] Provided the Person or Persons so to be authorized and appointed, will take the risk of the Province's paying to him or them, all such sum or sums of money so by them paid, laid out or expended for the purpose aforesaid".

The Governor said that this Proviso defeated the purpose of the Advice, and was intended to defeat it, as every one must be well assured that no person would undertake to advance money at such a risk. His Excellency was told, that without such a Proviso, an undertaker would have an equitable, if not a legal demand, on the Council, to make good all damages, in Case the General Court should refuse to repay him the money advanced. That it would be unreasonable to expect the Council would subject themselves to such a demand; and that in Case they were not subjected by Law, it would be deceiving the undertaker, and be a manifest Act of injustice not to inform him of the Risk: for a risk it must be, as it was impossible for any one to determine what the General Court would do, either in this, or in any other case whatsoever. Whereupon the Governor proposed, in a manner very dictatorial, that the proviso should stand thus, That such Person should undertake this business, upon the Credit of the General Assembly of the Province, according to the intent and meaning of the said Act of Parliament, and not upon the Credit of the particular Persons of the Governor and Council. But this proposed alteration not taking off the risk from the undertaker but in words, and it not being in the power of the Council to pledge the Credit of the General Assembly, it was rejected. It was very unfortunate to the Province, and to his Majesty's Service in general, that the General Court could not be sitting at a time when their aid was so essentially necessary.[26]

On the 12th: of October a full Council was advised to be called on the 26th: in order to consider divers matters of importance which the Governor said he had to lay before the Council.[27] In the mean time General Gage came to Town from New York viz[t]: on Saturday October 15th: and on Monday the 17th: the Governor called a Council,[28] and introduced the General, and here begins the concluding part of the Governor's narrative of his Endeavours to get quarters for the Kings troops, as appears by a Copy of his Letter to your Lordship, dated November 1st: 1768,[29] on which Letter we beg leave to make a few remarks.

It appears by the said Letter the General demanded quarters in Town for the two Regiments then here; and that he should reserve the Barracks at the Castle for the two Irish Regiments expected, or such part of them as they would contain.

The Council represented to the Governor that they had already given their sentiments fully on this subject, in their Answer delivered to him on the 24th: of September, and referred him to that: but this being not satisfactory, they desired him to postpone the Affair to the 26th: when a full Council was expected, agreeable to his appointment. This was refused. Whereupon the Governor proceeded, as he observes, in a Course of Questions, which finally issued in a vote of six against five, that the Governor be desired to order the Manufactory house to be cleared of it's present inhabitants, that it might be fitted up for the reception of such part of the Irish Regiments as could not be accommodated at the Castle Barracks.__ On this affair the Governor observes that the whole was a Scene of perversion, to avoid our doing any thing towards quartering the Troops, unworthy such a Body.[30] We deny that any thing was done to avoid quartering the Troops; on the contrary every thing was done, in the power of the Council, consistent with their ideas of the Act of Parliament; and consistent with what seemed to be the Governors Idea of it on the 19th: of September, when the affair of quartering was moved: for when the Act was produced, and some of the Council had expressed their opinion that, according to the Act, quarters could not be demanded before the Barracks at the Castle were full, the Governor afterwards, in the course of the debate upon it, implicitly acknowledged the propriety of that opinion, by urging it as the Council's duty in the case they were considering, to pay no regard to the Act:[31] which if they had done, he might have justly charged them with perversion unworthy such a Body. __ The Governor having charged the Council with perversion, proceeds immediately to charge them with lying. He says, "that in the course of the Questions he put to them, they denied that they knew of any building belonging to the Province, in the Town of Boston, that was proper for Barracks, and they denied that the manufactory house was such a Building."[32] This was ^so^ notoriously contrary to truth he says, that some Gentlemen expressed their concern that it should remain upon the minutes, and to induce him to consent to its being expunged a motion was made and agreed to relative to the manufactory house: Whereupon he ordered the former answers to be expunged.[33] It was to very little purpose to make this Bargain with the Governor, which it seems was done to save our Char^ac^ter,[34] as he has been the means of spreading the knowledge of it to the whole British Legislature, and with that knowledge the Infamy his representation tends to fix upon us. 'Tis true the Council denied and still ^deny^ that the Manufactory house was proper to be statedly used for Barracks, tho' in that Exigency they consented it should be improved for that purpose, It is capable of being improved in that manner, and so is any other house: but it is not proper that it should be so improved, for many reasons, which it would be impertinent to offer to your Lordship. The concern therefore did not arise from our answer to the Governors Questions being notoriously contrary to truth, but from the Impropriety of the Questions, and the dishonor they would reflect on the Questioner, if entered upon the Records.__ We should not have troubled your Lordship with any observations on a Business so trifling in itself, but it is rendered important to us by the Governors introducing it to traduce our moral character.

"The next thing to be done, says the Governor, was to clear the manufactory house, the preventing of which was a great object of the Sons of Liberty." But of this matter we shall take no farther notice than as it concerns a member of the Council, who is an Overseer of the Poor, and as such with the other Overseers, had the oversight and direction of the Workhouse. "For this purpose (of preventing the clearing the manufactory house) when the report of the Troops coming here was first confirmed, all kinds of People, says the Governor, were thrust into this Building; and the Workhouse itself was opened; and the People confined there were permitted to go into the manufactory house. This was admitted (continues the Governor) to be true in Council, by one of the Board; who is an Overseer of the Poor, and a principal therein." __

This representation is wholly without foundation, and was so far from being admitted to be true by the Gentleman refered to vizt; M^r. Tyler, that he told the Governor when he mentioned it in Council, there was no truth in it; and that he had been greatly imposed on by his informers, Therefore the Governor had no reason to say, in the winding up of his story about the manufactory house "[35]thus this building belonging to the Government and assigned by the Governor and Council for his Majesty's use, is kept filled with the Outcast of the Workhouse, and the Scum of the Town, to prevent it's being used for the accommodation of the King's Troops." [36] We beg leave to refer your Lordship to the Deposition of M^r: Tyler and the other Overseers on this Subject, herewith enclosed.

The Governor next proceeds to narrate his negotiation with the Justices on the Subject of Billeting; But their Conduct it is their own Business to justify, if they think proper. We shall only observe on this part of his Letter, that he has thrown out several censures upon the Council without Foundation, on some of which we shall presently remark.

The Governor concludes this Letter by saying he has already shewn to your Lordship how the order of Council for the purpose of Providing for the two Regiments at Boston, according to act of Parliament, was annulled and avoided in the origination of it; and that the Council have refused to make such an order for providing for the Troops at Boston, as has been made by them for the Troops intended to be stationed at Castle William. __ We have already given your Lordship an account of our Proceedings in this matter, by which we persuade ourselves it will appear to your Lordship, that the Council have done all that was in their power to do, without the aid of the General Assembly, which, from a Clause in the Governors Letter dated November 5, it appears probable he was at liberty to call. Supposing this to be the case, and whether it was so in fact is well known to your Lordship, he ought rather to censure himself than the Council, for neglecting this measure of affecting the thing which measure he has been often solicited to go into.

The Governor's Letter of the 5th: of November[37] is wholly taken up censuring the Conduct of the Council with regard to the Commissioners of the Customs, At a General Council held the 26th: of October[38] he says he "put a very embarrassing Question to them, viz[t]: whether the Commissioners might return to the Town and resume their functions with Safety to themselves and their Officers? If they answered yea, they would be chargeable with advising the return of the Commissioners: if they said No, they would contradict all their assertions, that there was no occasion for Troops to support the Civil Power."

This very embarrassing Question my Lord, had no embarrassment in it: for even on the Supposition that what the Governor in one of his Letters has said be true, that the Council are always for humouring the People, they were however no way apprehensive of being charged by them with advising the return of the Commissioners, if they answered the question in the affirmative. Nor have we any reason to think the Council have been so charged, notwithstanding they did answer so.

The Council did not apprehend themselves obliged to give opinions, and their answer to such a question could be nothing more than an opinion, which the Governor implicitly acknowledges they were not held to give; and tho': he altered the form of the question,[39] and it might be put as he says viz[t]; Whether they would advise him to assure the Commissioners that they might return with Safety? the Answer to it, which was given in the Affirmative, amounts only to this, that he himself, should give his opinion to the Commissioners that they might return with safety for his assuring them that they might return tho': done in consequence of our advice, and our assurance (if it had been added to it) would still be only a matter of opinion: But the principal reason why so much time was spent in this Affair, and in the other proceedings of that Council, the Governor might have found in himself—in his own austerity and incivility.

The Governor has found great fault with the Conduct of the Council towards the Commissioners. "The virulence with which they have been treated seems, he says, to be too violent to be the effect of public zeal only, without the interference of private animosity". The Council, my Lord, even if they had been influenced by meer motives of Resentment, could justify all they have either said or done with regard to the Commissioners, who in divers of their Letters to the Governor, which he laid before the Council, have treated the Council in a very unbecoming manner: one of which Letters,[40] in the time of it, the Council would have animadverted on, but to prevent their doing themselves justice, the Governor withdrew it. They have not however been actuated by resentment or private animosity, but by a regard for the Town and Province: both which the Commissioners, whatever they may have done by their Letters and memorials to Administration, have greatly abused by their retiring (under the pretence of Safety) on board one of his Majestys Ships and afterwards to the Castle: intending hereby that their memorials should have the stronger effect. __ But my Lord, their retiring was voluntary they were not com-pelled to it — they had never been attacked, and 'tis highly probable never would have been, unless they themselves had first concerted the plan of the attack; and that they had concerted such a plan seems probable, from their ordering the Sei-zure of the Sloop liberty on the 10th: of June, with such circumstances of violence, and at such a time of the day, as indicated a design to create a disturbance, which accordingly happened; tho:' trifling in comparison to what it has been represented, they improved as a plausible reason, on which to justify their voluntary flight.[41]

If this has been the Conduct of the Commissioners, which there is too much reason to believe, is it wonderful my Lord, the Council should animadvert upon it? or that they should endeavour to prevent the evil consequences to the Town and Prov-ince, which it had a tendency to bring upon them, and which in fact it has brought.

This is the reason my Lord, on which the proceedings of the Council with regard to the Commissioners are grounded, and not any private animosity, which is basely suggested by Governor Bernard.

These proceedings of the Council which first gave offence to the Governor were on the 27th: and 29th: of July last at which times the Behaviour of the Governor to the Council was so extraordinary,[42] that we beg your Lordship's indulgence to give some account of it. __

On the 27th: of July the governor laid before the Council, with an injunction of Secrecy, a Paper relative to riot[43] in Boston on the 10th: of June, to the proceedings in consequence of it, and to an offer of troops from General Gage: in which paper were a very imperfect account of those proceedings, and some unjust Censures upon the Council.

The Council thought it reasonable they should have time to place those pro-ceedings in a true light; and by so doing, show that they were unjustly censured. But notwithstanding the reasonableness of it, he refused it; and kept them the whole day (saving a short interval for dinner) treating them in a most abusive manner, and worrying them for an immediate answer. But as he could not prevail he adjourned the Council to the 29th: when he had the answer: which by the Votes of the house of Commons it appears the Governor has communicated to your Lordship.

With regard to the injunction of Secrecy it was objected, that from the tenor of the Councellors Oath, and from the nature of the thing, the Governor had no right (exclusive of the Council) to lay any such injunction; and besides, as it was apprehended by people in general, that the calling of that Council was for the purpose of bringing Troops into the Province, it could answer no good end to keep the proceedings (which were against that measure) secret. But the Governor in a manner inconsistent with decency, insisted on the injunction, and the affair was kept Secret to the great and unnecessary uneasiness of the Community. __ The Conduct of the Governor, as it is manifest there was a concerted plan between him and the Commissioners to introduce Troops here, can be accounted for no other way than this, that he apprehended the Publishing those proceedings might possibly retard or prevent the sending of the Troops, which we humbly conceive it probably might, if those proceedings, without the Governors Comments, could have reached your Lordship before his Majesty's orders had been issued.[44]

The sending for Troops has long been a favorite measure with the Governor, who has however appeared desirous it should be thought he has not sent for Troops, and has repeatedly said so: but if he has taken care that the measures of others should be effectual for that purpose, which we have reason to believe, the effect is still the same; and he becomes chargeable with an unmanly dissimulation.

The Governor, not content with censuring the Council for their Conduct in Council, steps beyond his line to bestow his Censures upon them: which he does in a very illiberal manner for their addressing General Gage. __

There are several very exceptionable things previous to his observations on the address; which was unanimous notwithstanding the Governor informs your Lordship that four refused to sign it: for these four were not present when it was settled; and three of them who lived in the country and whose business called them home had never seen it. But with your Lordship's leave we will pass over these things and come to the observations. "It is well known to your Lordship (says the Governor) that this kind of writing is designed for the People and this is notorious in the present Case". __ We acknowledge my Lord, that this address was designed for the people — the people of this Province in general, and of the Town of Boston in particular, who we had reason to think had been grossly vilified and abused by certain memorials and Representations sent from hence to Administration at home, particularly with regard to what have been called the Riots in Boston, on the 18th: of March and 10th: of June 1768:[45] and for the good of this people it was our indispensable duty to endeavor to place those proceedings, with the Cause of them, in a just light; and in this way to abate the resentment such memorials and representations had a tendency to excite against the Town and Province: and with this View, and to prevent a further accession of Troops the address to the General was undertaken and determined on: and with no . . . .[46] design to abuse the Commissioners (who are mentioned but incidentally) notwithstanding Governor Bernard assures your Lordship this was our principal design. His other observations therefore, which are built upon this supposition, are like the baseless Fabrick of a Vision;[47] and which, that we may avoid retorting his unjust reflections, and especially that we may not give your Lordship any unnecessary trouble, we shall take no notice of. __

Now we have had occasion to mention the Riot of the 10th: of June, we cannot refrain mentioning one circumstance concerning it, which is, that the morning after it happened being Saturday, the Governor with advice of the Council appointed a Committee, of such members of the Board as were qualified to act as justices of the Peace in the County of Suffolk, to make enquiry into the particular facts as soon as may be, and report to the Governor in Council, that so they might take proper measures on so interesting an occasion and the Governor desired the Committee to meet him on Monday morning, in order with him to proceed on the Enquiry: but on that morning instead of proceeding on the enquiry he postponed it, as appears by the Council minute[48] and never after resumed it. This seemed strange in the time of it, but the reason appears more clearly since our seeing the printed votes of the House of Commons, where among the Papers on American affairs, laid before the House, there are mentioned Depositions relative to said Riot: enclosed to your Lordship in Governor Bernards Letter dated 14 June 1768[49] and mentioned in the said Votes.

Now my Lord, is it any way uncharitable to suppose the Governor postponed the Enquiry with the said Justices, in order that there might be no contradiction between the Depositions that might have been thus jointly taken, and such as he had enclosed to your Lordship? was it not more likely my Lord, that a true State of the Facts might have been brought forth by such a joint enquiry, than by a seperate one? On the one hand, it might be said the Justices without the Governor would be most inquisitive after Facts and circumstances that would place the delinquents in the most favorable Light; and on the other hand, that the Governor might run into the Contrary extreme, which would place them in the worst light: and if this should be thought probable on both hands, from both of them conjunctly the exact State of Facts might have been expected. It is therefore greatly to be regretted, and argues a disposition and design in the Governor to represent things in the worst light, that he postponed, and never after resumed the enquiry: And the Representations, contained in Authenticated Copies of his six Letters transmitted to us, are a demonstration of such a disposition; and of a disposition, under the pretence of magnifying the Kings power, to make his own arbitrary and uncontrolable.

In the Governors' Letter of the 12th: of November[50] he reports to your Lordship how he proceeded in admonishing the justices: and expresses his displeasure,"[51] that the Council would not act with him in this Business; nor advise to any method of enforcing the order contained in your Lordship's ~~in your Lordships~~ Letter; and that he could make nothing of them but passive associates." The Council my Lord, apprehended it highly proper, that before the justices were censured, they should be informed of the charges against them, and heard in their defence. And because the Council desired to be excused acting in this business before such information and hearing, they are thus most grossly abused, and misrepresented by the Governor. He insinuates that the Council impeached the truth and justice of your Lordships Letter, both of which, he says, he observed to them were founded on notorious facts. This charge they deny. They might doubt and had great reason ^to doubt^ the facts on which your Lordship's letter was founded, and which were represented by the Governor, without impeaching your Lordships truth or Justice.

In the Course of the two last Conferences with the Council,[52] "he had an opportunity he says, to Observe upon and lament the Servility, in regard to the people, with which the Business of Council was now done in Comparison to what used to be."

Whatever character former Councils may have been of, the present Council humbly trust my Lord, that such an unworthy one as this does not belong to them; but if it should they will not add to the indignity of it by any Act of servility to his Excellency. The Governor would prove the Servility of the Council by saying that one Gentleman said, he did not enter the Council Chamber with that free mind he used to have; but as he liked to be concerned in public business, he must be content to hold his place upon such terms as he could. A Gentleman of the Council has divers times said that he did not enter the Council chamber with the same pleasure he used to, and the reason he assigned was, the angry disputes which had subsisted for some time between the Governor and the Council: he has likewise said he liked to be concerned in in[53] Public Business but he absolutely denies his saying and there's no one of the Council remembers he ever said, that he must be content to hold his place upon such Terms as he could; or anything tending to convey such an Idea. This is the whole matter upon which the Governor builds the infamous Character he has given of the Council to your Lordship. The anecdotes ~~will~~ ^which^ the Governor calls trifling are really so in themselves; and not only trifling but untrue, and discover great malignity towards the Council, not only as a Body, but as individuals. Tho:' the anecdotes are trifling in themselves, they are not so with regard to the purpose he intended they should answer: for if the Council be such Servile wretches as he has represented them to your Lordship if they would be content to hold their places upon such terms as they can — it is high time my Lord, they should be removed: and if a Seat at the Council Board, under the present form of Government, can be held by no other tenure, it is become quite necessary (as the Governor observes) "that the King should have the Council Chamber in his own hands."

The Governors next letter to your Lordship is dated November 14th:[54] in which he considers that part of his orders which he relates to the reforming the Bench of Justices: in which letter, as in all the rest, he is very liberal in his abuses of the Council — "They make he says the humouring of the People their chief object — the majority of the Council has avowed (indirectly at least) the same principles and now appear to Act in concert with that party from whence the opposition to Parliament originated."__ "They are the Creatures of the People and will never join with the Governor in censuring the overflowings of liberty, &c". But we shall pass them as undeserving further notice. __ There are several other things in this letter worthy of remark, which we beg leave here to mention.

It is a great defect he says in this Government, that the King has no Power over the Commissions, which are granted in his name and under his Seal. __

But if this be a defect, there's a similar defect in the Government of England, with regard to similar Commissions, But your Lordship is sensible, this is so far from being a defect with respect to some Commissions, particularly those of the Judges in England, that the King having no power over them is esteemed the strongest security to the Liberties and property of the subject. The removal of the pretended defect here would put all the Judges justices and other Civil Officers under the Power of a Governor, whose power already, if a good Governor, is apprehended to be sufficiently extensive; and if an arbitrary and oppressive one, much too extensive.[55]

The Governor next attempts to prove that there is such a defect in this Government: but his argument is cloudy and wholly inconclusive.

He observes in it, "the Council of this Province is as much out of the controul of the King, as the House of Representatives is".[56] But this is a very great mistake, as his Majesty's Governor has a negative annually upon the Choice of every Member of the Council; and has none at all upon the Representatives. It is also a mistake in him to say, "that when the Governor has once set the King's Seal to a Commission, it is forever out of the hands of the Crown; and the person who has obtained it may thenceforth defy the King, oppose his Laws and insult his Government, and be in no danger of losing his Commission for as the Governor himself adds the Governor with the Advice of the Council can Supercede him. But if he acts in a popular cause the Council, who are themselves the Creatures of the People will never join with the Governor in censuring the overflowing of Liberty".

The Council my Lord are no more the Creatures of the People than of the Governor, as his approbation of the election is necessary to their existence; and they are much more likely to be under the influence of a Governor than of the People; and therefore much more likely to join with him in censuring the overflowings of Liberty,[57] than the contrary. But my Lord, at the worst, supposing such a magistrate should escape censure thro': the fault of the Council, would it not be better that an instance of that sort should now and then happen, than that a Governor a thousand leagues distant from the throne, should be entrusted with a power so exorbitant and uncontrolable, as Governor Bernard is endeavouring to acquire; but which we humbly hope our gracious Sovereign will never entrust either with him or any of his Successors.

This exorbitant power M[r]: Bernard is for extending to all the Governors in his Majesty's Colonies, and proposes or rather dictates, that it should be done by a general act of Parliament, vesting such a power in the Crown. But "it will not be necessary he says, that such an act should be general. it is more wanted in this Government than in all the other together: and even here the defect will be cured by a Royal Council".

This is the least my Lord, that will content him. But we humbly trust in his Majesty's Goodness that the Charter of the Province with all the rights and Priviledges, granted by it to this People, will be continued to them, notwithstanding the machinations of Governor Bernard and all other enemies of the Constitution.

The Governors letter of the 30th: of November[58] being wholly relative to the Conversation between the Governor and M[r]: Bowdoin on the prayer of the Councils petition to his Majesty, M[r]: Bowdoin will have the honor of writing to your Lordship on that Subject. __[59]

The Governors Letter of the 5th: of December[60] Relative to the Councils' Petitions to the two Houses of Parliament[61] is principally designed to frustrate them; to give your Lordship a wrong idea of many of the circumstances attending the agreeing on them; and to let you know that the Council is brought under such awe of their Constituents by the frequent removal of the friends of Government, as that there is very little exercise for private judgment in popular Questions. __ We thought till the Receipt of this Letter of his, that the whole of your Conduct in this matter at least was in no instance excepted to by him: But we have found ourselves mistaken .__ There is nothing in this Letter very material and therefore without taking further notice of it, we beg leave to give your Lordship some Account of the origination of these Petitions. __ Your Lordship will therefore please to be informed, That at the last Sitting of the General Court, the Council thought it necessary to petition his Majesty, and both Houses of Parliament, on the Subject of the Acts of Parliament for raising a revenue from the Colonies, and divers times considered it. As it was apprehended the Session would be a long one on account of the Settlement of the valuation of Estates through the Province, the Council did not appoint a Committee to prepare the petitions, before the Governor Communicated on the 24th: of June, the latter part of your Lordship's letter[62] Signifying his Majesty's pleasure relative to the dissolution of the General Court. The Committee reported the draft of the petition to the King on the 29th: when it seems the Governor had determined to Prorogue the Court.

The Petition had been read, and was under consideration when the Message to the Governor from the House in Answer to the requisition for rescinding certain Resolves, interrupted the proceeding in it: But after receiving the said message the Governor would not suffer it to be resumed thô: earnestly requested, and without any necessity immediately Prorogued the Court, which prevented the Council petitioning in their legislative Capacity: in which capacity the Governor could not dispute the Council's right to petition independent of him. __ They thought it very unkind and very unjust, that he would not suffer them to compleat their petitions, which might have been done the next day; and they cannot account for that very hasty and abrupt prorogation but by supposing it proceeded from an intention to prevent or frustrate the said Petitions, and to stop a remonstrance to his Majesty against him, which was then debating in the House of Representatives.__ With regard to the said Petition immediately after the Prorogation it was moved in Council to proceed upon them, but the Governor interposed and insisted that the Council had no right to do it without him. __ A Committee after much Altercation was finally with his Consent appointed to prepare a Petition to the King and the King only, the Governor insisting that the Committee should not be Authorized to prepare Petitions to the Lords and Commons: which shewed his intention to prevent the Petitions to the two Houses of Parliament: and in regard to the Petition to his Majesty it has been apprehended he designed to frustrate that. __ This last mentioned Petition, at the Council's desire, was by the Governor, in whom they then thought they could place some confidence, transmitted to your Lordship,[63] with their humble request, that your Lordship would lay it before his Majesty. In the Prayer of it a word is used which the Governor is apprehended to have laid hold of to draw a sense very different from what he knew the Council intended; and that accordingly in writing to your Lordship he introduced the prayer of it in such a manner, as to make it seem that the Council intended to petition against the Revenue money being drawn, or sent from America, rather than for the Repeal of the Revenue Acts.[64] But however this may be (about which we are not yet Satisfied, notwithstanding the Governor is pleased to say we are) it occasioned our petitions to the two houses of Parliament, in which, that we might not be misapprehended from any reasonings of the Governor on the Prayer of our Petition to his Majesty, we have prayed for the repeal of those Acts in the most explicit manner. __ With regard to the Councils Petition transmitted to your Lordship by the Governor, we take this occasion to thank your Lordship for laying it before his Majesty.[65]

And now my Lord, having given your Lordship a general Account of the Councils Proceedings, in which they have acted (in a manner his Majesty expects they should act) agreeable to their Oaths and Consciences, and with an unremitting regard to his Service honor and Government, they humbly beg leave to express their deep sorrow and distress on account of his Majesty's displeasure, which the Town and Province at present experience.

The Dissolution of the General Court — the Ships of War stationed here — Troops in possession of the Town — the precautions taken to prevent any intelligence coming hither of the embarking of the Troops from Halifax, and the circumstances attending their landing here, as if in an Enemy's Country — all indicate the frowns and displeasure of his Majesty. __ We do not yet certainly know all the means by which this has happened: nor do we yet certainly know all our accusers. But we apprehend the representations and memorials, that have been made by Governor Bernard, the Commissioners of the Customs, and some other Persons, concerning the disorders and riotous proceedings, which happened in the Town of Boston in March and June 1768, have brought upon them that misfortune. What happened in March was of no consideration, and it must indicate a great degree of malevolence to represent it to the disadvantage of the Town.__ What happened on the 10th: of June, thô: highly unwarrantable and unjustifiable, was attended with circumstances, that make it probable a riot was planned, and hoped for, by some of those persons, who most exclaimed against it, and have made it the Subject of those Memorials and representations.__ But for a fuller detail of those disorders and the apprehended occasion of them, we beg leave to refer your Lordship to the proceedings of Council on the 29th: of July last,[66] and to their Address to General Gage of the 27th: of October[67] both which have been communicated to your Lordship by the Governor,[68] and which we humbly hope, notwithstanding they were accompanied with his animadversions, have induced his Majesty to look upon the Town of Boston, in a more favourable light than the Authors of the aforesaid memorials and representations are desirous he should.

Upon the whole my Lord we are constrained to say that Governor Bernards great aim (as evidently appears by his Letters) is the destruction of our Constitution derived to us by Charter, and as Englishmen; and that in his Letters to your Lordship he hath stuck at nothing to affect this purpose. A Constitution dearly purchased by our ancestors, and dear to us, and which we persuade ourselves will be continued to us notwithstanding the Representations in his Letters; the Truth of which depends solely upon his own averment.[69] The most material things charged upon the Council are, their not doing their duty with respect to the providing Quarters for the Kings Troops posted at Boston: and a general omission of duty arising from their Servility to the Populace, the pleasing of whom hath according to his Representation been the rule of their conduct — both without foundation, or even a colour of Truth. In addition to what has been already observed, we beg leave further to remark that such hath been the zeal of his Majesty's Council for his Majesty's Service that they have done every thing within their power or rather have exceeded the Authority given them by the Act for Punishing Mutiny and Desertion to promote it.[70]__ About the Beginning of the late War, when there arrived a number of his Majesty's Troops in the Harbour of Boston, immediately and without the least hesitation the Barracks at Castle William within the Territory's of Boston and but three miles from the Center of the Town were built by the Province for the accommodation of the King's Troops and were the best and most commodious of any in North America in the Judgment of Sir Jeffry Amherst when he was here.__[71] These were by the Council provided for those Troops, and furnished with every thing that by the Act aforesaid was required, and even beyond its demands, and the like provision has been made divers times since as Troops have occasionally arrived here. And now again, upon the news that his Majesty had ordered Troops hither,[72] the Council directed the Provincial Commissary General, that the Barracks aforesaid should be put into proper order for their reception, and that Barrack Utensils &c should be provided with the utmost expedition, which was done accordingly.__ These are facts that no one can deny. But it has been said that the Council did not exert themselves for the provision of the Troops in Boston__ to which it is answered that if they did every thing that by the act of Parliament they were obliged to or might do, surely they did their duty; and are not to be blamed, this was the Case, nor did they omit anything within their department. __

By the preamble of the Act it appears plain that the public Houses and Barracks are first to be filled. By the first enacting clause the Constables, Tithing men &c are required to quarter and Billet the Soldiers and in their absence or default a Justice of the Peace is to do it, they and *no others*: consequently if the Council had quartered any Soldiers at any place even in Inns or Livery Stables against the mind of the owner, he could maintain Trespass and no order of Governor and Council could have defeated the Action. But in case there should not be sufficient room for the Officers and Soldiers in such Barracks Inns &c; that in such and no other case, and upon no other Account it shall and may be lawfull for the Governor and Council to order quarters: from whence it clearly appears the Council exceeded their Authority in Favor of his Majesty's Troops rather than otherwise. Is it not manifest my Lord that the Governor and Council had no right to meddle in the quartering aforesaid, excepting it was for the residue of such Officers and Soldiers for whom there might not be room in such Barracks, Inns and public places? Then, and in that case, upon that Account, and in no other case, had the Governor and Council any right power or Authority to give Orders touching the quartering the said residue: but this never took place, none were quartered as directed by said Act Saving those at the Barracks at Castle William: this is the Act of Parliament, which is a penal Statute, and every penal Statute, is to be construed strictly. It never was in the intention of the Council to evade the Act in the least measure, or give it such a construction as would render it of no effect in this Province, notwithstanding what the Governor hath most injuriously suggested to the contrary.___ This act respects his Majesty's Troops either when at Winter Quarters, or when upon their March or both; it is not to be imagined that the Parliament of Great Britain when they made this Act, had in contemplation, that there would be a great number of the Kings troops sent to the Plantations to keep the Kings peace there which the Troops have no Authority to do, simply considered as the Kings troops, but only as part of Posse Coramitatus[73] under the direction of the Civil Majestrate; but whether this was the intention of Parliament or not, the King has a right to send his Troops where he in his great wisdom shall think best, and to resist the Kings troops in their landing, on their march or at quarters is Rebellion and High Treason; and it would be very unbecoming his Majesty's Council not to give them all that assistance they were Commanded by Law to give them. __ The sentiment of the Council is this, that when the Troops are at quarters in the same Town where there are good Barracks provided, these must be filled first. But the Council never were so absurd as to construe the Act that when the Kings Troops were upon the march a hundred miles from such Barracks that then no provision should be made for them on their march; in such case my Lord the same Provision ought to be, and would be made for them as if no Barracks had been in the Province.

As to the omission of Duty particularly with regard to the suppressing Riots, Mobs, Disorders, or the like, the Council can with truth say, it is not in the Governors Power to give one instance, wherein they have not exerted themselves to the utmost to suppress them; In proof of their having done so, they can appeal to their Answer to the Governor relative to a libell published against him; to the Proclamation they have advised him to issue; to the orders they have given the Attorney General to prosecute those who have been Rioters, or otherwise, Disturbers of the Peace; and to the Rewards offered to induce persons to bring them to Justice.[74] The Governor never laid any thing of this matter before the Council, wherein they were not as fond of having the Transgressors brought to condign Punishment as the Governor himself; and of taking every legal measure to effect it.__ Nor do we know any instance of any majistrate being complained of before the Governor and Council, but what the Council carried their Resentments as high against him as the Governor and some of them much higher: Why then should the Tenure of such Officers commissions depend on the Will of the Governor, which is what he greatly desires and which will be the Case, should he succeed in his desire, such a dependence is quite Contrary to the Tenure by which the Judges in England before the Accession of His present Majesty held their Commissions; and much more so now, since their Commissions continue in force notwithstanding the Demise of the King. If there has been no instance since the Charter of a Difference in Sentiment between the Governor and Council to the present time relative to the displacing or superceeding any Civil Officer (and we don't know of one) what foundation can there be for the Governors Complaint and the representations he has given, but what arises more from unjust and ungrateful prejudice against the Province than a Real Regard to the Kings Authority? How he cou'd write to your Lordship that his Informations to you were founded on the strictest truth and Candour is truly Surprizing; and to declare as he has divers times done that he never wrote to the prejudice of this Country, shews what Credit his Letters deserve, If the Governor knows there are any Persons in the Magistracy that have acted a part unworthy or inconsistent with their Office, was he not in Duty to His Majesty bound to exhibit a complaint against such to the Council, and when he should observe any failure on the part of the Council to Remove such persons, it would have been early enough for the Governor to represent the Council in the unkind and unjust light he hath done. It hath been the Happiness of his Majesty's Council from the Grant of the Charter till lately to be on the best terms with the Kings Representative; There have indeed be frequent disputes between the Governor and the House of Representatives but never (that we know of) between the Governor and the Council till now. That it is so at this day is our unhappiness not our Crime; Never was there a Council that have born so much from a Governor as the present Council have born from Governor Bernard; How often, have they been threatned by him that in case they would not come into his measures, he would lay their Conduct before the ministry, How often hath he demanded answers to his Questions immediately, purely to insnare them, without allowing them time to consider the Subject, or to assign the Reasons of their Answers? The answer must be given immediately either Yes or No; In how many Instances has He demanded the Advice of the Council on their Oaths, relative to matters of no publick Concern, and altogether foreign to the true Intention of their Oaths as Councellors, and on which they were not obliged by their oath of Office to give their advice or to make any answer? How often hath he upon his asking advice refused receiving it because it did not suit him? And thô: nothing can be more absurd than to ask advice, and tell the person of whom it is asked, that it must be in this or the other manner (in which case it is the Advice of the person asking advice, and not the advice of them from whom it is demanded) yet this has been very much his Practice. __

How kind and just would it have been in Governor Bernard to let the Council have previously known the several articles of his intended Complaint against them[75] and of his purpose (as far as in him lay) to bring about such essential and Fundamental Alterations in the Constitution of this Government, as he had endeavoured to do, that they might have had oppertunity of answering for themselves and their Country, and not to be condemned (as he intended they should be) unheard: especially at a Time when there was no House of Representatives to defend the Province. Had he been, what his Station required him to be, the Father of this People, He would have done it; and by so doing have had the applause of the King his Royal master, who delights in nothing so much as in doing Justice himself and seeing all in Authority under him immitating his Royal example. __

It is Plain my Lord that the People of this Province of all Ranks, Orders and Conditions (with but few exceptions) have lost all Confidence in Governor Bernard and He in them: Wherefore, from the Highest sense of Duty to his Majesty (whose Honor and Interest is very near our Hearts) and from a just regard to this Province and to all the Colonies and Provinces on this Continent, we most humbly Submit to your Lordship whether His Majesty's Service can be carried on with advantage during his Administration.

We have the honor to be with the most perfect regard —
My Lord Your Lordship's most obedient & most humble Servants

Members of his Majesty's Council[76]

Samuel Danforth
Isaac Royall
John Erving
Wm Brattle

James Bowdoin
Thos Hubbard
Harrison Gray
James Russell
Royal Tyler
James Pitts
Saml Dexter

The Right hon^ble. the Earl of Hillsborough

RC, LS   CO 5/758, ff 90-104.

Minor emendations not shown. In handwriting of John Cotton. The document was probably drafted by James Bowdoin.[77] The quotations refer to the authentic copies of FB's six letters that had been sent to Samuel Danforth by William Bollan with a cover dated 30 Jan. 1769 (**Appendix 2**). The quotations in **Appendix 4** are not wholly accurate transcriptions but are generally faithful to the wording and intent of the governor's letters. Missing quotation marks have been supplied, as indicated. Endorsed: Boston 15 April 1769 M^r: Danforth and Ten others Members of the Council R 29th May from Mr Bollan. B. 22. Enclosed a deposition of the overseers of the poor of Boston, 15 Apr. 1769 (MsS, RC), CO 5/758, ff 106-107. The package was enclosed in Samuel Danforth to William Bollan, 15 Apr. 1769 (not found).[78] The letter was later published in *Letters to Hillsborough* (1st ed.), 23-43; *Letters to Hillsborough* (repr.), 44-86.

William Bollan personally delivered this letter to the earl of Hillsborough at his London residence, but upon being refused admission left it with his servant. At a second meeting, probably in mid-June, Bollan was admitted and engaged the secretary of state in "a conversation of some length & freedom." Bollan urged the repeal of all the revenue acts, in accordance with the Council's position, but was unable to elicit Hillsborough's personal views on the topic. Hillsborough did "express . . . a very high regard for the conduct of Gov.ʳ Bernard, consider'd in relation to this kingdom and the Province." But he refused Bollan's request for copies of the governor's correspondence, insisting that "no copies of state papers cou'd be given without the King's order." However, other "political consultation[s],"convinced Bollan that Hillsborough "has not the chief ministerial direction of American affairs" and that, provided the colonies gave no further offence, the administration could move the repeal of the Townshend Revenue Act in the next session.[79]

Bollan was not far off the mark in presuming that the secretary's influence was waning. The cabinet and king had already contained Hillsborough's eagerness for taking punitive measures against the Massachusetts Whigs (see source note to **No. 743**), though it would be a while before they decided on repealing the Revenue Act. But Bollan was naive to think that Hillsborough might distance himself from FB, now that he had recalled him, even though the secretary of state probably did not yet know about Bollan's part in exposing the Bernard Letters.

---

1. **Nos. 706**, **708**, **709**, **711**, **717**, and **718**, all enclosed in **Appendix 2**.

2. In coming to this conclusion, the Council were not only following the contents of FB's six letters. In only one of the letters did FB openly recommend reforming the Council, the province's upper legislative chamber and advisory body to the governor, by proposing that the Crown appoint members directly: the "King should have the Council chamber in his own hands. How this can be done may be a question; the Exigency of it is none." (**No. 709**). This came after weeks of delay and obstruction in finding quarters for the British regiments stationed in the town. The proposal was also made in the context of reconstituting the province's magistracy by an act of Parliament, which councilors would have deemed an unprecedented intervention. (**No. 711**.) Such phrases likely resonated in the private conversations of the Massachusetts Whigs with the same frequency as TH's reflective comment that sustained opposition might result in an "abridgement of what are called English liberties." Like FB, TH delivered his damning judgment in private (on 20 Jan. 1769, three days before publication of FB's letters in the *Boston Gazette* and two months before the Council received Bollan's first "parcel" of authenticated copies); his observation was accorded *ex post facto* infamy when the letter was published in 1773.* Councilors probably found FB's blunt language just as shocking as they would TH's. The discovery confirmed what many already suspected was FB's enthusiasm for reforming colonial government, at least what could be gleaned from the governor's public pronouncements. As yet, the Whigs had not accessed FB's previous or recent correspondence in which he discussed his reform ideas in more detail. *Bernard Papers*, 3: 99-101, 108-109, 118, 188, 214-215; 293, 368; for 1768 see **No. 736**.

    * *Copy of Letters Sent to Great-Britain, by His Excellency Thomas Hutchinson, the Hon. Andrew Oliver, and Several Other Persons, Born And Educated Among Us: Which Original Letters Have Been Returned to America, and . : . In Which . . . the Judicious Reader Will Discover the Fatal Source of the Confusion and Bloodshed in Which This Province Especially Has Been Involved, and Which Threatned Total Destruction to the Liberties of All America* (Boston: Edes and Gill, 1773), 16.

3. **No. 706**.

4. See **Nos. 700** and **703**, which were among the second "parcel" of Bernard Letters dispatched by Bollan in June.

5. **No. 661,** *Bernard Papers*, 4: 271-276; for the proceedings see CO5/827, ff 59-60.

6. **No. 675,** *Bernard Papers*, 4: 304.

7. 10 Sept. 1768, *Reports of the Record Commissioners of Boston*, 20: 307-308.

8. The Quartering Act, 5 Geo. 3, c. 33 (1765).

9. The position taken by the Council and Boston selectmen was legally correct, and thus provided some justification for delaying the quartering of troops within Boston. But a strict interpretation of the law in this case did nothing to resolve FB's problem of finding suitable billets before the onset of winter, since putting soldiers in public houses was only likely to increase friction with the local residents. See 5 Geo. 3, c. 33, sect. 1 extracted in **No. 686**n4, *Bernard Papers*, 4: 336.

10. Proceedings in CO 5/827, f 60. FB's account is in **No. 706**.

11. Thus in manuscript.

12. CO 5/827, ff 60-61.

13. The chronology is correct. The Council's answer was published in the *Massachusetts Gazette*, 26 Sept. 1768. But FB's main objection, not addressed by **Appendix 4**, was that he interrupted "one of the Council [*James Bowdoin*] with the printer [*Richard Draper*] correcting the press: after which & not before, the paper was delivered to me." **No. 690**, *Bernard Papers*, 4: 347-351.

14. Printed in the *Boston Weekly News-Letter*, 7 Apr. 1769.

15. 28 Nov. *HCJ*, 32: 74-76.

16. **No. 690**, *Bernard Papers*, 4: 347-351.

17. The chronology explained here was probably correct but the Council's answer, along with a note of proceedings between 23 and 26 Sept., was printed in the *Boston Gazette* later the same day. The House of Commons' record of 28 Nov. is wrong: FB did not enclose the *Boston Gazette* with **No. 693** but the *Massachusetts Gazette*. The House of Commons' clerk of papers probably assumed FB was referring to the *Boston Gazette* when he described the Council's answer as a "most inflammatory Paper" in **No. 690**, having depicted the paper in similar terms in other letters listed among Parliament's American correspondence. *Bernard Papers*, 4: 347-351; *HCJ*, 32: 76.

18. CO 5/827, f 62.

19. The Council's main objection in the answer delivered on 26 Sept. was that barracks should be filled before any troops were quartered in public buildings, as the Quartering Act stated; that would have meant locating both the 14th and 29th regiments in the barracks on Castle Island. Both FB and Dalrymple argued that this would defeat the purpose of Dalrymple's orders, which stated that troops were to be billeted within the town. All parties were well acquainted with the law. The Council's strict constructionist position was legally correct, and was restated forcefully in the letter to Hillsborough; whereas FB and Dalrymple considered this approach a delaying tactic. CO 5/827, ff 60-63.

20. These "minutes" were rendered as **No. 693**, enclosed with **No. 690**, *Bernard Papers*, 4: 347-351, 355-356.

21. **No. 694**, ibid., 63-68.

22. CO 5/827, f 63.

23. CO 5/827, ff 63-64.

24. **No. 700**.

25. 5 Geo. 3, c. 33 (1765).

26. FB had dissolved the General Court in accordance with Hillsborough's instructions in **No. 608**, *Bernard Papers*, 4: 149-152.

27. CO 5/827, f 64.

28. CO 5/827, ff 64-65.

29. **No. 706**.

30. Thus in manuscript.

31. This is the only account of what was said in the debate of 19 Sept., which is unreported in the official minutes CO 5/827, ff 60-61.

32. Closing quotation marks supplied.

33. This word is written over an erasure; the first form is indistinct.

34. The first written form "save our Charter" may be symptomatic of the scribe John Cotton's own concern that the imperial government might revoke the Province Charter, as Bowdoin and the other councilors feared.

35. Editorially supplied for this quotation.

36. Editorially supplied.

37. **No. 708**.

38. CO 5/827, ff 65-66.

39. The official record notes the Council's affirmative answer to the first form of the question only: "Whether they would advise him to acquaint the Commissioners that in their opinion they may resume the execution of their Office in the Town without resistance or danger to themselves and Officers?" CO 5/827, ff 65-66.

40. Not identified.

41. The notion that the commissioners of Customs had had a settled plan to provoke crowd action was a key feature of Whig political literature. The trigger of the riot of 10 Jun., according to the Council's deliberations on 29 Jul. (CO 5/827, ff 53-56), was the commissioners' anchoring the *Liberty* alongside HMS *Romney* in Boston harbor. Whether or not at the time the Council truly believed the commissioners' plan went beyond the seizure of the sloop and the pursuit of its owner, John Hancock, is probably beside the point; they little doubted that the commissioners would justify their retreat to Castle William by representing Bostonians as hostile and violent. The accusation in **Appendix 4** that the commissioners determinedly misrepresented the town was a counter-offensive against the commissioners' memorials in which the town had been "grossly vilified and abused" (the Council rightly assuming that the *Liberty* riot was condemned as seditious) and FB's exaggerated claims of violent disorder in *Letters to Hillsborough*. Later in the document, the Council implicated FB and the commissioners in a "concerted plan" to bring British Regulars to Boston. But it was not until August that that they acquired documentary evidence to justify the accusations, found among the second "parcel" of Bernard Letters received from William Bollan.

42. CO 5/827, ff 52-56. Here the Council reveals that FB showed them a "Paper" on 27 Jul. This is not recorded in the minutes and may have been FB's letter to Gage of 18 Jul. **No. 655**, *Bernard Papers*, 4: 257-258. FB's intention may have been to demonstrate that he would not request troops without the Council's agreement (see **No. 660**n9, ibid., 270). Yet the Council, then and later, thought him more mendacious than maladroit in his dealings, complaining to Hillsborough in **Appendix 4** of the governor's "unmanly dissimulation" in getting the British to send troops direct to Boston.

43. Thus in manuscript.

44. This paragraph amounts to a defence of the Council's decision to publish their proceedings of 27 and 29 Jul. and 3 and 5 Oct. 1768 in the province newspapers, on 10 Oct. 1768. As such it anticipates FB's criticism of James Bowdoin's liaison with the printers, in **No. 703**, which the Council would not read until Aug. 1769.

45. The Council acquired the American Board of Customs' memorial on the *Liberty* riot (**Appendix 6,** *Bernard Papers*, 4: 377-378) in August, but not the memorial in which the Board discussed the disorders of Mar. 1768 (**Appendix 3**).

46. Thus in manuscript; the ellipses may have represented a space into which another word was to be inserted after the scribe had finished writing out the fair copy.

47. The seriousness of the moment was lightened by the optimism of this quotation from William Shakespeare, consigning FB to history.

> . . . . be cheerful, sir.
> Our revels now are ended. These our actors,
> As I foretold you, were all spirits and
> Are melted into air, into thin air:
> And, like the baseless fabric of this vision
> . . . . shall dissolve

> (*The Tempest*, 4.1.151).

48. 13 Jun 1768, CO 5/827, f 48.

49. **No. 630**, *Bernard Papers*, 4: 201-205.

50. **No. 709**.

51. Editorially supplied.

52. On 9 and 10 Nov 1768. CO 5/827, f 67.

53. Thus in manuscript.

54. **No. 711**.

55. FB had recommended the Crown reconstitute the commission for the justices of the peace, thus allowing the governor to appoint magistrates anew. He also considered the benefits of a royally-appointed Council. While FB did not address provincial judges in **No. 711** the principle still applied, as the Council argued: provincial judges appointed directly by the Crown would not have the safeguards of judicial independence that Crown-appointed judges in England enjoyed.

56. The starting quotation marks have been editorially supplied for both quotations in this paragraph; the closing marks are present in the manuscript.

57. As the letter moved toward its climax, the Council countered FB's accusations of populism with a classic formulation from Whig political theory: as the upper legislative chamber and advisory body to the executive, the Council properly maintained the balance of power in the province's mixed constitution, correcting the excesses of both people and governors. Here FB was exhibited as the archetypal, grasping governor—redolent even of the Roman tyrant Verres—whose misdemeanors would continue to jeopardize good government unless he were removed. The intimation of impeachment was an appeal to Hillsborough's political sensibilities that scapegoating FB would at least encourage others to do their duty.

58. **No. 717**.

59. **Appendix 3**.

60. **No. 718**.

61. Petitions of the [*major part of the*] Massachusetts Council to the House of Commons and the House of Lords, c. 30 Nov. 1768. There is a signed copy of the Council's petition to the Lords in Bowdoin and Temple Papers, Loose MSS; the petition to the Commons is in *Letters to Hillsborough* (1st ed.), 70-73.

62. **No. 608**, *Bernard Papers*, 4: 149-152.

63. **Appendix 11**, *Bernard Papers*, 4: 392-396, enclosed in **No. 654**, ibid., 255-257.

64. For more detail see the source note to **No. 717**.

65. Tactically, this was tactfully evasive. While Hillsborough received the petition on behalf of the king he presented it to Parliament on 28 Nov., as an enclosure to **No. 654**, *Bernard Papers*, 4: 255-257. Thus, he denied the Council the opportunity of communicating directly with the His Majesty in Council. *HCJ*, 32: 75.

66. Minutes of the Massachusetts Council of 29 Jul. 1768. FB had enclosed a copy to Hillsborough with **No. 660**, *Bernard Papers*, 4: 251. It is filed in CO 5/757, ff 366-368.

67. **Appendix 1**.

68. The minutes of 29 Jul. were enclosed in **No. 660**, *Bernard Papers*, 4: 266-270; a newspaper copy of the address to Gage was enclosed with **No. 708**.

69. That is, his own reading of the evidence and interpretation in relation to the law. *OED*.

70. The Quartering Act, 5 Geo. 3, c. 33 (1765).

71. The province spent over £800 in building the barracks and repairing the out-buildings during 1754 and 1755. *Acts and Resolves*, 16: 254, 293. Subsequent improvements to the Castle's defences are discussed in FB's letter to Jeffrey Amherst of 28 Dec. 1761, **No. 84**, *Bernard Papers*, 1: 169-170.

72. First written as "here".

73. Probably a scribal error for "comitatus".

74. See **No. 672** for FB's account of the failure of these measures, *Bernard Papers*, 4: 295-300.

75. Thus in manuscript. The intended meaning was probably: "How kind and just would it have been in Governor Bernard to let the Council *know previously* the several articles of his intended Complaint against them . . . ."

76. Signatories with dates of election to Council*: James Bowdoin (1726-90), 1757-68, 1770-73; William Brattle (1706-76), 1765-86, 1770-73; Samuel Danforth (1696-1777), 1739-74; Samuel Dexter (1726-1810), 1768-73; John Erving (c.1692-1786), 1754-74; Thomas Hubbard (1702-73), 1759-72; James Pitts (1710-76), 1766-74; Isaac Royall (c.1719-81), 1752-73; James Russell (1715-98), 1761-73; Royal Tyler (1724-71), 1764-70.

     *Elections were conducted at the beginning of the assembly's legislative year, in May, votes being cast by the new House of Representatives and the outgoing Council. Appointments to the mandamus Council in Aug. 1774 have been excluded.

77. According to **No. 765**.

78. According to Bollan to Danforth, et al., Henrietta Street, 21 Jun. 1769, *Bowdoin and Temple Papers*, 145.

79. Ibid.

Appendix 5

SAMUEL DANFORTH TO THE EARL OF HILLSBOROUGH

Province of the Massachusetts Bay Boston June 12th. 1769.

My Lord,

M[r]. Danforth, the President of the Council for the last and the present year, having communicated to this Board a Copy of a Letter, dated April the 15th:1769[1] sent to your Lordship, subscribed by eleven Gentlemen, being the major Part of the members of the Council for the last year in answer to six Letters wrote to your Lordship by Governor Bernard, dated November the 1st. 5th. 12th. 14th. 30th, and December the 5th: 1768.[2] They have unanimously resolved, that they approve of the measures taken by the major Part of the members of the last year's Council &c. Copy of which Resolve, we have the Honor to inclose to your Lordship.

As the Gentlemen who wrote that Letter, have been so full and explicit in defending themselves and the Province against the Governor's groundless and injurious Charges, we have the less Reason to enlarge upon such a disagreeable Subject. However my Lord, if it appears to us that there is any Charge against the Council in either of the aforementioned Letters, to which there [has][3] either been no answer, or if mentioned, not so fully dilated upon the nature of the Offence with which the Board were charged does require; Your Lordship will indulge us the Freedom first to address you.

Permit us then, my Lord, with all due Deference to your Lordship's high Rank and Station to animadvert with Freedom upon some Part of the Governor's aforementioned Letters.

The Governor says in one of his Letters, "The Council is under awe of their Constituents by the frequent Removal of the Friends of Government &c_"[4] Aspersions of the like nature are several Times cast upon the Council in some of his other Letters, which for the Sake of avoiding Prolixity we shall not repeat.

My Lord, if our Fondness for a Seat at the Board could possibly influence us to vote and advise contrary to the real Sentiments of our Hearts, the Governor's wanton Exercise of Power, in his frequent negatives put upon Councellors of the best abilities, either because they differed from him in their political Sentiments in some Instances, or from Resentment to the House of Representatives for dropping some of his Friends,[5] would have a much greater Influence upon us to fall in with his measures; than any Risque we run from the honorable House in what he calls *supporting Government*. It being more in the Power of a Governor to remove a Councellor, than it is in the House; consequently if we had any great Fondness for a Seat at the Board, we should act inconsistently with our political Interest to oppose the Governor in his measures. But, my Lord, we can with great Truth say, that while we have had the Honor to be members of his Majesty's Council, we have endeavoured to discharge a good Conscience, and acted our Part with Uprightness and Integrity, having never been awed into undue Conduct, either by the House or the Governor; and the Governor's Insinuations to the contrary are unkind, and without Foundation, and unless we can act with the same Freedom as usual, we cannot esteem it an Honour to be of that Body.

That the Council have appeared of late more engaged in defending the Rights of the Province than formerly may be a Fact, which we have no Disposition to controvert: But be that as it may we beg Leave to observe, that it never was so much the incumbent Duty of the Council as it was the last year, to defend the Rights of the People; for upon the Dissolution of the General Court, the Governor and Council are by the Charter to manage the Affairs of the Province; so that the last years Council had double Duty devolved on them; therefore it was justly expected, they should exert themselves in Defence of the civil Rights and Liberties of the People; tho' at the same Time they did, and we hope we ever shall, treat the Governor with that Respect that is due to the King's Representative. And your Lordship may depend upon it, that the present Council will be as free to assert and maintain the just Prerogatives of the Crown, as to defend the Rights of the People.

We beg Leave further to observe, my Lord, that the Governor in his Letter dated November the 5th. speaking of the address to General Gage, says, "It was signed by fifteen of the Council, among whom were five who knew not enough of the Town to vote for the Safety of the Commissioners Returning, but knew enough to join in an Invective against them."[6] This Observation of the Governor's, was no Doubt made with a Design to ridicule the Conduct of those Gentlemen, and to represent them as having acted an inconsistent Part. But we cannot conceive by what Rules of Logic he can charge them with Inconsistency. For, my Lord, may not the Gentleman say with Great Propriety, as they were not inhabitants of the Town of Boston, but lived at a great Distance from it; that they knew not enough of the Temper and Disposition of the Town to say that it was safe for the Commissioners to return; and at the same Time from the Evidence they had of the Commissioners Behaviour and Conduct ever since they have been in Office, to join in what the Governor is pleased to call an Invective against them? For our Part we can see no Inconsistency in their Conduct, for certainly the Commissioners haughty and insolent Behaviour may be such, as to expose them to the Resentments of the People; and yet it does not necessarily follow, that the People will offer the least Insult or Violence to them. They may, or they may not; and therefore as it was a matter of uncertainty, the five Gentlemen might well be excused from voting in Favour of the Safety of the Commissioners Return. And the Governor's Remark upon their Conduct, shews rather the Defect of his Reasons than any Inconsistency in them.

With a View to defeat the good Ends proposed by the major Part of the last year's Council in their Petitions to the two Houses of Parliament, and for other unjustifiable Reasons, the Governor acquaints your Lordship that he cannot "conceive that all the Persons who met at the several Meetings upon the Occasion of preparing the Petitions put together amount to the number of twelve"; which he tells your Lordship made the majority of the whole and after insinuating that by a majority might only be meant for Persons out of seven, who make a Quorum of the Council; in his Poscript[7] he gives your Lordship what he calls a List of the names of those members who passed upon the Petitions; which together make no more than eight. We persuade ourselves, my Lord, that you will not imagine, that the Council of last Year endeavoured to impose on the two Houses of Parliament, by asserting their Petitions to ^have^ been the Doings of a major Part, when in Fact they were not. Who furnished the Governor with the List he mentions, we cannot say, but we can take upon us to assure you, my Lord, that the names of Lincoln, Brattle Gray and Russell ought to have been inserted therein, they having also agreed to the Petitions, who, with the eight Persons in the Governor's List, made the number twelve, being as he mentions a Majority of the whole.

This Information, will among a Multitude of other Things, serve to convince your Lordship, that Governor Bernard has spared no Pains to vilify the Council, and prevent the Success of their applications for the Redress of the Grievances which the Colonies labour under; and that he never lost Sight of his favorite Object, the obtaining of a Council by Mandamus[8] from the Crown. And the Board are at a Loss how to reconcile his Conduct with what he declares and promises to your Lordship in his Letter of the 30th: of November last, in which he says, "your Lordship may depend upon it that "my Informations have been, and shall be dictated by the Spirit of Truth and Candor"; when there is scarcely any Thing in either of his Letters but is in direct Opposition to both.[9]

It gives us the deepest Concern to find by one of the Resolutions, passed by the Lords, and afterwards agreed to by the Commons, that the Council of this Province, have been censured as not exerting themselves in suppressing of Riots.[10] And we are firmly persuaded, that the Council would have escaped the Displeasure of the two Houses of Parliament, had it not been for the gross Misrepresentations of Governor Bernard transmitted to your Lordship; which we are constrained to say, we consider not only as extremely cruel with respect to the Council, but a high Imposition on your Lordship, and even on Majesty itself.

You will allow us to say, my Lord, that no Council on the Continent, not even those appointed by the King, have a greater aversion to Riots and Disorders, nor have any of them exerted themselves more to suppress them than his Majesty's loyal Subjects the Council of the Massachusetts Bay. Had their Conduct been truly represented, instead of Censure, they would have met with the highest approbation. And if those whose immediate Business it is to suppress Mobs and Riots (against whom no Complaint has been exhibited by the Governor) had done their Duty, some of the Disorders might have been prevented.

The Council, my Lord, have now done with their Observations on Governor Bernard's Letters, and they doubt not your Lordship will consider what they have written in Answer to his Charges against the Council as equally applicable to what has been objected against them, of the same Nature, by his Excellency General Gage, in his Letter to your Lordship of the 31st. of October last;[11] on which we shall only make this further Remark, that the General being a Stranger in the Province; and but just arrived, could ^not^ possibly speak from his own knowledge, but must have received his Account of the People, and of the Council in particular, from a Quarter, which it is needless to point out to your Lordship.

We will not further trespass on your Lordship's Patience. In Truth, my Lord, our own is almost exhausted. The Council have had such repeated Occasions to observe upon and lament the unkind Treatment of Governor Bernard towards this People, that the Subject is become extremely disagreeable to us.

We have only to add, that we apprehend it needful to acquaint your Lordship, that Samuel White Esqr., one of the last year's Council, dying[12] between the Time of passing on the Petitions above referred to, and the Time of writing the Letter to your Lordship of the 15th. of April last, eleven at the last mentioned Time made a majority of the whole

We have the Honor to be with great Truth and Regard My Lord, Your Lordship's most Obedient & most humble Servant

In the name & by order of the Board;

Samuel Danforth, President[13]

The Right Honble. the Earl of Hillsborough.

In Council June 12th: 1769.

The Committee appointed the 8th. Instant to prepare the Draft of a Letter to the Right Honorable the Earl of Hillsborough on the Subject of six Letters from Governor Bernard to his Lordship, having reported the aforegoing Draft. Which being Read.

Resolved unanimously That the same be, and hereby is accepted, and that Samuel Danforth Esqr sign the same as President on behalf of the Board and transmit it to his Lordship accordingly

A Oliver Sec^y

LS, RC   CO 5/758, ff 136-141.

Endorsed: Massachusetts Bay 12th June 1769. Mr Danforth President of the Council R 24 July B.30. Marked "Cop^d."   The loose copy made by the clerk has not survived but there is an entry-book version in CO 5/767, ff 341-352 (L, RLbC). Andrew Oliver was allowed to make a copy for his own files but not to retain the original, which was sent to the Council's agent William Bollan for transmission to Hillsborough.[14] Oliver's copy is in Prov. Sec. Letterbooks, 2A: 180-183 (L, LbC). The Council's letter was included in *Letters to Hillsborough* (1st ed.), 48-52 and *Letters to Hillsborough* (repr.), 95-103. The RC enclosed a copy of the minutes of the Massachusetts Council of 12 Jun. 1769, at CO 5/758, f 142.

FB had intended commenting upon the Council's letter but was prevented by the demands of other business (**No. 779**). He certainly would have questioned the legitimacy of the Council communicating directly with the king's secretary of state. The designation "major Part" of the Council had no governmental authority, for it referred to a majority of councilors acting collectively as individuals and not in the name of the Council. Yet, as the appended resolution[15] made clear, the letter was approved unanimously at a Board meeting. The term "president" recognized that Samuel Danforth was the eldest and most experienced member of the Board and would have been expected to chair the Council in the incapacity of the governor or lieutenant governor. These men might have supposed their collective action had some constitutional legitimacy akin to their responsibilities to assume temporary executive authority in the event of the death of the governor and lieutenant governor;[16] perhaps they supposed that FB and TH had rendered themselves symbolically *persona non grata* by reason of their having misrepresented the province and of FB refusing to withdraw the soldiers. The Council asserted that, whatever the case, they had a responsibility to protect popular rights from encroachment by the governor.

1. **Appendix 4**.

2. **Nos. 706**, **708**, **709**, **711**, **717**, and **718**.

3. Obscured by tight binding.

4. End quotation marks supplied. In **No. 718**, FB had accused the councilors of "Very little Exercise of private Judgement in popular Questions."

5. Thomas Hutchinson, Andrew Oliver, and others who failed to win election in 1766 and subsequent years.

6. **No. 708**. End quotation marks supplied.

7. Thus in manuscript, referring to the postscript to **No. 718**. Corrected to "postscript" in printed versions.

8. A writ commanding action.

9. **No. 717**.

10. The fourth resolution complained that the Council and province magistrates failed to "exert their Authority for suppressing . . . Riots and Tumults." Adopted by the House of Lords on 15 Dec. and approved by the House of Commons on 8 Feb. *HLJ*, 32: 209.

11. Printed in *Copies of Letters from Governor Bernard to Hillsborough*.

12. He died on 20 Mar. 1769.

13. Autograph.

14. It may have been enclosed in John Erving's letter of 26 Jul. 1769 confirming Bollan's appointment as Council agent. However, the letter is not mentioned alongside other enclosures, including *Letters to Hillsborough. Bowdoin and Temple Papers*, 149-150.

15. Omitted in the printed versions.

16. *Acts and Resolves*, 1: 10-11.

Appendix 6

PETITION OF THE HOUSE OF REPRESENTATIVES TO REMOVE GOV. FRANCIS BERNARD

To the King's most Excellent Majesty.

Most Gracious Sovereign

We your Majesty's most dutiful and faithful Subjects, the Representatives of your ancient and loyal Colony of the Massachusetts Bay, impressed with the deepest Gratitude to Almighty God for calling to the British Succession your illustrious Family, and so firmly establishing your majesty on the Throne of your royal Progenitors: And being abundantly convinced of your Majesty's Grace and Clemency, most humbly implore the Royal Favour, while we briefly represent our Grievances, which your Majesty alone under God can redress.

We are constrained in Duty to your Majesty, and in Faithfulness to our Constituents to lay before your Majesty our Complaints of his Excellency Sir Francis Bernard Baronet, your Majesty's Governor of this Colony, whose whole Administration appears to have been repugnant not only to your Majesty's Service, and the Welfare of your Subjects in the Colony, but even to the first Principles of the British Constitution.

From his first Arrival here, he has in his Speeches and other publick Acts, treated the Representative Body with Contempt.

He has in his publick Speeches charged both Houses of the General Assembly, expressly with Oppugnation against Royal Authority, declaring that they had left Gentlemen out of the Council, only for their Fidelity to the Crown.

He has from Time to Time indiscretely and wantonly exercised the Prerogative of the Crown, in the repeated negative of Councellors of an unblemished Reputation, and duly elected by a great majority; some of them by the unanimous Suffrage of both Houses of Assembly.

He has declared, that certain Seats at the Council Board shall be kept vacant, 'till certain Gentlemen who are his Favorites shall be reelected.[1]

He has unconstitutionally interfered with and unduly influenced Elections, particularly in the Choice of an Agent, for the Colony.[2]

He has very abruptly displaced divers Gentlemen of Worth, for no apparent Reason, but because they voted in the General Assembly with Freedom and against his measures.

He has in an unwarrantable manner taken upon himself the Exercise of your Majesty's Royal Prerogative, in granting a Charter for a College; contrary to an express Vote of the House of Representatives, and without even asking the advice of your Majesty's Council.[3]

He has practised the sending over Depositions to the Ministry privately taken against Gentlemen of Character here, without giving the Persons accused the least notice of his Purposes and Proceedings.[4]

He has very injuriously represented your Majesty's loving Subjects of this Colony in general, as having an ill Temper prevailing among them, as disaffected to your Majesty's Government, and intending to bring the Authority of Parliament into Contempt. And by such false Representations, he has been greatly instrumental, as this House humbly conceives, in exciting Jealousies, and disturbing that Harmony and mutual Affection which before happily subsisted, and we pray God may again subsist between your Majesty's Subjects in Great Britain and America.[5]

He has in his Letters to one of your Majesty's Ministers unjustly charged the Majority of your Majesty's faithful Council in the Colony with having avowed the Principles of Opposition to the Authority of Parliament, and acted in Concert with a Party from whence such Opposition originated.[6]

He has also in his Letter to another of your Majesty's Ministers falsely declared that a Plan was laid, and a number of men actually enrolled in the Town of Boston, to seize your Majesty's Castle William in the Harbour of the same, out of your Majesty's Hands.[7]

Such Representations of the State and Circumstances of this Colony from a Gentleman of the highest Trust in it, will of necessity be received with full Credit, till they are made to appear false. And in Consequence thereof, your Majesty's true and loyal Subjects have suffered the Reproach as well as other Hardships of having a military Force stationed here to support your Majesty's Authority, and the Execution of the Laws; which measure has been approved of by your Majesty's two Houses of Parliament, as appears in their Resolutions, that the Town of Boston had been in a State of Disorder and Confusion, and that the Circumstances of the Colony were such as required a military Force, for the Purposes above mentioned.

Having been a principal Instrument, as we apprehend, in procuring this military Force your Majesty's said Governor, in an unprecedented manner, and as tho' he had designed to irritate to the highest Degree, ordered the very Room which is appropriated for the meeting of the Representatives of the General Assembly, which was never used for any other Purpose, and where their Records are kept, to be employed as a Barrack for the common Soldiers: and the Centinels were so posted as that your Majesty's Council and the Justices of the Courts of common Law were daily interrupted, and even challenged in their Proceedings to the Business of their several Departments.

He endeavoured contrary to the express to the express Design[8] of an act of Parliament to quarter your Majesty's Troops in the Body of the Town of Boston, while the Barracks provided by the Government at the Castle within the Town, remained useless: and for Purposes manifestly evasive of said Act, he unwarrantably appointed an Officer to provide Quarters for the Troops, otherwise than is therein prescribed.[9]

After having dissolved the General Court, at a most critical Season, and while they were employed in the most necessary and important Business of the Colony, he arbitrarily refused to call another for the Space of ten months, and until the Time appointed in the royal Charter for the calling a General assembly, against the repeated dutiful Petitions of the People.

It appears by his Letters to the Earl of Hillsborough,[10] your Majesty's Secretary of State, that he had endeavored to overthrow the present Constitution of Government in this Colony, and to have the People deprived of their invaluable Charter Rights, which they and their Ancestors have happily enjoyed, under your Majesty's Administration, and those of your royal Predecessors.

By the means aforesaid, and many others that might be enumerated, he has rendered his administration odious to the whole Body of the People, and has intirely alienated their Affections from him, and thereby wholly destroyed that Confidence in a Governor, which your Majesty's Service indispensably requires.

Wherefore we most humbly intreat your Majesty, that his Excellency Sir Francis Bernard Baronet may be for ever removed from the Government of this Province: and that your Majesty would be graciously pleased to place one in his Stead worthy to serve the greatest and best monarch on Earth.

And the Representatives of the Colony of the Massachusetts Bay, as in Duty bound, shall ever pray In their name and by their Order

Signed Thomas Cushing Speaker

AMsS, RC

TNA: Privy Council and Privy Council Office: Miscellaneous Unbound Papers, PC 1/3142.

In the handwriting of Thomas Cushing, for the House of Representatives of Massachusetts. Endorsed: Presented to His Majesty by Dennys Deberdt Esq[r] Sep[r]. 14. 1769. The petition was both proposed and unanimously adopted by the House of Representatives on 27 Jun., indicating that it had been prepared in advance, in this case by Samuel Adams, the clerk of the House.[11] This version was entered in *JHRM*, 45: 197-199. The engrossed copy printed here was sent to DeBerdt, the House agent, under cover of a letter from Cushing dated 30 Jun. 1769 (not found), and transmitted to the Privy Council office on 22 Sept.[12] Upon receipt, DeBerdt left a copy of the petition at the London house of the secretary of state for the Colonies, the earl of Hillsborough, who was absent at his estates in Ireland.[13] This version is filed in CO 5/758, ff 182-185. There is a letterbook copy in CO 5/767, ff 22-28. FB published his own version in *Select Letters*, 89-94. He also compiled an *Answer* to the complaint, Feb. 1770, filed at PC 1/3142 and printed in *Select Letters*, 95-115. Endnotes below identify correspondence published in the Bernard Letters series[14] that the

House of Representatives would have been aware of when they prepared the petition and would have used to justify their prayer if called upon to do so.

The House of Representatives already knew that FB had been recalled to Britain when they composed this petition. In part it was an insurance of sorts to prevent the British government returning him to the province, for FB still remained titular governor. More importantly, the petition was a logical instrument with which the House could contest the many criticisms their governor had made the letters recently acquired by the Council and published in Boston.

FB's conduct in office was subject to the provisions of an act for punishing governors for crimes committed in the Plantations, 11 and 12 Will. 3, c. 12 (1698). Penalties for maladministration were dismissal, a life-time ban on holding Crown office, and a fine of one thousand pounds. Malfeasance and criminality could also be decided in a court of law. The most important threat to FB's reputation, however, was political: that the Grafton administration might blame the failure of its American policy upon FB and/or Hillsborough.[15] Impeachment by the Privy Council was one possible outcome, as FB's enemies knew. Indeed, after some delay, a hearing was eventually held on 28 Feb. 1770. But the privy councilors stoutly defended FB and rode roughshod over the House agent Dennys DeBerdt, who floundered in presenting the case. The Privy Council finally dismissed the House of Representatives' allegations on 7 Mar. as "groundless, vexatious and scandalous."[16] FB did not return to Massachusetts and in his stead the British appointed TH as governor on 28 Nov. 1770. In form and style, however, the accusatory list prepared by the Massachusetts House of Representatives anticipated the American Declaration of Independence of 1776; thus, the grievances against the king were an escalation of those cited in justification of removing a governor.

---

1. While the House was not in possession of FB's letters detailing these issues, they were, of course, fully able to document the governor's veto of councilors in successive elections since May 1766.

2. Again, the House did not have copies of FB's correspondence on this matter.

3. Queen's College, Hampshire Co., Mass. The bill for incorporating a western college (1762) was rejected by the House of Representatives in 1762. *Bernard Papers*, 1: 190-191, 217-281.

4. This was a general accusation.

5. This was another general accusation.

6. **Nos. 706**, **708**, **709**, **711**, **717**, and **718**.

7. This might have been deduced from FB to Conway, 28 Sept. 1765, which was laid before the House of Commons on 14 Jan. 1766. **No. 397**, *Bernard Papers*, 2: 369. On Parliament see *Bernard Papers*, 3: 128.

8. Thus in manuscript.

9. **Nos. 706** and **708**.

10. *Copies of Letters from Governor Bernard to Hillsborough*; *Letters to Hillsborough* (1st ed.).

11. *JHRM*, 45: 168-172. The version printed in Cushing, *Writings of Samuel Adams*, 1: 349-354, is based not on the official record or the engrossed copy but on FB's transcript published in *Select Letters*, 89-94. The differences are not substantive.

12. According to CO 5/758, f 185.

13. DeBerdt to Cushing, London, 15 Sept. 1769, Matthews, "Letters of Dennys DeBerdt," 378-380.

14. *Copies of Letters from Governor Bernard to Hillsborough*; *Letters to Hillsborough* (1st ed.).

15. See Nicolson, *'The Infamas Govener'*, 205-206.

16. Ibid., 206; *APC*, 5: 211-214.

Appendix 7

LIST OF CORRESPONDENCE

To the Earl of Hillsborough, Boston, 1 Oct. 1768. CO 5/757, ff 434-436 (dupLS, RC). **No. 694**.
——CO 5/767, ff 119-124 (L, RLbC).
——BP, 7: 67-70 (L, LbC).
——HLL: American Colonies Box 3 (L, Copy).
——*Letters to the Ministry* (1st ed.), 66-68.
——*Letters to the Ministry* (repr.), 89-92.
To Thomas Gage, Roxbury, 1 Oct. 1768. MiU-C. Gage, vol. 81 (ALS, RC).
  No. 695.
——BP, 7: 203-204 (L, LbC).
——CO 5/86, ff 205-206 (L extract, Copy).
To William Dalrymple, Roxbury, 2 Oct. 1768. BP, 7: 209-211 (L, LbC). **No. 696**.
To William Dalrymple, Province House, 2 Oct. 1768. BP, 7: 209 (L, LbC).
From Thomas Gage, New York, 2 Oct. 1768. BP, 11: 315-318 (ALS, RC).
  No. 697.
——CO 5/86, ff 198-200 (L extract, Copy).
To the Earl of Hillsborough, Boston, 3 Oct. 1768. CO 5/757, ff 439-440
  (ALS, RC). **No. 698**.
——CO 5/767, ff 124-126 (L, RLbC).
——BP, 7: 70-72 (L, LbC).
——HLL: American Colonies Box 3 (L, Copy).
——*Letters to the Ministry* (1st ed.), 69.
——*Letters to the Ministry* (repr.), 92-93.
——*Boston Evening-Post*, 11 Sept. 1769.
——*Providence Gazette*, 16-23 Sept. 1769.
——*Georgia Gazette*, 1 Nov. 1769.
From Lord Barrington, Beckett, 3 Oct. 1768. BP, 11: 319-321 (ALS, RC).
  No. 699.
To the Earl of Hillsborough, Boston, 5 and 6 Oct. 1768. CO 5/757, ff 442-444
  (ALS, RC). **No. 700**.
——CO 5/767, ff 126-132 (L, RLbC).
——BP, 7: 72-76 (L, LbC).
——HLL: American Colonies Box 3 (L, Copy).
——*Letters to the Ministry* (1st ed.), 70-72.
——*Letters to the Ministry* (repr.), 94-97.

To the American Board of Customs, Boston, 8 Oct. 1768. BP, 7: 211 (L, LbC).

To Henry Smith, Boston, 8 Oct. 1768. BP, 7: 212 (L, LbC).

To Thomas Gage, Jamaica Farm, 9 Oct. 1768. MiU-C. Gage, vol. 81 (ALS, RC).
  No. 701.

——BP, 7: 204-207 (L, LbC).

From the Earl of Hillsborough, Whitehall, 12 Oct. 1768. BP, 12: 1-4 (LS, RC).
  No. 702.

——CO 5/765, ff 43-44 (L, LbC).

——CO 5/757, ff 386-387 (LS, AC).

——HLL: American Colonies Box 3 (L, Copy).

To the Earl of Hillsborough, Boston, 14 Oct. 1768. CO 5/757, ff 492-495
  (ALS, RC). **No. 703**.

——CO 5/893, ff 86-90 (dupLS, RC).

——CO 5/767, ff 139-147 (L, RLbC).

——BP, 7: 76-83 (L, LbC).

——HLL: American Colonies Box 3 (L, Copy).

——BL: Add 35912, f 151 (L extract, Copy).

——*Letters to the Ministry* (1st ed.), 72-75.

——*Letters to the Ministry* (repr.), 97-101.

To the American Board of Customs, Roxbury, 19 Oct. 1768. Temple Papers,
  1762-1768: JT Letterbook (L, RLbC).

——BP, 7: 212-213 (L, LbC).

To the American Board of Customs, Roxbury, 22 Oct. 1768. BP, 7: 213-214
  (L, LbC). **No. 704**.

To Lord Barrington, Boston, 22 and 29 Oct. 1768. BP, 6: 156-163 (L, LbC).
  No. 705.

To the Archbishop of Canterbury,[1] Boston, N.E., 24 Oct. 1768. BP, 6: 148-149
  (L, LbC).

To Joseph Goldthwait,[2] 27 Oct. 1768, CO 5/757, ff 509-510.

To John Pownall, Boston, 29 Oct. 1768. BP, 6: 155-156 (L, LbC).

To John Pownall, Boston, 30 Oct. 1768. BP, 6: 153-155 (L, LbC).

To Richard Jackson, Jamaica Farm, 31 Oct. 1768. BP, 6: 149-152 (L, LbC).

To the Earl of Hillsborough, Boston, 1 Nov. 1768. CO 5/757, ff 497-502
  (ALS, RC). **No. 706**.

——CO 5/767, ff 152-162 (L, RLbC).

——BP, 7: 83-93 (L, LbC).

——Bowdoin and Temple Papers, Loose MSS (L, Copy).

——BL: Add 35912, ff 132-137 (L, Copy).

——*Boston Gazette, Supplement*, 23 Jan. 1769.

——*Copies of Letters from Governor Bernard to Hillsborough*.

——*Boston Chronicle*, 13-17 Apr. 1769.

——*New-York Gazette, and Weekly Mercury*, 22 May 1769.

——*Letters to Hillsborough* (1st ed.), 3-7.

——*Boston Gazette*, 31 Jul. 1769.

——*Letters to Hillsborough* (repr.), 3-11.

From Lord Barrington, Cavendish Square [*London*], 1 Nov. 1768. BP, 12: 5-8
  (ALS, RC). **No. 707**.

——BL: Add 73634, ff 63-63 (ALS, LbC).

To the Earl of Hillsborough, Boston, 5 Nov. 1768. CO 5/757, ff 513-516
  (ALS, RC). **No. 708**.

——CO 5/767, ff 163-169 (L, RLbC).

——BP, 7: 93-99 (L, LbC).

——Bowdoin and Temple Papers, Loose MSS (L, Copy).

——*Boston Gazette, Supplement*, 23 Jan. 1769.

——*Copies of Letters from Governor Bernard to Hillsborough*.

——*Boston Chronicle*, 13-17 Apr. 1769.

——*Providence Gazette*, 22 Apr. 1769.

——*New-York Chronicle*, 22-29 May 1769.

——*Letters to Hillsborough* (1st ed.), 7-10.

——*Boston Gazette*, 31 Jul. 1769.

——*Letters to Hillsborough* (repr.), 12-17.

To John Pownall, Boston, 7 Nov. 1768. CO 5/757, ff 520-521 (ALS, RC).

——CO 5/767, f 170 (L, RLbC).

——BP, 6: 164 (L, LbC).

From Lord Barrington, Cavendish Square, 9 Nov. 1768. BP, 12: 9-10 (ALS, RC).

To the Earl of Hillsborough, Boston, 12 Nov. 1768. CO 5/757, ff 524-525
  (ALS, RC). **No. 709**.

——CO 5/767, ff 171-174 (L, RLbC).

——BP, 7: 100-103 (L, LbC).

——Bowdoin and Temple Papers, Loose MSS (L, Copy).

——*Boston Gazette, Supplement*, 23 Jan. 1769.

——*Copies of Letters from Governor Bernard to Hillsborough*.

——*Providence Gazette*, 22 Apr. 1769.

——*New-York Chronicle*, 29 May-5 Jun. 1769.

——*Boston Chronicle*, 17-20 Apr. 1769.

——*Letters to Hillsborough* (1st ed.), 10-11.

——*Boston Gazette*, 31 Jul. 1769.

——*Letters to Hillsborough* (repr.), 18-21.

To the American Board of Customs, Jamaica Plain, 12 Nov. 1768. BP, 7: 214-215
  (L, LbC). **No. 710**.

To the Earl of Hillsborough, Boston, 14 Nov. 1768. CO 5/757, ff 526-529 (ALS, RC). **No. 711**.

——CO 5/767, ff 175-181 (L, RLbC).

——BP, 7: 103-109 (L, LbC).

——Bowdoin and Temple Papers, Loose MSS (L, Copy).

——*Boston Gazette, Supplement*, 23 Jan. 1769.

——*Copies of Letters from Governor Bernard to Hillsborough*.

——*Providence Gazette*, 22 Apr. 1769.

——*New-York Chronicle*, 15-22 May 1769.

——*Letters to Hillsborough* (repr.), 21-26.

——*Boston Gazette*, 31 Jul. 1769.

——*Letters to Hillsborough* (1st ed.), 12-14.

From the Earl of Hillsborough, Whitehall, 15 Nov. 1768. BP, 12: 11-16 (LS, RC). **No. 712**.

——CO 5/765, ff 48-52 (L, LbC).

——CO 5/757, ff 454-457 (Dft, AC).

——HLL: American Colonies Box 3 (L extract, Copy).

To Samuel Hood,[3] Province House, 18 Nov. 1768. BP, 7: 215 (L, LbC).

From the Earl of Hillsborough, Hanover Square [*London*], 19 Nov. 1768. BP, 12: 17-20 (ALS, RC). **No. 713**.

From John Pownall, Whitehall, 19 Nov. 1768. BP, 12: 21-24 (ALS, RC). **No. 714**.

To John Pownall, Boston, 25 Nov. 1768. BP, 6: 165-168 (L, LbC). **No. 715**.

To John Pownall, Jamaica Plain, 26 Nov. 1768. BP, 6: 168-173 (L, LbC). **No. 716**.

To the Earl of Hillsborough, Boston, 30 Nov. 1768. CO 5/767, ff 185-188 (L, RLbC). **No. 717**.

——BP, 7: 109-111 (L, LbC).

——Bowdoin and Temple Papers, Loose MSS (L, Copy).

——*Boston Gazette, Supplement*, 23 Jan. 1769.

——*Copies of Letters from Governor Bernard to Hillsborough*.

——*Providence Gazette*, 22 Apr. 1769.

——*New-York Gazette, and Weekly Mercury*, 29 May 1769.

——*Boston Chronicle*, 27 Apr.-1 May 1769.

——*Letters to Hillsborough* (1st ed.), 14-16.

——*Boston Gazette*, 31 Jul. 1769.

——*Letters to Hillsborough* (repr.), 27-29.

To the Earl of Hillsborough, Boston, 5 Dec. 1768. CO 5/758, ff 25-26 (ALS, RC). **No. 718**.

——CO 5/767, ff 189-192 (L, RLbC).

——BP, 7: 111-114 (L, LbC).

——Bowdoin and Temple Papers, Loose MSS (L, Copy).

——BL: Add 35912, ff 148-150 (L, Copy).

——*Boston Gazette, Supplement*, 23 Jan. 1769.

——*Copies of Letters from Governor Bernard to Hillsborough*.

——*Boston Chronicle*, 27 Apr.-1 May 1769.

——*Boston Gazette*, 31 Jul. 1769.

——*Letters to Hillsborough* (1st ed.), 16-17.

——*Letters to Hillsborough* (repr.), 30-33.

To the Earl of Hillsborough, Boston, 12 Dec. 1768. CO 5/758, ff 31-34 (ALS, RC). **No. 719**.

——CO 5/893, ff 92-94 (dupLS, RC).

——CO 5/767, ff 194-199 (L, RLbC).

To Lawrence Monk,[4] Boston, 14 Dec. 1768. BP, 7: 251 (L, LbC).

To the American Board of Customs, 22 Dec. 1768. T 1/465, ff 311-312 (L, Copy). **No. 720**.

To John Pownall, Boston, 24 Dec. 1768. BP, 7: 252 (L, LbC). **No. 721**.

From the Earl of Hillsborough, Whitehall, 24 Dec. 1768. BP, 12: 25-28 (LS, RC). **No. 722**.

——CO 5/757, ff 522-523 (L, AC).

——CO 5/765, ff 53-54 (L, LbC).

——*Letters to the Ministry* (1st ed.), 76-77.

——*Letters to the Ministry* (repr.), 102-103.

From John Pownall, Whitehall, 24 Dec. 1768. BP, 12: 29-32 (ALS, RC). **No. 723**.

To the Earl of Hillsborough, Boston, 26 Dec. 1768. CO 5/758, ff 38-40 (ALS, RC). **No. 724**.

——CO 5/893, ff 96-97 (dupLS, RC).

——CO 5/767, ff 202-204 (L, RLbC).

——BP, 7: 118-121 (L, LbC).

From Lord Barrington, Cavendish Square, 2 Jan. 1769. BP, 12: 33-36 (ALS, RC). **No. 726**.

From the Earl of Hillsborough, Whitehall, 4 Jan. 1769. BP, 12: 37-40 (LS, RC). **No. 727**.

——CO 5/765, ff 54-55 (L, LbC).

——CO 5/758, ff 1-2 (L, AC).

——*Letters to the Ministry* (1st ed.), 76.

——*Letters to the Ministry* (repr.), 103.

To the American Board of Customs, 6 Jan. 1769. T 1/471, ff 83-86 (L, Copy). **No. 728**.

To John Pownall, Boston, 13 and 19 Jan. 1769. BP, 7: 252-254 (L, LbC).
No. 729.

To the Earl of Hillsborough, Boston, 23 Jan. 1769. CO 5/758, ff 48-49
(ALS, RC). **No. 730**.

——CO 5/893, ff 98-99 (dupLS, RC).

——CO 5/767, ff 206-209 (L, RLbC).

——BP, 7: 121-123 (L, LbC).

To Lord Botetourt[5], Boston, 23 Jan. 1769. BP, 7: 216 (L, LbC).

To the Earl of Hillsborough, Boston, 24 Jan. and 4 Feb. 1769. CO 5/758, ff 50-51
(LS, RC). **No. 731**.

——CO 5/893, ff 100-101 (dupLS, RC).

——CO 5/767, ff 209-213 (L, RLbC).

——BP, 7: 123-126 (L, LbC).

To the Earl of Hillsborough, Boston, 25 Jan. 1769. CO 5/758, ff 56-57
(ALS, RC). **No. 734**.

——CO 5/893, ff 108-109 (dupL, RC).

——CO 5/767, ff 213-215 (L, RLbC).

——BP, 7: 126-128 (L, LbC).

To the Earl of Hillsborough, Boston, 26 Jan. 1769. BP, 7: 128-132 (L, LbC).
No. 735.

——BP, 7: 261 (L extract, LbC).

——BP, 12: 41-48 (dupLS, AC).

To the Earl of Hillsborough, Boston, 4 and 19 Feb. 1769. CO 5/758, ff 58-64
(ALS, RC). **No. 736**.

——CO 5/893, ff 110-114 (dupLS, RC).

——CO 5/767, ff 215-224 (L, RLbC).

——BP, 7: 132-138 (L, LbC).

From Samuel Venner, Boston, 10 Feb. 1769. Mass. Archs., 25: 292-293
(LS, LbC). **No. 739**.

From Lord Barrington, Cavendish Square, 12 Feb. 1769. BP, 12: 49-52
(ALS, RC). **No. 740**.

From the Selectmen of Boston, 16 Feb. 1769. *Reports of the Record Commissioners of Boston*, 23: 6-7 (transcript, PC). **No. 741**.

To the Selectmen of Boston, Province House, 18 Feb. 1769. *Reports of the Record
Commissioners of Boston*, 23: 7 (transcript, PC).

——Coll. Mass. Papers, 1769 (L, Copy).

To John Pownall, Boston, 18 Feb. 1769. BP, 7: 255-258 (L, LbC). **No. 742**.

From John Pownall, London, 19 Feb. 1769. BP, 12: 53-56 (ALS, RC). **No. 743**.

To Lord Barrington, Boston, 20 Feb. 1769. BP, 7: 258-261 (L, LbC). **No. 744**.

From the Earl of Hillsborough, Whitehall, 20 Feb. 1769. BP, 12: 57-60 (LS, RC).
No. 745.

——CO 5/765, ff 55-57 (L, LbC).

——CO 5/758, ff 36-37 (LS, AC).

To the Earl of Hillsborough, Boston, 21 and 28 Feb. 1769. BP, 7: 141-148 (L, LbC). **No. 746**.

From the Selectmen of Boston, 22 Feb. 1769. *Reports of the Record Commissioners of Boston*, 23: 6-7 (transcript, PC). **No. 747**.

To the Selectmen of Boston, 24 Feb. 1769. *Reports of the Record Commissioners of Boston*, 23: 9 (transcript, PC).

To the Earl of Hillsborough, Boston, 25 Feb. 1769. CO 5/758, ff 72-73 (dupLS, RC). **No. 748**.

——CO 5/767, ff 232-235 (L, RLbC).

——BP, 7: 148-150 (L, LbC).

To the Rev. Samuel Seabury, Boston, 27 Feb. 1769. BP, 7: 216 (L, LbC). **No. 749**.

To the Earl of Hillsborough, 28 Feb. 1769. CO 5/758, f 74 (L, RC).

——CO 5/767, f 235 (L, RLbC).

To Edward Hawke,[6] Boston, 28 Feb. 1769. BP, 7: 150-153 (L, LbC).

From the Earl of Hillsborough, Whitehall, 1 Mar. 1769. BP, 12: 61-64 (LS, RC).

——CO 5/765, f 64 (L, LbC).

——CO 5/758, f 44 (LS, AC).

To Thomas Gage, Boston, 2 Mar. 1769. BP, 7: 217-219 (L, LbC). **No. 750**.

To Benning Wentworth, Boston, 2 Mar. 1769. BP, 7: 219-221 (L, LbC).

To John Pownall, Boston, 5 Mar. 1769. BP, 7: 262-263 (L, LbC).

To Lord Barrington, Boston, 15 Mar. 1769. BP, 7: 267-270 (dupL, LbC). **No. 751**.

To Philip Stephens,[7] Boston, 15 Mar. 1769. BP, 7: 153-155 (L, LbC). **No. 752**.

To Lord Barrington, Boston, 18 Mar. 1769. BP, 7: 263-264 (L, LbC). **No. 753**.

From Lord Barrington, Cavendish Square, 21 Mar. 1769. BP, 12: 65-68 (ALS, RC). **No. 754**.

From the Earl of Hillsborough, Whitehall, 22 Mar. 1769. BP, 12: 69-72 (ALS, RC). **No. 755**.

To Thomas Gage, Boston, 23 Mar. 1769. BP, 7: 221 (L, LbC). **No. 756**.

Instruction from the Earl of Hillsborough, Court at St. James's, 23 Mar. 1769. BP, 12: 73-76 (LS, RC).

From the Earl of Hillsborough, Whitehall, 24 Mar. 1769. BP, 12: 77-80 (dupLS, RC). **No. 757**.

——CO 5/765, ff 64-66 (L, LbC).

To John Pownall, Boston, 25 Mar. 1769. BP, 7: 270-274 (dupL, LbC). **No. 758**.

To the Earl of Hillsborough, Boston, 27 Mar. 1769. CO 5/758, f 76 (ALS, RC). **No. 759**.

——CO 5/893, f 118 (dupLS, RC).

——CO 5/767, f 236 (L, RLbC).

——BP, 7: 155-156 (dupL, LbC).

From Lord Barrington, Cavendish Square, 5 Apr. 1769. BP, 12: 81-82 (ALS, RC).
No. 760.

To Richard Jackson, Boston, 8 Apr. 1769. BP, 7: 274-276 (L, LbC). **No. 761**.

To John Pownall, Boston, 8 Apr. 1769. BP, 7: 276-277 (dupL, LbC). **No. 762**.

To Lord Barrington, Boston, 12 Apr. 1769. BP, 7: 278-279 (L, LbC). **No. 763**.

To Richard Jackson, Boston, 12 Apr. 1769. BP, 7: 279-280 (L, LbC). **No. 764**.

To John Pownall, Boston, 12 Apr. 1769. BP, 7: 280-282 (dupL, LbC). **No. 765**.

To John Pownall, Boston, 23 Apr. 1769. BP, 7: 282-285 (dupL, LbC). **No. 766**.

To Guy Carleton,[8] Boston, 28 Apr. 1769. BP, 7: 222 (L, LbC).

To Thomas Gage, Boston, 29 Apr. 1769. BP, 7: 222 (L, LbC).

To the Earl of Hillsborough, Boston, 29 Apr. 1769. CO 5/758, ff 114-115
(ALS, RC). **No. 767**.

——CO 5/893, ff 126-127 (dupLS, RC).

——CO 5/767, ff 315-317 (L, RLbC).

——BP, 7: 160-161 (L, LbC).

To the Earl of Hillsborough, Boston, 1 May 1769. BP, 7: 156-157 (dupL, LbC).
No. 768.

To the Earl of Hillsborough, Boston, 8 May 1769. CO 5/758, ff 116-117
(ALS, RC). **No. 769**.

——CO 5/893, ff 128-129 (dupLS, RC).

——CO 5/767, ff 317-320 (L, RLbC).

——BP, 7: 161-163 (L, LbC).

To John Pownall, Boston, 9 May 1769. BP, 7: 286-287 (L, LbC). **No. 770**.

To Thomas Pownall, Boston, 11 May 1769. BP, 7: 288-289 (L, LbC). **No. 771**.

To Richard Jackson, Boston, 11 May 1769. BP, 7: 289-291 (L, LbC). **No. 772**.

Circular From the Earl of Hillsborough, 13 May 1769. BP, 12: 87-90 (LS, RC).
No. 773.

To Thomas Gage, Jamaica Farm, 15 May 1769. BP, 7: 223 (L, LbC). **No. 774**.

——CO 5/767, ff 326-328 (L, LbC).

——CO 5/893, f 134 (L, Copy).

——CO 5/758, f 126 (L, Copy).

——CO 5/87, ff 115-116 (L, Copy).

To the Earl of Hillsborough, Boston, 15 May 1769. CO 5/893, ff 130-131
(ALS, RC). **No. 775**.

——CO 5/758, ff 122-124 (dupLS, RC).

——CO 5/767, ff 320-325 (L, RLbC).

——BP, 7: 163-166 (L, LbC).

To John Pownall, Boston, 15 May 1769. BP, 7: 291-293 (L, LbC). **No. 776**.

From Thomas Gage, New York, 15 May 1769. BP, 12: 91-94 (LS, RC). **No. 777**.

From Thomas Gage, New York, 22 May 1769. BP, 12: 95-98 (LS, RC).

——CO 5/87, ff 117-119 (L, Copy).

To the Earl of Hillsborough, Boston, 25 May 1769. CO 5/758, ff 112-113
  (ALS, RC). **No. 778**.

——CO 5/893, ff 124-125 (dupLS, RC).

——CO 5/767, ff 314-315 (L, RLbC).

——BP, 7: 157-159 (dupL, LbC).

To Count d'Ennery,[9] Boston, 26 May 1769. BP, 7: 223-224 (L, LbC).

To Benning Wentworth, Boston, 30 May 1769. BP, 7: 224-225 (L, LbC).

To Lord Barrington, Boston, 30 May, 1 and 17 Jun. 1769. BP, 7: 293-299
  (L, LbC).

To the Earl of Hillsborough, Boston, 1, 8, 10, and 17 Jun. 1769. CO 5/758,
  ff 128-133 (ALS, RC). **No. 779**.

——CO 5/893, ff 136-141 (dupLS, RC).

——CO 5/767, ff 328-340 (L, RLbC).

——BP, 7: 166-175 (L, LbC).

To John Pownall, Boston, 1 Jun. 1769. BP, 7: 295-296 (L, LbC). **No. 780**.

From Count d'Ennery, Guadeloupe, 2 Jun. 1769. Mass. Archs., 56: 561-562
  (ALS, RC).

From Lord Barrington, Cavendish Square, 4 Jun. 1769. BP, 12: 99-102
  (ALS, RC). **No. 781**.

From Thomas Gage, New York, 5 Jun. 1769. BP, 12: 103-106 (ALS, RC).
  No. 782.

To Samuel Hood, Province House, 8 Jun. 1769. BP, 7: 225-225 (L, LbC).
  No. 783.

From Alexander Mackay, Boston, 10 Jun. 1769. BP, 12: 108-110 (ALS, RC).

To John Pownall, Boston, 12 Jun. 1769. BP, 7: 296-299 (L, LbC). **No. 784**.

To Thomas Gage, Boston, 12 Jun. 1769. CO 5/87, ff 128-130 (L, Copy).
  No. 785.

——BP, 7: 226-226 (L, LbC).

From James Robertson,[10] Boston, 13 Jun. 1769. Mass. Archs., 56: 559-560
  (ALS, RC).

——Mass. Archs., 56: 557-558 (L, Copy).

From Thomas Gage, New York, 18 Jun. 1769. BP, 12: 111-114 (ALS, RC).
  No. 786.

To Thomas Gage, Boston, 19 Jun. 1769. BP, 7: 226-228 (L, LbC). **No. 787**.

——CO 5/87, ff 130-132 (L extract, Copy).

To Thomas Hutchinson, Boston, 19 Jun. 1769. BP, 7: 228-229 (L, LbC). **No. 788**.

To Thomas Hutchinson, Jamaica Farm, 21 Jun. 1769. BP, 7: 229 (L, LbC).
   No. 789.
To the Earl of Hillsborough, Boston, 25 Jun. 1769. CO 5/758, ff 152-154
   (ALS, RC). **No. 790**.
——CO 5/893, ff 142-143 (dupLS, RC).
——CO 5/767, ff 353-356 (L, RLbC).
——BP, 7: 175-177 (L, LbC).
To John Pownall, Boston, 25 Jun. 1769. BP, 7: 300 (L, LbC).
To Thomas Gage, Boston, 26 Jun. 1769. BP, 7: 230-231 (L, LbC). **No. 791**.
——CO 5/87, ff 132-134 (L, Copy).
To the Earl of Hillsborough, Boston, 1, 7, 11, and 13 Jul. 1769. CO 5/758,
   ff 154-159 (ALS, RC). **No. 792**.
——CO 5/893, ff 144-149 (dupLS, RC).
——CO 5/768, ff 1-13 (L, RLbC).
——BP, 7: 177-185 (L, LbC).
From Thomas Gage, New York, 2 Jul. 1769. BP, 12: 115-118 (ALS, RC).
To Thomas Gage, Boston, 3 Jul. 1769. BP, 7: 231 (L, LbC).
To John Pownall, Boston, 3 Jul. 1769. BP, 7: 300 (L, LbC).
To Henry Bellew,[11] Boston, 3 Jul. 1769. BP, 7: 231 (L, LbC).
To Thomas Gage, Boston, 5 Jul. 1769. BP, 7: 232-233 (L, LbC). **No. 793**.
To Lord Barrington, Boston, 8 Jul. 1769. BP, 8: 1-3 (L, LbC). **No. 794**.
To James Cockle,[12] Boston, 8 Jul. 1769. BP, 8: 5 (LS, LbC).
From Thomas Gage, New York, 9 Jul. 1769. BP, 12: 119-122 (ALS, RC).
   No. 795.
From Thomas Gage, New York, 10 Jul. 1769. BP, 12: 123-126 (ALS, RC).
   No. 796.
From Joseph Chadwick,[13] Fort Pownall, 10 Jul. 1769. BP, 12: 127-130
   (ALS, RC).
To Oliver Partridge,[14] Boston, 11 Jul. 1769. BP, 7: 233-234 (L, LbC).
To Lord Barrington, Boston, 13 Jul. 1769. BP, 8: 3-4 (L, LbC).
To Messrs. Johnson, Boston, 15 Jul. 1769. BP, 7: 234-235 (L, LbC).
To the Earl of Hillsborough, Boston, 17 Jul. 1769. CO 5/893, ff 155-157
   (dupALS, RC). **No. 797**.
——CO 5/758, ff 175-178 (dupLS, RC).
——CO 5/768, ff 13-19 (L, RLbC).
——BP, 7: 185-190 (L, LbC).
To Guy Carleton, Boston, 25 Jul. 1769. BP, 7: 235-237 (L, LbC).
To Thomas Hutchinson, Boston, 19 Jul. 1769. Mass Archs., 25: 321-322
   (LS, RC). **No. 798**.

1. Frederick Cornwallis (1713-83) had succeeded Thomas Secker (1693-1768) as archbishop of Canterbury. FB wrote of "being known" to the new archbishop. BP, 6: 148

2. Joseph Goldthwait (1730-79) of Boston, later a prominent Loyalist and refugee.

3. Samuel Hood (1724-1816), a British naval officer and commander of the North Atlantic Station from Jul. 1767 to Oct. 1770. He did not see active service in the American War of Independence until his promotion to rear admiral and deployment to the West Indies in 1780.

4. FB corresponded with Monk about a bill of exchange for £40 drawn upon Monk by one Mr. Gibbs, recently settled in Boston. When Gibbs sought credit from Boston merchant Nathaniel Appleton, Appleton requested that FB endorse the bill, which FB did not normally do as a matter of course; instead, FB showed Appleton recent correspondence from Monk, which enabled Gibbs to obtain credit, and urged Monk to consider providing additional bills in order to help him set up in business in the year following. BP, 7: 251. Monk's identity cannot be established with certainty, but one possibility is Lawrence Monk of Caneby, Lincs., and a sheriff in FB's home county.

5. Norborne Berkeley (c.1717-70), fourth Baron Botetourt, and governor of Virginia from 1768 until his death.

6. Edward Hawke (1705-81), the first Baron Hawke, had a distinguished service record as a Royal Navy officer during the Seven Years' War, 1756–1763, and served as first lord of the Admiralty from 1766 to 1771.

7. Philip Stephens (1723–1809), first secretary of the Admiralty 1763-95.

8. Guy Carleton (1724-1808), an Anglo-Irish soldier and later the first Baron Dorchester, was governor of Quebec from 1768 to 1778, and a leading British general during the American War of Independence.

9. Victor-Thérèse Charpentier (1732-76), comte d'Ennery and French colonial administrator, was governor general of Martinque between 1765 and 1768 and concurrently governor of St. Domingue and the French Windward Islands, from 1768 to 1772.

10. James Robertson (1717-88), a Scottish-born British army officer, had served during the French and Indian War and had been the colonial administrator of the Floridas after their acquisition from Spain.

11. Henry Bellew was a Royal Navy officer and captain of HMS *Beaver.*

12. James Cockle had been dismissed from the customs service in 1764 after a long running dispute with John Temple, then his superior, who accused him of corruption and fraud. The affair, in which FB was implicated, is discussed at length in the second volume of the *Bernard Papers.*

13. Joseph Chadwick had undertaken a major survey of the Maine interior at FB's direction, which resulted in the production of the first maps of the region. See *Bernard Papers*, 3: 79; Chadwick's Survey of the Interior Parts of the Country from Penobscot to Quebec, 1765, CO 700/MAINE19.

14. Oliver Partridge (1712-93), a wealthy farmer and former representative for Hatfield, and FB's business partner in several New Hampshire land grants.

INDEX

CROWD ACTION

GOVERNMENT

and Boston, 75
boundary disputes. *See under* Boundary Disputes between Massachusetts and
and British Empire, 132
British government's views on, 9, 11, 17, 28, 31, 35, 50n, 122, 208, 343
British regiments
    and deployment of, 337
    and quartering of, 288, *See also* Government of Massachusetts:Quartering Act, obligations under
    and withdrawal of, 277, 289, 294, 317
charter of (1629), 166n, *See also* Province Charter (1691)
climate of, 157n
colonists of, 30
constitution of, 6, 351n, *See under* Government of Massachusetts: constitution
as "country," 26, 97, 113, 126, 157n, 158, 167, 227, 305, 346
courts. *See under* Law Courts
disorders in. *See under* Civil Disorder
FB does not return to, 33, 362
FB leaves, 2, 34, 225, 303n, 362
FB prepares to leave, 5, 27, 35, 200, 223, 234, 249, 259
finances of. *See under* Public Finances
fortifications in, 352n
friends of government in, 185, 210
Gage visits, 315
gentlemen of, 3, 185
governors of. *See under* Governors, Colonial: Massachusetts
interests of, 321
"internal Police" of, 300
and King-in-Parliament, 274
laws of, 267
lawyers, 49n, 97, 136–37, *See also* Lawyers
legislature. *See under* General Court
loyalty of, 286n
magistrates. *See under* Justices of the Peace
mentioned, 201, 221n, 235n, 279n
merchants. *See under* Merchants
misrepresentations of, 21, 175, 178, 197–98, 316–17, 326, 324–28, 337, 328–52, 362
mobs. *See under* Crowd Action
newspapers of, 58n, 76n, 123, 175–76, 195, 201n, 213n, 350n
officeholders, about, 136, 141
oppression of, 105, 178n
and Parliament, 35, 131, 153, 177, 200, 208
    resolutions of, concerning, 11–13, 126, 144, 153, 196, 238n, 242n, 300

peace and order in, 173, 181
people of, 26, 246
    and FB, 33–34, 37
    FB, no confidence in, 347
    inflamed, 248
    rights and liberties, 132
    as subjects, 327, *See also* King, The:subjects of
politics. *See under* Politics
province agent. *See under* Province Agent
public buildings, 96, 333, 344, *See also* Faneuil Hall, Boston; Manufactory House, Boston; Town House, Boston,
radicalism in, 14
reimburses, British, 51n
royal charter. *See under* Province Charter (1691)
settlers of, 172
shipping. *See under* Shipping
silver mines, 86n
social elite, membership of Council for, proposed, 186
"state" of, 27, 36, 102, 115, 140, 153, 182, 234, 239n, 262, 276, 283–84, 315
and taxation, 302n
towns. *See under* Towns
treason in
    accusations of, 196
    commission proposed, 28
    investigations of, 12, 194, 228
treasury of. *See under* Province Treasury
trials in, 204
valuation of estates, 341
vindication of, 36
welfare of, 141, 267
Whig party. *See under* Whig Party
Massachusetts Gazette
    cited, 258n
    Council, minutes of (26 Sept. 1768), prints, 89n, 349n
    as enclosure, 278, 349n
    mentioned, 214n
Massachusetts Gazette and Boston News-Letter
    Council, address to Gage from, prints, 318n
    Hatfield selectmen, letter to Boston selectmen from, prints, 81
    Parliament, presented to, 81
Massachusetts Gazette and Boston Weekly News-Letter
    cited, 57
    Letters to the Ministry, advertises, xxiv
Matthew, Book of
    cited, 56n